PERSONALITY TYPE

On The Hudson

Jung

BOOK SERIES

The New York Center for Jungian Studies presents
conferences and seminars in the U.S. and abroad,
including its Jung On The Hudson seminars held
each summer in the historic Hudson Valley. The
N.Y. Center seminars, book series and continuing
education programs are designed for individuals
from all fields as well as mental health professionals
who are interested in exploring the relevance of
Jung's ideas to their personal lives and/or professional
activities. The Center offers individual, couple and
group counseling, and provides consulting services
and mediation for family businesses and corporations.

For more information, please contact:
The New York Center for Jungian Studies
121 Madison Avenue, New York, NY 10016
Telephone: 212-689-8238 or Fax: 212-889-7634

PERSONALITY TYPE

An Owner's Manual

Lenore Thomson

SHAMBHALA
Boston & London
1998

Shambhala Publications, Inc.
Horticultural Hall
300 Massachusetts Avenue
Boston, Massachusetts 02115
www.shambhala.com

9   8   7   6   5   4

Printed in the United States of America
⊗ This edition is printed on acid-free paper that meets
the American National Standards Institute Z39.48 Standard.
Distributed in the United States by Random House, Inc.,
and in Canada by Random House of Canada Ltd

Library of Congress Cataloging-in-Publication Data

Thomson, Lenore.
    Personality type: an owner's manual/by Lenore Thomson.
  —1st Shambhala ed.
      p.   cm.
   ISBN 0-87773-987-0 (pbk.: alk. paper)
    1. Typology (Psychology)   2. Myers-Briggs Type
Indicator.
   I. Title.
   BF698.3.T46   1998   98–10700
   155.2'64—dc21   CIP

For my ESTJ father—
who doubts that type means much of anything . . .

my INFP mother—
who fervently hoped I'd write a book on the Enneagram . . .

and my ENFP husband—
who can't believe I'd invest so much time in one project.

Contents

Foreword

Over thirty years ago, C. A. Meier, one of the giants in the field of analytical psychology, delivered a provocative address at the Fourth International Congress for Analytical Psychology, in effect challenging his colleagues to administer psychological type tests to each of their patients. Of all the basic concepts of Jung, Meier declared, his notion of psychological type was not only the most neatly defined, but arguably the most important. Indeed, Meier suggested, perhaps membership in the International Association for Analytical Psychology ought to be limited to analysts who test their analysands at the start, during, and at the end of their analysis, as a way of determining whether or not Jungian therapy affected one's type.

For Meier, and Jung, understanding one's own type is the alpha and omega of the individuation process. Without this insight, one stands little chance of any true self-realization or development as an individual. Moreover, Meier's belief was that, since one's psychological type is not static, a shift must inevitably take place in order for any in-depth analytical work to be judged effective.

True to this challenge, Meier often administered the Myers-Briggs Type Inventory (MBTI) to those he worked with—myself included. While I am far from certain how much my own type shifted over the years, I have a profound respect for this aspect of Jung's thought, and I incorporate it into my own work with clients—both as a therapist and as a business consultant. Indeed, Jung's typology is widely understood and valued for its practical applications in an almost unlimited range of fields. Mental health professionals, literary critics, sociologists, and career counselors, among others, relate to this unique concept of Jungian psychology, which is in fact quantifiable and measurable. From its function in the business world, to its insights in the humanities and in the helping professions, over the years such well known and highly respected authors, analysts, and scholars as Arnold Toynbee, Marie-Louise von Franz, and Thomas

Moore, to name but a few, have written about and been interested in psychological type.

Nevertheless, the area where Jung's work on type has been most widespread is in the field of career and business consulting. The MBTI, developed almost fifty years ago by Isabel Briggs Myers and her mother, Katherine Briggs, is administered by personnel directors, career counselors, and business consultants, among others, to some two million individuals each year in the United States alone. In this context, the MBTI, along with other type tests such as the Gray-Wheelwright Psychological Type Questionnaire and the Singer-Loomis Inventory of Personality all owe their inspiration and conceptualization to Jung's groundbreaking work *Psychological Types*, first published in 1921. Lenore Thomson, in *Personality Type: An Owner's Manual*, has continued this tradition for us by providing an in-depth yet easily understandable overview of what psychological type is all about on the cultural, collective, and personal levels.

Ms. Thomson's tour-de-force will remain a standard work for many years to come. This will come as no surprise to those who know her past work as managing editor of *Quadrant: The Journal of Contemporary Jungian Thought*. Additionally, as both acknowledged and unacknowledged editor of numerous books by highly regarded authors in the field of psychology today, she has garnered considerable respect over the years. Personally, having had the benefit of working with Lenore Thomson on a number of projects, including coauthoring with her the article "In Search of the Essential John Lennon" (on understanding the Beatles' musician through the application of Jung's typology), I am pleased that her creative contributions to the field of psychological type will finally be available to the wider audience they deserve.

Notwithstanding the originality of Ms. Thomson's approach to type in general and this book in particular, I am pleased to have played some role in having her work see the light of day. A number of years ago, in response to a request to produce a psychological type quiz that would be self-scoring, accurate, easily taken, and computer-scored, I began developing such an instrument. First published in *McCall's* magazine in 1989, the Maidenbaum Personal Identity Test has been taken by well over five thousand individuals to date. Lenore

Thomson was my editor on this project. With over twelve thousand lines of text, a myriad of different possible analyses based on the results of computer-generated responses, I could not have completed this project without her valuable input and suggestions.

Following this project, I was invited by Shambhala Publications to write a book on the topic—a book that would include a self-scoring type test and that would make psychological type understandable and accessible to a wide audience—an audience that would include such diverse groups as educators, the lay public, career counselors, clergy, mental health professionals, and business consultants. I approached Lenore Thomson to coauthor just such a book with me. Fortunately, she agreed. As had been the case with our collaborations in the past, the process began by my submitting a chapter to her with the goal of having her add and edit. My own work came back so improved, so changed, and with such depth added, that I came to realize that her voice needed to be heard by itself. The result, including her vastly expanded type test, is evident in this book—one that I am pleased inaugurates the Jung on the Hudson book series presented by Shambhala Publications.

As readers of *Personality Type: An Owner's Manual* will discover, despite the myriad books, monographs, and articles on the subject of psychological type, Ms. Thomson's work stands in a category of its own when it comes to originality and depth. Drawing on her strong background in such fields as psychology, literature, and popular culture, utilizing her knowledge of computer technology, and injecting a most impressive creative element in the combination of thought and image, Lenore Thomson has given us a rare gift. This book will close the door to such arguments that one need be a particular type or from a specific field to understand, appreciate, and, most important, apply Jung's concept of type to one's daily life and professional activities.

Aryeh Maidenbaum, Ph.D.
Director
NEW YORK CENTER FOR JUNGIAN STUDIES

PART ONE
The Personality Type System

1

This Door Is Not the Door

▲ THIS BOOK IS FOR THOSE WHO BELIEVE that living can be an art—a project whose outcome is ourselves, the person we are meant to be. But how does this happen? How do we become uniquely "ourselves"? Is it possible to create a life in which we are acting from our deepest values—doing the best that we know how? How do we figure out what those values are? Where do they come from?

It may seem strange that these questions should even arise. Why is it so hard to figure out "who we really are"? A Chinese wisdom story addresses this question with particularly subtle insight.[1]

An evil warlord has kidnapped a young woman. In an ostensible attempt to demonstrate goodwill, he offers her a choice between two doors. One door, he tells her, leads to his garden. If she chooses that door, she may follow the path beyond it to freedom and sunlight and he will never bother her again. The other door leads to his bedroom. If she chooses that door, she must stay with him forever.

Now, the young woman knows very well that the man is lying. Both doors in fact lead to the bedroom, and it doesn't matter which one she chooses. For a long time she's silent, contemplating her options. Finally, she makes her choice. She points to one of the doors and says, "This door is not the door that leads to the garden."

Like the young woman in the story, we can't choose something that doesn't yet exist. If our potential is not being lived out, it doesn't have any external form. It's simply raw possibility. Raw possibility comes to our awareness only when we realize that something is missing. It takes our attention away from the things we already know and do and love.

We usually experience this diversion of attention as a vague feeling of boredom or restlessness—the sense that our lives aren't what they could be. Sometimes this happens because circumstances have pushed us to develop traits and values that aren't consistent with our real personality. But it happens for another reason as well—to all of us.

We're born with many possibilities for development, and one lifetime is too short to make the most of all of them. Thus, we usually concentrate on the ones that come easiest to us, cultivating our strengths—the possibilities that feel most "like us." When we do this, we're filled with energy and engaged with life.

In the process, however, we necessarily sacrifice other possibilities, which are equally valuable and part of our human heritage. Thus, we're likely to feel that something is missing even when we've done exactly what we set out to do! We all contend with potential left behind, and it's not easy to figure out how to deal with it.

For one thing, our society is relentlessly external. When we feel frustrated or dissatisfied, our first impulse is to blame our job, partner, or environment for our lack of interest. We're encouraged at every turn to solve the problem by embarking on a new career, finding a more exciting love life, or starting a hobby.

Usually, however, a feeling of restlessness or dissatisfaction occurs not because our outer situation has lost its appeal but because our unexpressed potential has no other way to get our attention. If anything, our unlived possibilities claim our attention most insistently when we've built an outer life strong enough to withstand their realization.

The theory of psychological types offers a kind of vocabulary for recognizing and talking about the different ways this sort of thing happens to people. It tells us how our personalities take shape, depending on the gifts and strengths we put into play, and what kinds of inner possibilities may be trying to get our attention.

The Theory of Psychological Types

In the 1920s, Carl G. Jung, the Swiss psychiatrist and philosopher, was attempting to understand why he and Sigmund Freud were moving in different theoretical directions. Jung had once been Freud's protégé, but he was coming to disagree with Freud's ideas, and he eventually developed his own theory of personality development.

The cornerstone of Freud's theory was his belief that most human motives derive from an unconscious sexual drive—the body's relentless search for pleasure. Jung had come to believe that this approach was too limited. As he saw it, we are motivated by the need to adapt to our environment, and the search for pleasure is only one aspect of our adaptational equipment.

During the same time period, psychoanalyst Alfred

Ziggy ©1995 Ziggy and Friends, Inc. Dist. by Universal Press Syndicate. Reprinted with permission. All rights reserved.

Adler had advanced a competing theory of personality development. He believed that all human motives are derived from the need to establish power. Jung gradually realized that the human personality encompasses all these things: the need for pleasure and relationship, the drive for power and control, and the motivation to adapt. Freud, Adler, and Jung had each emphasized motives that reflected his own outlook.

This led Jung to the idea that each of us sees reality according to his or her own "psychological type." He began to construct a unifying theory that would allow each view its own integrity. As he explored the many theories of personality that have been devised throughout human history, he was struck by the fact that so many of them describe human character in terms of four basic classifications.

Astrology, one of our oldest personality theories, classifies character in terms of the four elements: water, air, earth, and fire. Greek medicine classified people in terms of bodily secretions and gave us our words phlegmatic, sanguine, choleric, and melancholic. The tarot cards relate personalities to the four suits: wands, cups, swords, and pentacles, or our modern clubs, hearts, spades, and diamonds. The Neo-platonists also described four ways of interacting with reality.

Greek Medicine	Neoplatonic Emanations	Tarot Suits	Astrological Elements
Sanguine	Spirit	Wands	Fire
Choleric	Mind	Swords	Air
Phlegmatic	Soul	Cups	Water
Melancholic	Senses	Pentacles	Earth

Jung began to realize that the four possibilities in each scheme are fairly consistent, representing four basic human ways of approaching reality. Freud, Adler, and Jung himself had been emphasizing only one of the four—the one that corresponded to his own way of approaching reality.

The Four Functions

Ultimately, Jung concluded that we are all born with four psychological functions—four distinct ways of knowing and interacting with the world around us.

▲ Sensation ⟍
          for direct experience
▲ Intuition ⟋

▲ Thinking ⟍
          for organizing experience rationally
▲ Feeling ⟋

Just as we can locate a place geographically by noting its relationship to the four directions, Jung thought of our functions as compass points for the personality, by which we are oriented to our immediate situation. For example, people who are well developed in Sensation or Intuition prefer direct experience. They live in the present, and they are alert to situations that require an immediate response. They may resist situations that require them to organize their experience systematically or to follow a plan.

Calvin and Hobbes   by Bill Watterson

People who are well developed in Thinking or Feeling prefer to organize their experiences and plan for them. Once they've established a plan, they can be irritated by the unpredictability of the direct experience.

Calvin and Hobbes   by Bill Watterson

We experience each of our functions from two distinct perspectives—one that involves the person we are inside (the Introverted view) and one that involves our relationship to others (the Extraverted view). We struggle all our lives to pull these two viewpoints together into a picture of the "whole."

Jung, with his strong interest in this whole, had been taking an Intuitive approach to inner reality. Intuition gives us the ability to see how individual elements are actually part of larger patterns.

Freud had been seeing people in terms of Feeling—the human need to divide experience into things that feel good and things that feel bad. On this foundation he built a theory concerned with our negotiation of individual pleasures in light of social ideas about civilized behavior. Alfred Adler had been emphasizing people's Thinking motives—the desire to know something in order to predict and control it. His theory extended, therefore, to questions of power and justice in social systems.

Type and Psychological Wholeness

Although our typological functions are inborn, it takes a long time to adapt raw possibility to our particular time and place. By the time we're realizing the potential of our strongest functions, the behaviors they shape feel like "us." So other functions get left behind and don't mature in the same way.

It's this preference for certain functions and not others that constitutes our particular psychological type. Because we all seek out situations that allow us to use our best skills, knowing our type can help us to understand why we negotiate reality the way we do. No particular combination of functions is inherently better or preferable to another, but each way of seeing the world has its own advantages and disadvantages.

For one thing, societies tend to favor some type configurations more than others. Types that are well represented will have more options for using their strengths, but they are also less likely to see the limits and possibilities of social institutions. Conversely, types that are uncommon may have to work harder to be understood, but they are also less likely to be seduced by a collective illusion.

Because we all develop some functions better than others, we are all contending with unlived potential of one sort or another. This is one reason certain fourfold schemes in popular culture come to seem archetypally perfect and become part of our social mythology. They appear to represent psychological wholeness in ways that we intuitively recognize.

The Beatles, for instance, are an interesting example of a typological quaternity. John came across as the acerbic Thinker, George as the mystical Intuitive, Paul as the romantic Feeling type, and Ringo as the earthy Sensation type. It may be their attempt to balance themselves in a group context that gave them such power to affect culture.

More recently, Marvel comics has launched a storyline for its popular character Spider-Man, called "Identity Crisis." It seems that Spider-Man is a marked man, so he's forced to assume four separate crime-fighting guises. Each suggests one of the four functions in his personality: Hornet, the man who loves science and gadgets (Thinking), Prodigy, the man who fights for what's right (Feeling), Richochet, the light-hearted guy who likes to have fun (Sensation), and Dusk, the man who moves in the shadows and sees new possibilities (Intuition).

Types Theory and Science

Once Jung recognized that personality difference is largely a matter of functional preference, he looked forward to a time when the typological elements he defined would be corroborated by hard science. He didn't live long enough to see this happen, but he was right.

Extraversion and Introversion are now regarded as biological markers, more consistent than any other factors in predicting people's behaviors. Moreover, the advance of brain-imaging techniques has allowed us to see how Sensation, Intuition, Thinking, and Feeling operate neurologically. Using one function instead of another has distinct and measurable consequences.

The brain contains many billions of nerve cells, each of which contains hundreds of branchy fibers that allow it to reach out and communicate with other cells. When we use a particular function, the nerve cells in those activated areas of the brain begin to make connections with each other. The more we use a function, the more complicated the neural connections become, and the more rapidly communication takes place among them.

As a result, our best functions become easier and easier to use, and the growing network of cells form an architecture of extraordinary complexity. When this happens, the neural circuitry, in a sense, takes off on its own, combining ideas, images, and memories associated with our preferences in creative and personally distinctive ways.

One of the reasons for learning about type is to recognize that we are constantly motivated, simply by the way we've established our neural networks, to shape reality along particular functional lines. Another is to recognize the possibilities for growth and change that exist within—and apart from—the framework we have created for ourselves. Even small changes in our usual way of doing things can make big differences in the way our brain is operating. We develop the ability to think in new ways, and this stimulates creative change in all areas of our lives.

A Note on the Terms Used in This Book

During the 1950s, Katherine Briggs and her daughter, Isabel Briggs Myers, used Jung's work as a foundation for their own research, and their collaboration with career counselors and college placement officers resulted in a personality inventory now administered annually to two million people, the Myers-Briggs Type Indicator (MBTI).

The MBTI establishes criteria for what are, in effect, sixteen different psychological types—sixteen basic patterns for approaching the world. All deal with normal psychological behavior. They are not designed to characterize people as right or wrong in the choices they have made. They are designed to show how the various mental processes we have as human beings combine to make up different ways of understanding reality. These sixteen types remain the standard for the field, and the Myers-Briggs research is invaluable for insights on and refinements of Jung's theory.

On the other hand, one can neither administer nor take the MBTI outside of a professional counseling relationship, and it is here that this book can make a contribution. One does not have to be in a counseling situation to understand and apply the insights of psychological types theory. Jung spent the last years of his life attempting to make his theories accessible to an audience unfamiliar with the field of psychology. Moreover, areas of research exist today that were unavailable to the Myers-Briggs team a generation ago.

Although much of this research is neurological and beyond the scope of my expertise, the conclusions that have been drawn from it, particularly with respect to the right and left brain, can be integrated with Jung's theory in a way that extends typology's usefulness and potential. However, for the sake of consistency, I've maintained the typological categories that have become standard in the field since the MBTI was developed.

Postscript

Although types theory has very real neurological correlations, it should be recognized that Jung's was not a strictly scientific enterprise. It was an attempt to invent a vocabulary for unseen dimensions of psychological reality—to capture an experience otherwise difficult to talk about.

Type theory, in this respect, is a *description of*—not a prescription for—human behavior. It's useful in the way that wisdom stories are useful. It points us to certain truths about the human condition, and can tell us something important about our particular way of knowing and interacting with the world. One might even say that it's a more complicated version of the old story about four people and an elephant in the dark:

> An elephant belonging to a traveling exhibition had been stabled near a town where no elephant had been seen before. Four curious citizens, hearing of the hidden wonder, went to see if they could get a preview of it. When they arrived at the stable they found that there was no light. The investigation therefore had to be carried out in the dark. One, touching its trunk, thought that the creature must resemble a hosepipe; the second felt an ear and concluded that it was a fan. The third, feeling a leg, could liken it only to a living pillar; and when the fourth put his hand on its back he was convinced that it was some kind of throne. None

could form the complete picture; and of the part which each felt, he could only refer to it in terms of things which he already knew. The result of the expedition was confusion. Each was sure that he was right; none of the other townspeople could understand what had happened, what the investigators had actually experienced[2]

Like the people in the story, each of us knows a specific piece of a much larger picture. Our particular combination of functions helps to form our identity and conditions the way we seek and find satisfaction in life. We may not fully appreciate people who have made different choices than we have.

The enduring worth of types theory is its capacity to show us the common intersection of our varied paths. The people we understand least usually represent the parts of our psychological heritage that we've left behind. Indeed, our most persistent relationship problems are a valuable resource. They can offer us glimpses of "the whole elephant."

Being true to ourselves is not just a matter of honoring our own motivations. It's also acknowledging the views and resources we've set aside. Beyond our own boundaries, we are inextricably linked with people whose motives, choices, and unlived potentials are different from our own.

Whether we're feeling pushed beyond a secure situation to risk greater engagement with life, moving beyond a familiar identity to find ourselves anew, or recognizing that deeper meaning lies beyond the things we've already accomplished, types theory can tell us how our preferences relate to the larger human story.

2

Casting Types

▲ BEFORE PROCEEDING WITH THIS BOOK, it might be best to get an idea of your own psychological type. The test in this chapter (developed in collaboration with Jungian analyst Aryeh Maidenbaum, Ph.D.) will help you do that.[1] Answer each question by choosing between A and B, and mark your choices on the answer sheet on page 19.

Although this type evaluator will probably reflect your genuine preferences, don't worry if your type designation seems inaccurate. Sometimes circumstances don't favor the functions that come to us naturally. If this happens, you may not identify with the description of your type as a whole (see chapters 14 through 21).

Don't underestimate a result of this kind! It can tell you about the way you're currently organizing your life—perhaps in an effort to maintain a job or relationship. You might read the different type descriptions to see whether another reflects your true preferences. Similarly, if you are going through a transition period, your scores may be too close in a number of categories to determine a clear-cut psychological type. This result, too, should be heeded. It's telling you about a shift in your situation or identity.

Once you have a four-letter type designation, go on with the rest of the book.

Read each question and its pair of answers. Choose either A or B and place a mark in the appropriate column of the answer sheet on page 19. Note that the numbers are progressing *across* the columns of the answer sheet, not down. Your answers should reflect how you actually see yourself, not how you would like to be. Even if you feel that neither answer applies to you, or that either applies under different circumstances, choose the one that you most agree with right now. No answer is right or wrong, or better or worse. The more honest you are with yourself, the more the test will tell you.

1. When you meet new people, do you
    A. talk as much as you listen?
    B. listen more than you talk?
2. Which statement characterizes your general approach to life?
    A. Just do it.
    B. Check out the alternatives.
3. Which do you like more about yourself:
    A. your cool-headed, logical approach?
    B. your warm, understanding approach?
4. Which are you better at:
    A. shifting gears when necessary?
    B. focusing on one task until it's done?
5. Do you prefer a social life that includes
    A. many friends and acquaintances?
    B. a few people that you feel close to?
6. When you're trying to understand something, do you
    A. press for specifics?
    B. get an overall picture and fill in the details later?
7. Which is more interesting to you:
    A. knowing how people think?
    B. knowing how people feel?
8. What kind of job do you like better:
    A. one that allows you to react quickly and improvise?
    B. one that allows you to determine goals and take steps to meet them?
9. If a heavy snowfall keeps you from going to school or work, do you
    A. wonder what you're missing?
    B. enjoy the unexpected time alone?

Which statement are you more likely to make?

10. A. I'm interested in people's experience—what they do, who they know.
    - B. I'm interested in people's plans and dreams—where they're going, what they envision.
11. A. I'm good at making a plan that will work.
    - B. I'm good at getting others to agree with a plan and cooperate in the effort.
12. A. I may try something impulsively, just to see what happens.
    - B. I want to know what's likely to happen before I try something.
13. A. I usually think on my feet, as I'm talking.
    - B. I usually reflect on what I'm going to say before I say it.
14. A. I'm almost always aware of how things look.
    B. I may not notice much about how things look—at least not right away.
15. A. I tend to be an analytical sort, maybe a little skeptical.
    - B. I'm interested in people and care about what happens to them.
16. A. I like to leave room for new options, even after plans have been made.
    B. Once plans have been made, I want to be able to count on them.
17. A. People who know me are generally aware of what's important to me.
    - B. I don't talk about what's really important to me unless I feel close to someone.
18. A. If I enjoy a particular activity, I'll engage in it frequently enough to do it well.
    B. Once an activity is familiar to me, I want to change it or try something new.
19. A. When I'm making a decision, I weigh the pros and cons of my choices.
    B. When I'm making a decision, I'm interested in what others have done in similar situations.

20. A. I tend to learn by experience, so I often have my own way of doing things.
    B. I generally learn by following instructions and adapting them to my needs.
21. A. I get restless when I'm alone too long.
    B. I get restless when I don't have enough time to myself.
22. A. I'm not much interested in ideas without some practical application.
    B. I like ideas for their own sake and enjoy playing with them in my imagination.
23. A. When I negotiate, I depend on my knowledge and tactical skills.
    B. When I negotiate, I establish common ground with the other person.
24. A. I need a break now and then when I'm working on something.
    B. I would rather not be interrupted when I'm working on something.
25. A. When I'm having a good time with others, I get energized and keep on going.
    B. When I'm having a good time with others, my energy runs out and I need space.
26. A. My physical surroundings are important to me and affect how I feel.
    B. Atmosphere isn't all that important to me if I like what I'm doing.
27. A. People can count on me to be fair and to treat them with respect.
    B. People can count on me to be there when they need me.

When you're on vacation, are you more likely to

28. A. take things as they come, doing whatever you feel like at the moment?
    B. work out a tentative schedule of things you want to do?
29. A. spend time doing things with others?
    B. take time to read or walk or daydream alone?

30. A. return to a vacation spot you love?
    B. go someplace you've never been before?
31. A. take a work- or a school-related project with you?
    B. renew relationships that are important to you?
32. A. forget about your everyday routines and concentrate on having fun?
    B. think about things you need to prepare for when the vacation is over?
33. A. see famous landmarks?
    B. spend time in museums and quieter places?
34. A. have a good meal at a restaurant you really enjoy?
    B. explore new cuisines?

Which word best describes the way you see yourself?

35. A. levelheaded
    B. idealistic
36. A. spontaneous
    B. systematic
37. A. open
    B. reflective
38. A. factual
    B. conceptual
39. A. knowledgeable
    B. understanding
40. A. adaptable
    B. organized
41. A. expansive
    B. intense
42. A. down-to-earth
    B. imaginative
43. A. questioning
    B. questing
44. A. enthusiastic
    B. deliberate
45. A. well-rounded
    B. deep

46. A. seasoned
    B. spirited
47. A. just
    B. merciful
48. A. open-ended
    B. goal oriented
49. A. straightforward
    B. reserved
50. A. realistic
    B. visionary
51. A. impartial
    B. sensitive

Would you rather

52. A. put off unpleasant chores until you're in the right mood?
    B. get unpleasant chores out of the way so they're off your mind?
53. A. be admired for your work, even though you're not satisfied with it yourself?
    B. create something of lasting worth, but remain unknown?
54. A. have extensive experience in an area that pleases you?
    B. have many options to choose from?

Which slogan better captures your point of view?

55. A. People are apt to mistake the strength of their feeling for the strength of their argument.
    B. Logic is the art of going wrong with confidence.
56. A. He who hesitates is lost.
    B. Look before you leap.

When you've finished marking the columns, as described on page 19, add downward and place the total number of A and B answers in the boxes at the bottom of each column. Then go on to the next step to figure your type.

Answer Sheet

	A	B		A	B		A	B		A	B
1		✓	2		✓	3		✓	4		✓
5		✓	6		✓	7		✓	8		✓
9		✓	10		✓	11		✓	12		✓
13		✓	14	✓		15		✓	16	✓	
17		✓	18	✓		19	✓		20		✓
21		✓	22		✓	23		✓	24		✓
25		✓	26	✓		27		✓	28		✓
29		✓	30	✓		31	✓		32		✓
33		✓	34		✓	35		✓	36		✓
37		✓	38		✓	39	✓		40		✓
41		✓	42		✓	43		✓	44		✓
45		✓	46		✓	47		✓	48		✓
49		✓	50		✓	51		✓	52		✓
53		✓	54	✓		55	✓		56		✓
	0	14		5	9		4	10		1	13
	1	2		3	4		5	6		7	8

Determining Your Psychological Type

Insert the numbers from columns 1–8 of your answer sheet into the corresponding boxes on the next page. In each pair of numbers, one number will probably be higher than the other. Mark the letter underneath the highest number in each pair. This will give you your four-letter type designation. If the numbers in a pair are even, you'll probably need to read more about the two possibilities to figure out your most likely preference.

1	2		3	4		5	6		7	8
E	I		S	N		T	F		P	J
O	14		5	9		4	10		1	13

E = Extraversion S = Sensation T = Thinking P = Perceiving
I = Introversion N = Intuition F = Feeling J = Judging

Now that you have your type designation, you may wish to read the description of your type (found in chapters 14 through 21) and see how it relates to your self-experience. Some types will want to read about type theory first; others won't. Some will read all the type profiles; others will concentrate on their own. There is no right or wrong way to use this book.

If you choose to read your type description and it doesn't capture the way you see yourself, see if another fits you better. In particular, if the scores in a type category are close or even, take a look at both possible type profiles.

THE FAR SIDE   By GARY LARSON

The four basic personality types

3

Interpreting the Type Evaluator Results

▲ THE FOUR LETTERS IN A PSYCHOLOGICAL TYPE stand for the two functions and two attitudes we use most often. These letters can result in sixteen possible type combinations:

ESTP	ENTP	ISTP	INTP
ESTJ	ENTJ	ISTJ	INTJ
ESFP	ENFP	ISFP	INFP
ESFJ	ENFJ	ISFJ	INFJ

By convention, the four letters are set up as a kind of sandwich. The two outer letters, the first and the fourth, are the bread slices. They represent our attitudes:

E or I			P or J

E or I = Extraversion or Introversion
P or J = Perceiving or Judging

In the middle of the sandwich are the two letters that represent our strongest functions—that is, the ones we usually rely on:

	S or N	T or F	

S or N = Sensation or iNtuition
T or F = Thinking or Feeling

What Do the Letters Mean?

Each of the functions and attitudes will be covered in more detail as the book goes on. The following, however, is a quick overview of the "type sandwich":

The first letter represents our primary attitude.

E or I			

▲ Extraverts define themselves in light of externals—the aspects of their lives that others will recognize and respond to.

▲ Introverts consider their own viewpoint the final arbiter of reality and define their external situation in terms of it.

The second letter describes the way we *Perceive*—that is, the way we process direct experience or new information.

	S or N		

▲ Sensates process new experience by comparing it to past experience.

▲ iNtuitives process new experience by imagining its future possibilities.

The third letter describes the way we *Judge*—that is, the way we organize familiar facts or experiences so they're predictable and can be understood rationally.

		T or F	

▲ Thinkers organize information impersonally and logically.

▲ Feelers organize information personally, in terms of relationship.

The fourth letter tells us which function we generally rely on when we're dealing with *external reality*.

			P or J

▲ P types rely on the direct Perceptual experience of Sensation or Intuition.

▲ J types rely on the rational Judgment provided by Thinking or Feeling.

Functional Preference Is Like a Native Language

Although we need all of our functions and attitudes to be fully engaged with life, we gradually learn by experience and preference to use some better than others. As these functions become more developed, we begin to understand ourselves in light of the skills they make possible. Our personality consolidates around them, and they help to determine our accustomed approach to reality—our beliefs about relationship, our interests and inclinations, the contributions we make to society, and so forth.

On the other hand, our type does not define who we "really are" any more than using a particular language defines the nature of the soul. It simply characterizes the way we've learned to participate in life—to understand and be understood by the world around us.

Nature equips us in most spheres with more potential than we can actually develop in a lifetime. We are born with a broad range of adaptive possibilities. For example, every infant—from China to Mexico to New Guinea—babbles in exactly the same way, using every sound that occurs in every language spoken on earth. It's only as we begin to imitate the sounds we hear around us that certain linguistic combinations become reinforced and others are set aside. If we attempt to learn another language later in life, we can usually recover some of that sacrificed potential. But we may find it difficult to lose the accent derived from our native language.

So it is with the typological functions. Although we are born with the capacity for many different combinations, we adapt to our environment by developing only one or two—usually the ones that come easiest to us, modified by opportunity and social expectation. The process is very much like becoming fluent in a language. When we've developed a particular way of interacting with the world, we tend to use other, less-developed functions with something like a behavioral accent.

For example, people who prefer to use Sensation most of the time depend on acquired experience for their knowledge of reality. If they can't apply an idea to a real-life situation, they may find it difficult to accord it significance. With enough motivation, they can get past that resistance, but they'll always feel more comfortable with immediate sensory feedback. For Sensates, that's what "real life" is all about.

Because each function and attitude encourages a specific approach to reality, it's possible to make broad generalizations about the different types. These generalizations, however, should not be construed as stereotypes. Psychological type is not an internal tape loop that irrevocably determines people's options. Even when two people share a common language, they each create sentences unique to themselves. Type is only a description of how we've learned to communicate. What we communicate is another matter entirely.

In the last analysis, psychological type is the way humans adapt to cultural reality. Thus, the strength of our two best functions is not in the boundaries they dictate but in the flexibility of the behaviors they shape. It's only the overdevelopment of one function to the exclusion of others that constricts a personality and limits possibility. When two strong functions are working well together, our adaptive potential is astonishingly varied.

Opposing Forces

Stability in nature is often based on the union of opposites, whose tension makes for creative variation and change. Research into the brain suggests that this basic structural framework is also characteristic of our adaptive resources. For example, we need both predictability and variation, security and independence. Such tensions ultimately make for evolutionary momentum. We can adapt to almost any environment on earth; but we are never entirely satisfied. We are "hardwired" for the kind of tension that makes change possible.

As an adaptive mechanism, psychological type is very much a part of this natural economy. Each of the four categories consists of conflicting choices for behavior. Significantly, each choice also activates a different part of the brain. To choose one necessarily precludes the simultaneous use of the other—rather like going up the stairs instead of down.

▲ We can *either* adjust ourselves to the external situation (Extraversion) or relate the external situation to ourselves (Introversion).
▲ We can *either* focus on what's right in front of us (Sensation) or see other possibilities in our imagination (Intuition).
▲ We can *either* analyze impersonally (Thinking) or evaluate personally (Feeling).
▲ We can *either* experience events directly as they happen (Perceiving) or organize events rationally and prepare for them (Judging).

Life *always* places us at a typological crossroads. Whenever we employ a function or attitude, we are axiomatically choosing *against* its opposite. In a very real sense, life pushes us to make this choice—and to grow and evolve as we contend with the consequences.

Sometimes, when people are just learning about type, they assume that the point of type development is perfect balance—that is, close scores in all type categories. It's worth noting, however, that in the realm of nature, perfect balance is not a good thing. A physical system reaches equilibrium when it has lost its energy and can no longer change.

Insofar as type is concerned, close or even scores in a category (8/6 or 7/7) tend to suggest that the person hasn't developed a clear-cut sense of self. This is particularly true for people under thirty. Such scores may also indicate that the demands of a relationship or career is pushing a person away from his or her usual self-experience. For example:

▲ ETPs sometimes find themselves pushed by social expectations to soften an otherwise aggressive, impersonal approach to others, and such types may get nearly even scores on T and F.
▲ ITJs who take a job that rewards good "team" players may get close scores on P and J.
▲ An ENFP who marries another ENFP may assume more Sensate responsibilities than he or she wants to, resulting in close scores on S and N.

If both middle letters are too close to call, the person may be trying to please someone else, struggling with a lifestyle choice that does not have social approval, or adapting to a situation that conflicts with his or her true preferences. FPs and FJs, in particular, need a certain degree of social support to feel comfortable. Without it, they're reluctant to express their actual preferences, and most of their scores may be 8/6 or 7/7.

For people over thirty-five, close scores tend to indicate a period of transition. This is frequently the point in life when the ghosts of lost choices come back to haunt us, and the experience can result in test scores that are nearly even in every category. Close scores may also indicate an interior search—a quest for meaning and spiritual depth.

It should be recognized, of course, that all these interpretations must be inferred. A type test can't get at the content of one's inner life. Close scores merely indicate the absence of a developed exterior form. This point is an important one.

The theory of psychological types is largely concerned with the development of *conscious* awareness—the sensations, perceptions, moods, and mental formations that interact to compose an everyday understanding of reality. We develop conscious awareness precisely in the struggle to define who we are and who we are not. The test is measuring the relative strength of this kind of self-definition.

To be sure, a deliberate attempt to quell the struggle "for" and "against" is often part of a search for "higher" awareness, but such attempts have little meaning before we've developed our conscious approach to life as well as we know how. This is why many traditions restrict the interior quest to people who have already achieved some tangible success in matters of work and love.

It should also be recognized that types theory is first and foremost a *psychological* approach to meaning and growth. It can tell us about the ways in which different people experience life, including the stirrings of faith and purpose beyond psychological satisfaction and development. However, its province is human nature, no more and no less. We grow typologically by establishing a well-differentiated and focused personality, with boundaries clear enough to enable choice, relationship, commitment, and all the human satisfactions thereof.

4

The First Type Category

Extraversion or Introversion

▲ THE FIRST LETTER OF A PSYCHOLOGICAL TYPE IS E OR I, which stands for our primary attitude: Extraversion or Introversion.

Extraverts	Introverts
▲ define themselves in terms of externals—things that others will recognize and respond to	● consider their own view-point the arbiter of reality and define externals in terms of it
▲ are stimulated by the claims, pleasures, and obligations of the outer world—the people, things, and events that constitute external reality	● are more aware of purely mental phenomena—the impressions, facts, ideas, and reactions that constitute an inner world
▲ act before reflecting	● reflect before acting
▲ are influenced by and gauge their worth by the expectations and attention of others	● may defend themselves against the expectations and attention of others
▲ are straightforward, understandable, accessible	● are reserved, complicated, private
▲ are outgoing, sometimes highly expressive, but may not recognize their own needs	● are self-aware, sometimes passionately intense, but may not realize their effect on others

How the Attitudes Develop

If someone tells us that we have an "attitude," we may not take it as a compliment. The phrase is often used to describe people who have a chip on their shoulder—that is, who are unnecessarily hostile or combative. On the other hand, we also say that someone's music or art "has attitude," and we mean something positive—something like aggressive self-awareness, a quality that transcends the role or genre to which the phenomenon belongs.

The various uses of the word *attitude* in pop culture can be helpful when we're trying to understand what Extraversion and Introversion are all about. In the domain of psychological types, our attitude is our way of negotiating the inevitable gap between self-determination and the expectations of others.

We begin to recognize this gap the moment we come squalling into the world, abruptly and brutally aware of our own needs and appetites. In the early stages of life, reality has meaning for us largely in those terms—the constant alternation of wanting and having, presence and absence, pain and satisfaction. This, in its rawest form, is Introversion—knowledge of reality as it relates directly to our own priorities, without compromise.

Primitive Introversion is always infantile in nature. It takes the form of accommodating external reality to our own immediate wishes, needs, and impressions. As Introversion develops, however, we recognize beneath the surface of our immediate relationship to the outer world a deeper level of the human psyche—the universals that exist in all of us, inherited across thirty thousand generations of human existence. When we get to know ourselves in an Introverted way, we recognize not only the shifting kaleidoscope of hopes, values, dreams, and mysteries that belong to our individual "self" but also the collective aspect of consciousness that Jung called the Self, which determines our fundamental unity with others, beyond external differences.

Of course, the external world has its own reality, apart from us. As children, our comfort and security, the growth of our mental and physical abilities, our pleasures and our possibilities—all depend quite literally on our surroundings and the people who interact with us. Our nerve cells are making thousands upon thousands of connections in our brains, simply from the way that we are touched and held and sung to and played with. We learn to sleep and wake and eat according to the needs and schedule of a particular household.

Gradually, we begin to recognize that relationship to this larger world is a two-way street. We may depend on others, but our behaviors also have an effect on them. We experiment with these effects— employing stratagems, seduction, tantrums, and demands, gradually modifying our attempts in light of the reactions we get. This is the ground floor of Extraversion. We're adjusting to our outward situation so we can interact with it. Throughout our lives, certain kinds of adjustments are reinforced and rewarded by the people around us, and others are not.

In its most primitive form, Extraversion is also self-oriented, in that it prompts us to make a place for ourselves in light of others' expectations and responses. When Extraversion is undeveloped, it encourages us to insist on that place and to bring attention to ourselves. But, like Introversion, this attitude matures as we do. Over time, we recognize the value of consensual reality—the ability to understand and interpret the behaviors of others, and the assurance that others will recognize and respond to us in familiar terms.

▲ In general, Introversion helps us to realize individual responsibility. When we judge our situation by relating it to our own ideas, impressions, hopes, and values, we are not at the mercy of our environment.

▲ Extraversion helps us to risk ourselves and to discover what we lack. When we judge ourselves in light of the values and reality of others, we learn to trust and to be vulnerable. We also learn how to work within the bounds of what exists to bring about change.

Too much Introversion will deprive us of our ability to share our views and ourselves with others. Too much Extraversion may keep us from recognizing our own needs and potential, particularly if others don't acknowledge them.

The Attitudes and Biology

Although most of us feel more comfortable with one attitude or the other, all of us are Introverted in some ways and Extraverted in others. We have to be. The brain is set up that way. As soon as our senses take in information, they send it directly to the Introverted part of the brain. Practically speaking, when we "Introvert," we process the data we've taken in and see how it relates to our own agenda.

If our Introverted reflections lead us to formulate an outward goal, the Extraverted part of the brain gets involved. Say, for example, that our senses have informed us that we're about to be hit by a runaway supermarket cart. The Introverted part of the brain, having considered this information in light of immediate self-interest has likely established an obvious goal: avoid the collision! The Extraverted part of the brain responds to this goal somewhat like Superman recognizing a piece of kryptonite. "Quick," it says, "got to get away!"

How we carry out this course of action, however, depends very much on the concrete reality of our circumstances. Are we standing in a supermarket aisle? Do we have enough room to leap aside? Should we flatten ourselves against the nearest shelf of tuna? Did we get the name of that TV lawyer who specializes in collision suits?

In other words, our Extraverted actions may be based on our Introverted reflections, but they have to be adjusted to the limitations and potential of our actual situation. This is why we need both attitudes—to determine our needs, as we understand them, in light of our present circumstances, and to accept and interact with those circumstances on their own terms. No one can be entirely Introverted or Extraverted.

The different behaviors of Introverts and Extraverts are the result of emphasizing either the reflective or the active side of the process.

▲ Introverts emphasize the inner viewpoint. They are most comfortable in situations that allow for sustained reflection and a certain amount of privacy. If the satisfactions possible in a situation aren't well enough related to their needs, they may carve out a space for themselves that allows them to participate on their own terms.

▲ Extraverts emphasize the influence of outward circumstances. They interact with most situations in terms of the satisfactions possible to them—even if those satisfactions have no immediate relationship to their Introverted reflections.

The primary difference between the two seems to be biological—a matter of how much stimulation we need to feel comfortable. When researchers studied attitude preference in young infants, for example, they confirmed two distinct patterns of behavior. Confronted with a new and exciting toy, some babies reacted with initial interest but were quickly bored and shifted their attention elsewhere. Other babies reacted with great intensity, became overwhelmed, and burst into tears.

Although our stereotypes of Introverts and Extraverts might lead one to assume that the babies who lost interest were Introverted, the truth is exactly the opposite. The babies who lost interest were Extraverted.

If we consider again the brain's division of labor, this distinction should be clear.

▲ The Extraverted part of the brain requires an outward goal to stay involved. Thus, Extraverts become restless below a certain level of external stimulation.

▲ The Introverted part of the brain is constantly processing sensory input and relating it to an internal agenda. Thus, Introverts can be quickly overtaxed by too much external input unrelated to their needs.

It's important to note that the converse is also true. Extraverts feel depleted and overtaxed by the kind of inner mentation that motivates and energizes an Introvert. Introverts can happily sustain their focus and concentration long after the Extraverts have yawned, stretched, gotten up, and started conversations about sports and relationships with their coworkers.

What's Culture Got to Do with It?

Although biology does push us in a particular direction, different cultures appear to value and support the attitudes in their own ways. If Jung's writings are any indication, the Swiss consider Introverted Thinking a masculine trait and Extraverted Feeling more common to women. Americans are a decidedly Extraverted lot—in a ratio of three to one—but we also tend to associate Extraverted socialization with women and Introverted reflection with men.

Popular books on relationship, for example, insist that women need to talk about their feelings in order to recognize them, whereas men "retreat to their caves" to work out their problems. Given our strong cultural preference for Extraversion, the association is probably an artifact of restricted gender roles rather than an indication of gender-specific traits.

One can see our general Extraverted bias simply by reading the advice columns in the newspaper. For example, when Ann Landers counsels that "most of our problems in life are the result of saying yes too soon or no too late," she's clearly speaking to the Extraverted majority, who are inclined to adjust to others' expectations and take action before they've reflected long enough to know what they really want. An Introvert's problems are more likely to stem from the reverse inclination—to say no too soon or yes too late.

Many Extraverts don't even acknowledge their Introverted side until midlife, when changing physical and social circumstances encourage them to think more seriously about what "it all means" to them. Introverts may take the opposite path. Some Introverts spend the first half of life trying to make a place for themselves that won't compromise their inner reality. Such Introverts usually feel that they've just "found themselves" at midlife.

What If Extraverted/Introverted Scores Are Too Close to Call?

If a person's Introverted and Extraverted scores are nearly equal, he or she is likely to be an Introvert who is feeling pushed to develop more Extraversion.

▲   Introverted men, in particular, often get scores that indicate slight Extraversion (8/6). This is because American men are socialized to display certain Extraverted traits and regard them as part of a masculine identity.

On the other hand, if a person has close E and I scores but has marked column A on questions 5, 17, and 25, the type is probably an Extravert. Such Extraverts might be

▲   feeling some uncertainty about their ability to take direct action under their present circumstances;
▲   in a committed relationship with someone more Extraverted than they are;
▲   in a transition period—for example, between jobs, or trying to understand themselves in a new way.

Types whose E/I and P/J scores are both very close may be

▲   feeling pressure to conform to someone else's image of them;
▲   in a new job or school or marriage, whose demands are playing havoc with an accustomed self-image;
▲   recently retired or divorced, or attempting to redefine an accustomed identity.

5

Our Two Strongest Functions

▲ THE TWO MIDDLE LETTERS of our psychological type tell us which two (of our four) functions we usually rely on for our approach to life.

The Perceiving Functions: Sensation and Intuition

	S or N		

The letters S and N stand for Sensation and iNtuition. These are the Perceiving functions, so called because we use them literally to perceive. That is, we use these functions when we encounter new information or circumstances that are unpredictable. When something is unpredictable, we don't know what to expect, and we can't make plans in advance. We have to be response-ready, so we can deal with the situation as it occurs, adjusting and improvising as we go along.

Thus, when we use Sensation or Intuition, we're taking in as much direct information as we can. We're alert to new opportunities. We may resist making final decisions, and we may lose track of time and limitation.

Although both Sensation and Intuition encourage us to live life in an immediate way—as it's happening to us—the two functions are in conflict with each other. That is, they can't be used at the same time. This is why a preference for one or the other can tell us something about the kinds of experiences we regard as definitive.

▲ Types who prefer Sensation generally focus on direct sensory experience. They're aware of appearances, facts, and details, and their surroundings have a direct impact on them.

▲ Types who prefer Intuition generally ignore the material surface of things and consider the larger picture. They're interested in meaning and future possibility, not facts and details. Intuitives may be so focused on a situation's potential that they overlook present obstacles.

Sensation gives us	Intuition gives us
▲ an appreciation for objective facts and circumstances, as perceived by the senses	● an appreciation for the larger picture or underlying pattern, beyond the reach of the senses
▲ excellent powers of observation	● vivid powers of imagination
▲ an investment in life as it exists right now, in all its glorious particulars	● an investment in future possibility, the wonder of things to come
▲ satisfaction in the pleasures and security of material reality	● a fascination with the unknown, the hidden, the unseen
▲ pragmatism and precision	● inspiration and enthusiasm
▲ an emphasis on utility and literalism	● an emphasis on originality and alternate meaning
▲ a need to absorb all the facts, no matter how long it takes, before attempting to understand	● a tendency to get "the whole picture" on the basis of a few salient facts
▲ a reliance on past experience when solving problems	● a reliance on ingenuity when solving problems
▲ the inability to believe or rely on something without sensory evidence	● the inability to feel motivated unless something new can be anticipated

Sensation gives us	Intuition gives us
▲ a sense of joy in consuming, possessing, and using things as they were meant to be used	● some resistance to material possession and responsibility as potentially entrapping

How the Perceiving Functions Develop

Sensation   As infants, our initial information about the world is primarily physical—we're hungry, tired, cold, warm, comfortable, uncomfortable, and so forth. This is the ground floor of the Sensation function. As our sensory information changes, our experience of reality changes.

Sensation, in this respect, should not be confused with simple awareness—that is, with the ability to receive information from the world. Sensation is ultimately the ability to adapt to and make use of what we're taking in with our senses. When we employ this function in an Extraverted way, we interact physically with the data in our immediate environment. For example, we might use it to catch a ball, get out of the rain, change a tire, play a guitar.

When we Sense in an Introverted way, we retain and make use of facts, statistics, and information about the physical world, particularly as they relate to a specific field of interest.

People who use Sensation for most of their interactions with

Peanuts

Peanuts reprinted by permission of United Feature Syndicate, Inc.

reality are highly observant and deeply influenced by what they see and hear around them. An exclusive reliance on Sensation, however, can tie us to the material surface of life. For example, we may find it difficult to deal with theories or abstract concepts unless we can apply them directly to our own experience.

Intuition   Even as infants, we aren't locked into an eternal present. We spend a great deal of time anticipating the future. We hear footsteps in the hall and realize that someone's about to come into the room. We see sunlight on the dresser and know that the household will soon be in motion. Research into infant behavior indicates that parents instinctively support a child's ability to envision the future. For example, as soon as a baby shows an inclination to sit up, a parent is likely to help the child into that position and name the anticipated behavior.

This is how Intuition first makes its appearance. It encourages us to see things not as they are but as they might be. When we use Intuition in an Extraverted way, we recognize what exists in front of us as meaningful not in its own right but because it suggests the larger picture—a pattern, an emerging possibility.

When we Intuit in an Introverted way, we also recognize patterns. But Introverted Intuition is more cerebral. It enables us to understand that meaning is relative. The same information can suggest many different patterns, depending on one's perspective.

People who use Intuition for most of their interactions with reality are imaginative and forward looking. They anticipate and may

Gilbert

Dilbert reprinted by permission of United Feature Syndicate, Inc.

push for change. An overreliance on Intuition, however, can keep us from understanding the value of stability and perseverance. We may jump to conclusions too quickly or confuse possibility with fact.

Type Trekking

An easy way to see the difference between our two Perceiving functions is to think about the crew of the Starship *Enterprise* on the classic *Star Trek* series. Scotty, the ship's engineer, behaves like a Sensation type. He is persuaded by nothing less than actual experience, and his focus is always on objects and conditions as they really exist—fuel, dilithium crystals, and not having enough time to repair the ship.

His direct opposite is Captain Kirk, the quintessential Intuitive, whose focus is squarely on the possible—the not-yet-tried. Like most Intuitives, Kirk is a master of the Great Idea but has little sense of the details or strategy needed to bring it about. He expects to solve problems as they happen, under the pressure of the moment.

Many of the heated arguments on board the *Enterprise* occur between Kirk and Scotty, because their approaches to life are fundamentally alien to each other. "Mr. Scott! More warp drive—NOW," says Kirk, in another last-ditch attempt to extricate the ship from peril with a brilliant but untested plan of action, to which the redoubtable engineer objects with his legendary Sensate rejoinder, "I canna' give you more'n she's got, Cap'n!"

Ultimately, if the crew is to survive, both characters must compromise.

▲ Scotty, like most Sensation types, needs to be reminded that the future can be different from the present—even though direct experience suggests otherwise.

▲ Kirk, like most Intuitives, needs to recognize the reality, limits, and value of what already exists.

The Judging Functions: Thinking and Feeling

		T or F	

The third letter of our psychological type, T or F, stands for Thinking or Feeling, which are known as the Judging functions. In the great

38

adventure of life, we're not going to spend all our time hacking our way through the thickets of firsthand experience. Sometimes it's better to know where the path is and whether something horrible is likely to eat us on the way.

Unlike Sensation and Intuition, which encourage us to keep our options open and to acquire more information, the Judging functions prompt us to note how things usually happen and to organize our behaviors accordingly. This is why Thinking and Feeling are considered rational functions. Rational behavior is always based on predictability—things we know to be true because they happen regularly in the same way.

Although Thinking and Feeling both prompt us to focus on the predictable, they encourage conflicting ideas about how predictability is reckoned. This is why a preference for one or the other can tell us something about how we manage life and attempt to keep things under control.

- When we use Thinking, we organize our behaviors in terms of general, impersonal predictability: rules, laws, principles, logical or numerical sequence, definition, hierarchy, and so forth.
- When we use Feeling, we organize our behaviors in terms of specific, personal criteria: the signs and rituals that convey our shared beliefs, values, moral sensibilities, identification with others, and social relationships.

Thinking gives us	Feeling gives us
the ability to make decisions impersonally, based on logic, analysis, and efficient tactics	the ability to make decisions personally, based on shared values and relationship
an interest in how things work	an interest in how people feel
a reliance on justice, ethics, fair play, and equality	a reliance on consensus, morality, mercy, and loyalty

Thinking gives us	Feeling gives us
▲ a commitment to intellectual freedom, freedom of conscience, and individual rights	● a commitment to social obligation, empathy, and responsibility to others
▲ the ability to anticipate and plan for obstacles realistically	● the ability to anticipate people's needs and reactions
▲ an interest in causal relationships and the general laws they imply	● an interest in human relationships and the values they illustrate
▲ a good sense of narrative structure and sequence—how the beginning leads, step by logical step, to a conclusion	● a good sense of body language and vocal intonation—how something was said and why

How the Judging Functions Develop

Feeling   In our early years, as we're acquiring Sensing experiences and learning to Intuit their potential, we are also beginning to develop "ideas" about experiences that occur with some regularity. Some of them feel good, and we like them. We smile and laugh and show our pleasure, attempting to make them happen again. Some of our experiences feel bad, and we try to avoid them. We fuss and cry and push people away.

This is our first, natural use of the Feeling function. We're not only building up our ideas about "how things are" and using those ideas to give our world rational coherence; we're also making judgments about what is happening to us. We're deciding what's important to us. In a primitive, infantile sense, we're expressing our values.

It should be recognized, however, that these personal evaluations are visible to others—in our displays of pleasure or distress. As such, they have a social component. They become part of our relationship with the people around us. They engender responses, which become part of our external environment. When we use Feeling in an Extraverted way, it facilitates a complex social vocabulary, by which we express and recognize the values we hold in common with others.

When we use Feeling in an Introverted way, it operates as a kind of inner flame—a sense of personal values that may be difficult to explain or express directly but whose character informs our choices and inclinations.

People who use Feeling for most of their interactions with reality are usually people-oriented and empathetic. They attempt to foster consensus and cooperation. An exclusive reliance on Feeling, however, can lead us to depend too much on social display for our understanding of relationship or on private ritual behaviors for our sense of identity.

cathy®   **by Cathy Guisewite**

Cathy ©1994 Cathy Guisewite. Reprinted with permission of Universal Press Syndicate. All rights reserved.

Thinking   Although evaluation is our first, natural response to our experiences, as we increase in cognitive development, we begin to recognize that certain experiences share features in common, whether we value them or dislike them. Footsteps in the hall and the sound of a key in the front door both suggest that someone is arriving. Teddy bears are soft, like blankets. Toys can be arranged by size or shape or kind.

This penchant for impersonal categorization is the rudiment of the Thinking function. Over time, observed properties—such as softness, warmth, loudness, redness—become separated from the things themselves, and we use them as touchstones to describe and recognize new experiences. That is, we try to fit new information into the categories we've already established.

When we use Thinking in an Extraverted way, we work within the categories society provides for describing and understanding situations impersonally. This enables us to analyze information logically, in terms of cause and effect, rather than personally, in terms of social relationship.

When we use Thinking in an Introverted way, we get a mental image of the logical relationships in an entire system. For example, if we're crocheting an initial into a sweater, we're likely to draw a picture rather than work out the logical relationships analytically.

People who use Thinking for most of their interactions with reality are likely to have a clear sense of how things happen—or should happen. They're good at finding solutions to problems impartially and logically. An overreliance on this function, however, can lead to a dependence on analytical observation, blinding us to truth that can't be expressed in terms of logical cause and effect.

Dilbert

Dilbert reprinted by permission of United Feature Syndicate, Inc.

Type Trekking

Again, the classic *Star Trek* crew can give us some insight into how conflicting functions operate. Indeed, one of the most helpful aspects of looking at type through the lens of a cultural myth is that we can see some things more clearly than we might by applying the theory to ourselves.

For example, because of the way the terms are normally used, it's easy to assume that Thinking and Feeling concern themselves, respectively, with the provinces of reason and emotion. Typologically, however, both Thinking and Feeling are methods of *reasoning*. Both enable us to make decisions based on what we know to be predictable.

The actual distinction becomes quite clear, in the *Star Trek* episodes, in the ongoing conflict between Dr. "Bones" McCoy, the ship's physician, and Mr. Spock, its half-Vulcan, half-human science officer. Both are eminently reasonable men, technically proficient and scientifically knowledgeable. The primary difference between them is the criteria on which their reasoning is based.

Spock, the Thinking type, reasons by way of logic. He aggressively seeks the most expedient solution to a problem, unencumbered by the need for approval or attention to other people's beliefs or opinions. Dr. McCoy, the quintessential Feeling type, reasons by way of human values, which dictate that relationships and people's reactions be taken into account when solving a problem.

Although Spock stereotypes him as a sentimentalist, McCoy's behavior is not guided by romantic notions or by immediate emotional responses to life. His rationale is consistent and predictable, based on a lifetime of experience with people and cultural assumptions.

To be sure, McCoy is often querulous and moody, but why shouldn't he be? His Feeling-oriented expectations are usually frustrated by the other crew members' motives and behaviors. Within the context of the series, his role is to serve as the moral conscience of the group by offering a humane counterpoint to pragmatic decisions already made.

For example, when McCoy, Spock, and others have crash-landed on a primitive planet, McCoy is horrified to find that Spock is willing to leave the dead behind unburied. Spock has reasoned that survival of the group is a more logical aim than an unnecessary ritual service. McCoy has reasoned from a different perspective. He believes that Spock will forfeit the group's cooperation, even in the interest of their own survival, if he does not show the proper respect for human life conveyed by the ritual.

This is not an issue of reason versus emotion. Both men are approaching the situation rationally; but one is focused on the impersonal criteria of logic, the other on the personal criteria of values.

▲ Spock, like most Thinking types, needs to be reminded that the desire for approval, acknowledgment, and support may be illogical, but it is not unreasonable. He needs to take it into account, like any other data expedient to his objective.

▲ McCoy, like other Feeling types, needs to be reminded that a purely causal approach to problem solving may be impersonal, but it is not inhuman. He could scarcely practice medicine without recourse to impersonal laws and principles.

In the climax of the aforementioned plot, McCoy hardens his jaw and stands firm. He reminds Spock that "life and death are seldom issues of logic." "Perhaps," Spock acknowledges, "but attaining a goal always is." This is really the heart of the Thinking/Feeling distinction.

Logic, which underlies the operation of Thinking, is an impersonal method of determining causal relationship. It can be applied to any situation in which one's only concern is the attainment of an end. Human values, on the other hand, which underlie the operation of Feeling, are apparent only in the specific behaviors that give them expression. Their universality notwithstanding, they are usually embedded in the sometimes unconscious ways that people understand the world—in assumptions that people hold in common.

When four crew members, including McCoy, find themselves in a parallel universe, forced to survive among barbaric and violent versions of the colleagues they once knew, the only character who is consistent in both universes is Spock. Because he sees life as governed by mathematical logic, once the rules of the game are clear to him, he can survive anywhere, as a warrior or as a peacemaker.

McCoy, on the other hand, has no resources in the parallel universe. In a culture where power is taken by force and discipline is savage authoritarianism, the Federation-honed values he's brought with him—respect for sentient life, military discipline, nonviolence—have no Extraverted means of expression. If he acts on them, he strikes the other members of the society as weak and stupid.

Feeling types who pursue careers in Thinking-oriented fields, like business or law, can easily find themselves in McCoy's position. Their expressed values may be misunderstood by Thinking types as lack of aggression and self-esteem.

For example, a Feeling type usually attempts to soften a critical remark by prefacing it with a polite disclaimer, such as "I'm not sure I'm understanding this correctly, but . . ." The type expects a reply that acknowledges the effort—something along the lines of "Yes, of course you've understood correctly; I was unclear." A Thinking type, however, is likely to take the disclaimer at face value and hear it as an indication of the speaker's insecurity.

A Thinking-oriented approach to life can operate as a kind of common language in cultures otherwise divided by specific customs and values. On the other hand, the price of a one-sided Thinking orientation, as Spock's various story lines indicate, may be quite high.

6

The Fourth Type Category

Perceiving or Judging

▲ AS I SAID IN THE LAST CHAPTER, the two middle letters of our type stand for the functions we use most in everyday life.

▲ The first of these middle letters designates our Perceiving function (Sensation or iNtuition), which encourages a response-ready mode of behavior: action right now, as a situation is happening.

▲ The second designates our Judging function (Thinking or Feeling), which prompts us to hesitate before we act—to recognize the predictable and to anticipate consequences.

The fourth letter of our type, P or J, tells us which of these two functions we use in an Extraverted way—that is, to understand and relate to our external conditions.

▲ P types use their Perceiving function (Sensation or Intuition) to understand and relate to external conditions:
- ESTPs, ESFPs, ISTPs, and ISFPs use Extraverted Sensation.
- ENTPs, ENFPs, INTPs, and INFPs use Extraverted Intuition.

▲ J types use their Judging function (Thinking or Feeling) to understand and relate to external conditions:
- ESTJs, ENTJs, ISTJs, and INTJs use Extraverted Thinking.
- ESFJs, ENFJs, ISFJs, and INFJs use Extraverted Feeling.

The function we use to interact with the external world helps to determine what we take for granted about outward reality in general. Whether we're Extraverted or Introverted types, we all use our Extraverted function to fit into society and to carry out our goals. Thus, the P or J at the end of our type tells us a great deal about the way we understand the pleasures, problems, and purpose of life.

Because our Extraverted function characterizes our expectations of others and our visible behaviors, it also influences the way others see us. P types, who are response-ready, display different characteristics than J types, who like to know what to expect before they act.

Acting Naturally

In chapter 3, I mentioned the fact that our typological architecture mirrors other natural systems, in that stability is founded on the union of opposites. In the physical world, this structural arrangement allows for creative variation within the constraints of natural law. To a large extent, P types and J types illustrate the psychological correlates of this dynamic process. P types are drawn to novelty and variation; J types focus on boundary conditions and direction.

Some researchers believe that this distinction has its roots in evolutionary development. For hunter-gatherers, P traits were crucial to survival. Rapidly shifting attention, hands-on intelligence, and hair-trigger responses ensured the ability to exploit opportunity and to defend against predators in a dangerous prehistoric environment. J traits, by contrast, developed in a more secure environment, which encouraged focused attention, structural maintenance, and the development of long-term goals.

One can see the same distinction, from a radically different perspective, as it exists in information theory, which deals with the accurate transmission of communication signals. A message that's been converted into electrical signals is difficult to reconstruct if the pattern of signals is too highly varied. Too many interpetations are possible. The only way to ensure correct interpretation is to reduce a message to its essentials and to repeat the signals most important to its understanding.

One might say that P types emphasize variation and multiple options over exactitude of communication. They want all the information they can get and diverse possibilities for understanding and response. J types are more inclined to introduce redundancy into a system, focusing on essentials, and anticipating regular occurrences of the same event over time.

It should be remembered that P and J traits are most pronounced in our dealings with the outer world. When we're alone, doing exactly what we want to do, we may exhibit some traits that conflict with our P or J designation. For example, TJs may be highly task-oriented in their career objectives, but somewhat indecisive in their personal lives. FPs may be highly flexible in social situations, but exacting in areas important to themselves. This outer/inner division is the normal state of affairs—for all types.

Extreme Extraverts, therefore, may find that their self-experience coincides almost entirely with their P or J traits. For extreme Introverts, the opposite is true. That is, high-scoring Introverts generally find that their self-experience coincides strongly with many traits *opposed* to their P or J designation.

P types	*J types*
▲ never feel they have enough information to decide, and may seek new options even after deciding	● may decide before all the facts are in or limit their options just to have things settled and off their minds
▲ react fully and quickly to whatever happens to catch their attention	● want to know what's going to happen so they can prepare for it
▲ are ready for anything but may depend too much on chance and circumstance	● are self-motivated but may be unprepared to deal with the unexpected
▲ resist structure; may not start a project until motivated by the arrival of a deadline	● prefer structure; will organize time and efforts to meet goals and deadlines
▲ may take on too many projects or keep going until they're overloaded and unable to do it all	● do exactly what they say they're going to do, and will renegotiate if more is required

P types	J types
▲ may experience their emotions as physical states and become run down	● may not be aware of their physical needs until they have a real problem
▲ are curious, adaptable, masters of improvisation, but may not follow through or stick to something very long	● are responsible, firm, true to their word, but may be unwilling to change, even when things are going badly
▲ are enthusiastic, engaged, impetuous	● are decisive, committed, determined
▲ can be reckless—may not consider risks or time constraints when drawn to something exciting	● can be controlling—may take authority instinctively, certain they know what needs to be done

The P Types

Because P types use Sensation or Intuition for their outward behaviors, the goals they formulate usually emphasize direct engagement. When people consistently take action in Perceiving terms, they develop a way of looking at reality that colors their behaviors and is apparent to others. These traits are more pronounced in the Extraverted P types, but Introverted P types also display them.

For example, because they value the immediacy of direct engagement, P types tend to be flexible and will change directly easily if something else seems more interesting or more exciting at the moment. A very high P score may even suggest resistance to time constraints and external limits.

Given their openness to experience, P types may avoid making decisions until circumstances force their hand. They don't want to "push the river" or close off other options that might turn up. Such types may believe that the right choice will simply happen to them or become apparent to them in the process of living their lives. As author Alice Walker says, in fine Perceiving tradition, "Expect nothing; live frugally on surprise."

Surprise, for these types, doesn't mean being startled or forced to contend with the unknown. It means leaving room for life to happen without too much predetermination. Perceivers are like surfers in this respect. The goal may be the perfect wave, but you can't control the wind or the tides or the weather. What's important is to recognize the moment when the wave is beginning to build and to go with it in a glorious leap of faith, cocreating the experience as it's unfolding.

For this reason, P types can be discouraged by too many obstacles. They may not anticipate problems realistically, figuring they'll improvise if they need to when the time comes. If they can't do this successfully, they may be frustrated and impatient, as though life were being unfair to them.

Most P types have some difficulty shutting down their perceptual receptivity. For example, they can be influenced by the views and ideas of each new person they talk to, or each new article or book they read. They get restless when their attention is not fully engaged, and they tend to change direction and careers more often than J types.

Their moods, accordingly, seem to run in cycles—periods of enthusiasm and receptivity alternating with periods of overload and withdrawal. P types often experience their legitimate need to withdraw as a feeling of disappointment and depression.

The J Types

Because J types use Thinking or Feeling for their outward behaviors, they don't believe for one minute that the right things will "just happen" to them naturally. As Lois Lane, the very decisive female reporter, once said to Clark Kent: "You're wrong about me. I really *like* surprises. I just want to know about them in advance."

J types handle outward events rationally, by anticipating the predictable and being prepared for it. They don't want their hand forced by unanticipated circumstances. They want to organize their experience in advance so they know what's essential and can attend to it in terms of their goals.

P types generally misunderstand a Judging approach as restrictive and controlling. From their perspective, J types are conformists, intent on imposing the very limitations that P types regard as suspect—the dull security of rules and systems that tell people what to do and how to feel. It's important to recognize that this distinction—between P types as free spirits and J types as authority freaks—is a stereotype. *All* types cherish freedom. And all types crave security. It's just that P types and J types understand these things in different ways.

P types, who are response-ready, naturally understand freedom as the absence of constraint. They want the ability to take immediate action, as a situation is occurring, without having to explain it to themselves or reckon with prior limits.

J types understand freedom from the opposite perspective. Without plans or expectations, one has no *choice* but to be response-ready, constantly alert to all the data available in a situation. This lack of choice makes J types feel trapped. It forces them to react, and only to react, without recourse.

From this point of view, the ability to establish priorities doesn't limit one's options. It creates options that don't exist in nature, thus freeing one from the mercy of chance and circumstance. If a course is worth pursuing, then immediate information is important only when it has some bearing on the issue.

Accordingly, J types react badly to a change of plans. They don't want to entertain new options when a decision has already been made. On the other hand, J types are more philosophical than P types when implementation of a plan goes awry.

As suggested earlier, P types are a bit like surfers. They make decisions by recognizing the right wave and "going with it," relying on their natural skills and past experience to handle problems as they arise. Like a surfer shifting to maintain balance, P types count on their ability to improvise, and their reflexes are often keen.

If improvisation doesn't work, however, the experience is simply ruined. Once you've fallen off the board, there's nothing more to be done. The moment is gone. P types in this situation are crushed and disappointed and feel exposed as inadequate. Indeed, when P types find themselves contending with circumstances in which they have neither skills nor experience to count on, they die a thousand deaths, anticipating all manner of awful things that could go wrong.

J types aren't like this. Not that they react well to failure. No one does. But they have more patience with obstacles. They don't invest their self-worth in the successful outcome of one moment. They make plans with an eye toward using them again, and they expect to refine them over time. If a system doesn't work, a J type will get frustrated, but ultimately regards the failure as a useful piece of information. It suggests a way to anticipate the problem or prevent it before it happens.

Our Introverted Function

Although the P or J at the end of our psychological type tells us which function we use for our Extraverted behaviors, there is a good deal more to us than meets the eye. Inside ourselves another world exists, in which we reflect on and interpret our experiences, relating them to our individual needs and point of view. We don't use our Extraverted function for these tasks. We use our other function, our Introverted function.

- ▲ P types use their Judging function (Thinking or Feeling) for Introverted reflection:
  - ● ESTPs, ENTPs, ISTPs, and INTPs use Introverted Thinking.
  - ● ENFPs, ESFPs, ISFPs, and INFPs use Introverted Feeling.
- ▲ J types use their Perceiving function (Sensation or Intuition) for Introverted reflection:
  - ● ESTJs, ESFJs, ISTJs, and ISFJs use Introverted Sensation.
  - ● ENTJs, ENFJs, INTJs, and INFJs use Introverted Intuition.

For all practical purposes, our psychological division of labor sees to it that our two strongest functions offer us two entirely different perspectives on reality.

As suggested in the last chapter, P types who are easygoing and flexible in an Extraverted social situation can be ruthlessly self-critical or hold very stubbornly to a set of values in those Introverted areas of life that apply to themselves and their own priorities. Many a Perceiving comedian, athlete, or performer is responsive, spontaneous, and improvisational onstage or in the field but quite decisive and even controlling about things at home that involve personal time and space.

In contrast, a J type may be a high-powered manager among colleagues or in a club or organization but display a surprising lack of boundaries where immediate personal satisfactions are concerned. Part of our development, typologically, is learning how to bring our inner and outer worlds into balance.

The P/J Split in Pop Culture

In Willy Holtzman's stage play, "Sabina: The Untold Story of Sigmund Freud, Carl Jung and Sabina Spielrein" the following exchange occurs between Freud and Jung:

> CARL JUNG: You declined the invitation to America?
> SIGMUND FREUD: I was inclined to. But an entire nation half Puritan and half savage—what analyst could resist?

I can think of few characterizations that capture more succinctly the stereotypes that Judgers and Perceivers maintain about each other in this country. Indeed, Freud's observation was downright Jungian. Our political and social conflicts are often framed in terms of the polar distinctions within us.

Simply at the level of popular culture, an extraordinary number of movie and TV plots are fueled by the particulars of the puritan/ savage (Judging/Perceiving) opposition. Apart from such obvious examples as *The Odd Couple, Simon and Simon, Starsky and Hutch,* or *Cagney and Lacy,* the tension between the two approaches is also a staple of the cop/cowboy genre, which often pits direct action against principled decision making.

In fact, media detectives are almost invariably hard-knuckled Perceiving types whose code of honor is entirely situational. Our films, TV shows, and novels tend to represent such men as woefully misunderstood by the rule-driven J types overseeing their cases from behind the safety of a desk. In the Perceiving-oriented world of entertainment, Judgment types are almost invariably played as uptight hypocrites devoid of physical passion.

In the short-lived series *Kindred: The Embraced*, a story about five clans of modern vampires, a young musician of the Toreador clan, known for being free spirits and artists, says disparagingly of the Vendru clan, "They're not like us. They're power brokers and bankers—suits with sharp teeth." The P/J split apparently reigns even among the undead.

Not surprisingly, many of our popular films represent the P/J split in terms of gender issues. *Pretty Woman* and *The Bodyguard*, which might be regarded as popular fairy tales, both tell the same basic story: a Judging male, accustomed to life as an emotionally controlled pragmatist, is gradually thawed by the playful, vulnerable, sexually open immediacy of a Perceiving female.

For the most part, however, Perceiving qualities are more likely to be represented as masculine—as in the popular novel *The Bridges of Madison County*, which pairs a dissatisfied but loyally committed J housewife with an itinerant P photographer, surprised by love in midlife.

Such Perceiving heroes are almost always represented as latter-day Huck Finns who suspect that females are "out to civilize" them. For example, in *Moonlighting*, Maddie Hayes spends all her time setting rules (Judgment), while her partner, David Addison, regards escape from the rules as a declaration of personal freedom (Perception).

On *Cheers*, sports-jock-turned-bartender Sam Malone is the classic Perceiving type of the Peter Pan variety, while his intellectual snob of a barmaid, Diane Chambers, is the classic Judging type who won't tolerate even her stuffed animals' being out of order.

On *Remington Steele*, Laura Holt, a smart, aggressive, Judging-oriented detective with a strong moral code, is forced to rely on a mysterious cat burglar whose Perceptive style has unaccustomed him to moral considerations and long-term commitment.

In all plots of this sort we are meant to recognize the sexual tension between the principals, fueled, in part, by their mutual antagonism. And we have a stake in the characters' discovery that they are falling in love, somewhat despite themselves. We instinctively recognize in their situation an image of our own P/J conflicts.

On the other hand, we also recognize the potential for growth in the characters' fundamental polarity. A film like *Pretty Woman* can end at the point of climax, so to speak, and we are left with a feeling of exhilaration. In a TV show, however, which continues season after season, sexual resolution of a P/J conflict nearly always drains the energy from the couple's relationship. This is because, typologically, the tension between our P and J functions is the source of our creativity and psychological evolution. If we resolve it by way of merger, we become less conscious.

7

Our Dominant and Secondary Functions

▲ AS DISCUSSED IN THE LAST CHAPTER, the P or J at the end of our psychological type tells us which of our two best functions we use for Extraversion—that is, for interacting with others and adjusting to our outward circumstances. We use our other strong function in an Introverted way—for reflection and the maintenance of our own viewpoint.

For most of us, one of these functions predominates. Using it feels natural and comes easily to us. This is our *dominant* function. It determines our general approach to life, and it colors our understanding of life's purpose and satisfactions.

Our other function is *secondary*. It, too, encourages skills that come easily, but using them requires more deliberate effort. This is because our secondary skills not only complement but also limit our dominant ones. The effect of using both is like looking through a stereoscope. We see the same situation from slightly different angles, and bringing them together gives us perspective.

One of the basic tasks of typological development is to develop our secondary function well enough to get this perspective. It's normal, particularly between adolescence and early midlife, to refine the skills of our dominant function and to use our secondary function only when it supports them. Eventually, however, the circumstances we create by doing this push us toward other dimensions of our personality.

Extraverts

Extraverts, of course, use their Extraverted function most of the time—the one indicated by the P or J at the end of their type. This is what makes them Extraverts. Their Extraverted function is *dominant*. Their Introverted function is *secondary*.

These are the eight Extraverted types:

ESTP = Extraverted Sensation type with secondary Introverted Thinking.

ESTJ = Extraverted Thinking type with secondary Introverted Sensation.

ESFP = Extraverted Sensation type with secondary Introverted Feeling.

ESFJ = Extraverted Feeling type with secondary Introverted Sensation.

ENTP = Extraverted Intuitive with secondary Introverted Thinking.

ENTJ = Extraverted Thinking type with secondary Introverted Intuition.

ENFP = Extraverted Intuitive with secondary Introverted Feeling.

ENFJ = Extraverted Feeling type with secondary Introverted Intuition.

Because American culture favors Extraverted personality traits—outgoing behaviors, a strong interest in others, attention to externals—we tend to think of them as products of healthy socialization. And they can be fostered, up to a point, by cultural training and expectations. At bottom, however, Extraversion isn't a choice so much as it is a biological need. It derives from a high threshold for external stimulation and the ongoing attempt to get enough to stay comfortable.

Because Extraverts are motivated to seek external stimulation, they naturally see reality as something outside themselves—something that claims their attention and is encountered in the material world. An Extravert's sense of identity reflects this other-oriented viewpoint. It develops in the meeting of self and world, and the result is a "local habitation and a name"—a place and persona that others recognize and acknowledge as one's own. Indeed, for most Extraverts, self-esteem depends on understanding and being understood in light of others' expectations and behaviors.

This doesn't mean, of course, that Extraverts simply accept the ideas and assumptions that prevail in their jobs, family, society, or country. They may quarrel with them or try to change them. The point is that Extraverts take them for granted as given data. Reality is whatever happens to exist—people, places, events, things, opportunities—and the self-evident purpose of life is engagement.

This is why Extraverts regard Introverted personality traits as a social deficit. As far as they're concerned, maturity and normalcy are evidenced by the ability to find satisfaction and derive meaning from outward engagement. They associate their inner "self" with unpleasant experiences of isolation and overload—all those impressions, impulses, and uncivilized tendencies put aside for the sake of relationship. This association is not so much inaccurate as it is limited in scope.

Introverted self-experience has many levels, just as Extraverted identity does. Among other things, it comprises needs, values, talents, intuitions, dreams, ideas, and potential that existing opportunity and engagement will not satisfy. Without some active awareness of this inner realm, Extraverts have little perspective on the general social compact. They become dependent on feedback from others to formulate their beliefs and opinions. As an executive producer once said to a TV series writer, "I don't know whether I like your script or not. No one else has seen it yet."

In other words, Extraverts can get stuck in their dominant approach to life. The outer world both names and defines them, and they lose track of the unique perspective that makes them who they are. Accordingly, most Extraverts benefit from a deliberate attempt to react less and reflect more.

Such benefit, however, may not be apparent immediately. Extraverts identify with their dominant function, which is like depending on one eye for visual input. The process of opening the other is potentially enriching, but it initially creates an experience of conflict. Introverted reflection may, for example, suggest alternative options for constructing a life—options that cannot be pursued without undermining commitments and responsibilities already assumed.

Our very Extraverted culture tends to regard inner conflict as a problem, and therapists' offices are filled with people attempting to make it go away. But, in truth, this is what growth is about for an Extravert—learning to live with psychological ambiguity long enough to recognize inner conflict as a valuable source of perspective.

Our two best functions are meant to work together, but because their attitudes are opposed, the images they offer us are difficult to integrate. The attempt to use both creates a certain amount of mental and emotional friction. We need this friction. It helps us to stay conscious, no matter what type we are.

An unopposed dominant function is tantamount to instinct. It moves us to adapt to our environment in the same way, over and over again. Our secondary function ensures some independence of our circumstances as well as our relationship to them.

Extraverted P types   Extraverted Perceivers use Extraverted Sensation or Extraverted Intuition most of the time, which moves them to react immediately to external stimulation. These types depend on direct experience for their primary understanding of life, and they're likely to be accomplished change masters. They enjoy the challenge of improvising as a situation is happening.

Accordingly, these types can find it difficult to defend themselves against overstimulation or depletion. They adapt to reality by participating fully in whatever turns up, and they'll invest as much time, energy, and attention as they have—until it runs out. This is one reason Extraverted Perceivers need to cultivate their secondary Judgment function, Introverted Feeling or Thinking.

Without some awareness of their own limits and priorities, their only recourse is escape from the expectations of others. Extreme P types are like the flock of birds in the old Disney cartoon who always flew backward. They never knew where they were headed, but they definitely knew where they didn't want to be anymore.

It's not that Extraverted P types don't realize what matters to them personally. They do. In fact, they can be quite strong about taking some space for themselves. For example, an ESFP bishop of my acquaintance spends the lion's share of his time responding to crises in his diocese but insists on having Mondays off to play golf, no matter what else is going on. This is the way many Extraverted Perceivers use their Introverted Judgment—to withdraw from others' needs and demands and do something that makes them feel good. They get the relief they need, but their dominant Perceiving style remains unmodified.

The growing edge for Extraverted P types is to bring their Introverted Judgment into dialogue with their accustomed approach to life—for example, by recognizing their limits *before* they get invested in a new situation, or by sticking with something, despite the absence of reassurance or satisfaction, because it's the right thing to do.

Such exercises can easily strike such types as chores. Indeed, simply *intending* to try them can give them a feeling of accomplishment. They get irritated and bored with ongoing pursuits whose rewards are not immediate.

Extraverted Perceivers need to recognize their boredom as a positive sign—rather like the soapy-headed man in the old commercial for dandruff shampoo who knew the product was working because it tingled. If they contend with the conflict they're experiencing, even in one small area of their lives, they begin to see things from a broader angle. They recognize their very real power to affect others and to make a difference in the world.

Extraverted J Types   Extraverted Judgers use Extraverted Thinking or Extraverted Feeling most of the time, and they depend on rational predictability for their primary experience of life. These types make it their business to know how things are supposed to happen. They're directed and organized, and they know how to set goals and meet them. In fact, they may not be able to rest until they're confident a situation's well in hand.

Accordingly, these types may find it hard to contend with the unpredictable or irrational side of life. They can spend too much of their time trying to keep things under control, opting for perfectionism when the situation requires risk or making the most of an opportunity.

Extraverted Judgers need their secondary function, Introverted Intuition or Introverted Sensation, to stand in the middle of their own lives and simply have the experience—without trying to fit it into a schedule or predict its outcome. Where Extraverted P types become overloaded with information and are forced to set limits by escaping, Extraverted Js get pushed by fate (exhaustion, mortality, other people's decisions) to deal with the unexpected and to take in more data. To paraphrase the late John Lennon, life happens to them while they're busy making other plans.

Being pushed into Introverted Perception unawares is almost always a negative experience. When illness, fatigue, or a personal crisis forces Extraverted Judgers to take time for themselves, they feel guilty, as though they're letting others down. Thus, they tend to divide life experience into three basic sorts: situations that are reasonable and require their time and attention, situations that are unreasonable and can be ignored, and situations that are out of control but must be endured. It is the latter category to which such types generally apply their Introverted skills, because they have no other options.

The problem with this division of labor is that the latter category too easily extends to situations that are not really out of control but whose disposition is simply not rational. For example, such types may believe that the standards they maintain in their public life have no bearing on their private satisfactions. Or they may tolerate a bad job or relationship because taking action involves too many variables, and they can't organize the information to their satisfaction. They explore their possibilities and watch for the "right moment," but they're hoping that some outside force will provide a sudden and unexpected solution to the problem.

The growing edge for these types is to bring their immediate experience of a situation into dialogue with their accustomed approach to life—for example, by recognizing the effect of their schedule and routines on themselves or the people around them, or by making room for needs unrelated to the goal at hand.

Extraverted Judgers tend to regard these kinds of exercises as an indulgence they can't afford, but the effort to take immediate experience into account eventually rewards them with both wisdom and empathy. It gives them a way to identify with others, and their ability to recognize the predictable becomes an ability to see with genuine clarity.

Introverts

Introverts construct their typological house differently from Extraverts. The P or J at the end of their type represents their Extraverted function, but this function is not dominant in their personality. It's secondary. Introverts are Introverted because they use their Introverted function most of the time.

This is one reason Introverts are harder to "read" than Extraverts. Their motives cannot be deduced as readily from their relationship to outward circumstances.

Here are the eight Introverted types:

ISTP = Introverted Thinking type with secondary Extraverted Sensation.

ISTJ = Introverted Sensation type with secondary Extraverted Thinking.

ISFP = Introverted Feeling type with secondary Extraverted Sensation.

ISFJ = Introverted Sensation type with secondary Extraverted Feeling.

INTP = Introverted Thinking type with secondary Extraverted Intuition.

INTJ = Introverted Intuitive with secondary Extraverted Thinking.

INFP = Introverted Feeling type with secondary Extraverted Intuition.

INFJ = Introverted Intuitive with secondary Extraverted Feeling.

As in Extraversion, Introverted traits can be fostered by cultural expectation and formative experience. In general, however, Introverts don't tolerate as much external stimulation as Extraverts do. Their most prominent characteristics—their ability to focus at length on one thing, their tendency to observe and reflect, their need for time alone—are the direct result of a lower threshold for environmental input.

Because Introverts don't depend as much as Extraverts on external motivation, they regard their internal motives and reactions as primary. This doesn't mean that Introverts have no interest in others or put their own concerns first. It means they regard the meaning and influence of a situation to rest ultimately with the individual. From an Introverted perspective, the self cannot be defined by its circumstances. On the contrary, reality is what we bring to it from within.

Introverts do, of course, establish an Extraverted identity, just as Extraverts recognize the contribution of the self to outward meaning. Like all types, their Extraverted side develops as they adjust to, interact with, and find a place for themselves in the world. Unlike Extraverts, however, Introverts don't regard their Extraverted identity as the most important part of themselves. Introverts reflect before they Extravert, attempting to understand how the situation relates to their accustomed viewpoint.

Although Extraverts tend to mistake this hesitation for diffidence or uncertainty, it's really a form of self-assertion. An Introvert's first order of business is to protect the integrity of the inner world and to respect the authority of its claims. One can see this quite clearly by considering another character from the *Star Trek* series: Captain Jean-Luc Picard of *Star Trek: The Next Generation*.

Picard's taciturn reserve and underground passion are nothing like the aggressive derring-do of Captain Kirk in the classic *Star Trek* series. Yet fans recognize both men as strong, curious, and capable of inspiring and leading others. The difference is in their respective attitudes toward the same position.

Kirk, the Extravert, requires a great deal of external input. He thrives on new dangers and new love affairs, wanting to gauge directly the effect of his actions on the people (and humanoids) around him. Thus, he tends, somewhat imprudently, to leave his ship in the care of crew and subordinates, while he beams down to explore the outer terrain. This is generally how Extraverts use their Introverted function—to take care of the technical details while they relate to the outer world.

By contrast, the Introverted Picard considers himself the focal point of the reflective, decision-making process. He doesn't risk himself needlessly in new or unknown situations. He stays aboard the *Enterprise* as his staff explores the outer terrain. They provide him with the information he needs to understand the situation and to determine a reaction. This is how Introverts generally make use of their Extraverted function. They regard it as a subordinate whose job is to supply data and to carry out the Introverted agenda.

Of course, Picard's ability to establish an effective inner agenda depends on the kind of Extraverted data his scouts are bringing in. For example, if Picard dispatches a Klingon to relay information about a planet's terrain and inhabitants, the data he gets back will necessarily reflect a Klingon's militaristic point of view. In the same way, the Extraverted function dispatched by an Introvert to relate to the outer world will bring back information on its own terms.

Take an ISFJ, whose dominant function is Introverted Sensation. When Sensation is Introverted, its area of concern is concrete facts— mental content that will remain stable over time. The kind of facts an ISFJ acquires, however, is determined by the type's secondary function, Extraverted Feeling, which prompts an interest in human relationship. This is why ISFJs are usually characterized by their interest in meeting people's concrete needs. Such types often go into service occupations.

It should be granted that Introverts have little choice in the matter of developing their secondary function. Where Extraverts can ignore their Introverted side for half a lifetime before they run into major problems, Introverts usually establish enough Extraversion to realize their Introverted aims and goals. Indeed, when Introverts are involved in a situation congenial to their inner world, they even look like Extraverts.

This is particularly true of Introverts who like dealing with people—teachers, social workers, receptionists, and so forth—and of Introverts who enjoy performing, such as preachers, athletes, actors, and politicians. Introverted types are also likely to seem more Extraverted in the company of friends, family, or other Introverts.

The challenge for most Introverts is to use Extraversion in situations not congenial to their inner world. Because they are not energized by active stimulation, and, in fact, can be depleted by it, they need a certain amount of time alone—rather like Odo, the shape-shifter on *Star Trek: Deep Space Nine*, who can maintain his social form for only so long, until he must return to his original state and replenish his energies. This impels the typical Introvert to restrict genuine Extraverted adjustment to situations that further Introverted goals.

In most other situations, Introverts use a kind of Extraverted persona, which both accomplishes the tasks at hand and protects the inner self from unnecessary or unwanted engagement. Recall again the taciturn Captain Picard, who dispatches an away team to deal with conditions on a planet's surface, while he maintains his own counsel. Involving Picard directly in a problem becomes necessary only when the away team encounters a situation that goes beyond their authority or expertise. Because Extraversion can be used in this way—to resist rather than adjust, Introverts can easily learn to rely on their persona and never really develop the ability to adapt to others.

In fact, a very high P or J score (12 to 14), for an Introverted type, doesn't usually indicate balanced Extraverted development. It suggests an attempt to keep the inner self intact by meeting others' surface expectations.

Introverted P Types   Like Extraverted Perceivers, Introverted P types understand outward reality by way of direct experience, and they may have a similar resistance to limiting their options in areas that interest them. Their inner world, however, is characterized by Introverted Judgment (Introverted Feeling or Introverted Thinking), which determines their primary motives.

Introverted Judgment is not like Extraverted Judgment, which fosters a concern with outward standards, goals, and organization. Introverted Judgment is immediate and contextual. It encourages a person to recognize the underlying pattern of an ongoing situation and to respect its likely implications.

What I mean by *respect* is the sense that one's own actions are part of the larger pattern or have a hand in its unfolding. The resulting behavior can be as simple as appreciating a piece of music, as complicated as performing surgery, or as aesthetic as designing a set for a play. The way Introverted Judgment is expressed depends entirely on a person's talents and environment.

The types who use it, however, almost always have an artist's approach to what they do. They don't count on things staying the same way each time they're repeated, the way Extraverted Judgers might. They regard every moment as unique, with its own character and possibilities. A musician of this type might practice the same song for ten hours a day, and each time experience it as a new creation, with new possibilities for improvisation.

Because the values of an Introverted P type are linked to the experiential context in which they're being expressed, the inner life of the type may be otherwise diffuse. That is, such types may not focus their attention unless they're engaged by something that compels or obliges them. They need to develop their Extraverted Perception (Extraverted Sensation or Extraverted Intuition) well enough to provide some meaningful outlet for their Judgment in the outer world.

Deprived of such an outlet, Introverted P types will almost invariably realize their drive for contextual structure in the private realm, by ritualizing everyday experiences or regarding certain routines as all but sacred. Such rituals can benefit an *Extraverted* P type, who generally needs more experience with Introverted Judgment. But Introverted P types can get locked into their dominant function. They can be fiercely protective of their privacy and personal space—to the point of cloistering themselves from situations they regard as alien to their needs and values.

A P score of 12 or more can indicate this kind of development. It suggests that the type is using Extraverted Perception to shield a deeply personal experience of life against the expectations and judgments of others. Although practicing artists sometimes obtain scores like this, because they've deliberately constructed a life that allows periods of unfocused consciousness, a very high P score, for Introverts, more often suggests an inner life that has no directed means of public expression.

To be sure, this may happen for good reason. For example, the type's self-experience may be at odds with social convention. Or the type may have a spiritual vocation unsatisfied by organized religious institutions. Even when defensive Extraversion is warranted, however, Introverted P types run the danger of keeping too much of themselves in reserve.

Although this strategy does protect their inner world, it can render that world formless and inaccessible, even to themselves. It can also isolate them from genuinely satisfying relationships. For example, these types sometimes develop the habit of "going along" with outward situations from which they have actually distanced themselves, and their self-image becomes rather hazy. They're friendly, adaptable, and do what's expected—but in the manner of deep-sea divers swimming with a passing school of fish.

Introverted P types need to use their Extraverted Perception more actively, to give shape to their inner values. They don't need to articulate them so much as engage in experiences that have real meaning for them. If they can't do this vocationally or spiritually, they often benefit from avocational involvement in drama, the arts, or music.

When Introverted P types develop their Extraverted Perception well enough, they usually experience a discrepancy between their inner ideals and the real potential of external circumstances. But they need this conflict in order to grow and to fully recognize their own strengths and boundaries.

Introverted J Types   Like Extraverted Judgers, Introverted J types feel most comfortable when they can establish predictable reference points in the external world. Their inner world, however, is characterized by Introverted Perception (Introverted Sensation or Introverted Intuition), which determines their primary motives.

Unlike Extraverted Perception, which encourages an immediate response to direct experience, Introverted Perception dictates an interest in *represented* experience—words, facts, numbers, signs, and symbols: the kind of data that can be acquired or explored in the mind. For this reason, Introverted J types don't take systems of thought for granted, as Extraverted Judgers do. They are constantly taking in new information, and they may be single-minded in their attempt to accommodate it to existing procedures or to change the system accordingly.

Like Introverted Judgment, the expression of Introverted Perception depends largely on the type's interests and talents. It can make for careers in fields as varied as science, law, the ministry, and astrology. Almost all Introverted Js, however, will accumulate more information than a situation actually requires. They are constantly analyzing what others believe and think in terms of their own reflective process.

In fact, such types can find it difficult to limit and organize the data of their inner world without an external reference point to guide them. For example, unless given a specified amount of time or space to present their ideas, they may not know how much or how little to say. They are frequently surprised to find that they've overestimated others' interest in a project or overmet others' expectations.

For this reason, a J score of 12 or more usually suggests that Extraverted Judgment (Extraverted Thinking or Feeling) is being used defensively—to establish an outer environment that can be taken for granted, thus to serve, analyze, improve, or deconstruct it. These types can be decisive, even exacting, about time, plans, and goals when dealing with others, but they may not know how to set priorities or direct their energies where their personal space, ambitions, and interests are concerned.

Introverted Js need to apply their Extraverted Judgment less to the systems of others and more to the data of their own minds. When they do this well enough, they inevitably experience a conflict between their need to acquire more information and the effort to articulate what they already know. But in their attempt to resolve the conflict, these types often develop new ways of looking at an issue that make a genuine contribution to society.

8

Personality Types
Are Also Brain Types

▲ ONE OF THE MORE INTERESTING RESULTS of research into psychological types is the finding that each function operates in a different area of the brain. Each type not only activates a distinct set of neurological sites but also favors one side of the brain over the other.

Most of this research has been done with positron-emission tomography, or PET scanning, which allows technicians to see the brain at work. When the brain's nerve cells are active, the body produces enough glucose to support them. Researchers can tell from this increase in glucose which parts of the brain are working hardest when different functions are being used.

Even the simplest of human skills, of course, requires complex neural connections in many areas of the brain. To speak of a function's locus of activity is an extreme generalization. Roughly speaking, however, PET technology indicates that our functional capacities are distributed as follows:[1]

Front of Left Brain	Front of Right Brain
Extraverted Thinking	Extraverted Intuition
Extraverted Feeling	Extraverted Sensation
Introverted Sensation	Introverted Feeling
Introverted Intuition	Introverted Thinking
Back of Left Brain	**Back of Right Brain**

Because these findings suggest that different types are developing their strongest skills in one brain hemisphere or the other, it's worth summarizing what we currently know about right- and left-brain processing.

The Two Hemispheres of the Brain

In an episode of the now-defunct TV series *John Grisham's The Client*, a preoccupied accountant is helping an attractive young woman to organize her finances. In hopes of moving the relationship into a more romantic vein, the woman offers him tickets to a sports event, but the accountant hasn't a clue.

After the woman leaves, the office assistant, who knows the accountant is attracted to this client, confronts him with exasperation. "What is it with you?" she asks. "Is your right brain not paying attention or is your left brain not explaining anything to you?" This is as good a way as any to characterize the brain's division of labor. One hemisphere attends to immediate experience; the other looks for explanations.

The brain's two halves are roughly equal in size, connected in the middle by a nerve cable that allows for communication between them. Until the mid-sixties, neurologists believed that the left side of the brain, the side responsible for language and analytical thought, was dominant, and that the right side didn't do much of anything. Surgeons could remove the entire right brain from a fully conscious patient, and the person wouldn't even realize it was missing!

Further research, however, proved these initial assumptions mistaken. The left side of the brain isn't dominant or more important than the right. It simply isn't aware of things that happen only to the right brain. In fact, it isn't aware of anything that can't be put into words. The right brain, on the other hand, is aware in a direct, immediate way. It processes data in terms of images and patterns.

We now know that both hemispheres have a great deal of flexibility. For example, some left-handed people rely more on the right brain for language skills than do their right-handed compatriots. In general, however, each hemisphere handles information in its own way, and we learn to integrate the two streams of data—at least in some areas of behavior. There are many cases in which one side of the brain is better suited to a task than the other.

Consider the cook who tosses a hunk of pizza dough into the air, twirls and catches it, and shapes it without poking a fist through it. He isn't explaining to himself how people usually make pizza. He's using right-brain skills to respond to events as they happen. In the popular catchphrase of our right-brain-oriented sports culture, he's "just doing it."

Indeed, when an experience happens too rapidly or is too complex to put into words, the left brain simply backs off and ignores it. This is why right-brain knowledge can seem instinctive or even magical. When we know something by way of the right brain, we don't have much sense of how we know. We just do.

Conversely, the right brain will lose interest when the left brain is reducing a situation to its essentials and assigning them to categories. This is why left-brain knowledge seems so cut-and-dried. When we know something by way of the left brain, we're concentrating on what we can define and talk about. All the asymmetrical aspects of life, the things that make us unique, the truths we can't express—are left out.

How Brain Hemisphere Relates to Psychological Type

One of the first things apparent about left- and right-brain characteristics is how closely they correspond to the traits associated with J and P psychological types.

Left side of the brain (J)	Right side of the brain (P)
idea oriented	event oriented
general and abstract	concrete and specific
uses words and numbers	uses patterns or pictures
seeks exact conclusion	content with approximate, evolving solution

Left side of the brain (J)	Right side of the brain (P)
reductive and analytic	synthesizing and insightful
symbolic	imaginal
temporal	unaware of time limits
proceeds one step at a time	perceives all at once
little appreciation of tone	evaluates intonation
specializes in language skills	specializes in musical and artistic skills
controls speech	controls spatially related activities

There is good reason for this correspondence.

▲ J types use Extraverted Thinking or Extraverted Feeling for their outward behaviors. These functions activate more areas in the *left* hemisphere of the brain.

▲ P types use Extraverted Sensation or Extraverted Intuition for their outward behaviors. These functions activate more areas in the *right* hemisphere of the brain.

Once it's clear that J and P styles of behavior have a relationship to left- or right-brain processing, we can better appreciate the worldviews of the J and P types.

The left brain processes information one thing at a time. If it has to deal with many issues, it will organize them sequentially or numerically. Accordingly, J types like to finish one thing before starting another, and they rely on systems based on memory, repetition, and standards.

Because they depend on the left brain's linguistic propensities,

▲ TJs may need to hear something verbalized or see it written before they'll entirely credit its existence.

▲ FJs may need behavioral signs or symbols to tell them that someone's heart is in the right place.

The right brain is designed to process many things at once and to apprehend them in whole patterns. It does not recognize sequence or abstraction. Accordingly, P types are more unstructured than J types, less concerned with step-by-step planning and temporal boundaries.

Because they depend on the right brain's preference for images,

▲ SPs may not appreciate theories or explanations. They prefer illustrations or examples when trying to learn something new.

▲ NPs respond better to metaphor than to exposition or narrative thought.

The Introverted Functions and Brain Hemisphere

One of the most useful findings of current type research is the surprising fact that *Introverted and Extraverted versions of the same function activate on opposite sides of the brain.*

▲ Extraverted Thinking and Extraverted Feeling activate more areas in the *left* brain, but Introverted Thinking and Introverted Feeling activate more areas in the *right* brain.

▲ Extraverted Sensation and Extraverted Intuition activate more areas in the *right* brain, but Introverted Sensation and Introverted Intuition activate more areas in the *left* brain.

This information is useful for several reasons. For one thing, it makes clear that each function can operate in a right- or left-brain manner. For another, it suggests that our dominant and secondary functions are compatible because their primary activity takes place in the same brain hemisphere. Indeed, we may resist our less-developed functions, in part, because they require us to process information in an unaccustomed left- or right-brain way.

Rethinking Our Functional Definitions

Perhaps the most important implication of these findings involves our persistent cultural mythology. For example, most of us associate Thinking with verbal analysis and abstract logic. As it turns out, these skills characterize only Extraverted Thinking, a left-brain, linguistic manner of reasoning. The right brain also Thinks, from an Introverted standpoint, by way of visual, tactile, or spatial logic.

THE LOCKHORNS by Bunny Hoest & John Reiner

"WHY CAN'T YOU EVER USE THE SAME SIDE OF THE BRAIN I'M USING?"

The Lockhorns. Reprinted with special permission of King Features Syndicate.

Along the same lines, we generally associate Feeling with subjective ideas about human value. But this is largely an aspect of Introverted Feeling, a right-brain function. Extraverted Feeling makes use of left-brain skills, prompting us to recognize signs of relationship and to draw rational conclusions about people's behavior.

More dramatically, we usually associate Sensation with physicality and material investment, but this is true only of Extraverted Sensation, a right-brain function. The left brain also Senses, from an Introverted perspective, prompting us to acquire mental content in the form of facts and impressions.

Intuition, often described in self-help literature as a holistic right-brain activity, operates this way only in its Extraverted form. The left brain also Intuits, in an Introverted, language-oriented way, encouraging us to move beyond the boundaries of accepted terms and explanations.

The second section of this book will discuss each of the type categories more fully. As the specific functions are covered, these distinctions will become more apparent.

9

What Happens to the Functions We Don't Prefer?

▲ BECAUSE OUR FUNCTIONS AND ATTITUDES COME IN OPPOSING PAIRS, our preference for some necessarily entails the forfeiture of others. We attend to our promises, but dream adventure; companion others, but covet self-discovery; ensure our independence at the expense of emotional support.

Mythologies throughout the world tell us that this sacrifice of "the whole" is a universal phenomenon that serves the evolution of consciousness. Odin, for example, the ancient Teutonic god, pawned an eye to drink from the waters of knowledge. Eve, the ancestral mother of Genesis, acquired powers of discrimination but lost Paradise in the bargain.

By setting ourselves a direction, we surrender a great deal of our generic potential, but in return, we develop what Jung called differentiated strengths. We adapt our strongest function to our own needs, specialize it for a particular place and time. The paradox of the typological journey is that if we do this well enough, the functions we left behind begin to claim our attention, and we can differentiate some of them as well.

It's interesting to look at this journey in light of what we now know about right- and left-brain processing. Much of this knowledge was gained during the last generation by studying so-called split-brain patients—epileptics whose seizures stopped when the nerve cable between their brain hemispheres was severed.

Once communication between the two hemispheres ceases, the two sides of the body work separately. The left eye, controlled by the right brain, recognizes faces and patterns. The right eye, controlled by the left brain, recognizes words and letters.

More significantly, when the left and right brains are no longer cooperating, it becomes clear that each hemisphere has a distinct personality of its own—memories, experiences, self-awareness, and goals that conflict with those of the other hemisphere. Neurologists recognized this latter phenomenon when some split-brain patients developed a condition known as "alien hand" syndrome. Their left hand literally interfered with things the right hand was attempting to do.

As pointed out in the last chapter, most of us favor functions governed by one side of the brain or the other, which ensures that the "alien side" of our personality receives little attention. Eventually, we reach a state of typological imbalance. Much as the "alien hand" of a split-brain patient stops the other hand from opening a door or putting on a sock, our least-developed function asserts its own priorities, flooding us with impulses that interfere with our usual goals.

The Typological Journey

It should be emphasized that typological imbalance isn't a sign that something has gone wrong. It's the natural result of the human path of development. At puberty, strong hormonal drives impel us to channel our strongest functional skills into a social identity, and we need that identity to make our way beyond the family circle, to establish a place for ourselves in the world.

However, once we've accomplished some of what we set out to do, the identity we established in hormonal crisis isn't adequate to our continuing development. The problems and possibilities we're encountering require the use of other, less accessible functions, and the psyche pushes us, inevitably, to recognize their value.

The way this push occurs is admirable in its economy. When we concentrate most of our attention on our strongest function, its direct opposite gradually gets out of our control, and it plays havoc with our dominant aims and goals.

For example, if our dominant function is Extraverted Feeling,

76

most of our conscious choices will favor relationship and interaction with others. As a result, the impersonal goals encouraged by Introverted Thinking (Feeling's direct opposite) will seem cold and negative to us, and we won't recognize them as part of our personality.

The more firmly we identify with our dominant choices, the further our disowned function gets from our awareness, until it splits off and severs communication with us. Like an alien hand interfering with its opposite, it begins to work against us, encouraging primitive behaviors in direct conflict with our accustomed goals and self-image.

We may not experience these impulses as such, but we're very much aware of their effects. The energy we normally invest in our favorite pursuits is being siphoned off, and we experience a loss of interest in them, or we feel that our goals are being thwarted by others.

Hagar the Horrible

Hagar the Horrible. Reprinted with special permission of King Features Syndicate.

To be sure, no one enjoys an experience of this sort, but the subversive efforts of our least-developed function are probably our best safeguard against complacency and automatic behavior. When our usual way of doing things isn't satisfying, or is no longer working, we're forced to rethink our priorities. We ask ourselves questions, try new strategies, discover strengths we didn't know we had.

In consequence, we unearth more of our functional potential. We see ourselves a little differently. We risk new behaviors. Everyday existence is filled with ordinary conflicts that are really calls to assimilate more of who we are.

The Argument from Pasta

One reason for learning about psychological type is that the system tells us which function we've developed well and which one is likely to split off and get out of control. Even more, it tells us which functions are most helpful to us when it's time to grow. So let's stop here for a minute and take a look at how the different types organize their functional preferences.

Traditionally, a type profile is set up like a slab of lasagna. The functions are assumed to arrange themselves in layers—like noodles, tomato sauce, ricotta, and mozzarella. As in a lasagna, they all blend together to make one entity.

Conscious awareness, however, is a top-down affair. What we believe about ourselves and what we want for ourselves is reflected by the layers near the surface of the lasagna.

- ▲ The top layer is our dominant function, which governs most of our conscious behaviors. It's subject to our will, and the traits it encourages feel like "us."
- ▲ The next layer down is our secondary function, which is less conscious, but supports and advances our dominant aims and goals.
- ▲ At the very bottom are the two functions directly opposed to the top two: the tertiary and inferior functions. These are our least-conscious functions.

Opposite is a "type lasagna" for each of the sixteen types, showing our two extremes: our two strongest and two weakest functions.

In the logic of this analogy, most of us get a conscious fork into the top layer of our type lasagna, but we don't have much control over the layers at the bottom. In fact, our inferior function generally gets stuck in the pan and we leave it behind.

As already suggested, this situation is not only normal, but ensures that we go beyond the skills that come naturally to us. Our dominant function, after all, is easy to use, and we tend to avoid situations in which we can't depend on it. It's only the push from the "other side" of ourselves that wakes us up and tells us there's more to life than what we already know.

	ENFP		INFP
dominant	Extraverted Intuition	dominant	Introverted Feeling
secondary	Introverted Feeling	secondary	Extraverted Intuition
tertiary	Extraverted Thinking	tertiary	Introverted Sensation
inferior	Introverted Sensation	inferior	Extraverted Thinking

	ENTP		INTP
dominant	Extraverted Intuition	dominant	Introverted Thinking
secondary	Introverted Thinking	secondary	Extraverted Intuition
tertiary	Extraverted Feeling	tertiary	Introverted Sensation
inferior	Introverted Sensation	inferior	Extraverted Feeling

	ESFJ		ISFJ
dominant	Extraverted Feeling	dominant	Intraverted Sensation
secondary	Introverted Sensation	secondary	Extraverted Feeling
tertiary	Extraverted Intuition	tertiary	Introverted Thinking
inferior	Introverted Thinking	inferior	Extraverted Intuition

	ESTJ		ISTJ
dominant	Extraverted Thinking	dominant	Intraverted Sensation
secondary	Introverted Sensation	secondary	Extraverted Thinking
tertiary	Extraverted Intuition	tertiary	Intraverted Feeling
inferior	Introverted Feeling	inferior	Extraverted Intuition

	ESFP		ISFP
dominant	Extraverted Sensation	dominant	Introverted Feeling
secondary	Introverted Feeling	secondary	Extraverted Sensation
tertiary	Extraverted Thinking	tertiary	Introverted Intuition
inferior	Introverted Intuition	inferior	Extraverted Thinking

	ESTP		ISTP
dominant	Extraverted Sensation	dominant	Introverted Thinking
secondary	Introverted Thinking	secondary	Extraverted Sensation
tertiary	Extraverted Feeling	tertiary	Introverted Intuition
inferior	Introverted Intuition	inferior	Extraverted Feeling

	ENFJ		INFJ
dominant	Extraverted Feeling	dominant	Introverted Intuition
secondary	Introverted Intuition	secondary	Extraverted Feeling
tertiary	Extraverted Sensation	tertiary	Introverted Thinking
inferior	Introverted Thinking	inferior	Extraverted Sensation

	ENTJ		INTJ
dominant	Extraverted Thinking	dominant	Introverted Intuition
secondary	Introverted Intuition	secondary	Extraverted Thinking
tertiary	Extraverted Sensation	tertiary	Introverted Feeling
inferior	Introverted Feeling	inferior	Extraverted Sensation

This is why psychological conflict is often a gift in disguise. It tells us that it's time to move beyond the top layer of our typological preferences. In terms of the lasagna theory, it's time to get our conscious fork more deeply into the second layer of our personality: our *secondary function*.

But Why? Shouldn't We Be Trying to Develop our Inferior Function?

Logic might suggest that our inferior function is the one to work on. After all, that's the one that's out of control, right? But concerted efforts to identify with our least-developed point of view never work out the way we think they will.

For one thing, we don't really know what we're after. Our inferior function is inferior because its approach to life opposes everything we've tried to be. Making 180-degree turns, even for good reason, is dangerous business. Instead of raising our least-developed function to consciousness, we can sink our personality to a more unconscious level of operation.

Trying to Get to the Bottom of the Pan

The problems with trying to develop the inferior function directly, by using it more often, can be illustrated by the story of Maggie, an INTJ researcher who thought she could get "out of her head" and more into life by deliberately using Extraverted Sensate skills. This is Maggie's type lasagna:

INTJ	
dominant	Introverted Intuition
secondary	Extraverted Thinking
tertiary	Introverted Feeling
inferior	Extraverted Sensation

Because she associated Sensation with concrete physical pursuits, Maggie bought a rowing machine and started an exercise program.

She taught herself to crochet. To her surprise, she found that she enjoyed both, but she couldn't say that she felt more engaged or embodied. Like most of what she did, she easily adapted these enterprises to her dominant perspective. They became part of her Introverted identity.

So she stopped thinking about her development project—until marriage took her from Manhattan into one of the bedroom communities of Long Island. For the first time in her life, she recognized a genuine need for Extraverted Sensation.

Every morning, Maggie would catch a train on the Long Island Rail Road to get to her job in the city. And every day as the train pulled in, the distinguished executives in nice suits and cashmere scarves seemed to become a veritable horde from hell, pushing and gouging and shoving her aside or trampling right over her to get to their usual seats on the car. She felt like one of those cartoon figures where the crowd rushes by en masse and all that's left of the heroine is a big flat person-shaped pancake.

Here, Maggie decided, is a situation that cries out for a quick physical response to immediate sensory phenomena. Either she'd develop a few Sensation skills or spend the rest of her days standing all the way into Manhattan while everyone else got to sit and fold and unfold the New York Times.

The first thing Maggie found out is how hard she had to work to put her plan into action. Accustomed to losing herself in daydreams or books when she had time to kill, she had to force herself to pay attention to her outward situation. She kept reminding herself to stay alert. She noted the way people moved when they rushed onto the train, the way they calculated space, held their ground. She took in as many details as she could and pushed herself to put into practice the physical strategies that seemed required.

To her chagrin and irritation, none of this did her any good. There was always some determined individual with a briefcase who'd wedge his way past her and all but trip her for the last seat. So she decided to go the whole nine yards. She bought her own briefcase, and within a week or two, she got surprisingly good at wielding it to advantage. So good, in fact, that she began to get a seat more often than not, and she was feeling very proud of herself—as though she'd tapped right into the Extraverted Sensation skills she needed and solved her problem.

It wasn't long, however, before she noticed that the people she was competing with every morning were looking at her a little strangely, as though they found her frightening. At first she thought it was because she was participating as a female in what seemed to be a male executive ritual. But as the weeks went on, she began to notice something that truly puzzled her.

Every day, as soon as the train started to move, everyone else calmed down and settled in to their financial pages and crossword puzzles. In fact, Maggie remembered that her reason for wanting a seat in the first place had been for the opportunity to read comfortably on her way into the city. Now it never occurred to her. She didn't even look out the window. She was too pumped. Her heart was pounding, she was out of breath, and she was infuriated by the people who had managed to push in ahead of her. Everyone was talking and snoozing and reading and daydreaming, and she was replaying strategies in her head as if she'd been in a prizefight.

It was as though these people had developed control over broader permutations of anger than she could even identify. Maggie scarcely recognized herself. As soon as the train doors opened, her adrenaline level shot up, liberating feelings that were a good deal more than hostile. She felt like a character in a Mad Max movie, wedging her briefcase for the sheer malicious pleasure of keeping someone at bay.

Taking It from the Top

As cautionary tales go, this one may seem a little flimsy. New York, after all, is full of people more volatile under ordinary circumstances than Maggie became in a very contained situation. The point, however, is that our inferior function isn't merely undeveloped. Its point of view is genuinely inferior. The approach to life it fosters has no relationship to our conscious position or to the assumptions of others.

Our psyche, remember, is millions of years old—as old as the human race. When we differentiate our best functions, we're adapting them, making them useful in our particular life situation. The functions we haven't differentiated are still archaic and primitive. They haven't been refined by the trial and error of real experience.

Extraverted functions, in particular, become adapted as we test them in the arena of consensual reality. Maggie's only experience with Extraversion was her secondary function, Extraverted Thinking, and she used it largely to support her Introverted cerebral goals—to organize her intuitions and to test them against others' ideas. It scarcely occurred to her to use Extraverted Thinking in its own right—as a means of dealing with the objective world logically and responsibly.

In consequence, she had no idea what an Extraverted Sensate view would really entail. She used her Sensate skills in an Introverted way, to force the outer environment to accommodate her dominant aims. Indeed, Maggie's frantic need to control her situation made her seem out of control rather than outgoing or empowered.

Apart from the Paul Gauguins among us, who abruptly realize that they should quit their boring jobs, move to Tahiti, and take up painting, most types don't solve their problems by making choices diametrically opposed to their accustomed identity. If anything, the aspiration is a classic sign that the secondary function hasn't had enough attention.

How the Secondary Function Helps Us Grow

Our secondary function needs attention not just because of the skills it offers, but because of its attitudes. It may be recalled that we have four attitudes altogether: Introversion, Extraversion, Perception, and Judgment. Each offers a distinct approach to life:

▲ Extraversion encourages adjustment to others.
▲ Introversion encourages responsibility to the self.
▲ Perception gives us the wisdom of direct experience.
▲ Judgment gives us rational understanding.

An adequate relationship with reality requires all four.

Although our dominant function feels "natural" to us and is

compatible with our biological resources, it provides only two of the four attitudes we require. The other two belong to our secondary function, and they don't come as easily to us. This is why we generally use our secondary skills only to support our primary aims.

The time comes, however, when that psychological arrangement isn't enough. We need to use our secondary attitudes to modify our dominant function as well as support it. Otherwise, we have a hard time recognizing the part we're playing in the situations we're trying to deal with. Consider Maggie, who concluded that the problem she needed to address could be solved by turning her briefcase into a weapon.

When we rely on our dominant function for all our answers, we usually wind up like Alice, running hard just to stay in place. Or we feel stuck, without options, unable to decide what to do. *This feeling of being stuck is always the give-away.* It tells us that our attitudes need work. We're not seeing the situation from a broad enough perspective.

Accepting Psychological Conflict

Although our secondary function is accessible to us, it isn't possible to use it reflexively. We have to use it deliberately, and it may take some effort. As soon as we're making that effort, however, we get results. We're immediately aware of the conflict inside us, and we're obliged to come to terms with it.

One can see how this happens simply by reading the letters that appear in columns like Dear Abby and Ann Landers. A good percentage of the questions are from people contending with what might be called a crisis of the secondary function. Although these columnists don't use typological terms, they invariably persuade their correspondents to make the necessary shift in attitude.

For example, a retiree who feels lost without the outward structure of his job (Extraverted Judgment) is advised to rediscover himself—to do something he loves but had no time for when he was employed (Introverted Perception). A widow whose husband was her best and only friend (Introverted Judgment) is advised to look outside and explore new options (Extraverted Perception).

Because our secondary attitudes are not our strongest suit, sometimes we do need an objective observer to tell us how to proceed. But even a half-hearted attempt in this direction inevitably makes us more conscious. We stop thinking that the world has it in for us and start to take responsibility for ourselves.

For example, if Maggie had thought out her problem logically, with Extraverted Thinking, she might have solved it easily enough, by getting up earlier and catching a less crowded train. And it may be noted that Maggie habitually avoided her secondary attitudes for just this reason. They brought her face to face with her impractical side, her disinclination to accept the world on its own terms.

By reaching for her inferior function, Maggie didn't become more conscious of her Extraverted side. She simply lost touch with rational Judgment altogether. She pulled an alternate Perceiving personality to the surface of her behaviors—a crude, primitive one, directly in conflict with the Intuitive skills she'd worked hard to differentiate.

This is hardly an effective way to integrate and humanize a weaker function. It just manages to alienate us from our greatest strengths. It can't be denied, however, that it may get us a seat on the Long Island Rail Road—and very likely, a seat to ourselves.

10

Type Dynamics

▲ ALTHOUGH THE TYPE LASAGNA IMAGE IS A USEFUL ONE, it doesn't really tell us enough. Whenever I've taught a class on psychological types, the students always want to know what happens to the *other* functions—the four sandwiched between the layers at the top and the layers at the bottom. Don't they play a part in our personalities?

In a sense, these remaining functions are like genes in a differentiated cell. Every cell in the body contains all the genetic data needed to produce a whole organism. But when a cell differentiates, it concentrates on one particular task—like making organ tissue or producing milk. As soon as this happens, the information offered by the other genes is blocked out biochemically. The only genes that remain active are the ones that permit the cell to perform its task.

In roughly the same way, our psyche contains all the functional information we need to become human beings. When we develop our dominant function, we learn to block out information from functions that won't support the direction we're taking. These blocked-out functions are the two at the bottom of our type lasagna.

The others behave like the genes that remain active in a differentiated cell. We use them to support our specialized aims and goals. They don't exert much influence on our choices as such, unless we make a deliberate effort to see life from the perspective they offer.

When a cell is close to death, it eliminates the biochemical blocks on its genes and thus acquires the potential to start again. This is the sort of thing that happens typologically when it's time for us to grow. We don't actually start over, but we become more vulnerable to the influence of our tertiary and inferior functions, the ones that *don't* support our accustomed goals.

As I say, the lasagna image is a good one, but it's too static. It doesn't give us a clear enough picture of how the functions work together in a real-life situation. To that end, I'd like to suggest a supplementary analogy, simply to illustrate the process: the psyche as a ship that we learn to pilot with our dominant function. Our remaining functions play different roles on the ship, but they operate within the constraints of our dominant course.

The Ship's Roster

In the years when we're consolidating our place and powers through some combination of love and work, we identify with our dominant function and captain the ship in terms of the views it encourages. Most of our other functions hire on as a crew, and we need them to administrate our primary goals.

Our secondary function is the most important of these crew members. It operates as a kind of petty officer, who follows our orders, but also brings alternate perspectives to our attention. The views of the petty officer are crucial to the success of our journey, and we need to take them into account. However, until we're in a crisis situation, we may treat this function as more of a servant than a counselor.

Our inferior function strikes us as a troublemaker—a would-be captain who opposes the course we're taking. This function sows enough dissension among the crew that we have no choice but to supply it with a lifeboat and put it off the ship. Unknown to us, the lifeboat is attached by a long rope to the ship's hull, and as the disgruntled inferior function makes its way back to shore, the rope is playing itself out.

Our tertiary function doesn't like our agenda either, but its strategies are opportunistic rather than oppositional. When the ship is in motion, this function is happy to water-ski behind it, shouting rude remarks. A good petty officer will advise us to consider some of these comments, as long as they're not distracting the crew from their posts. But we're more likely to forget the water-skier is even there.

The Functions in Between

The four functions between our strongest (the captain and the petty officer) and our weakest (the water-skier and the would-be captain) have their own roles on our typological ship. But the best way to see how they work is to introduce a specific example.

Grant, a fifty-nine-year-old ESTJ, had been an accountant for thirty years in a church-related lending institution. This is Grant's type lasagna—with the four additional functions sandwiched in the middle:

ESTJ	
dominant	Extraverted Thinking
secondary	Introverted Sensation
left-brain alternatives	**Extraverted Feeling**
	Introverted Intuition
right-brain double agents	**Extraverted Sensation**
	Introverted Thinking
tertiary	Extraverted Intuition
inferior	Introverted Feeling

Grant captained his typological ship as an Extraverted Thinker, so his course was an impersonal, logical one, based on his social roles as an accountant, husband, father, and church elder. The lion's share of his self-image was coincident with his professional identity.

Introverted Sensation, Grant's secondary function, helped him to invest himself in his outward roles. In its own right, this function prompts us to keep our external arena consistent with what matters to us individually. As a secondary function, however, Introverted Sensation supported Grant's Thinking agenda, and it encouraged a reliance on his social roles, particularly his job, to define who he was and what he stood for.

Grant had, accordingly, anchored his religious priorities to the role he played in the company. He saw his job as a form of mission, and he was trying to keep his identity intact, even when a more conservative church body acquired his company and began to edge the "old guard" out.

Like most ESTJs, Grant interpreted threatening situations in light of his disowned inferior function, Introverted Feeling. He saw the new board members as dangerous—practitioners of situational morality, which he regarded as unprincipled and irrational.

The Crow's Nest Functions   Let's take a look now at the four middle functions of a type profile. The top two occupy the crow's nest on our typological ship. Their perspectives compete with our preferred way of seeing life, but when we run into problems our dominant skills can't handle, they're the first functions we turn to for solutions. As Grant tried to adapt to the changes at work, he turned to his own crow's nest functions, Extraverted Feeling and Introverted Intuition.

Extraverted Feeling offered Grant an alternative to his dominant function, Extraverted Thinking. As a Thinking type, Grant was most comfortable analyzing things logically, by way of general rules and principles. Extraverted Feeling encouraged him to assess others' reactions and to pay more attention to his relationships.

Although these functions compete with each other, they both activate areas in the left brain, encouraging adaptation to others' standards. So Grant used his Feeling skills fairly well—when he recognized their logical utility. In his current situation, it was important to him to get along with the new board members and to be appreciated, so he socialized with them and tried to foster loyal personal connections.

In the same way, Introverted Intuition offered Grant an alternative to his secondary Introverted Sensate skills. This skill was barely developed for Grant. He preferred to see reality as factual and consistent over time. Introverted Intuition encouraged him to see reality as a matter of viewpoint—relative and arbitrary.

As his work relationships changed, however, Grant used his Intuitive skills more often to support his dominant aims. He tried to explain to himself why he saw things so differently from the new board members, and he wanted those members to know that his understanding of the job had meaning and utility.

Although we generally use our crow's nest functions to shore up our dominant position, it should be noted that a well-developed secondary function helps us to use their perspectives more expansively, to broaden our options. For example, if Grant had realized, by way of Introverted Sensation, what priorities were unconditional for him, his Introverted Intuitive crow's nest function might have counseled him to explore new avenues for their maintenance and expression.

The Double Agents The remaining two middle functions are what I call double agents. The skills they provide share common ground with our preferred ones, but double agents activate the opposite brain hemisphere. Serving largely as a maintenance crew on our typological ship, they tend to mutiny when they get the chance.

Under normal circumstances, Grant's double agents, Introverted Thinking and Extraverted Sensation, served his dominant goals well enough. Their right-brain skills did not come easily to him, but they gave him needed balance when things were going smoothly in his life. In particular, they encouraged him to "go with" things as they happened rather than analyze them beforehand—to enjoy sports, to be spontaneous, and to use his sensory skills as well as his cerebral ones.

As his situation changed, however, Grant began to use his double agents more defensively, to keep himself from feeling anxious. His crow's nest functions had solved none of the problems he was having, and he was experiencing a classic crisis of the secondary function. He felt stuck.

In terms of our analogy, Grant had taken his typological ship as far as it could go in one direction. The inferior function, which he'd put off the ship long ago, had reached shore, and the rope between the lifeboat and the ship's hull was becoming taut. Indeed, this disowned function had tied its end of the rope to a monster truck, and was now starting to drive it inland.

As his ship came to a standstill, Grant's double agents recognized a potential power shift, and they got out of his control. In consequence, Grant sometimes acted like an inferior ESP. He was impulsive and self-indulgent rather than spontaneous. And he felt trapped, like an inferior ITP, by the new rules he was supposed to be following. This is how double agents generally switch allegiance—by pulling us away from our strongest tendencies toward our less conscious side.

Let's stop for a minute to add these four middle functions to our type lasagnas:

ENFP	
dominant	Extraverted Intuition
secondary	Introverted Feeling
right-brain	**Extraverted Sensation**
alternatives	**Introverted Thinking**
left-brain	**Extraverted Feeling**
double agents	Introverted Intuition
tertiary	Extraverted Thinking
inferior	Introverted Sensation

INFP	
dominant	Introverted Feeling
secondary	Extraverted Intuition
right-brain	**Introverted Thinking**
alternatives	**Extraverted Sensation**
left-brain	**Introverted Intuition**
double agents	Extraverted Feeling
tertiary	Introverted Sensation
inferior	Extraverted Thinking

ENTP	
dominant	Extraverted Intuition
secondary	Introverted Thinking
right-brain	**Extraverted Sensation**
alternatives	**Introverted Feeling**
left-brain	**Extraverted Thinking**
double agents	Introverted Intuition
tertiary	Extraverted Feeling
inferior	Introverted Sensation

INTP	
dominant	Introverted Thinking
secondary	Extraverted Intuition
right-brain	**Introverted Feeling**
alternatives	**Extraverted Sensation**
left-brain	**Introverted Intuition**
double agents	Extraverted Thinking
tertiary	Introverted Sensation
inferior	Extraverted Feeling

ESFJ	
dominant	Extraverted Feeling
secondary	Introverted Sensation
left-brain	**Extraverted Thinking**
alternatives	**Introverted Intuition**
right-brain	**Extraverted Sensation**
double agents	Introverted Feeling
tertiary	Extraverted Intuition
inferior	Introverted Thinking

ISFJ	
dominant	Introverted Sensation
secondary	Extraverted Feeling
left-brain	**Introverted Intuition**
alternatives	**Extraverted Thinking**
right-brain	**Introverted Feeling**
double agents	Extraverted Sensation
tertiary	Introverted Thinking
inferior	Extraverted Intuition

ESTJ	
dominant	Extraverted Thinking
secondary	Introverted Sensation
left-brain	**Extraverted Feeling**
alternatives	**Introverted Intuition**
right-brain	**Extraverted Sensation**
double agents	Introverted Thinking
tertiary	Extraverted Intuition
inferior	Introverted Feeling

ISTJ	
dominant	Introverted Sensation
secondary	Extraverted Thinking
left-brain	**Introverted Intuition**
alternatives	**Extraverted Feeling**
right-brain	**Introverted Thinking**
double agents	Extraverted Sensation
tertiary	Introverted Feeling
inferior	Extraverted Intuition

ESFP

dominant	Extraverted Sensation
secondary	Introverted Feeling
right-brain	**Extraverted Intuition**
alternatives	Introverted Thinking
left-brain	**Extraverted Feeling**
double agents	Introverted Sensation
tertiary	Extraverted Thinking
inferior	Introverted Intuition

ISFP

dominant	Introverted Feeling
secondary	Extraverted Sensation
right-brain	**Introverted Thinking**
alternatives	Extraverted Intuition
left-brain	**Introverted Sensation**
double agents	Extraverted Feeling
tertiary	Introverted Intuition
inferior	Extraverted Thinking

ESTP

dominant	Extraverted Sensation
secondary	Introverted Thinking
right-brain	**Extraverted Intuition**
alternatives	Introverted Feeling
left-brain	**Extraverted Thinking**
double agents	Introverted Sensation
tertiary	Extraverted Feeling
inferior	Introverted Intuition

ISTP

dominant	Introverted Thinking
secondary	Extraverted Sensation
right-brain	**Introverted Feeling**
alternatives	Extraverted Intuition
left-brain	**Introverted Sensation**
double agents	Extraverted Thinking
tertiary	Introverted Intuition
inferior	Extraverted Feeling

ENFJ

dominant	Extraverted Feeling
secondary	Introverted Intuition
left-brain	**Extraverted Thinking**
alternatives	Introverted Sensation
right-brain	**Extraverted Intuition**
double agents	Introverted Feeling
tertiary	Extraverted Sensation
inferior	Introverted Thinking

INFJ

dominant	Introverted Intuition
secondary	Extraverted Feeling
left-brain	**Introverted Sensation**
alternatives	Extraverted Thinking
right-brain	**Introverted Feeling**
double agents	Extraverted Intuition
tertiary	Introverted Thinking
inferior	Extraverted Sensation

ENTJ

dominant	Extraverted Thinking
secondary	Introverted Intuition
left-brain	**Extraverted Feeling**
alternatives	Introverted Sensation
right-brain	**Extraverted Intuition**
double agents	Introverted Thinking
tertiary	Extraverted Sensation
inferior	Introverted Feeling

INTJ

dominant	Introverted Intuition
secondary	Extraverted Thinking
left-brain	**Introverted Sensation**
alternatives	Extraverted Feeling
right-brain	**Introverted Thinking**
double agents	Extraverted Intuition
tertiary	Introverted Feeling
inferior	Extraverted Sensation

Recognizing the Impetus to Grow

Grant's story may seem more like a saga of midlife frustration than an illustration of ordinary typological growth. But this is often the pattern in our culture. Many types recognize the need to change or grow only when an important part of their life seems to be getting out of control. This may not happen definitively until midlife.

And it's not that Grant should have lived his life some other way. By following the lead of his dominant skills, he had forged a satisfying identity for himself. He was a decent man, with a high moral fiber, who loved his wife and children. He'd achieved moderate success, security, good relationships, and the opportunity to help others.

The point is that Grant's dominant function had served its purpose, and it was time to expand his identity. His children were growing up, his parents were growing old, and a new generation was entering the workforce, fueled by the energy and optimism of youth. His psyche was prompting him to go beyond his accustomed identity—to broaden his conscious options, to modify his direction. To that end, his inferior function, Introverted Feeling, was pulling him backward, undermining his usual aims and goals.

Grant had felt the effects of this unconscious pull long before the takeover at work. He had been increasingly dissatisfied with the old board's religious philosophy and was advocating lending money to church outfits his superiors thought questionable. He was bored with his bookkeeping routines. He wanted to make a difference in the world.

Unpleasant as the takeover was, the new, even more conservative policies gave him a perfect external focus to explain his feelings to himself. Indeed, he gained a new sense of ambition for a time. He was anxious about keeping his job, and he increased his efforts to do what made him feel powerful and most like himself.

In other words, he held to his dominant Extraverted Thinking course. He figured the board would need his knowledge and his expertise even if they didn't agree with his religious views. He treated the problem as a purely external one—and his task, as he understood it, was to stay in control: to be objective, logical, and diplomatic, no matter what else was happening.

All of this sounds sensible enough. But when life is pushing us to grow, focusing on the external problem generally makes things worse. What Grant actually needed was more contact with his secondary function, Introverted Sensation. He needed to figure out what was truly important to him, to recognize the tenuous connection of his job to his genuine faith experience and potential. He needed to ask himself what would truly fulfill him in the years ahead. He needed real information about his resources and his possibilities, given the existence of commitments already made.

Grant had always resisted questions of this sort, because his primary goal was to *adapt* to the conditions of his job and his marriage. He wanted to know what to expect, and he wanted to stay true to his obligations. He didn't want to reexamine the path he was taking.

But his inner life was also real, and acknowledging its existence would have changed his view of the problems he was encountering. Indeed, by using his secondary Introverted function deliberately, he would have satisfied some of the Introverted demands of his inferior function. Under such circumstances, the inferior function loses some of its negative leverage.

If we don't turn to our secondary function at this point—that is, if we insist on doing what we've always done—we eventually reach a point where our water-skiing tertiary function takes over the ship. Our tertiary function has been coasting on our dominant momentum for a long time, and that arrangement is now in jeopardy. So this function frantically climbs aboard, tosses the secondary function over the side, and insists that we get out of this mess at any cost.

Grant's tertiary function was Extraverted Intuition, and he rarely used it in a fully conscious way. Intuitive motives struck him as irresponsible and illogical. Now, as Extraverted Intuition gained more access to his decision-making process, Grant was filled with adolescent daydreams about running away.

He reasoned that he'd been meeting others' expectations all his life. When was it going to be his turn? He longed to do something adventurous and exciting, something new, something that didn't involve the social roles that were draining his forces. While his wife baby-sat the grandkids on weekends, he haunted the used-car lots, looking at pickup trucks and entertaining dreams about heading west.

The tertiary function is dangerous in a crisis because the point of view it encourages is not so much wrong as it is misplaced. Grant *had* been meeting others' expectations all his life—as a good provider, a successful son, a decisive man. He did need more contact with his Perceiving skills, with the self that existed apart from his social identity.

But Extraverted Intuition was not useful to Grant in this regard. Its outward focus kept him from looking within, and it encouraged him to believe that the pressure he was feeling from his inferior function was being caused by other people.

Once we're persuaded that our inner conflicts are outside enemies, our only options are fight or flight. And the tertiary function *always* counsels flight. Its solutions can't be implemented without jettisoning a good deal of what we've already established.

Some types actually follow this shortsighted advice, but most of us are like Grant. We fight for our present way of doing things. And given the fact that all our inferior aims have been projected onto others, we credit ourselves with taking the high road against impossible odds. Meanwhile, our inferior function keeps pulling us backward, and we're certain that it's only strength of character that's keeping us afloat. We're no longer dealing with dissatisfaction and frustration. We feel decisive and strong, primed to do battle with dark forces.

Indeed, Grant became consumed with self-oriented idealism, envisioning himself as a lone fighter for justice in a corrupt situation. In reality, his inferior function, Introverted Feeling, was subverting his more developed ideas about the logical consequences of his actions. He opted for a prophetic stand at work and got fired.

If Grant had been using his Introverted Feeling function in a conscious way, he would have recognized the distinct possibility of this outcome. But his feelings of justification were actually a product of diminishing consciousness. Rather than expand his identity as an Extraverted Thinker, he'd stopped thinking altogether.

The problems we create when our personality moves too close to the unconscious side are almost always dramatic. We get a good hard kick from life, which forces us, ironically, to use the very secondary skills we've been resisting.

11

The Tertiary Problem

▲ As DISCUSSED EARLIER, developing our secondary function usually takes a deliberate conscious effort. As soon as we're using it, however, we get immediate results. We feel the tension between our preferred attitudes and the ones that come less naturally, and we're forced to wrestle with competing aims inside ourselves. We find ourselves asking some variation of the following questions:

▲ How do I stay true to myself and also honor my relationships with others?
▲ Is it better to be loved for what I do or to do what I love?
▲ Can I trust my own sense of values when others see things differently?
▲ Should I follow the rules or follow my heart?

We can't answer these questions in any final way. Each time we come to terms with them, we assimilate a little more of our functional potential, thereby ensuring their return in some new form. And with each return, they're more complicated, the resolutions more subtle. They touch on issues of purpose, responsibility, intimations of the spirit.

This cycle of disharmony and resolution, like the great wheel of stars and seasons, is a tried-and-true pattern of nature. It allows for variation and new combinations of elements within the framework of a stable structure.

In a physical system, the price we pay for creative variation is the potential for disorder. In a psychological system, the price we pay for change and growth is the experience of conflict—the struggle between mutually exclusive intentions. When we feel stuck or have run out of options, it usually means that we're resisting the kind of conflict that makes growth possible. We're trying to hold on to what has worked in the past.

We mature typologically by learning to live with periods of disorganization in ourselves and by sustaining the kind of consciousness they require. This is what typological balance is all about. We're impelled by opposing perspectives to spiral alternately between stability and new options.

Good type development, in this respect, doesn't mean using all our functions equally well. It means establishing a psychological structure strong enough to contain and unify them in a shared enterprise. Although we begin the process by limiting our focus to our dominant viewpoint, the result is a base of conscious operations— a platform from which we can redeem and integrate what we've left behind, piecemeal, according to our own preferences and timetable.

There doesn't seem to be any way to do this except by the long process of sacrifice and redemption. We bargain the undifferentiated wholeness of childhood for the power to choose, then recover it again, as a unified perspective on life. Our youthful optimism, the expectation that things will turn out well, gives way to inner conviction: the sense that some things are worth doing, however they turn out. The first requires material evidence to be sustained. The other is a state of awareness, a way of being.

The process of integration is always a hard one—if for no other reason than the fact that we begin, like plants, by germinating in the dark. We don't know that we're contending with unconscious potential; we're simply impelled to grow. This impulse always seems, initially, to be coming from outside us, threatening to shatter what we already are. The misconception is so universal, so utterly human, that hundreds of psychological strategies have evolved for dealing with it.

All of them, in one way or another, ask us to "take responsibility" for what happens to us, whether or not it appears to be our fault. The reason for this is clear. If we persist in seeing conflict as a problem that others are causing, we invariably use our dominant function to deal with it. By taking responsibility, we, in a sense, trick ourselves into developing our secondary attitudes.

The Tertiary Function

In some respects, it's easier to recognize what happens if we *don't* take responsibility. Taking responsibility is a matter of conscious individuation. Its forms are many and varied. But when the psyche is trying to impose balance on us unconsciously, by pulling us toward our least-developed function, things tend to go wrong in a fairly predictable way.

One might recall Grant, who used all the strategies at his disposal to solve his problem in the outer world. For ordinary, everyday adaptation, these strategies would have worked. We all use our crow's nest functions to support our dominant agenda in situations that require more than our preferred skills. When it's time to grow, however, implementing our standard agenda won't work. Expanding our dominant identity requires a different kind of effort.

Grant is a good example of what happens when we cycle back to the familiar rather than moving toward new sites of typological growth. The psyche steps up its efforts to push us away from our dominant position. Our inferior function gains more unconscious influence over us.

Grant responded to this pressure by defending himself against it. This is a natural way to proceed. If we're in pain, we want to make it stop. But this defensive maneuver is ultimately a surrender of conscious awareness. It empowers the tertiary function to direct our subsequent course.

The tertiary function, remember, is hardly developed at all. It's been along for the ride, coasting on our dominant energies. We haven't applied it to our actual situation and tested its limits. If we're coming to a psychological standstill, it will frantically advise us to do whatever we have to do to get rid of the problem. But it will also shape our understanding of the problem in a distorted and defensive way.

In fact, when it substitutes for our secondary function, the tertiary function will tell us *exactly* what we want to hear: that the conflict we're experiencing is not our fault, and that we're absolutely justified in our defensive strategies. The more we heed these rationalizations, the more our inferior function pulls us backward, until we're actually using our least-developed tendencies unawares. It's the voice of the tertiary function that makes extreme types so oblivious to the effects of their behaviors.

The Tertiary Problem for Extraverts

In general, when we're not using enough of our functional potential, some parts of life do get out of hand. So it's easy for Extraverts who need to develop their secondary skills to believe that their problems are being caused by outside forces. The unconscious Introversion of their inferior function increases their self-orientation, and their normal Extraverted outlook becomes defensive. They may assume, for example, that others are working against them, or misunderstand them, or don't care enough about their needs.

A conscious, developed Introverted function doesn't have this egocentric quality. It simply prompts us to reflect before we act—to weigh our outer situation against our subjective point of view. Such reflection doesn't ensure that we get our own way; it preserves our independence from environmental influence. Our ethics may be stronger, for example, than others' expectations can or will define. This is the sort of thing an Extravert's secondary function is designed to address.

Inferior Introversion is very different. In an Extraverted personality, it's all mixed up with the shadowy things that get pushed out of awareness—uncivilized predilections, impossible dreams, the tiny agonies of childhood, magnified by time. Under its influence, Extraverts feel that they're not getting what they really need. They don't feel satisfied; they're not living the life they want to live.

These perceptions are not inaccurate so much as misattributed. Such Extraverts aren't being met by life, but it's because they're in touch only with the dominant surface of their personality. In order to see their options clearly, they need the input of their secondary attitudes. However, when inferior impulses are pulling Extraverts away from their dominant identity, the tertiary function quickly steps in to protect their accustomed self-image.

Jake

Jake was a staff writer on a travel magazine for about fifteen years, and like many ENFPs, he enjoyed the pace and the challenges of a journalistic career. He loved the feeling of being plunged into life, dealing with whatever came to hand. He used his secondary function, Introverted Feeling, as a situation unfolded, to gauge his immediate experience of interest or boredom.

Indiscriminately curious and willing to do almost anything for a story, he was identified early in his career as a charismatic go-getter. But now, in his mid-thirties, he was beginning to run into problems. Here is Jake's complete type lasagna:

ENFP	
dominant	Extraverted Intuition
secondary	Introverted Feeling
right-brain alternatives	**Extraverted Sensation**
	Introverted Thinking
left-brain double agents	**Extraverted Feeling**
	Introverted Intuition
tertiary	Extraverted Thinking
inferior	Introverted Sensation

Jake had a genuine flair for writing, but he didn't have much interest in reworking what he wrote—or even thinking through an article a second time. When he had an assignment, he wrote off the top of his head and depended on the pressure of a deadline to spur him into finishing. It was his skills as an improviser that kept him afloat most of the time. He was a charmer who could talk his way into and out of anything.

Lately, however, he wasn't "getting over" as well as he wanted to. His managing editor was questioning too many of his decisions, and she was increasingly annoyed by the idiosyncrasies of Jake's writing style. Jake regarded these idiosyncrasies as personal trade-marks, off-limits to criticism or editing, and he was feeling both resentful and unappreciated.

His home life was also beginning to irritate him. His wife seemed to be angry with him most of the time. She said she couldn't count on him, an accusation he thought unfair and insulting. He had been faithful to his marriage for ten years now, proof enough that his intentions were solid.

The idea that he should come home when he said he would, or follow through on his promises, made him furious. How could he possibly know he was going to be late until he already was? How could anyone know whether tomorrow's circumstances would favor yesterday's promises? He wondered if he should look for another job, perhaps one that got him home on time, but he didn't want to start at the bottom somewhere else, and his wife reminded him (as if he'd forgotten) that he'd run into the same general problems at every job he had. He felt stuck.

This is the sort of external conflict that serves as a typological wake-up call. Jake was having problems because he wasn't using enough of his functional skills. His priorities were determined almost exclusively by what came at him from the outer world. Usually if things went wrong, he'd draw from his crow's nest functions, Extraverted Sensation and Introverted Thinking. They helped him to think quickly and to get through a crisis, but they offered no perspective on his Intuitive aims and goals.

What Jake needed was more input from his secondary attitudes. He wasn't reckoning with the tension between his response-ready strengths (Extraverted Intuition) and the guiding force of his inner values (Introverted Feeling).

Indeed, Jake's priorities took shape around whatever person he happened to be with at the time. He was all but instinctive in his ability to identify with others' feelings and to establish immediate relationships. But figuring out what was truly important to him made him uncomfortable. It threatened to limit his open-ended approach to life.

In consequence, Extraverted Intuition was his only developed conscious position, and his psyche was striving for balance. His inferior function, Introverted Sensation, was pulling him away from his accustomed aims and goals, undermining his image of himself as a free agent.

As pointed out in the last chapter, Introverted Sensation prompts us to anchor our outward situation to consistent inner priorities.

When we use this function in a dominant way, we have a feeling of rootedness and continuity. Grant, the ESTJ discussed earlier, used Introverted Sensation in a secondary way, to support his Extraverted identity. He associated his job with the constants of his inner life and depended on it to define who he was and what he stood for.

Jake didn't use Introverted Sensation much at all. His Extraverted Intuition had taken him in the opposite direction. He wasn't interested in factual continuity or the consistency of his responses to life. He was interested in the broad sweep of things, the possibility of change, the realization of potential.

Thus, his Introverted Sensation was unadapted and egocentric. Under its unconscious influence, he expected others to provide him the constants he needed to keep his identity intact. That is, he expected others to provide him with assignments, deadlines, and limits, but he also expected these tasks and boundaries to support his Intuitive goals. If they didn't, he felt used and controlled.

The more he was influenced by unconscious Introverted Sensation, the more he was convinced that people were trying to rein him in and keep him from realizing his intentions. Ultimately, Extraverted Thinking, his tertiary function, jumped on board to help him deal with this perceived external problem.

As a dominant Extraverted Perceiver, Jake needed the perspective of his *secondary* function, Introverted Feeling. He needed a sense of personal values that would move him to set priorities, and to stay on track because a goal mattered to him. Jake resisted this course because he didn't want to be controlled, even by his own values. He didn't realize that a constant influx of information actually *deprived* him of control.

In fact, he had so little awareness of his own power that he interpreted others' tentative suggestions as demands for his immediate response. New obligations seemed to come at him constantly, cheating him of time, intimacy, and the opportunity to realize his best intentions. His tertiary function stepped in at that point.

Extraverted Thinking is a Judging function, like Introverted Feeling. But the Judgment it offers is other-oriented, which moved Jake to train it on the outer world. He became convinced that people were asking too much of him and didn't appreciate his efforts. This gave him a logical reason to dispense with guilt when he didn't meet their expectations.

Again, the advice of the tertiary function is not so much wrong as it is misplaced. It offers platitudes—ideas that are true in general but have no productive relationship to the situation we're actually in. Jake *was* overwhelmed by others' values and expectations. He did need to set priorities. But Extraverted Thinking couldn't help him do that. It merely rationalized his accustomed Intuitive standpoint. He used it defensively, to prove that others were being narrow-minded or manipulative when their expectations conflicted with his own.

It should not be construed that Jake was badly out of control or unlikeable. He was mercurial in the best of circumstances, but he was also smart, funny, and ambitious, and he displayed many of the gifts and strengths of an Intuitive personality. On first meeting him, people were charmed and engaged.

His defensiveness became apparent only as he interacted with others over time. As inferior Introversion gained more power in his personality, he was almost childishly self-centered. He had the idea that he should be rewarded for meeting others' expectations, that people should go out of their way to support and affirm him uncon- ditionally. If they didn't, he was nearly irrational, believing them to be unfair or to have a stake in denying his value. This struck others as a flaw in his character, a refusal to grow up, and the problems it caused became more difficult for him to solve.

The fact is that Jake's tertiary strategy had done its job, insofar as it alleviated his sense of anxiety. Although his outer life was in- creasingly beyond his ability to manage, Jake felt little conflict within himself. Given his certainty that others were causing his problems, he felt justified in his refusal to consider their point of view. But as a result, he shut out data that he needed to use his Intuition well. His dominant and inferior functions were, quite sim- ply, canceling each other out.

Extraverts like Jake generally become aware of the need for change only as the social price of unconscious balance becomes higher than they're willing to pay. Jake lost a series of jobs and quite nearly lost his marriage before he realized that he was part of the problem.

Solving the Real Problem

As with many types, Jake finally recognized the need to do something about his life when a good friend suggested an attitude adjustment. Take some time off, he said. Figure out what you really want to do with yourself.

Jake was out of a job anyhow, feeling burned-out and mistreated, so he took that advice. He went on a short camping trip. He had expected his wife to object to the plan, but to his surprise, she was more than ready for a break from his company. He found himself wondering if she'd be there when he got back. He realized, for virtually the first time, how much he depended on his marriage. In the course of that realization, he bumped into his secondary function. He valued his marital life, and the emotional investment was important to him.

He took the time alone, trying to figure out what else was that valuable to him. What was worth doing or maintaining, even if things got hard or went wrong? One thing that occurred to him was the idea of writing for its own sake. He was always willing to invest his time in poems and letters and projects outside his job at the magazine. He thought it was important to do that kind of personalized writing.

The notion struck him as annoyingly vague, so he tried to work out a way that he could write from the heart and also manage to support a family. As he considered his options, he realized that he had never really been committed to his job at the magazine. The assignments had given him flexibility and the opportunity to travel, but the articles themselves had no contact with what he believed or what he felt. They had no lasting effect on anyone. He wanted to have that kind of effect. He thought he could help others to clarify their beliefs and their values.

He decided to teach a creative writing course at a local college, and he volunteered some time overseeing the campus political journal. To his pleasure, he found that the work energized him. It drew on his talents, gave him more immediate interaction with people, and kept him in touch with some of his abiding beliefs.

To be sure, sometimes considered reflection does move us to trade one identity for another. The point is that such changes can't be made until we've wrestled with the questions our secondary attitudes raise for us. Otherwise, we're likely to use our tertiary function to decide what to do.

As stated, tertiary solutions will work for a while, but only because they help us to escape from our conflicts. They don't change our perspective or push us to grow. Secondary solutions are different. They require that we "own" our inner conflicts and find some way to integrate our competing aims and goals. For example, although Jake was energized by the new job, the consistency of its routine was almost intolerable for him. He hated submitting to the rules and bureaucratic nonsense of another institution, and he had a hard time reconciling the authority of his position with his secret respect for the iconoclasts and free spirits in his classes.

But this was a job in which he had little choice in the matter. He had to show up on time and prepare for his students or he couldn't do what he wanted to do. And he loved what he was doing enough to tolerate the irritation. He found that he had a real gift for seeing and bringing out talent in others. More important, he saw his value reflected in his students' progress, so he didn't need to explore new options constantly or seek reassurance that his choices were meaningful and important.

As his Introverted Feeling function became more differentiated, Jake felt a little more amenable to his wife's requests for limits and schedules. He didn't turn into a J type by any means. But he began to engage his tertiary Thinking skills more consciously and productively—not for defensive purposes, but to organize his time and ideas.

The Tertiary Problem for Introverts

Unlike Extraverts, Introverts can tell you exactly where their social roles end and their real self begins. One might call this the Clark Kent mindset. They make a very clear distinction between their Extraverted image and their "true identity." When it's time to grow, therefore, Introverts are contending with the pull of an inferior Extraverted function, which plays havoc with their usual Introverted behaviors.

Under the unconscious influence of inferior aims, Introverts are certain that the outer world is preventing them from expressing, perhaps even from defining, their true nature. They try to address this problem by becoming more assertive, making sure that external situations conform more closely to their self-experience.

They may, for example, relate largely to people who need them, which allows them to define the nature of these connections. They may be disruptive or obstructionist in a group situation, or behave in a way that forces others to deal with their needs or views. Indeed, unconscious Extraversion often prompts these types to call attention to themselves, to set themselves apart in a visible way.

Just as inferior Introversion is self-centered and defensive in an Extraverted personality, inferior Extraversion is other-oriented and aggressive in an Introverted one. It's all mixed up with the psychological ghosts of adolescent biological drives: the will to power and acquisition, the desire to be seen and admired and wanted.

A conscious, developed Extraverted function isn't like this. It doesn't prompt us to make our environment congenial to ourselves. It prompts us to make our contribution to the world as it exists. In the process, we find out who we are and what we're made of.

It should be recognized that extreme Introverts are seeing something real. They aren't connecting well enough with the outer world. Not because the environment is hostile to their self-experience, but because they haven't accorded the world its own reality, its legitimate "otherness." They're not looking far enough outside themselves.

It's hard for Introverts to see their options clearly, however, until they get more experience with their secondary attitudes. When inferior impulses are pulling Introverts away from their dominant identity, the tertiary function quickly steps to protect their accustomed sense of self.

Maggie

I introduced Maggie in chapter 9, as the private and bookish INTJ who couldn't get a seat on the morning train. This is Maggie's complete type lasagna:

INTJ	
dominant	Introverted Intuition
secondary	Extraverted Thinking
left-brain alternatives	**Introverted Sensation**
	Extraverted Feeling
right-brain double agents	**Introverted Thinking**
	Extraverted Intuition
tertiary	Introverted Feeling
inferior	Extraverted Sensation

Even as a child, Maggie had a deep connection to her inner life. Like many Introverted Intuitives, she created imaginary friends, spent long hours reading and drawing, and dreamed dreams that stayed with her for weeks.

As she grew older, she found that her curiosity took her in more directions than she knew how to satisfy. Her dominant function literally entertained her with speculative theories, inspirations, fantasies, and hunches that always seemed worth considering further. Moreover, all her interests seemed to intersect in a way that had profound but unarticulated meaning for her.

In college she had a hard time with her assignments. Her ideas took her in too many directions, and she didn't know how to limit them. Her essays, accordingly, had little narrative structure.

Most Introverts experience a certain disinclination to make their private world public, but Introverted Intuitives can find it difficult to stay in contact with their intuitions unless they shut out others' expectations and opinions. Accordingly, they may not get the Extraverted experience they need in order to know who they are and how their inner agenda relates to what actually exists.

Maggie was nowhere near midlife, and she had scarcely realized her Introverted gifts, but she had so little Extraverted perspective that her psyche was pushing her to get more balanced. She began to experience an unconscious pull toward her least-developed function, Extraverted Sensation.

Under force of this pull, she became hyperaware, and she didn't know how to shut down anymore. She had frequent migraines, unusual dreams, and insight into others' lives that made her wonder if she had psychic ability. She started to collect her dreams, and before long she was deeply invested in the process, waking three or four times a night to catch all of them, and spending hours each day just writing them into her dream tablet.

Indeed, she had no time to analyze them—or to do much of anything else. This is how unconscious Extraversion can affect some Introverts. They need not become active in the larger social arena to come to the attention of others. Some, like Maggie, simply engage in behaviors that strike others as eccentric. Her favorite professor took her aside and asked if something was wrong. Her best friend tried to persuade her to go out more often.

Maggie, predictably, became irritated with others' concern and advice. Their anxiety gave her a convenient way to deny her own. What she was doing felt important to her, even cosmically important, and she didn't expect anyone to understand. Her tertiary function, Introverted Feeling, stepped in at this point. It imbued her inner world with something like magical import. She felt caught up in a larger purpose she couldn't share with anyone.

One might recall, in this regard, the way Introverted Feeling worked for Jake, who used it as a secondary function. As an Extraverted Perceiver, Jake *needed* Introverted Judgment. It helped him to focus his Extraverted energies by giving him contact with his inner values. It kept him on track when his dominant tendencies encouraged him to respond to the next thing that turned up.

Maggie, as an *Introverted* Perceiver, needed a way out of herself. Her Introverted Feeling function couldn't help her do that. It just encouraged her to rationalize her subjective viewpoint. It convinced her that what she was doing was so valuable and so right that everything else could be sacrificed to it.

Maggie had no way of seeing that her all-consuming attention to her dreams—writing them down, drawing pictures of them, getting just the right tablets for them, and so forth—was actually undermining her Introverted Intuitive skills. She was feeling more Intuitive than she ever had, but all her energies were devoted to the concrete Sensate mechanics of the task she'd set herself. Like Jake, she didn't recognize she had a problem until the price became too high.

For one thing, she was becoming nearly incompetent in areas of genuine practical concern. Her bills were piling up, unpaid. She'd forget to buy groceries. All her term papers became opportunities to raise questions about alternate consciousness and the paranormal.

What finally got her moving was the offhand remark of a professor, who said that her papers seemed deliberately obscure. She didn't have much respect for this professor. She didn't even like the class he taught. But for some reason, his opinion irked her. She didn't see herself as deliberately obscure. She saw the professor's understanding as limited.

Yet, for reasons she couldn't get hold of, she wanted to make him understand. What would happen, she wondered, if this professor really heard her and had to deal with her ideas? The question pushed her unexpectedly into her secondary function, Extraverted Thinking.

One could maintain, of course, that Maggie simply pulled herself together and began to grow up. But it's helpful, nonetheless, to see how this happened—to recognize that growing up is related to the specific construction of a personality. Once Maggie had acknowledged her desire to be heard and understood, she made a deliberate effort to use her Extraverted Thinking skills. She made a plan and stuck to it. She looked at the A+ papers on file in the library and worked out her ideas in terms of their format.

It may be granted that Maggie was embarrassed about her need for outside affirmation. She felt like some kind of a sellout. But she also found that she was enjoying the process of linear exposition. What she'd learned about dreams had given her unusual insight into the subject at hand, and she liked anticipating the arguments that could be made against her view.

Ultimately, she experienced a sense of vindication. Once she was operating in an arena of shared vocabulary, her professor had to contend with what she thought, and some of what she thought was original in a way that he hadn't foreseen. Other ideas were easily disproved by arguments that hadn't occurred to her, but Maggie realized it was important to her to know that. Her Introverted Feeling became necessary at this point, and she used it in a more conscious, adapted way to determine which ideas were worth pursuing further.

When Maggie was responding to unconscious Extraverted impulses, she tried to control her environment so that it reflected her inner agenda. As a result, she lost her usual perspective on life. But Extraverted Thinking, her secondary function, encouraged her to take responsibility for her inner life and to recognize the effects she had on others.

One might note, again, that Jake and Maggie used many of the same functions, but they used them in different ways and for different reasons. For Jake, Extraverted Thinking was a tertiary function. He employed it defensively to keep his Intuitive behaviors from being Judged by others. As an Extraverted P type, he had to develop Introverted Judgment first. Once Extraverted P types are in touch with their own values, they can deal productively with the standards and expectations of others.

For Maggie, Extraverted Thinking was a secondary function. As an Introverted J type, she *needed* to apply the Judgment of others to her Intuitive perceptions. Getting in touch with her own values, via Introverted Feeling, merely locked her into her own perceptual world. Once Introverted Js accept the reality of outward standards, they're more comfortable in an Extraverted role, and can make use of their values to determine their objectives.

The Tertiary Function in Everyday Life

Even when our secondary attitudes are relatively well developed, we encounter all kinds of circumstances in which we resist their perspective and use our tertiary function instead. Tertiary rationalizations defend us against psychological conflict by encouraging a flight-or-fight mentality.

Take the case of Sharlene, a very Extraverted ENFJ grammar school teacher. Sharlene enjoyed her work and was involved with most of the things that characterize an Extraverted Feeling approach to life: upholding the standards of her community, organizing her busy social life, serving her church as a deacon, participating in family and community rites of passage, and meeting her students' needs for approval, guidance, and encouragement. This is Sharlene's type lasagna:

ENFJ

dominant	Extraverted Feeling
secondary	Introverted Intuition
left-brain alternatives	**Extraverted Thinking**
	Introverted Sensation
right-brain double agents	**Extraverted Intuition**
	Introverted Feeling
tertiary	Extraverted Sensation
inferior	Introverted Thinking

Like many Extraverted Feeling types, Sharlene was conspicuously well-adjusted to the values and expectations of her colleagues and superiors. When she found herself in disagreement with the majority of the school board on an important issue, she was concerned but said nothing. She didn't want to be considered a troublemaker. She wasn't even sure her dissenting opinion meant anything. Yet the situation continued to bother her. She didn't know what to do.

This is the feeling of being stuck that gives us a clue to the secondary nature of the problem. Sharlene was relying so heavily on Extraverted Feeling in this context that she didn't know how to deal with her own views and opinions. She didn't want to create conflict by questioning shared Feeling assumptions.

Sharlene's crow's nest functions, Extraverted Thinking and Introverted Sensation, were of little help to her under these circumstances. She wasn't ready to explain to the group why she disagreed with them. And she didn't have enough facts at hand to make the explanation work.

So she enlisted the support of her tertiary function, Extraverted Sensation, which gave her an escape hatch. It told her that the only solution was to act on her impulses: to say what she thought and not consider the group's approval. Like most types, Sharlene decided to reject that counsel and opt for the "high road." She kept her opinion to herself and maintained the appearance of harmony, secretly concluding that the group was intolerant of new ideas anyhow.

What Sharlene actually needed was to sink her conscious fork into the *second layer* of her type lasagna and engage her secondary function, Introverted Intuition. She needed to wrestle with the group decision in terms of her own experience, observations, and impressions (Introversion). And she needed to recognize the potential of the group to envision new possibilities, given the opportunity (Intuition).

When ENFJs apply the Perceptive insights of Introverted Intuition to what they already know about maintaining harmony, they are highly effective motivators. They not only recognize potential; they also inspire people to cooperate in its development and use. This is one reason ENFJs are drawn to group work and the teaching professions in the first place.

Once Sharlene was in touch with her secondary attitudes, she recognized the possibility of phrasing her ideas in a way that would support the group's common objectives. At that point, Extraverted Sensation served her productively—not as a rationalization for conforming with the group, but as a check on her Intuition. In a group process, one can accomplish only so much. Extraverted Sensation kept her in touch with immediate reality, and prevented her from expecting too much.

Back to Lasagna

So, just how long are the tines on our hypothetical conscious fork? Can they actually reach the bottom of the pan? Perhaps the best answer is: They're long enough. The more we involve our first two functions in our life's dreams and goals, the more we will notice, at the very least, that our tertiary function is cooperating in the outcome.

Used in conjunction with our best two, the tertiary function doesn't offer rationalizations or strategies of defense. It grounds the aims of our stronger functions by introducing us to our genuine limitations—of time, ability, and opportunity, which must be taken into account as we set our goals and make our decisions.

As pointed out, Jake's tertiary function, which had defended him against others' expectations, checked unrealistic idealism once he was using Introverted Feeling. For example, it gave him a way to recognize the limits of a classroom situation and to organize his insights accordingly.

Maggie's Introverted Feeling function, which had kept her from sharing her ideas with others, began to help her once she was using Extraverted Thinking. It gave her a sense of what was truly important to her and worth accommodating to a common vocabulary in the outer world.

Responsible contention with the fourth, inferior, function is another matter, well beyond the scope of this book. For now, when you're reading about the functions and looking at type definitions, keep your own type lasagna in mind.

12

Getting Along with Other Types

▲ ONE OF THE MOST EFFECTIVE WAYS TO RECOGNIZE the influence of the inferior function on our behaviors is to pay attention to the problems that come up in our relationships. Our inferior function is like an untended yard. It gets littered with all sorts of things that drop out of awareness—pain, anger, fear, lost gifts, broken promises. So whenever it comes into play, we feel defensive and angry, without the resources to deal with our situation.

As the story about Sharlene makes clear, our inferior function gets involved in all sorts of life situations. We don't have to hit a crisis to experience its pull on our accustomed sense of self. The inferior function gets involved almost any time we feel stuck and don't know how to adapt. We're overwhelmed by negative impulses that pull us away from our usual strategies. If we know this is happening to us, we have the chance to grow.

Because we're so likely to project these impulses onto other people, it's easiest to recognize their influence in our relationships—particularly with people whose dominant approach to life conflicts with our own. Such people can raise our emotional temperature very quickly. We have a hard time getting along with them. We may not even want to get along with them. We'd rather change them, get them to see things our way. But learning to cooperate with our typological opposites—rather than persuade, argue with, or defend ourselves against them—is one surefire way to bring balance to our personality.

It should be apparent by now that cooperation with other types is not a matter of following the Golden Rule. If we treat other types the way we ourselves would like to be treated, the result is likely to be disaster.

The classic example is probably the Thinking type who tries to respond to a Feeling type's problem by solving it logically. For Thinkers, helping someone analyze a problem is an expression of interest and involvement. But Feeling types don't bring up problems in order to analyze them. They want to talk about them and find out what other people believe, so they know where they stand. They feel controlled by a Thinker's logic, boxed into a solution before they've had a chance to explore the territory for themselves.

It should be noted that Thinking types have no problem using Feeling *skills* when they recognize the situation as personal. And many Feeling types are highly developed in mathematical and scientific skills. What types find difficult to grasp is the *approach to life* a competing function encourages, the expectations it fosters, the needs it creates.

So, in the midst of an argument, both types end up feeling stuck. Their dominant perspective can't make any headway; it's taken them as far as it can. In consequence, each feels the pull of inferior aims and goals, and believes the opposition is coming from the other person.

Thinking types, influenced by inferior Introverted Feeling impulses, feel a threat to their self-sufficiency and logic, and believe the Feeling type is being manipulative and hysterical. Feeling types, contending with inferior Introverted Thinking impulses, feel a threat to their self-esteem and value, and assume the Thinking type is criticizing them and trying to make them feel inadequate.

Before long, each type's inferior function is in control, but neither realizes it. A Thinking type, for example, can end up sounding like a Feeling caricature, concerned with personal relationship: "You don't appreciate me! You don't want my advice; you want a damned mind reader!" The Feeling type responds by inferring a law and predicting the other's behavior: "Whenever I ask for support and understanding, you *always* make me feel stupid!"

Conflicts of this sort are usually described in self-help literature as gender related. Women are presumed to focus on relationship and men on logical principles. But the behaviors in question cut across sexual lines. Men and women are undeniably different, and culture socializes us in gender-specific ways, but one need only consider President Bill Clinton's FP orientation and Hillary Rodham Clinton's TJ one to recognize that gender and socialization are not the last word on typology.

Once we realize that we're catching reflections of our own undeveloped qualities in the behaviors that annoy us in other people, we can get some perspective on some of our most consistent relationship problems. The bottom line is that we need each other. We need input from viewpoints that we wouldn't ordinarily consider.

But as the foregoing interaction suggests, it's impossible to do this from the perspective of our dominant function. When we realize what's going on, we need to shift to our secondary function, or to some other function that won't create immediate typological conflict. This is why learning to cooperate with people who are not like us can give us practice with functions we may not otherwise use.

The Star Trek Solution

The Star Trek characters offer a surprisingly insightful look at how this typological strategy works. Many of the interactions in the various Star Trek programs involve competing types, and the solutions nearly always involve a shift to a more compatible function.

Sensation versus Intuition

Although their viewpoints are in competition, Captain Kirk and Engineer Scott, in the classic Star Trek series, are obliged to work together each time there is an impending threat to the Enterprise.

Kirk, the Intuitive, who relies on quick imaginative solutions, inevitably comes up with a Great Idea. Scotty's first instinct, as a Sensation type, is to focus on what exists right now and to dismiss Kirk's plan as unworkable.

Intuitives always start with the part of an idea that has transforming power; they figure they can deal with details and obstacles later. Sensation types are improvisers and risk-takers, but they build their conceptual houses from the foundation up. They won't take the next step until they're satisfied that everything so far accords with what they know to be true. Thus, Scotty's classic tag lines: "I canna' change the laws of physics, Cap'n," or "I got to have more TIME!"

Within the context of the stories, Kirk and Scott are usually at loggerheads in a crisis, when Scotty can't afford to dismiss Kirk's plans out of hand. Kirk also happens to be Scotty's superior. Thus, Scotty has no choice but to *make* the plan work by forcing Kirk to flesh out his Great Idea and to find a way to implement it. The way he does this is useful to us.

Rather than disparage Kirk's Idea as unrealistic, which simply pits Sensate priorities against Intuitive ones, he plays to Kirk's Introverted Thinking function. This is probably Kirk's secondary function, and it's likely Scotty's as well. He brings the conversation around to logical probabilities—the variables that have to be considered (the limits of warp drive, force field, power source, and so forth) before the Great Idea can be applied to the system.

Kirk responds well to this kind of challenge. He gets to think speculatively, which allows him to use his Intuition, but he's also considering the situation rationally, as it's happening. Gradually, Scotty's more detailed knowledge of the ship pushes Kirk into greater specificity, until Scotty sees how the original Idea relates to their actual context.

Two things are happening here that should be noticed: First, Scotty neither disparages nor appeals directly to Kirk's Intuition. He encourages him to use a function that isn't competing with his own dominant approach. Second, once the two are no longer in direct conflict, they can draw from their crow's nest functions and meet on common ground. Scotty can anticipate Kirk's potential solution to the obstacles he's pointing out, which draws on his Intuition. And Kirk can focus on material issues, as they exist, which draws on his Sensation.

Thinking versus Feeling

Let's look at this from the standpoint of the other two functions, and also from the standpoint of Introversion, where the secondary issue is somewhat different.

Tuvok, a Vulcan tactical officer on the spaceship *Voyager*, is probably an Introverted Sensate, but it's Extraverted Thinking that determines his outward relationships. He relies on logic to accommodate his knowledge of the facts to a reasonable course of action.

Stranded on a distant moon after a crash landing, Tuvok encounters three abandoned, childlike humanoids. They tell him that they were once part of a larger group, but a monster in a nearby cave has been abducting several of them each night. Tuvok reacts by looking for facts to support their claim.

Finding no evidence of monsters in the cave, Tuvok concludes that the three have misunderstood the nature of the situation. He tells them there is nothing he can logically do. The three react with frustration and terror, and they appeal to his protective Feeling instincts, but Tuvok can't connect their requests to anything objectively real. So he does what he considers best; he teaches them how to control their fear.

The next morning, when two of the three have disappeared, Tuvok recognizes that his conclusions were in serious error. The episode is instructive, however, for the way in which the remaining humanoid deals with Tuvok thereafter. She doesn't ask him to display remorse, nor does she attempt to change his priorities. She forms an alliance with him on different terms. She asks if she can help him repair his stranded ship.

To put this typologically, she stops relating to Tuvok's Thinking viewpoint in Extraverted Feeling terms. Instead, she appeals to his Introverted Sensate practicality.

The focus on a useful course of action suits Tuvok. It's compatible with his cause-and-effect approach to the outer world. But once they're working side by side, Tuvok also recognizes his companion's gift of service, which he values as an Introverted Sensate. As a result, he's more inclined to take the humanoid's need for protection into account as factual data.

As with Kirk and Scotty, two things are happening here that should be noticed. First, the humanoid does not appeal to Tuvok's Thinking function, nor does she encourage him to use more Feeling. Instead, she uses a function that can be allied with either. Second, once Tuvok's Thinking and her Feeling are no longer in conflict, they're both able to draw from their crow's nest functions. The humanoid is helping Tuvok to solve a problem logically (Thinking), and Tuvok is recognizing his obligations to their relationship. (Feeling).

PART TWO

A Closer Look at the Attitudes and Functions

13

The Attitudes

Extraversion and Introversion

▲ A MAJOR ARTICLE IN *PSYCHOLOGY TODAY* CLAIMS that happiness is a matter of three traits: self-esteem, optimism, and Extraversion. You might imagine, the author contends, that Introverts would be happiest of all, living, as they do, "in peaceful solitude," but no, study after study indicates that it's the "sociable Extraverts . . . who report more happiness." Thus, the author concludes, if you want to be happy, reprogram your inner operating system: feign Extraversion until going through the motions triggers the desired emotion.[1]

If typologists hadn't already told us that Extraverts constitute three-quarters of the American population, one might hazard a guess from the premise of this article. When Extraversion is taken for granted as the normal outcome of development, Introversion can't help but fall into the cultural unconscious. As a result, Introversion appears to have no definitive existence of its own. In the words of the author just quoted, it strikes people as peaceful but unhappy solitude—the failure of Extraverted socialization.

In the near century since Jung coined the words Introversion and Extraversion, they've tossed on the tide of our cultural assumptions until their original meanings have all but worn away. *Extraverted* has come to mean well-adjusted, people-oriented behavior—the gregarious nature one associates with being good-humored, friendly, and fun to be with. *Introverted* now serves as its darker antonym, the sort of thing we say about the mass murderer who "seemed so ordinary" but was "pathologically shy and mostly kept to himself." Such stereotypes may be predictable in a culture like ours, but they aren't useful to either type.

When Jung set out to describe Extraversion and Introversion, he understood them simply as two opposing ways of dealing with life, comparable to expending energy and conserving it. Because Extraverts regard objective reality as absolute, they will expend energy to relate themselves to it. Introverts, who emphasize what they bring to reality from within, will seek to protect their subjective point of view.

The two types are so consistent and recognizable that Jung believed them to be biological in origin—the psychological descendants of two adaptational strategies still operative in nature. Certain organisms are highly fertile but vulnerable—undefended against predators. Their lives are short, but they leave behind many offspring. Other organisms are less fertile, have many strategies of self-preservation, and live relatively long lives.

Jung thought that Extraverts, as self-propagating and subject to external influence, were adapting like the first kind of organism, whereas Introverts, as self-protective and defended against the claims of others, were adapting like the second.[2] This hypothesis has never been proved (nor can it predict reproductive destiny), but it does serve as a rather nice analogy.

▲ Extraverts strive to broaden their sphere of influence. They want to affect their circumstances in a way that is visible to others, and they are affected in turn by others' opinions and expectations.

▲ Introverts strive to consolidate their territory. They don't share their inner world right away and may resist the influence of others on their opinions and expectations.

As should be clear from the illustrations throughout this book, all types use both attitudes. It's the dominance of one or the other that makes a difference in the way we behave and understand life.

Extraverts

When we move from one climate to another, our bodies change. We adjust to the prevailing temperature and air pressure without even having to think about it. We may notice symptoms of discomfort as we make the transition, but eventually we're harmonized with our environment and take it for granted.

In the same way, our psyche makes adjustments to our social climate. We harmonize ourselves with our situation, absorbing the standards and beliefs that prevail around us, so we can understand and interact with others. These psychological adjustments are the province of our Extraverted functions.

One might even say that we're born Extraverted. We emerge from the womb ready and eager to engage the world and everyone and everything in it. In fact we must, or the brain won't have enough stimulation to develop and organize itself into patterns. Without consistent experiences of touch, play, communication, and loving attention, and the chance to explore, we forfeit curiosity and the capacity to learn from others.

Extraverted behavior is coordinated by this need for outside stimulation. For Extraverted types, negotiating reality is always a matter of engaging the external world: responding to what exists, interacting with it, being part of it. Accordingly, the behavior of Extraverts can always be explained by the nature of their outward situation.

This doesn't mean that Extraverts are conformists or believe what everybody believes. It means they relate to the world as it happens to impinge on them. If society defines reality in a particular way, Extraverts will accept that definition as given, then figure out where they stand in relation to it. The form such relationship takes varies as widely as people do.

Extraverts may enjoy their circumstances, dislike them, protect them, change them, see their potential, analyze them, care for them, destroy them, explore them, experiment with them, and invent new ways of understanding and dealing with them. The point is simply that such types regard the objective situation as reality itself. This is the realm in which they live and breathe and have their being.

In consequence, Extraverts know who they are in connection with others. Their identity is shaped by the varied claims of family, friends, career, possessions, politics, pleasures, hobbies, and so forth: the whole gamut of external existence. Most Extraverts need some consistent contact with a face-to-face community in which others are invested and participate: the family, the workplace, a faith community, a voluntary organization, a peer group. If such opportunities are not available, they will identify with other kinds of group experiences—sports events, fan clubs, street gangs, and the like.

Sally Forth

Sally Forth. Reprinted with special permission of King Features Syndicate.

The assumptions and expectations that prevail in a communal setting are the basis of an Extravert's character and conscience. Extraverts may not agree with these assumptions and expectations—particularly in areas opposed to their dominant function—but they will inevitably take them as their point of departure, assessing their behaviors and ideas in terms of them.

This assessment process constitutes the Extravert's claim to an independent inner life. That is, for Extraverts, the inner world consists of private reactions to collective assumptions, along with mental and emotional content that can't be accommodated to their outward situation. Their self-image, therefore, may be somewhat negative, because they associate their inner life with experiences of inadequacy or difference from others.

In fact, Extraverts have a hard time conceptualizing a self-experience that is not related to external options or to others' judgments. If self-reflection seems warranted, they do it by talking to people about their private inner life: sharing their feelings of inadequacy or exclusion, their shameful wishes and behaviors, their difficulties with jobs or relationships. Such things are, of course, part of an Introvert's inner life as well. But Introverts don't construct their inner life strictly in terms of their outward conditions. So their understanding of self-reflection is different from an Extravert's.

Extraverts assume that everyone sees life as a matter of relational adjustments. In conversation, they will ensure that others recognize what they consider important or valuable about themselves, so that people can take these conditions into account as part of their environment. And they expect others to do the same. It is this reciprocal give-and-take pattern among Extraverts that Americans regard as healthy assertiveness and sociability.

And, indeed, it is. The drawbacks for Extraverts are almost entirely the result of their being in the cultural majority. Extraverts easily define their needs and identity in terms of the situation they're in, without recognizing the price their adjustment can exact. Without sufficient Introversion, Extraverts can cut themselves off from gifts and potential that others don't recognize or appreciate.

This phenomenon is illustrated, rather poignantly, by the behavior of the Extraverts who signed up for the first few seminars I gave on psychological types. Most of the people who sign up for a types seminar are Introverts. The majority, in fact, are usually INFs, who are deeply interested in people and self-definition.

Because INFs constitute about 2 percent of the population, they tend to be in the minority of most group situations. So they're surprised and pleased to find a class in which their approach to life is understood and affirmed by others. Introverts in this kind of situation can become quite Extraverted—in their own way. They adjust because the environment is congenial to their self-experience. Such Introverts talk at their own pace, listen to each other, and develop a strong feeling of camaraderie.

The Extraverts who signed up for the course were also surprised. They weren't accustomed to an Introverted group experience. Until I understood what was happening to these Extraverts and could provide for their way of seeing the world, the same thing would occur every time I gave the seminar.

During the first session, I'd administer a type test, hand out type descriptions, and invite the students to react to them. The Introverts responded with excitement to this exercise. They enjoyed relating their type description to their inner sense of themselves. Their opinions were strong, and they asked lots of questions. The Extraverts, in contrast, said very little. But nearly all of them stayed behind after class. Each one asked the same question. They wanted to know whether I thought the type descriptions were accurate.

This struck me as peculiar, and it took a while to realize that their reaction was my own fault. I was conducting the class in light of my own Introverted assumptions, perhaps buoyed by the Introverted nature of the majority. But Extraverts don't use their self-experience as a primary reference point. They wanted me to give them an *external* reference point so they could *establish* their self-experience.

They wanted to know, first, how I expected them to react, so they could figure out where they stood in relation to those expectations, and second, whether the description of their type was a good enough standard of measurement, so they could figure out how well they fit. Even the Extraverted Thinking types, who genuinely enjoy the process of critical assessment, needed an objective point of departure before they'd venture an opinion.

Moreover, within two or three sessions, if I gave out another type test, virtually every Extravert in the room got close or even scores on Introversion and Extraversion! Some of the Extraverted Feeling types actually came out as full-fledged INFs. Why? Because the Extraverts were doing what they do best. They were Extraverting. They were trying to fit themselves into the situation as they understood it and gauging their self-worth by the expectations of the majority.

I've seen the same kind of thing happen when an Introvert learns about type and takes a test home to an Extraverted spouse. Although the two people are clearly different, the spouse apparently feels pressured to display the "right" type criteria and ends up with scores very much like the Introvert's or so close in every category that the type designation is impossible to determine.

I don't wish to imply that Extraverts will swim in any body of water they happen to fall into. My point is that their need to identify with others is very strong, so they learn to resist their inner life. It confronts them with self-experience that can't be defined in socially recognized terms, and entertaining it strikes them as an unpleasant and largely negative pursuit.

It's important for Extraverts to recognize that outward adjustment is a survivalist response, but survival also requires that we meet our fundamental needs. A plant that deforms itself to reach a small patch of sunlight has adjusted to its situation and may even thrive for a while, but eventually it must reckon with the laws of its own nature. We, too, may thrive by linking our fate to a particular social situation, but societies are not necessarily constructed to meet our individual human requirements. We become aware of such requirements by Introverting.

Introversion, in this respect, connects us more definitively with others than Extraversion can, because it links us with our common human heritage—the reality that exists beyond the visible tokens of outward identity. From an Introverted point of view, identity is a kind of group myth, a Procrustean trap that can stretch us out of shape or cut us off from our true nature if we aren't careful enough.

It often happens that Extraverts recognize their Introverted side only when an external situation falls apart. A crisis—divorce, loss of a job, catastrophic illness, a death in the family—will call into question the conditions that have helped to establish the type's experience of self. Extraverts taxed beyond their capacity to adjust are thrown back on resources a society may not acknowledge, and can, in the process, discover who they are apart from a particular complex of roles.

But Extraverts need to cultivate their Introverted function before a crisis forces the issue. Introversion offers a perspective on external conditions that has value in its own right. When we adjust too well to an external situation, we are at its mercy. We take too much for granted. We forget how to see apart from our conditioned expectations. Idries Shah tells a Sufi teaching story that makes this point:

> Nasrudin used to take his donkey across a frontier every day, with
> the panniers loaded with straw. Since he admitted to being a
> smuggler when he trudged home every night, the frontier guards
> searched him again and again. They searched his person, sifted

the straw, steeped it in water, even burned it from time to time. Meanwhile he was becoming visibly more and more prosperous. Then he retired and went to live in another country. Here one of the customs officers met him, years later. "You can tell me now, Nasrudin," he said. "Whatever *was* it that you were smuggling, when we could never catch you out?"

"Donkeys," said Nasrudin.[3]

Like most teaching stories, this story has a number of interpretations. However, in our particular context, it suggests that we can be so blinded by assumptions that we miss the obvious. This is often the cutting edge for Extraverted types. They need to stop from time to time and recognize the validity of their own perceptions.

Because Extraverts associate their inner life with needs and wishes they can't satisfy in their outward situation, their first attempts to develop their Introverted side are almost always self-assertive. Such types may, for example, insist that others accept their self-oriented desires and behaviors as a valid part of their social identity.

But this egocentric aspect of the Extravert's inner life is only its immediate, surface level. Such types don't reach the deeper levels of their inner world until they realize that accepting their Introverted side doesn't mean forcing it on others—by living it out or telling people about it. Accepting the inner world is very much like accepting the outer one. It exists. It's the hand we've been dealt.

The point of an inner quest, in other words, is not to make room in our outer lives for everything that occurs to us inside, but to take our real needs into account as we make our plans and choices. Even if our fundamental responses to life are difficult to reconcile with outward expectations, accepting their existence gives us the power to make responsible decisions differently, so we aren't struggling so hard to keep unsatisfied needs at bay. The process doesn't require determination so much as imagination.

Learning to deal with private wishes and needs gradually gives Extraverts a new perspective, which ushers in a deeper level of Introverted experience—gifts, potential, and feelings they've never realized in themselves. Because such things have no immediate relationship to the outer world as the Extravert has accepted it, they're not usually apparent right away. Extraverts need some experience with Introverted reflection before they recognize this part of their inner life.

Introverts

Just as the Extraverted functions adapt us psychologically to our environment, the Introverted functions accomplish the converse. They prompt us to evaluate our environment, to assess its congeniality to our self-experience.

As mentioned earlier, there is some biological basis for the attitude we find most comfortable. Introverts have a lower threshold for stimulation than Extraverts, so they're inclined to reflect more on external claims for their attention. This biological explanation is misleading, however, if it is understood only in terms of Extraverted priorities.

Because Introverts need less stimulation from the environment, their sense of identity is configured differently from an Extravert's. They have the distinct luxury of deciding which aspects of a situation to endow with meaning, and they try to do this in accordance with their own needs, potential, and expectations.

Such assessment has nothing to do with selfishness or poor socialization. Many Introverts are highly oriented toward people and service. Introverts simply don't establish a persona as well integrated with their environment as an Extravert's. Indeed, the idea that one should is an artifact of our assumptions as an Extraverted society.

Introverted cultures, such as the ones that exist in some of the Asian countries, generally provide a kind of ritualized Extraverted vocabulary, whose use conveys the proper social attitude without compromising individual privacy. In American culture, Introverts tend to develop ritual Extraversion on their own—a persona that conveys relationship while protecting the integrity of the inner self.

An Extravert easily hears this as self-entitlement, as though an Introverted approach precluded empathy and concern for others. This is because Extraverts take outward reality so much for granted.

They picture everyone's inner life as a repository for fantasies and impulses normally checked by external patterns of morality and ethics.

From an Introverted perspective, outer reality *can't* be taken for granted. It's no more than an influx of perceptual data—meaningless, unless we give it the capacity to signify: with our thoughts, impressions, values, ideas, and interests. Introverts feel a certain responsibility to keep the outer world informed by and integrated with this inner human design.

Introverted children usually discover their inner world as a "secret place" inside themselves, one that is part of them but also has a creative power of its own. For some Introverts, this is simply a matter of having their own unchallenged view of things. For others, the inner world is magical—full of stories and images and characters that all but invent themselves. For still others, it's a private space they can inhabit for thinking about problems and savoring memories. Like external reality, the internal world looks different to different types.

In a somewhat surprising interview soon after she became known for her aggressively sexual character in the film *Basic Instinct*, Sharon Stone said that she had always regarded grammar school recess games as a chore, until one day she realized that she could lean against a wall by herself and use the time to read. This is a typically Introverted awakening. A child will abruptly find that a group situation need not be accommodated on its own terms. The inner kingdom has its own reality and offers its own rewards.

Indeed, an unusual number of actors, musicians, and comedians are Introverts who recognize a performance as an external "space" that can be aligned with the inner self. The very way Introverted performers describe their approach to the task confirms what we now know about the brain activity of Introverted behavior.

Introversion is regulated by the part of the brain that takes in sensory data from the external world and evaluates it. Introverted actors appear to create a character in precisely this way—from the outside in. They observe or invent gestures and movements that seem to belong to the character, and then attempt to inhabit them, like an alternate body.

For example, Leonard Nimoy, in *Star Trek Memories*, describes how he created the character of Mr. Spock:

> I would ask myself, ". . . How can I get myself out of my own shoes and into this character's skewed point of view? How does he perceive any given event differently than I might?" I was also constantly on guard in making sure that my own everyday habits wouldn't creep in and water down the character.[4]

Introverted speakers and teachers often say they approach their jobs in much the same way: They see teaching or speaking or being in authority as a role they're playing. They inhabit it for a while and then go back to being who they really are. For an Introvert, this is essentially what Extraverted action is all about—taking on a social persona.

By contrast, Extraverted actors are inclined to say that a part enables them to freely express who they are without censure. That is, they get to act out all the (unsocialized) things they normally keep at bay.

In contrast to Leonard Nimoy, William Shatner says:

> I used my own experience to find the emotional core of any scene. I wasn't so much acting as I was reacting, using my own internal makeup as the spine upon which I was able to build the character of Jim Kirk. We were basically one and the same.[5]

This distinction tells us something important about how both types understand reality. Extraverts are reacting to what comes at them from the outer world. Self-reflection for these types is usually a process of acknowledging the parts of themselves that aren't integrated with the outer situation.

For Introverts, the inner world comes first. External behaviors that can't be integrated with an inner agenda generally constitute an Introvert's experience of a false self. Thus, Introverts are often caught between the need to create a persona in order to relate to others and the need to stay true to themselves. When they wrestle with these competing aims, they gain access to more of their functional potential. However, in our highly Extraverted culture, this conflict can also play havoc with an Introvert's self-esteem.

Introverts generally feel most comfortable when the environment is closely aligned with their self-experience, and they may seem quite Extraverted in such contexts. For example, when external boundaries are clear and congenial to an Introvert's needs—a dinner with friends, a classroom hour, preaching from the pulpit—the type can be outgoing and revealing, and talk at great length. Although this looks like Extraverted behavior, strictly speaking, it isn't. Extraversion moves us to adjust ourselves to outer reality, whereas an Introvert is usually content because the outer situation is well matched to his or her inner world.

This is why it's helpful to look at the behavior of Introverted artists, who deliberately create a controlled "space" for themselves in which they can, so to speak, Introvert in an object-oriented way. David Letterman, for example, seems entirely outgoing when he's onstage, because the performance space he's created is suited to his particular talents and sense of humor.

Letterman has said in many interviews that being in that space is like trying to be the best version of himself he can possibly be. But apart from that context, he's often described as guarded and reticent—words that Extraverts generally use to characterize an Introverted approach to others.

Just as Extraverts derive energy from other-oriented participation, Introverts are energized when their inner world is engaged. However, the kind of energy that Introverts experience is different from the Extraverted sort. Extraverts who feel energized are likely to seek more stimulation—talk to another person, stop off at one more place, sign another client, add something else to the mix.

Introverted energy prompts one to stay in one place and go deeper. This is precisely the kind of behavior that Extraverts find taxing. Introverts can concentrate on something (or engage in a near monologue about something) to the exclusion of all competing external stimuli for very long periods of time.

For this reason, Introverts are unlikely to describe their emotional state in the same terms that Extraverts do. The studies that "prove" Extraverts are "happier" generally require agreement with such statements as "I like to be with others" and "I'm fun to be with." Introverts are more likely to describe happiness in terms of knowing themselves, being comfortable in their own skin, realizing their potential, having enough space and privacy, and being free to pursue their own path.

Because Introverts perceive values and standards to come from the inside, they are territorial rather than expansive. Introverts will not generally share what they consider important or valuable about themselves right away. They may not share those things at all unless the situation strikes them as appropriate.

This is why the initial response of an Introvert to the unexpected invitation or offer is frequently negative. A negative response gives Introverts time to "try on" the idea of participation. As a result, an Introvert may seem indifferent or even hostile to a situation until he or she feels ready to take part.

For an Extravert, whose adjustments are made in terms of objective relationship, this process can look like a refusal to take risks or the tendency to be difficult unless accommodated. But Introverts are also making adjustments—in terms of others' presumed spatial needs: issues of privacy, possession, and boundaries.

The difference in adjustment criteria extends even to the area of conversational exchange. Introverts are highly aware of territorial imperatives, and they'll generally wait for cues that demarcate conversational space before they contribute to a discussion. For this reason, an Introvert can find an Extraverted group conversation tiring, because people take the floor largely by interrupting each other and often by changing the subject.

In a one-to-one exchange, Extraverts tend to misunderstand the Introvert's territorial behavior as receptivity—the willingness to adjust to another's conversational lead. Thus, Introverts can find themselves overwhelmed by information they weren't seeking or become the unexpected beneficiary of another's confessional story. It should be granted, on the other hand, that an Introvert determined to occupy a conversational space is likely to be indefatigable and oblivious to interruptions of any sort.

Extreme Introversion can have serious drawbacks—but not for the reasons Extraverts suppose. Introverts don't get lonely the way Extraverts do. Extreme Introversion causes problems because it eventually leads to a display of inferior Extraversion.

Like Extraverts who don't understand their undeveloped Introverted side, Introverts rarely understand the message of their unconscious Extraverted side. Instead of adapting more to others, they try harder to create a "space" they can control. In the process, they may strike others as being out of control themselves.

The late John Lennon, for example, was deeply connected to the inner world in a very positive way. But fortune accustomed him to a lifestyle in which he could adjust most situations to his own needs. As a result, his Extraversion was so poorly developed that it was not under his conscious control. When it surfaced, he invariably got into trouble. He made wild public pronouncements, got himself thrown out of public places, and engineered stunts that made others want to stop him.

A much more extreme example might be the Unabomber suspect. Although his motivations were clearly pathological, it's useful to consider their typological aspects. By all accounts, the man is a deeply Introverted mathematical genius, but his inferior Extraverted aims began to put pressure on him from within. Like most types, he didn't see that pressure as psychological. He saw the problem as an external one. Technological advancement began to strike him as a threat to individual self-awareness and self-determination.

In his attempt to create a "space" that he could control, he moved further and further away from society and its technological influence on him. In consequence, his unconscious Extraversion grew even stronger, until it all but merged with his Introverted aims.

One can see this merger clearly in the Unabomber's paradoxical behaviors. The further he moved from society, the more he became obsessed with having an irrevocable effect on it. It was his desperate need to publish his ideas for a mass audience that finally brought him to the attention of the country.

Well-developed Extraversion adapts us to the conscious position of society, and it can lead to a disconnection with self. But well-developed Introversion can align us with the unrealized potential of the human race, and this may lead to an exaltation of self. An extreme Introvert can come to believe that he or she is uniquely privy to the dance of archetypal truths.

There is a Sufi story, called "The Happiest Man in the World," that, among other things, addresses the Introverted need for Extraverted experience.[6] A man goes to a sage, reputed for his wisdom. He tells the sage that he's tried to be happy, but he can't come to terms with the world; his inner thoughts give him no answers. The sage advises him to find the happiest man in the world. "As soon as you find him," he says, "ask him for his shirt, and put it on."

The seeker, with no idea how to accomplish this task, begins to travel, and he does in fact find many happy men. But each says there's a man even happier. So the seeker spends many years on his quest. In the process, he meets remarkable people, sees different countries, acquires varied experiences.

Finally, he reaches the forest in which the happiest man in the world is said to live, and he follows the sound of laughter until he finds a hooded man. "Yes," the man says, "I'm the happiest man in the world." The seeker tells him why he's come and offers him anything he wants in exchange for his shirt.

The happiest man simply laughs. "Look more closely," he says. "I don't even own a shirt!" The seeker is crestfallen. "What should I do now?" he asks.

"You've already done it," the happiest man answers. "You've been striving for something unattainable, but in the process, you've done what you needed to do. You're like the man who manages to jump across a stream by picturing it far wider than it is and gathering his strength accordingly."

The happiest man then revealed his face, and the seeker recognized the very sage who had given him the original advice. "But why didn't you just tell me what I needed to know when I came to you all those years ago?" the seeker asked him.

"You weren't ready then to understand," the sage said. "You needed certain experiences, and I had to make sure you actually went through them."

I deliberately chose a story about a quest for happiness undertaken by a man who could "not come to terms with the world." It gives us another way to look at the article quoted at the start of this chapter, in which the author concludes that Extraverts are "happier" than Introverts. This conclusion is most certainly not true.

It may be suggested, however, that Introverts who *do* experience themselves as unhappy can benefit by doing exactly what the author suggests: "Feign" a little Extraversion until the problem gets solved. That is, an Introvert may have to take deliberate steps toward adjusting to objective reality—even if the process seems unrealistic or "not good enough" or feels like "selling out"—simply in order to develop an outward perspective strong enough to align with the Introverted agenda.

The Symbiotic Nature of the Attitudes

Jung once said that two personalities are like two chemicals. When they meet, both are transformed. Because we have such strong preferences for one attitude or the other, we are often attracted to our attitudinal opposites. The affinity is a natural one, and it leads to relationships in which both parties are able to grow and change. The partners help each other, by advice and example, to get in touch with their secondary functions.

Sometimes, however, when we've overdeveloped our dominant attitude, we're attracted to people who will actually "live out" our opposing attitude for us. This kind of attraction is also natural. It's part of an attempt to resist conflict within. The other person gives us contact with our unconscious side, but we're spared the ordeal of reconciling our own contradictions.

Although such attractions give us a sense of well-being in the initial stages of involvement, the connection inevitably generates conflict in its own right. The partnership is symbiotic rather than relational. In most cases, both parties depend on each other for their sense of wholeness and well-being, so the individual growth of either will threaten the arrangement.

Moreover, once symbiosis has been achieved, it becomes easier for the partners to disassociate themselves from behaviors in the other that don't feel like "themselves." The two can become locked into parallel lives, with no real sharing possible.

Take the case of Lorna, an Introverted artist who runs a small craft shop out of her home. Several years ago, she married Michael, a highly Extraverted journalist, who enjoys being on the road, meeting new people and seeing new places. At first the marriage was fulfilling and expansive for both parties. He was good at taking immediate initiative; she was observant and saw things he didn't notice. That first winter Michael taught Lorna how to ski; she introduced him to classical music.

But little by little, as the two came to depend on each other to carry the entire burden of their unconscious attitudes, their worlds intersected with less and less frequency. The skiing trips that Lorna had thought exciting and romantic when she was first getting to know Michael now seemed like expensive and time-consuming breaks from the work she really loved. The concerts that moved her to tears were more likely to put Michael to sleep.

Worse, Lorna realized that she hated the parties where Michael did most of his networking. He seemed to want her there with him, but as far as she was concerned, he spent the entire night mixing and glad-handing, while she was left to make her way alone among a roomful of strangers who meant nothing to her. Moreover, just when she was fading and wanted to go home, Michael seemed to perk up and start all over again.

When she finally told Michael how she felt, he was angry and defensive. "Here I was, laboring under the delusion that we were having a good time together," he said, "and now I find that you not only dislike these parties but also blame me for your inability to socialize. Why do you need me to hold your hand all night?"

For his part, Michael didn't understand Lorna's need to create an unimpeded cocoon for herself in the house. When he came home from work or an extended trip, she actually seemed to resent his presence. When he mentioned that to her one day, she said that he immediately took over whatever room he came into and didn't even consider her needs. For example, the second he walked in, he'd switch off her classical music and turn on the TV. This struck Michael as a simple refusal to compromise. After all, Lorna could listen to her music all day long. Why did everything have to happen according to her inner blueprint?

As time went on, Lorna became more involved in her work, and each time she was absorbed by a project that meant something to her, she was completely oblivious to the things she usually did with Michael. Michael felt jealous of her time and her attention, and felt that she was using her work to avoid him. Lorna couldn't make him understand that this was not unlike the kind of complaint she had about the parties he so valued.

Although these may seem like inconsequential problems, they were an indication of increasing polarization. The arguments got worse, and they never seemed to get resolved. Lorna said that Michael had no respect for her work or the things she cared about. Michael said that Lorna was blind to everyone's needs but her own. They weren't even sure they liked each other anymore, and they seemed to inhabit two different worlds. But they also realized they were deeply attached to each other.

This is a fairly typical attitudinal impasse that is often attributed in books on relationship to differences in male and female psychology. But the basic configuration works in the other direction as well. The classic cartoon illustration of marital misery is the Introverted husband caught midway between sinking into a favorite chair with a newspaper and his Extraverted wife's exasperated reminder that they've got plans to go to a wedding or have dinner with the new neighbors.

Similar problems can arise between colleagues in a business situation, or between siblings, or between parent and child. The merger involved need not be sexual; it's just easier to see it when it is. In none of these cases will the situation yield readily to technique. The solution lies squarely in the area of the secondary function. The more we remain unconscious of our secondary attitudes, the more our weaker functions will rush in to fill the gap. This is why the arguments Lorna and Michael were having were so difficult to resolve.

When two people have formed an attitudinal symbiosis, they are likely to experience each other as frustrating and impossible to change. But they also have a secret pact that keeps them from growing, so the arrangement stays the way it is.

For example, an extreme Introvert may welcome a stable relationship as a respite from having to maintain an Extraverted social life. In the case at hand, Michael's relentlessly outward focus allowed Lorna to regard him as orbiting about her still point at the center of the house. She was free to pursue her Introverted interests without having to Extravert at all.

But the more she ignored her own Extraversion, the more she saw Michael's Extraversion as inferior. Her unconscious attitude was alive and well inside her, and it pushed her to control the very behaviors in Michael that had drawn her to him. She couldn't see this in herself, so she assumed it was a problem with Michael. He wasn't respecting her needs.

Michael, for his part, had a barely realized investment in Lorna's inaccessibility, which he found both mysterious and attractive. More to the point, very little was actually required of him in terms of sharing who he was or developing genuine intimacy with her. But the more he ignored his Introverted side, the more he saw Lorna's Introversion as selfish and distancing. Because he couldn't see this in himself, he assumed that it was Lorna's problem.

Ultimately, both Lorna and Michael were drawing not from their dominant functions but from the functions they were least equipped to use in relationship. This is why the solution in such cases can be so elusive. What we need to do is *give up*. That is, we need to give up our expectations of the other. This is the only sure way to undermine a symbiotic dependence.

No one can do this all at once, of course. But the surrender of expectations even in a small area of a relationship can force a real change in a pattern of unconscious balance. It forces a crisis of the secondary function, and we may be induced to integrate more of our own potential.

As often happens, this occurred for Michael and Lorna not because they agreed to it but out of pure frustration. Lorna was tired of depending on Michael for all her social contacts. She felt misunderstood and angry with him and was secretly thinking about a separation. She decided to prepare for a life without him by developing more contacts of her own. She joined an organization related to her art work, and she accepted a few invitations to sell her pieces at craft fairs.

Michael, predictably, was not happy about any of this. He wanted more of her attention, not less. But after a number of very serious arguments, he realized that Lorna was intent on taking this direction. So he went to some of the fairs with her, and was surprised and impressed by the respect she had from her peers.

Lorna, meanwhile, began to recognize that Michael's knowledge of networking could be helpful to her in her new context. Some of what he had been saying about contacts made sense to her now, and she asked him for advice on the process. Michael liked being approached as an authority, and he turned out to be a good teacher. He was also discovering that he enjoyed the private space he had when Lorna was at her meetings. He used the time to build a small darkroom and learn more about photography.

In one respect, Michael and Lorna simply developed a little more in common. But this is surely the point. Once we stop expecting our partner to carry all of our undeveloped attitude for us, we create the potential for a genuine relationship. This is why even small changes in one area of life can have perceptible results in a short period of time.

It's important to recognize that neither Lorna nor Michael changed their fundamental type orientation. They didn't attempt to develop their weakest functions. They simply dipped into their secondary functions and brought their types more into balance. This, in turn, improved their interaction with each other.

To be sure, when one person gives up his or her expectations and the balance begins to shift, the other person may not welcome the opportunity to change. But this in itself makes for different problems than the ones that had seemed so insoluble.

The Perceiving Functions

- ▲ Extraverted Sensation
- ▲ Introverted Sensation
- ▲ Extraverted Intuition
- ▲ Introverted Intuition

14
Extraverted Sensation
E_STP and E_SFP Types

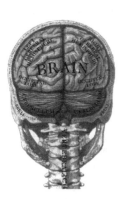

Left hemisphere

Tertiary function
Extraverted Judgment

Inferior function
Introverted Intuition

Right hemisphere

Dominant function
Extraverted Sensation

Secondary function
Introverted Judgment

▲ BECAUSE EXTRAVERTED SENSATION ENCOURAGES PHYSICAL ENGAGE-
MENT with the outer world, it's often described as sensory awareness—our knowledge that material things exist. But this function is
a good deal more than a means of acquiring perceptual information.
As a right-brain function, Sensation comes into play when events are
changing so rapidly that linear analysis is impossible. We respond
immediately, on the basis of visual and tactile information, guided
by what we've done before.

For example, we may learn to tango by following a chart of
steps, but once we actually know how to dance, we aren't thinking
about rules or instructions. We're directly engaged by our surface
perceptions—the rhythm of the music, the movements of a partner.
We're changing as our situation does.

Robert Pirsig, in *Zen and the Art of Motorcycle Maintenance*, describes Sensate experience this way, with regard to a mechanic working on a motor:

> The nature of the material at hand determines his thoughts and motions, which simultaneously change the nature of the material at hand. The material and his thoughts are changing together in a progression of changes.[1]

This is what happens whenever we're using Sensation. It happens when we're kneading bread and the pressure of our hands changes with the texture of the dough. It happens when we're moving a ball downcourt for a chance at the hoop. It happens when we're driving, alert to a whole field of sights and sounds. It happens when we're playing in a band. It happens when we're knitting a sweater. Every time our actions are changing immediately and directly in concert with our surface perceptions, we're drawing on Extraverted Sensation.

It should be clear from these activities that the only way to cultivate Extraverted Sensation is by hands-on involvement—by strengthening the link between sensory perception and neural response. *Our bodies have to get into the act.* For types who use this function as their primary approach to life, true knowledge is *always* concrete, a product of firsthand experience.

Such knowledge can't be acquired by reading instructions, taking a course, or considering the ramifications of our actions. We have to plunge in and do something often enough to get a "feel" for what it requires—whether it's sautéing garlic, shooting darts, competing in a race, serving a volleyball, making love, plunking a banjo, or doing a comedy routine at an improv club. In some aspects of life, direct experience is all that counts. We take action, see what happens, and make adjustments when we do it again.

Sensate types are not just active physically. They're active socially. They're deeply influenced by what's going on around them, and they want to take part in it. They have a "feel" for atmosphere, style, and image. They know what people are interested in and like being recognized as paradigmatic of the trend.

The ESP Types

	ESTP		ESFP
dominant	Extraverted Sensation	dominant	Extraverted Sensation
secondary	Introverted Thinking	secondary	Introverted Feeling
right-brain	**Extraverted Intuition**	right-brain	**Extraverted Intuition**
alternatives	**Introverted Feeling**	alternatives	**Introverted Thinking**
left-brain	**Extraverted Thinking**	left-brain	**Extraverted Feeling**
double agents	**Introverted Sensation**	double agents	**Introverted Sensation**
tertiary	Extraverted Feeling	tertiary	Extraverted Thinking
inferior	Introverted Intuition	inferior	Introverted Intuition

Although we all use Extraverted Sensation for at least some of our activities, the ESTPs and ESFPs depend on it for identity and relationship with others. The ISTP and ISFP types, for whom Extraverted Sensation is secondary, display some of the same personality traits, but they understand reality differently.

ESPs understand life by way of their surface perceptions, and they prefer situations that change quickly enough to hold their attention. Their senses may be so acute that they seem to be anticipating things before they actually happen.

Such types need hands-on experience to feel in contact with life. They may get bored or uneasy when a situation requires assessment without perceptual information to guide the process. Accordingly, they usually gravitate to professions, hobbies, and recreational pursuits that ensure some form of immediate sensory feedback.

An ESP firefighter puts it this way: "It's strange, but one of the things I love about my job is the sensation of heat on my skin, even if it hurts. Long before I even see the fire, I feel it; I know it's there. I know what I'm dealing with." Interestingly, this man also works part-time as a performer, and he says he feels the same way about that job: "I feel the 'heat' from the audience just like I feel the fire, and I love responding to it and knowing how they're going to respond in return."

Most ESPs understand the pleasures of that kind of interaction. In their social lives as well as their jobs, they're "in it to win it."

They gauge their performance, always, by its immediate effect. Many Sensates are drawn to politics, show business, and sales for this reason. They are often witty, entertaining communicators who quickly read and connect with an audience. They make excellent police officers, athletes, negotiators, diplomats, impresarios, restaurant managers, sales agents, real estate brokers, advertisers, publishers, stock traders, and public relations strategists.

Like the firefighter just quoted, ESPs often speak of that peculiar thrill of knowing their game, knowing when luck or timing or the cards or an audience is "with them." An ESP goes with this feeling, tries to stay with it—like a surfer coming in on a perfect wave. To paraphrase Pirsig, the nature of the situation determines the type's thoughts and motions, which simultaneously change the nature of the situation. The average ESP assesses what's going on, plays to it, and takes pleasure in the escalating sense of mastery.

For highly Extraverted types, this happens as naturally as a leaf turning its face to the sun. You can always tell from the ESPs in the crowd exactly what society currently regards as admirable, stylish, fascinating, outrageous, or exciting. These types will have so adapted themselves to generalized assumptions that they physically embody them.

Many ESPs seem to be striving for this—for the highest pitch of concrete actualization. They become the experiential standard by which others' image and attitude are measured. In fact, many attractive and engaging people are led to use Sensation as a dominant function precisely because their style and impact are their fundamental strengths.

Some ESPs have a kind of movie-star quality—a self-assurance, a charisma, an appetite for life—that others enjoy and find infectious. Magnetic, clever, full of energy and enthusiasm, they make a room come alive, thrive on attention, and are attentive in return. Billy Crystal satirizes this way of approaching reality with his character Fernando, who invariably greets people by observing, "It's better to look good than to feel good—and darling, you look marvelous!"

The ESP's need for sensory input is so strong that the type may find it difficult to recognize relationship apart from physical proximity and direct response. It was probably an ESP who first said, "Absence makes the heart grow fonder—of someone else." ESPs base their relationships on parallel sensory experience rather than on common ideas: doing things together, being in the same circumstances.

Calvin and Hobbes   by Bill Watterson

If they aren't getting enough feedback, they'll push for it, teasing people or goading them into some form of physical display—if only a disconcerted laugh. Unless they can see the raised eyebrow, hear the quick intake of breath, or feel the touch of someone's hand on their arm, they lose touch with the situation and don't know how to proceed. Even those ESPs who enjoy writing and publishing are always aware of their potential audience. They need responsive interaction, the sense that their words have connected and are having an effect.

More than any other type, ESPs believe that life is right now—explosive, impulsive, kinesthetic: a matter of doing, having, using things as they were meant to be used. In a social situation, they're outgoing and generous; in a crisis, practical and resourceful, immediately alert to the import of sensory data.

It should be noted, however, that a response-ready approach to life has its drawbacks. ESPs are stimulated by whatever comes to their attention, but they also lose interest quickly. They have little patience with information unrelated to their skills and interests. If a problem involves elements they don't understand or don't want to think about, they're likely to avoid it or let someone else take care of it.

Perceiving all relevant data to come from the surface of the external world, ESPs are not disposed to tolerate anxiety or feelings of inadequacy. They'll find a new situation and change themselves by adapting to it. Jon Krakauer, author of *Into Thin Air* (about the 1996 Mount Everest expedition that killed eight people) captures something of this viewpoint when he suggests that people who risk physical danger do so because they're looking for "something like a state of grace."

The climbers who lost their lives were hoping, he says, "for some kind of transformation. . . . Climbing something that big and difficult and mythic and huge is just so impossible. And if you do it, you assume in your heart that it has to change everything."[2]

ESPs are continually propelled, in this respect, beyond the reckoned limits of past accomplishment. They'll reinvent themselves to meet a challenge and become in the process the very embodiment of social aspiration. But a Sensate frame of mind also keeps ESPs in a constant state of physical expectancy. Unless ESPs develop their secondary function, Introverted Thinking or Introverted Feeling, they can't defend themselves against overstimulation except by withdrawing emotionally.

The ESP's Secondary Function

It should be granted that ESPs don't feel unduly vulnerable to external influence. Indeed, they cherish freedom and individuality. The worst fate they can imagine is to be trapped by others' ideas about normal or typical behavior. This understanding of freedom, however, derives largely from the type's resistance to *Extraverted* Judgment.

Extraverted Judgment is a tertiary viewpoint for ESPs, and they have little incentive to develop it well. To compare one person to another strikes these types as pointless. To be alive is to be yourself. Go for it, they say. Do it. Don't hide behind other people's doubts and expectations. And sometimes, as stated, ESPs become paradigms of what *can* be acquired, said, or done, notwithstanding accepted social wisdom.

What ESPs don't recognize is their need for *Introverted* Judgment.

A response-ready approach to life ultimately commits them to circumstances as they exist, here and now. Their only possible options are participation, resistance, or escape. Proactive change requires an Introverted viewpoint—the ability to stand back and measure a situation against one's inner needs and values.

Unlike the Extraverted Judging functions, which prompt us to apply general standards to individual situations, Introverted Judgment prompts us to see every situation as unique, subject to the dictates of our own experience. Roughly speaking, this is the difference between reading a manual of sexual techniques and reading the immediate needs of a partner.

The better ESPs develop their Introverted Judgment, the better they are at gauging probabilities as a situation is unfolding, and the better they are at improvising successfully. Conversely, the more likely they are to recognize the limits of their own experience. This is the point at which Extraverted Judgment makes sense to them. Once ESPs know something for themselves, they'll actively seek out the benefit of others' knowledge.

Like other types, ESPs normally use their secondary function only when it supports their dominant aims and goals. This is what keeps them from developing their Introverted point of view. Their main objective is to meet the outer world, to be received by it, and to have a perceptible effect on it. In youth, before their skills are equal to their aspirations, ESPs can be disruptive and restless; but they can also be shy and socially awkward. A surprising number of such types recall a time when they lacked confidence and were reluctant to take action apart from existing standards.

Once ESPs acquire enough experience to use Sensation well, they invariably discover the utility and power of their strongest skills. Their ability to read people and to establish a rapport with them is parallel to none. ESPs take pleasure in this aspect of their personality and they use it to their benefit.

Adolescent ESPs, in particular, may see life as a kind of game that requires equal measures of skill and luck, and getting over with people gives them a certain competitive advantage. For example, an ESFP of my acquaintance, having reached the ripe old age of twenty-one, finally admitted to his girlfriend that he was never really a vegetarian; he just liked the reactions he got with socially conscious women when he claimed he was.

Such types have a talent for being whatever they need to be in order to make a situation work for them. They may be so alert to probability in the social realm that they embody developing trends long before the popular tide has even turned. For this reason, it's hard for ESPs to recognize that being admired for their individuality is very often the opposite of being true to themselves.

When ESPs cultivate Introverted Judgment in its own right, their point of view is less conditioned by immediate material effects. They recognize that some experiences genuinely separate them from others and give them a unique way of seeing the world, but others are universal, linking them with values and aspirations shared by all human beings, no matter who they are or what they do. If ESPs don't find a way to honor both aspects of their Judgment, they aren't being true to themselves, and they eventually feel trapped by what they've accomplished.

Introverted Intuition: The ESP's Inferior Function

In our increasingly Sensate culture, our movies focus on the kind of quest that Introverted Judgment engenders. Some of our most popular film heroes are the ones who give up status and power for the sake of a higher purpose, but recoup them in the last frame, having discovered, in the process, the true meaning of life and love. In real life, the effects of Introverted Judgment are more subtle, and their rewards are a matter of character.

It should be emphasized that ESPs are generous and responsible, and they establish a strong code of honor within the context of their Sensate assumptions. They're deeply loyal to the people they care about and respond immediately when someone needs their help. However, they don't recognize the Introverted side of their personality until their Sensate assumptions are called into question—by failure, middle age, or an external situation so inhumane that it forces them to recognize unconditional inner values.

Moreover, when ESPs feel stuck or have run out of external options, they don't turn naturally to their secondary function. Like all types who take their dominant function as far as it can go, ESPs first feel the pressure of their least-developed function, Introverted Intuition, which has moved too far from their conscious control. Unexpectedly pushed away from their usual Sensate motives, ESPs feel thwarted, and they look to their outer circumstances to find an explanation.

Well-developed, Introverted Intuition is a valuable commodity. It helps us to recognize that "what you see" is not necessarily "what you get." The same information can be interpreted from many different, and incompatible, perspectives. ESPs have no problem using Introverted Intuitive skills when they need them. It's the Introverted Intuitive *approach to life* that plays havoc with a Sensate point of view.

A response-ready frame of mind presumes a world that has immediate perceptual import. Introverted Intuition suggests that absolute meaning is an illusion—the result of having incomplete information. ESPs don't recognize this point of view as part of their own make-up. It strikes them as dangerous and stupid, the province of ivory-tower theorists who fear to take action.

Thus, when ESPs are experiencing Introverted Intuitive impulses, they feel as though their way of life were being criticized from the standpoint of someone's abstract assumptions—someone who hasn't been there, doesn't know them or their circumstances. In a Sensate culture like ours, there are hundreds of ways this internal drama gets played out—between one generation and the next, between men and women, between one race and another.

ESPs can address the perceived problem by developing more Introverted Judgment, which draws their attention to unconditional human values—the needs and feelings that unite people, notwithstanding external distinctions. However, when ESPs are influenced by unconscious Intuition, they're certain that people are discriminating against them for something unconditional about their *surface identity*. So they turn to their tertiary function, Extraverted Feeling or Extraverted Thinking, to get social affirmation from people who share their Sensate self-understanding.

Tertiary solutions are always successful for a time, because they persuade us that all the difficulties we're having are being caused by others. Moreover, tertiary rationalizations always contain an element of truth. ESPs *do* need to honor their subjective experience of life. But Extraverted Judgment gives them no power to do this. It keeps them focused squarely on external reality—on externals that condition their identification with some people and not others.

Sensate Culture and Tertiary Judgment   Because our society has become increasingly Sensate, the development of Judgment has become a collective as well as an individual problem. It has taken only one generation for "the appearance of impropriety," a Sensate criterion, to become a more important standard of social judgment than the rational principle of "innocent until proven guilty."

Types who use Extraverted Sensation for identity and relationship have enjoyed greater numbers than other types for as long as type tests have existed. Social institutions, however, have been brought into line with Sensate priorities only recently, presumably by way of mass-market advertising, which targets the consumer majority and plays to its tastes and point of view. Thus, an entire generation has grown up in a wall-to-wall pop cultural atmosphere, with both communications overload and the idea that *everything* is essentially entertainment.

Although our educational methods have been gradually shifting to meet the Sensate hunger for perceptual variety and stimulation, there has been little corresponding shift in our transmission of cultural values and standards. We continue to inculcate moral responsibility from an Extraverted, left-brain perspective—in the form of laws, rules, and generalized standards of behavior. This, ultimately, in a Sensate culture, is to train an inferior, tertiary understanding of moral obligation.

For Sensates, moral judgment is Introverted. It's part of a person; it operates every time we take action. Rules and laws don't foster that kind of judgment. From a Perceiver's point of view, Extraverted Judgment merely ensures social order. ESPs will gladly point out the hypocrisy of meeting the demands of the law while violating the canons of human decency. Such apparent contradictions encourage these types to regard legal and political action as purely strategic, a means of getting others to support one's own priorities.

Sensates need more experience with their right-brain reasoning skills, in order to recognize their larger implications. Used well, Introverted Thinking and Feeling give us a sense of interdependence—the understanding that our local actions go beyond ourselves and our group loyalties to affect the whole, for good or ill.

One reason we lament the dearth of cultural heroes is our failure as a society to make this leap. The heroes we elevate by way of Sensate prowess or beauty—athletes, models, military leaders, and so forth—are too often torn down by negative revelations of individual character. Such fallen heroes inevitably defend themselves with tertiary Extraverted Judgment. They resent the obligation to be a role model as well as a good team player. It strikes them as unfair, depriving them of the freedom to be themselves.

Calvin and Hobbes   by Bill Watterson

Calvin and Hobbes ©1995 Watterson. Dist. by Universal Press Syndicate. Reprinted with permission. All rights reserved.

Moreover, like individual ESPs, a Sensate society can be undermined by the functions it has relegated to the cultural unconscious. Without a strong Introverted Judging perspective, Introverted Intuition gets out of society's control. Under its unconscious influence, we're moved to identify ourselves largely by external differences from others.

In consequence, we resist common consensus in the realm of ideas. Parallel external conditions—race, color, gender, nationality, and so forth—come to seem a more tangible foundation for our loyalties, a more equitable basis for moral judgment.

Undeveloped Intuition can also flood a Sensate culture with a high toleration for magical thinking. One can see it in a benign form in the growth of industries devoted to handling and selling totems associated with the rich and famous. But inferior Intuition has a dark side as well. When something contradicts the straightforward expectations dictated by direct experience, inferior Intuition will persuade people that the problem is one of hidden powers and influences.

These powers are invariably understood in a literal Sensate manner. Such understanding need not issue, say, in the certainty that aliens are abducting vulnerable segments of the population (although it can), but it tends to foster the suspicion of conspiracy where none exists. It becomes too easy to believe that people are plotting to impose their own agenda whenever the facts go afield of one's immediate personal interests.

Marvin

Marvin. Reprinted with special permission of North America Syndicate.

Developing Introverted Judgment

Once an ESP begins to make the effort to look within, he or she often blossoms in a way that is quite extraordinary. When such types fuse their perceptual experience with a deeper sense of human value, their potential to influence culture is enormous, and they can easily become genuine examples for others.

From time to time, a fictional character will embody Introverted Judging standards in a positive, individual sense, and it's worth using such characters to illustrate the kind of fusion I'm talking about. Significantly, such characters tend to be drawn as misfits. They're forced to Introvert because they've been separated from their group identity by circumstances. In the process, they recognize their common humanity with all people.

Kwai Chang Caine, the Chinese-American mystic/martial arts expert in *Kung Fu*, fits this description. So does Benton Fraser, on the little-watched program *Due South*. Transferred from the Royal Canadian Mounted Police to the angry streets of Chicago, Fraser is much like Caine. He, too, is deprived of collective support for his identity. He, too, has evolved a near-Zenlike approach to life.

Both characters are highly Sensate. In fact, they enjoy senses preternaturally keen from years of rigorous training. Fraser, in particular, relies on taste and smell in a way that his colleagues find eccentric and laughable. But these men also react to what they're taking in through the prism of unfailing compassion and honor.[3]

Because they're not concerned with the immediate image they're creating as they go about their work, both Caine and Fraser look, at first glance, to be innocents. But each is utterly, unshakably aware. Their assumption that we all share fundamental human values doesn't lead them to break rules for the sake of individual freedom; it leads them to do far more than the rules require. Their point of view becomes a beacon of morality in a world that no longer believes human values exist.

One might point in this respect to Oskar Schindler, the industrialist immortalized in the movie *Schindler's List*. Schindler was hardly a moral paradigm in the classic sense of the term. He seems to have been a successful ESTP pragmatist whose urbanity, intelligence, and nerves of steel had made him wealthy and accustomed him to all the creature comforts life had to offer. It was the inhumanity of his circumstances that forced him inward, and he struggled with the conflict between the identity he had formed and a larger sense of responsibility.

Sensates who struggle with Introverted Judgment don't evolve fight-or-flight strategies in response to perceived mistreatment at the hands of others; they recognize their responsibility to the situation, to the part they play in it, and they move to affect it for good. Schindler, in the manner of all ESPs, actualized his values in a direct, immediate, physical way and became a genuine role model.

Because we are inclined to elevate such people beyond their humanity, it's important to note that Schindler's personality, strengths, and gifts did not fundamentally change. What changed was his attitude. He remained essentially what he was—a charming opportunist, a hustler—but he used his well-honed abilities to mirror and to persuade in the service of a guiding moral purpose.

One thinks here of the ancient Sufi economy of salvation, wherein change is never escape or denial but the ability to see things exactly the way they are, so that even our flaws become useful to others. When Extraverted Sensation is leavened with the values of Introverted Judgment, we fully embrace the outer events that make us who we are—here, now, in time and space, with all their attendant problems and limitations; but we also recognize our responsibility to them, to the larger pattern of which we are a living part.

Another interesting example of this kind of "salvation" occurs in the movie *Peggy Sue Got Married*. At the time this film came out, critics understood it as a less compelling distaff version of *Back to the Future*, the movie in which a young man takes a time machine into the past and changes the outcome of his parents' history. He returns to his own time to find them no longer embarrassing misfits but attractive, blow-dried, physically vibrant cultural paragons. The perfect Extraverted Sensate conclusion.

Peggy Sue, by contrast, goes back in time the way Dorothy is blown over the rainbow—unexpectedly, as though unconscious forces had propelled her out of her everyday life and forced her to see things from a new perspective. Her story seems less exciting because, given the opportunity, she changes virtually nothing in the past.

She falls in love with the same man, despite all her efforts to do otherwise, conceives the same child, and realizes, finally, that her choices have woven the fabric of her life. They can't be unmade without collapsing everything else of importance to her.

This is an Introverted Judging view. It always reveals the interdependent nature of reality. It fuses the outer, phenomenal world and the human spirit. Such fusion is the ESP's unique contribution to human consciousness.

ESTP: Extraverted Sensation/Introverted Thinking

ESTP

dominant	Extraverted Sensation
secondary	Introverted Thinking
right-brain alternatives	**Extraverted Intuition**
	Introverted Feeling
left-brain double agents	**Extraverted Thinking**
	Introverted Sensation
tertiary	Extraverted Feeling
inferior	Introverted Intuition

ESTPs are realists of the first order. Like all Sensates, they are geared by their senses and enjoy action and stimulation. But unlike the ESFP, who is drawn by Introverted Feeling to an interest in people, the ESTP is galvanized by Introverted Thinking toward situations involving risk, strategy, and serious competition.

Although Sensation types are evenly divided among men and women, American culture has traditionally associated many of the characteristics of the ESTP with a cultivated but apparently effortless machismo, perhaps best demonstrated by the fictional characters of James Bond and Rhett Butler. It should be emphasized, however, that society's increasingly Sensate orientation has contributed to the rise of a strong ESTP female image—the gritty, sarcastic, self-possessed, karate-kicking woman who takes gender equality for granted and is determined to enjoy life on her own terms.

Whether male or female, these types are the quintessential adventurers. They like the thrill of the game, and they generally play out their need for action and challenge in fast-moving careers that require think-on-your-feet decisions and split-second coordination. Often as not, they take up professions that require both mental and physical agility: athletics, stunt work, choreographed performance, surgery, high-stakes negotiation, diplomacy, undercover operations.

Introverted Thinking gives ESTPs a talent for evaluating the variables in a crisis situation, and they invariably respond with action. They take in so much information at a glance that they may seem to have a sixth sense. They know far more than they're able to express about what's likely to happen and what they can do to prevent or support it.

For this reason, their competitive drive is very strong. They're accustomed to calculating the angles well enough to assure a successful outcome, and settling for less is more frightening to them than taking a risk. If their work doesn't satisfy their need for brinkmanship, they will find a sport or recreational activity that allows them to compete against themselves, to push themselves to the limits of their skills and senses. Lacking such outlets, the type can become reckless or even self-destructive, simply for the thrill of meeting a challenge, courting potential disaster, and coming out on top.

ESTPs are usually charismatic, often charming. Because they rely on firsthand experience for what they know, they are entertaining and tell a good story—about things they've done, people they've met, interesting events they've seen, any kind of tangible reality that will further their connection with their listeners. They read people very well, and they're always aware of the impression they're making.

Indeed, ESTPs are so alert to others' reactions that they can use this skill to advantage, negotiating ends favorable to their own interests. An ESTP may be ruthlessly pragmatic in this respect, fully capable of depersonalizing a situation, seeing others as players in a game that inevitably results in winners and losers.

A real-life example of the type is surely the late President John F. Kennedy, a well-bred diplomat whose charm, wit, and enthusiasm for life created an image that still has affective power today. Like all ESTPs, Kennedy was conscious of his style and appearance. He enjoyed the demands and challenges of negotiation and depended on his powers of persuasion and improvisation—both socially and politically. His sometimes ruthless pursuit of the Sensate pleasures of life has become the stuff of legend—as has his disinclination to follow through on details. The very idea of Camelot, where everything is perfect for one shining moment, appeals to SPs of all varieties.

A more modern image of the type may be a woman like Madonna, whose ability to reinvent her image is the direct result of her Sensate grasp of the popular imagination. One might also consider the larger-than-life character in the TV series *Xena*, whose style and charisma never take a backseat to her prowess as a warrior, her cool assessment of pertinent facts, and her appetite for sensory pleasure.

Like all Perceiving types, ESTPs are drawn to immediate achievement, but they may not care to build a structure on the foundations thus established. Once a situation is in hand, the type tends to lose interest and moves on to the next challenge. It should be emphasized, however, that ESTPs generally have their own code of honor. It may not accord with collective mores and expectations, but it is consistent and fiercely maintained—especially where loyalty to friends is concerned.

In relationship, the type is given to showing rather than saying. ESTPs handle their romantic lives with the same strategic drive that fuels their other activities. Their attention, timing, and sense of drama are often larger than life and may sweep the other person off his or her feet. The utter realism of the type, however, may not leave much room for discernment of a lover's unique qualities.

ESTPs seem alert to nuance because they are so aware of another's reactions, but in truth, they may not be seeing much beyond a person's ability to embody the traits that culture associates with a desirable partner. Once they've made a commitment, they're true to it in their fashion, but save for the initial thrill of attraction and challenge, they may believe that most relationships are basically interchangeable.

Romantic gestures are likely to strike them as a courting game. Far more persuasive are experiences of sensory excitement—a flare of anger, a dangerous liaison, an unexpected fright, a heart-pumping adventure, even an intense argument.

As right-brain types, ESTPs have little patience for or interest in the contemplation of abstract knowledge. They prefer concrete facts that have some kind of practical application. It was probably a scornful ESTP who invented the term *nerd*. These types are disinclined to explain their motivations or justify their behaviors, other than to shrug offhandedly and say something disarming.

Accordingly, ESTPs can be difficult to read and predict. They don't like problems that can't be solved as they arise, and they're likely to disappear if they feel trapped by unexpected obstacles. This is not due so much to unreliability as it is to their Sensate priorities.

A situation that conflicts with their expectations irritates them because they can't bring their experience into play.

Even when bored or unhappy, they are not inclined to seek out something entirely new. They enjoy action and excitement and the thrill of a new sensation, but only in terms of a familiar framework of perceptual experience. This is why ESTPs usually become masterful at variations on a particular type of activity.

One might consider the typical ESTP movie hero—the charming gambler, moving from town to town, looking for a new high-stakes game; the flinty-eyed warrior with instincts like quicksilver, seeking the next covert operation; the gritty detective who knows exactly who she is but whose strength and restless energy make anything but the job ultimately unsatisfying. Required to accept an entirely novel premise, an ESTP will test it against the experience and opinions of others but may well remain indifferent until it proves useful.

ESTPs experience regular periods of dissatisfaction, when their inferior function, Introverted Intuition, moves too far outside their control. They tend to interpret such feelings as restlessness, or the need for more stimulation, and they generally try to solve the problem by finding a new challenge. What they're actually contending with is a natural impulsion to go beyond their usual way of handling things.

ESTPs need to recognize dissatisfaction as a natural response to a constant diet of external stimulation. It offers them the space and time to reflect on the situations they've created, to figure out what matters to them and why. They need to come to terms with their secondary function, Introverted Thinking—that is, to stop calculating what they can get out of life long enough to realize what they want to bring to it.

Without some sense of their own purpose, ESTPs focus their feelings of unhappiness on the reactions they're getting from others. Their first instinct is to "go over" better—either by doing something different or by finding a new audience. To this end, they turn to their tertiary function, Extraverted Feeling, which offers strategies for gaining others' approval. Such types may develop a strong hail-fellow-well-met public persona or make grand gestures for the sake of image and style.

Intimacy, however, eludes them, and they're likely to confuse behavioral engagement with emotional connection. They may be increasingly remote in their private lives because they have no other means of handling sensory overload.

Very often, ESTPs wrestle with their secondary function when they have children and recognize their ongoing responsibility to people who need them. When they recognize that their individual choices can affect the outcome of other people's lives, they're more likely to set priorities, and they don't alternate between the extremes of absolute engagement and unreachability. Their view of life broadens, and they recognize their very real need to make a difference.

ESFP: Extraverted Sensation/Introverted Feeling

ESFP

dominant	Extraverted Sensation
secondary	Introverted Feeling
right-brain alternatives	Extraverted Intuition
	Introverted Thinking
left-brain double agents	Extraverted Feeling
	Introverted Sensation
tertiary	Extraverted Thinking
inferior	Introverted Intuition

ESFPs best illustrate Jung's description of the Sensation type as a lover—a "lover of tangible reality." Such types have a good eye for detail and are aware of and interested in anything that appeals to the senses: food, clothing, style, art, music, amusement, sports, and so forth. They generally enjoy "going with the flow" and will take pleasure in whatever is happening until it no longer seems enjoyable.

ESFPs tend to be generous sorts, and they may seem vulnerable, even naive, because they're inclined to surrender themselves to the moment without restraint. Whatever they're in, they're in wholeheartedly, and if they're not interested, they're likely to escape or create a humorous diversion. Thus, ESFPs may strike people as not taking life seriously enough, not caring enough about the consequences of their actions.

In truth, these types are usually ambitious and want to be admired and respected, but they don't make plans the way Judging types do; they don't think in step-by-step terms. They think perceptually, alert to the opportunities life offers them.

Introverted Feeling encourages ESFPs to be interested in people. They notice the way people say things, how they look when they say them, the intonation of their voices, the language of their bodies. For this reason, they often know more than they realize about others' states and intentions. Sometimes their response is so attuned to the emotional state of another that they seem quite intuitive. But they are actually alert and observant to a very high degree, often without realizing what they are taking in.

Such types, for this reason, can be natural salespeople. They adapt easily to the people around them, even mirror them, and enjoy the camaraderie they establish. It should be noted, however, that ESFPs are bona fide Perceivers. Connections with people are important to them only while they're happening; their attention is easily diverted by something else.

Because they adapt so easily to others' emotional states, ESFPs sometimes get overinvolved in helping others. They may, for example, drive friends to their appointments, fix people's cars, help neighbors put up storm windows—never thinking of their efforts as anything more than a natural response to their circumstances.

ESFPs rarely ask for anything in return for their involvement. They do, however, have a strong need to feel appreciated, and they want that appreciation demonstrated tangibly. They like gifts and surprises and the unexpected romantic gesture. They assume that others need the same kind of appreciation and attention they require, and for this reason, they are usually excellent hosts. They enjoy getting people together, whether for a party or for a joint effort of some kind, and are attentive to the comfort, pleasure, and goodwill of their guests.

Most ESFPs are engaging talkers. They like an audience, and they may have some talent for entertaining. They also enjoy, and even require, physical exertion, even if it's a matter of working around the house and garden and garage. They usually enjoy sports—either as players or as supporters, though it should not be supposed that every ESFP is a potential athlete. Sport may entail a regular game of bridge with the neighbors.

These types want to use their reflexes and adaptive abilities in a concrete physical way. Thus, ESFPs can be found in many service occupations that require constant adaptation and response—as police officers, firefighters, social workers, paramedics, receptionists, project editors, hairdressers, and so forth. They are particularly good at crisis intervention, which calls for an immediate, effective, and sympathetic response to unexpected circumstances.

Pop culture is filled with images of such types, all of them larger than life. Probably one of the best examples on television is the character of Hercules in the syndicated series that bears his name. Like many of the ESFP heroes of role-playing computer games, Hercules is a wanderer, moving from town to town solving people's problems and fighting various enemies. Like all ESFPs, he tackles difficulties as they arise, with a combination of skill and improvisation, neither seeking trouble nor avoiding it when it happens.

In fact, ESFPs are so accustomed to handling problems as they arise that intractable difficulties can make them feel anxious and want to get away as soon as possible. They don't like unpleasantness that can't be handled with immediate action. If they get trapped in a situation they don't want to be in, they will generally go along only until escape becomes possible. This can make ESFPs seem unreliable to people who care about them.

Their attitude, however, is really a matter of their Sensate priorities. ESFPs will resist experiences in which their adaptational skills have no value. Like ESTPs, they enjoy action and excitement only in terms of a familiar framework of perceptual experience. They want to be able to invest everything they have in a situation that interests them, and they can't do this without some familiar landmarks to count on.

This approach often results in the type's becoming an expert in a particular kind of activity. Unlike Introverted Sensates, who may possess a great deal of esoteric information about a subject, ESFPs may have unusually fine-tuned skills in a sport or profession. ESFP basketball players, for example, will accumulate as much experience as they can get in their particular field, which gives them the opportunity to improvise in a wide range of familiar situations.

Such types have a highly practical relationship to factual reality, and they're seldom wrong about information they know first hand. It takes ESFPs a long time, however, to accept a wholly novel idea, even if it involves the possibility of pleasure. They're likely to test new possibilities against the expectations and experience of people they know and trust before they consider acting on them.

Indeed, the very presence of other people in a pleasurable activity is important to ESFPs. They like doing things with people who are enjoying the same experience, and others' enthusiasm can carry them into situations they may not have otherwise thought much about. For most of these types, shared feelings and common ideas are less important than parallel perceptions or shared activities. They don't really understand people who genuinely prefer the sidelines.

Many of these types recall a time in adolescence when they felt "shy" or unsure of themselves, perhaps in the shadow of someone they regarded as brighter or more likable. They're determined to help others who seem shy to feel good about themselves and "come out of their shell," and they may initiate a campaign to bring such people out with humor or flirtation.

An interesting example of the type in this respect may be the late Princess Diana, whose image has extraordinary popular power but who reportedly experienced herself as the "ugly duckling" of her highly cultivated family. As she came into her own, Diana radiated the kind of charisma that is often characteristic of developed ESFPs. Her image was constantly evolving, in tune with popular appeal, but slightly ahead of mass acceptance. ESFPs are almost always aware of the effect they have on others, and it's important to them. They often choose partners who are physically attractive, dynamic, or in the public eye.

Like ESTPs, ESFPs experience regular periods of dissatisfaction, particularly when they rely on their Sensate skills to the exclusion of their Introverted side. Their inferior function, Introverted Intuition, moves too far outside their control, flooding them with impulses that oppose their usual immediate goals. They tend to interpret the resulting inner conflict as depression and confusion, and they try to solve the problem by withdrawing from others. What they're actually contending with is a natural push to go beyond their usual way of handling things.

Indeed, most ESFPs learn to rely on feelings of fatigue and depression as a way to escape the constant onslaught of external information they're trying to deal with. At these points, the type is not generous at all, and can seem quite self-absorbed. This kind of disengagement becomes necessary, however, when ESFPs haven't developed a strong enough Introverted perspective. Because they associate diminished energy with disinterest and disenchantment, such types are likely to have a particular problem with the effects of physical change or middle age.

ESFPs of this sort may attempt to start over again, trying to find a new lease on life. This often happens in conjunction with their tertiary function, Extraverted Thinking, which prompts them to find an external explanation for their lack of satisfaction. ESFPs are particularly susceptible to popular religious, political, or psychological theories that make sense of life and involve them with others who are having the same experience. These explanations give ESFPs the illusion that they've come to terms with their own convictions, but they've simply become "players" in a new arena.

ESFPs need to cultivate enough Introverted Feeling to look within—that is, to stop responding to life as it exists, and to consider what they themselves can bring to it. This is not the kind of question ESFPs generally ask themselves, which is why they need more experience with it. When ESFPs wrestle with this question, they begin to realize their considerable power to affect a situation for good or ill.

Indeed, without some internal code of honor, these types tend to be social chameleons. It's hard to tell who they really are apart from the people they're currently connecting with. They don't really know what they need or want for themselves, and they don't think much beyond their immediate situation. They respond to what comes at them—sometimes with great ingenuity, but with little sense of purpose.

When ESFPs bring their Sensate skills into line with their inner standards of Judgment, they discover that some experiences are more important than others, are worth the investment of their time and energy. In the process, they realize their own limits—their need to pace themselves, to say no, to be honest with others about their priorities. This keeps them from alternating between the extremes of "going along" and being completely inaccessible.

ESFPs often find that their strongest values involve compassion for the vulnerable, and their attempt to put them into action changes not only their lives but the lives of those around them. Such types can become role models, and their efforts make a genuine difference in the world.

15

Introverted Sensation

ISTJ and ISFJ Types

Left hemisphere		Right hemisphere
Secondary function		**Inferior function**
Extraverted Judgment		Extraverted Intuition
Dominant function		**Tertiary function**
Introverted Sensation		Introverted Judgment

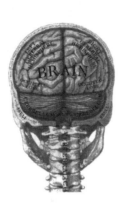

▲ LIKE ITS EXTRAVERTED COUNTERPART, Introverted Sensation is a Perceiving function, and its focus is on data received through the senses. However, the two forms of Sensation differ considerably in their effects. When we use Introverted Sensation, we don't adjust to our surface perceptions. We package them and take them with us—in the form of facts, numbers, signs, and memories.

Ask five people who saw the same movie to describe what it was about, and it's clear that each person is impressed by certain aspects of reality and not others. We don't remember—or even notice— everything we see, hear, taste, touch, and smell during the course of our lives. Only some things strike us as important, useful, familiar, or exciting enough to convert into mental content—that is, into facts that we retain over time.

Introverted Sensation guides this selection, and it prompts us to reconcile our new impressions with the ones we've already stored. In this respect, the function is a mirror image of its Extraverted equivalent.

▲ When we use Extraverted Sensation, our behaviors keep pace with our immediate sense impressions. We "lose ourselves" in whatever is happening, become part of it.

▲ When we use Introverted Sensation, we stabilize our immediate sense impressions by integrating them with the ones we remember and care about. We "find ourselves" in whatever is happening, because our perceptions are anchored by what we already know.

The two forms of Sensation are not directly opposed. Both encourage us to understand our immediate sense impressions by way of past experience. But the different locations they activate in the brain see to it that they produce inverse results.

Extraverted Sensation, as a right-brain function, *bypasses* the left brain's penchant for explaining things to itself. Our past experience helps us to respond quickly to an immediate situation. Introverted Sensation *relies* on the left brain's linguistic powers. What we know from past experience helps us to keep a situation consistent.

Introverted Sensation gives us the will to accumulate information—names, dates, numbers, statistics, references, guidelines, and so forth—related to the things that matter to us. And this is an important qualification. Such facts are highly selective, an attribute perhaps easiest to see in our stereotypes about gender. Everyone knows a man who can talk for hours about the wisdom of substitutions in the 1986 World Series but has to think hard to remember a friend's birthday. Or a woman who can name fifty different shades of eye shadow but can't tell one make of car from another.

The point is not to indulge in sexist generalizations but to emphasize that the facts we acquire by way of Introverted Sensation are more than information. They're part of our self-experience. They define the specific nature of our passions and interests. They become our basis for taking in new data.

When Introverted Sensation is our dominant function, selective acquisition is our primary arbiter of meaning. It's the prism through which we see reality. From an Introverted Sensate viewpoint, immediate conditions have no stable meaning. They're just an influx of data impinging on the senses. And our response to these impressions depends on our mood, our state of mind, our desires, our feelings. It's our commitments and priorities, the facts we hold inalienable, that give our circumstances enduring significance.

Knowing what matters, what's worth keeping or building again, gives us a sense of continuity and security. It gives us direction in the midst of a crisis, or helps us to weather a loss of faith that immediate feelings would not equip us to handle. All things flow away like water; the ground of our self-experience remains.

The ISJ Types

	ISTJ		ISFJ
dominant	Introverted Sensation	dominant	Introverted Sensation
secondary	Extraverted Thinking	secondary	Extraverted Feeling
left-brain	**Introverted Intuition**	left-brain	**Introverted Intuition**
alternatives	**Extraverted Feeling**	alternatives	**Extraverted Thinking**
right-brain	**Introverted Thinking**	right-brain	**Introverted Feeling**
double agents	**Extraverted Sensation**	double agents	**Extraverted Sensation**
tertiary	Introverted Feeling	tertiary	Introverted Thinking
inferior	Extraverted Intuition	inferior	Extraverted Intuition

Although we all use Introverted Sensation to reconcile new impressions with enduring beliefs and commitments, ISTJs and ISFJs depend on this function for their primary approach to life. ESTJs and ESFJs, who use Introverted Sensation in a secondary way, resemble ISJs in their reliance on concrete facts and standards of reason, but these types don't have the same view of reality.

ISJs have a strong, abiding, personal investment in the information that strikes them as important, and their behaviors reflect what they care about, both professionally and personally. Such types rarely acquire knowledge for its own sake. What they know is useful to them and directly related to what they like to do.

ISJs pursue their interests so intensively that they sometimes develop expertise of an esoteric sort, but they scarcely know this is happening to them. One day they simply find that they know more than most other people about an obscure area of experience.

An ISJ of my acquaintance, for example, devoted all his spare time to collecting turn-of-the-century cylinder phonographs. He haunted the museums, pored over catalogs and manuals, tracked down other collectors, and taught himself to repair the broken machines he acquired. Over the years, he accumulated so much information, skill, and contacts that his fascination became his life's work. Today a life-size image of Thomas Edison peers out at passersby from the front window of his restored nineteenth-century home/repair shop.

This tendency to acquire facts, objects, and a social role along the lines of one's inner priorities is typical of the ISJ, and it inverts the pattern more common to the Extraverted Sensate. ESPs adapt themselves so well to others' expectations that their behaviors and style can reflect the quintessence of popular taste and aspiration. ISJs adapt the external situation so well to their own interests and motives that even a conventional job, hobby, or alliance can become a uniquely tailored expression of who they are.

Among all Introverts, ISJs are the most likely to join clubs and organizations devoted to their specific field or fascination, and they may have a strong investment in the way the organization is run. If they have a particular hobby or avocation, they will go to some trouble to gather and share information in that domain—tracking down specialized bookstores, writing to fellow enthusiasts, publishing newsletters, taking classes, going to flea markets, attending collectors' conventions. The information that matters to them is nearly always part of their self-definition and social identity.

It should be recognized, however, that ISJs pursue their interests in a way that scarcely suggests the passion and curiosity that actually motivate them. ISJs organize and apply their information with their secondary function, Extraverted Thinking or Extraverted Feeling. No matter how excited they are about a job or a subject, they tackle it methodically, and somewhat myopically. Their attention is consumed by what they're doing, and they're concerned with every detail. They may be unable to finish a project until a particular detail strikes them as perfectly realized.

Questions of Judgment

Because ISJs are so exacting, conscientious, and deliberate in their outward behaviors, some typologists describe them as a more conservative species of ESJ. This is not a wholly inaccurate way to understand the type, but it focuses too much on surface traits. ISJs and ESJs are both left-brain types, and they share common strengths, so a certain resemblance is inevitable:

▲ Both count on established facts and concrete results.
▲ Both consider it a point of honor to discharge their responsibilities, to be on time, and to keep their word.
▲ Both are reassured by a defined place in a larger group—whether this is realized in a job, family, community, or social organization.

Some typologists have been persuaded by these outward similarities that ISJs and ESJs should be lumped together as "SJ" types, defined as conservative, rule-oriented, and intent on maintaining the status quo. But ISJs and ESJs don't really use their Judgment in the same way, and it's worth noting some of the differences between them.

ESJs   ESJs rely directly on their Extraverted Judging skills. They have a rational approach to life, and they're good at managing outward structural relationships: time, sequence, standards, procedures, causality. Such types use Introverted Sensation to support and identify with the social institutions in which their rational skills are valued. Accordingly, ESJs regard their professional and social roles as an important part of themselves, and they may ignore, or relegate to leisure time, activities that conflict with their responsibilities to these roles.

ISJs   ISJs, by contrast, rely on their Introverted Sensate skills. They have an experiential approach to life, and their primary sense of responsibility is to their inner priorities—to the facts and knowledge they've acquired about things that matter to them. They use Extraverted Judgment to manage their outward relationships rationally, in terms of what they regard as important. Such types don't require a specific job or role in order to do this. When they're relating to others, they have a hard time not doing it.

ISFJs, for example, who relate to others with Extraverted Feeling, are constantly alert to the practical needs of the people around them. As soon as they see a place for themselves, they offer help and get things organized—among friends, family members, colleagues, even strangers on an airplane.

ISTJs, who relate with Extraverted Thinking, are alert to people's need for logical management and principled counsel. No matter how busy they are with job and family, they'll volunteer their services to boards and organizations, administer a friend's financial affairs, or advise someone in trouble.

Preserving Order amid Change

It may be clear from the foregoing descriptions that ISJs don't understand the "status quo" in the same way that ESJs do, much less have the same ideas about its maintenance. Technically speaking, the status quo isn't maintained by anyone. It's a moving tide with which one swims, adjusting as it shifts and eddies.

This is what ESJs do. They swim with prevailing social standards, adjusting their pace and rhythm as necessary to deal with change. They can make such adjustments because they don't try to maintain a particular set of rules or laws.

What ESJs maintain, and maintain unconditionally, is their rational assumptions about reality. As far as these types are concerned, Judging standards reflect universal presumptions about reason and order. If circumstances change, Judging standards can change too, without violating the general principles of reason and morality.

ISJs are not like this. They don't believe for a minute that the universe is inherently rational. For these types, the outer world is a jumble of ever-changing perceptual experiences, dictating ever changing behavioral responses. What ISJs maintain, and maintain unconditionally, is their priorities, which stabilize perceptual reality and give it consistent meaning.

Judging standards are the means by which ISJs link their outward situation to meaningful priorities within. From this perspective, values and rules are not a tide with which one swims. They're specific forms of behavior, and enacting them is the only way to keep faith with the priorities they make manifest.

There's an old Jewish story about a man who gave money to a beggar every day on his way to work. One day he didn't, and the beggar called after him to ask why.

"I had a bad week," the man said. "I'm sorry."

And the beggar answered: "So? You had a bad week, and I should suffer?"

ESJs are likely to understand the beggar as an ingrate. After all, the man's contribution was voluntary. He wasn't obliged to give that money every day. His present actions are a reasonable response to changed circumstances. They don't cancel out his essential morality.

ISJs would immediately understand the beggar's position. Regardless of circumstantial change, you meet your obligations. The very proof of one's priorities is maintaining them when no one expects it of you or you don't want to.

ISJs make it their business to know how things are supposed to work in any Extraverted arena they care about, and they're concerned that others take these operating standards seriously as well. Their thoroughness in this regard propels many of these types into positions of authority, where their enforcement of regulations may be exacting.

It should be emphasized, however, that far from supporting the status quo, ISJs have very firm ideas about "how things should be," and they use rules and regulations to bring outer reality into line with them. Such types are most inflexible when they're not *enough* in touch with prevailing rational assumptions.

Think again about ESJs, whose faith in objective principles allows them to take changing circumstances into account. ISJs who insist on the letter of the law are not being guided by objective rational assumptions. They're using their Judgment to make a changing situation stable, to anchor it to uncompromising inner priorities.

Extreme ISJs, it may be noted, are not necessarily "conservative" in the political sense of the word. Such types can be diehard liberals, working hard for causes that no longer hold society's interest.

The point is that an ISJ's "conservative" behaviors have little to do with supporting the status quo as such. Without sufficient Extraversion, ISJs are relying on subjective criteria for decision making, so they feel personally responsible for keeping things under control. They don't trust anyone but themselves to do the job the way it needs to be done.

Subjects and Objects

When I say that ISJs are relying on subjective criteria, I don't mean they're guided by selfish impulses. On the contrary. ISJs are usually so busy managing other people's practical needs that they can easily ignore their own health and well-being. By *subjective* I mean that a person's ideas about what matters are unique to himself or herself.

Think again about five people coming out of a movie theater. The film they saw unquestionably exists. It's objective data. But those five people are likely to care about and remember very different things about it.

How something interests us, what aspect of it we find important, and what it means to us in the long run is often consistent for us. But being consistent isn't the same thing as being rational. Unless we have some objective standard to measure our priorities against, we simply don't know how subjective they are.

Like all Introverts, ISJs find it hard to train the Extraverted character of their secondary function on themselves rather than on others. They become so proficient at stabilizing things for the people around them that they can get trapped by their dominant function. They tie what they do in the world to their inner priorities and lose sight of objective reasons to do anything else.

It's easier to see this tendency in ISTJs, because they clearly identify with particular standards or principles and become offended when people question their importance or refuse to honor them. ISFJs usually identify with the needs of a person, so their attempt to manage a situation may not look like management. It may look like the need to please or serve or rescue.

The point is that ISJs are likely to use their Extraversion only to assess the ways in which others' situations can be stabilized, so they end up feeling guilty about having objective needs of their own. They need perspective on their priorities—to recognize that their desires and fears and immediate responses to life are *also* arbiters of meaning and should have an effect on their decisions.

This is the logic behind the famous Ann Landers question to women wrestling with a commitment to a bad marriage: "Am I better off with him or without him?" Objective reason will counsel us to break a promise if the toll on our health or other relationships becomes too high. ISJs sometimes need an objective outsider to help them accept the wisdom of that counsel. Holding to one's course may be a mark of integrity in one situation, but irrational and self-destructive in another.

Or, as Ann Landers puts it (quoting Joe E. Lewis in *The Prairie Rambler*): "Show me a man who has both feet on the ground, and I will show you a man who can't put his pants on."

The ISJ's Inner World

Like ESPs, ISJs are at the mercy of their immediate perceptions, but they don't usually realize this. Nor do the people around them. Extraverted Sensates respond to their sense impressions all at once, and their receptivity is obvious. When they "burn out," people don't need to ask why. ISJs are so cautious about their investment of time and energy that people are surprised when they reach a breaking point.

It should be noted, therefore that ISJs really are Sensation types—left-brain Sensation types. The left brain can't handle multiple perceptions—except by dispatching Extraverted Judgment to put them in sequential order. So ISJs are constantly absorbing new impressions, but they're sorting them one at a time, putting them into the various "meaning" boxes they've set up in their internal storage system.

When such types are faced with a decision, they literally examine every fact at hand, granting each its own integrity, examining it from every angle, trying to figure out which box it belongs in, or whether some other box will have to be set up and labeled. ISJs do this with *all* the facts involved before they're willing to draw any conclusions.

The best comparison I can think of is those tribal elders who won't sanction outward change in the community until they've located a precedent in the founding stories that embody their tradition. Until they can figure out where to store the information and what it's likely to affect, they have no basis for accepting or rejecting a proposal.

Most ISJs go over books, documents, and contracts word by word, and perhaps several times, before they're satisfied they know what's being said. Pushed to a premature decision, they will continue to think of exceptions and qualifications that hadn't occurred to them earlier.

Once they've decided change is warranted, however, ISJs are impossible to dissuade. If their decision is an unpopular one, they'll stand by it, come hell or high water. The relevant facts have become part of who they are, and they will insist that their outward situation be adjusted to reflect them. Even if they have little time, they will not delegate this implementation process to others. They want hands-on control over it.

Introverted Sensation on Its Own Terms   The outward behaviors of these types have contributed to their general reputation as careful, strong, faithful, persevering, and honorable—but perhaps a little dull. Even ISJs will describe themselves this way! But in truth, the inner world of an ISJ is often delightfully unconventional, even whimsical, and the type's private interests can be decidedly offbeat.

This is where ISJs definitively part company with the ESJs. Extraverted Judgers are inevitably well-adjusted to prevailing standards and assumptions, but they don't usually see themselves that way. Because they maintain a flexible relationship to those standards, they describe themselves as independent, even different from others. ISJs, by contrast, may have a thoroughly individual way of looking at life, but they rarely believe that their way of seeing things is unusual. They may feel alone, unable to make a decision, misunderstood, or unappreciated, but it almost never occurs to them that their views are idiosyncratic, much less unique to themselves.

The flavor of their inner world is not immediately apparent in an Extraverted context, but it's almost always visible in their hobbies, their personal letters, and their leisure-time pursuits. Such activities make clear the way these types naturally give form to their internal priorities, apart from managing life for others.

ISJs are quintessential collectors, and they acquire objects the way they acquire facts—one at a time, in a consistent domain of interest. Although these objects may be classic collectibles, like stamps or Hummels or first editions, they're more often specific and esoteric, as though the ISJ were giving outward expression to the Perceiving self within: the pleasures, passions, and humor that would otherwise go undetected.

ISJs attend toy soldier conventions, become experts on musical nutcrackers, fill their basements with arcade games from the 1950s, accumulate medieval maps, collect weapons, Snow White figurines, and artifacts from particular time periods. They show up at memorabilia auctions, book fairs, flea markets, and science fiction gatherings.

Their acquisition also takes the form of collecting experiences—or more accurately, variations on a particular experience. This, too, can occur in the classic sense of playing golf every day or boating every weekend. But it more often involves activities of a distinctive, even fanciful nature that, by virtue of ritual repetition, become nearly archetypal.

For example, a good friend, an ISFJ army operations engineer, spends his vacations riding roller coasters all over the world. A colleague, an ISTJ indexer, finds a way to attend every concert within a 500-mile area given by folk artist Richard Thompson. An acquaintance, an ISFJ social worker, reads every new Stephen King novel ten times in a row.

Such activities appear to make a stable bridge between consistent personal impressions and the constantly changing outer world. But unless one knows an ISJ well enough to be aware of the type's private pursuits, the deep, sometimes romantic attachment the type has to certain kinds of objects, information, and experience may be completely invisible. In fact, people who don't know an ISJ apart from a work context may regard the type as serious, predictable, and somewhat detached.

Actually, ISJs are almost helplessly engaged. Given the subjective nature of their perceptual reality, they're always aware of a certain discontinuity between their expectations and others' behavior. Most ISJs find this aspect of life amusing, if frustrating, and they may keep up a running Seinfeld-like commentary in their heads about the absurdities they encounter every day. Not long ago, the ISFJ engineer was complaining about how hard it is to find a decent classical section in popular music stores—he keeps finding *Frankie Valli's Greatest Hits* filed under Vivaldi's *Four Seasons*.

Ziggy ©1995 Ziggy and Friends, Inc. Dist. by Universal Press Syndicate. Reprinted with permission. All rights reserved.

ISJs tend to believe that others don't "get" their sense of humor, but this isn't necessarily true. When ISJs feel comfortable, they make all sorts of observations about perceived discontinuities, some of which are dead serious. But they aren't the kinds of observations that everyone would make. So it's not always clear what kind of reaction the type is looking for.

For example, ISJs may react with discomfort when someone's behavior is inconsistent with a stated or apparent obligation. Their feelings, however, may focus on something that other people regard as a mere technicality. They can be acutely embarrassed by social or economic misrepresentation—such as wearing the wrong clothes or displaying possessions beyond one's means.

Pop media is merciless in its depiction of such reactions. One thinks about Niles Frasier, of the TV program *Frasier*, who becomes apoplectic at the idea of anyone's wearing white shoes after Labor Day. ISJs in real life usually try to behave in a way that reflects precisely the role, station, obligations, and rights they perceive as their own. They may even present themselves neutrally, preferring to err on the side of underestimating their position.

The Push toward Growth

Because they are so concerned to anchor outward reality to their self-experience, ISJs can have a hard time understanding that others don't see reality in the same terms. It may strike them that any decent person would see reality in those terms. So the only possible response for many of these types is to establish a particular area of expertise, so they can have hands-on control over what happens in that arena or determine how the standards are met.

This is how ISJs unwittingly trap themselves in their dominant function. They turn into lone rangers, enlisted by friends, colleagues, employer, spouse, and children to rescue them from and discharge the tasks that others find tedious or difficult. ISJs nearly always comply, even when they feel overwhelmed or used, and others may come to take them for granted.

Some ISJs shrug and figure that their inner resources and sense of responsibility have doomed them to a life of unequal partnerships, but they need to take a closer look at the decisions they've made in this regard. Being of use can be tantamount for ISJs to intimate connection with others, so they can unknowingly keep others dependent for the sake of being needed.

ISJs who restrict themselves to circumstances in which they feel needed ultimately cheat themselves of necessary Extraverted experience. Their Extraverted environments are too well adapted to their inner life. They have no incentive to make decisions apart from their own priorities. These decisions have a selfless quality, because they're made on behalf of others, but they aren't objective, and they can create problems the ISJs aren't equipped to handle.

Such types may find, for example, that the people who depend on them react to their ministrations with an irritating mixture of resentment and appreciation—or with entitlement and increased demands. Colleagues may accuse them of being controlling or unreasonable. ISJs don't recognize themselves in these criticisms. Sticking to their guns strikes them as a matter of honor and integrity, not a matter of reason or relationship.

Ultimately, they get pressured by their psyche to develop a more Extraverted perspective. They're pulled in the direction of their inferior function, Extraverted Intuition, and the resulting impulses undermine their usual approach to life. Like all types, however, ISJs don't see this unconscious drama as part of themselves.

Extraverted Intuition directly opposes the ISJ's dominant aims and goals, so it's not well developed in these types. Introverted Sensation tells them that immediate sense impressions are part of a consistent pattern of inner meaning. Extraverted Intuition suggests, rather, that immediate impressions are part of an emerging external pattern, which will ultimately change their meaning.

Under the influence of unconscious Extraverted Intuition, ISJs become genuinely cautious. They have the impression that others are asking them to accept changes that require a compromise of their integrity, and they suspect that these people lack discipline or a sense of values. Inferior Intuition persuades them that the larger picture is at stake, and that accepting the change will collapse the whole structure.

What ISJs need at this point is the deliberate cultivation of their secondary function, Extraverted Thinking or Extraverted Feeling. This won't protect them from a sense of conflict, but it will keep them from mistaking competing psychological aims for outward battles in which their honor is at stake.

As stated earlier, ISJs usually need an outside viewpoint to understand how to do this. And it's worth noting that many of the letters printed in advice columns ask the columnist to arbitrate precisely the kind of outward battle ISJs are wont to conduct—between doing "the right thing" and compromising their integrity for the sake of relationship. A fairly typical letter of this sort is from a mother who objects to a church wedding for a daughter already living with her fiancé. The question is whether the mother should stand up for her morals and stay home or attend and thereby sanction what she regards as a dishonorable life choice.

Advice columnists invariably refuse to answer this kind of question, which is posed in solidly Introverted terms. Instead, they ask the writer to recognize the Extraverted side of the issue. They ask whether the exercise of subjective priority in this context is worth the probable loss of daughter and potential grandchildren in all the contexts to come.

Such advice does not beg the issue of personal integrity. It forces the mother to recognize that there is an objective moral issue involved—the relationship with her daughter and grandchild, which she values and needs. If Introverted Sensation insists that Judgment be used to manage the integrity of others' decisions, Extraverted Judgment suggests that the roles of mother and grandmother are also priorities, and they'll be lost unless the daughter is allowed to learn from her own decisions. This is where the real conflict lies—not between doing the right thing and sanctioning a bad thing, but between two honorable ways of understanding the same situation.

It takes a lot of work for ISJs to recognize that their very real virtues can be modified by external considerations without betraying them. It requires bringing their inner priorities into dialogue with their outer ones, rather than the other way around. By wrestling with this conflict, the mother in question may decide that family values means more than playing by the rules; they mean cherishing loved ones even when they appear to be wrong.

ISJs who learn how to train their Judgment on their outer needs as well as their inner ones gradually increase the range of both their options and their capacity for empathetic relationships. These types are highly respected and admired by others. They radiate a quiet, caring, but forceful sense of authority. They know exactly who they are and are assured in their direction, but they can hear what others say and make accommodations when they need to.

Some of our best public servants appear to be ISJs of this sort—most notably President George Bush and General Colin Powell. Their leadership derives, in part, from their ability to stay true to what they believe, to listen to others, and to direct people's energies productively in a crisis.

The Tertiary Function   Conversely, ISJs who resist their Extraverted side find it very difficult to take others' views into account. They're quite sure they're right, and they can be incensed by suggestions to the contrary. The more they resist an external standard of Judgment, the more Extraverted Intuition gets out of their control, and they reach for the comfort of their tertiary function.

The ISJ's tertiary function is Introverted Thinking or Introverted Feeling, which I talked about in the last chapter. This kind of Judgment operates in a right-brain manner. Developed well, it encourages us to maintain unconditional human values, even when doing so is not immediately gratifying.

This kind of morality is crucial for *Extraverted* Perceivers, who need contact with an internal sense of right and wrong. It can be disastrous for ISJs who lack an adequate Extraverted perspective. ISJs are already likely to regard their subjective priorities as internalized values. Introverted Judgment ultimately persuades the type that he or she is the only decent, moral, or reasonable person in the picture, whose mission is to maintain the still point at the center of a disintegrating universe.

Such types can seem almost Extraverted, because their behaviors are colored more and more by their inferior function. They take all sorts of social positions that give them the power to do what they think is right, or they're bustling back and forth between various people's houses, quite certain that things will fall apart if they don't take care of them personally. Their tireless efforts are usually rewarded by others, and they can appear saintlike—until someone questions their motives or strikes them as unappreciative.

This particular aspect of the ISJ is often stereotyped in our culture's Sensation-oriented myth cycle—on TV shows, in novels, and in movies. Big Nurse, the head of the psychiatric ward in the movie *One Flew Over the Cuckoo's Nest*, is a good example of an ISFJ who deforms external reality along the lines of her inner impressions, all the while believing herself to be a sane, calming, helpful manager of people. One might also consider all those unyielding, by-the-books ISTJ police captains in TV cop shows who make life difficult for the typical flamboyant ESP detective.

Such caricatures imply that ISJs are threatened by individuality and concerned to stamp it out wherever it rears its spirited head. But entertainment is an Extraverted Perceiving medium, and Perceivers always fear that rules and regulations are designed to curtail their personal freedoms. As I've tried to point out, ISJs themselves have a view of reality that is highly individual. The ones who lack Extraversion simply don't know how individual they really are.

One can see it in the way such types apply forms and rules. They aren't trying to make others conform to objective standards. They're trying to force life to adhere to their subjective impressions. Some infractions will strike them as meaningless, others a threat to civilized existence as we know it.

CRANKSHAFT   **by Tom Batiuk and Chuck Ayers**

Crankshaft ©1997 Mediagraphics, Inc. Reprinted with permission of Universal Press Syndicate. All rights reserved.

In fact, extreme types can become distinctly amoral, all the while believing themselves to be champions of society's moral values. Lately, medical shows have been portraying HMO directors in these terms—as the cost-conscious ISTJ who thinks he's saving the world, but whose bottom-line mentality is devoid of moral principle.

Like all Introverted functions, Introverted Sensation has an archaic human core—the unchanging psychic patterns, evolved over millions of years, that help to form and stabilize our individual frame of mind. ISJs who get seriously out of touch with their Extraverted side gradually become oriented by this collective psychic world, and their behaviors and emotions seem oddly stereotyped, as though they were playing a part in their own myth—as the Hero, the Strong Leader, the Savior, the Martyr, the Sage, the Victim, the Nurturer, the Protector, and so forth.

Ultimately, however, the archaic aspect of Introverted Sensation tells us something important about this function's distinct contribution to human awareness. If Extraverted Sensation suggests that we have our portion in constant phenomenal change, Introverted Sensation suggests that we are grounded by archetypal patterns beneath the threshold of consciousness.

In this respect, Extraverted and Introverted forms of Sensation bring together the two aspects of sensory existence that physicists call explicate and implicate order. We recognize the transcendent nature of this combination in many of our religious traditions, such as the taking of vows and the celebration of the sacraments. When we submit immediate sensory phenomena to static ritual boundaries, it grants them meaning. And that meaning helps to mark out our individual path.

ISTJ: Introverted Sensation/Extraverted Thinking

ISTJ

dominant	Introverted Sensation
secondary	Extraverted Thinking
left-brain alternatives	**Introverted Intuition**
	Extraverted Feeling
right-brain double agents	**Introverted Thinking**
	Extraverted Sensation
tertiary	Introverted Feeling
inferior	Extraverted Intuition

ISTJs are so task-oriented, and so conscientious in their handling of details and standard procedures, that they are often stereotyped as "establishment" types, weighed down by the gravity of institutional priorities. Although ISTJs are indeed careful, and concerned to preserve what has been proved to be worthwhile, these characteristics are only a part of the type's approach to the world—the part that most people see. ISTJs are fundamentally Introverted Sensates, with a highly subjective, original turn of mind.

As Introverted Sensates, ISTJs are unparalleled realists. However, they don't concern themselves with external reality as such. They relate to facts *about* external reality, and largely by way of the mental constructs determined by Extraverted Thinking: words, numbers, schemes, diagrams, hierarchies, methods, and codes of conduct.

Moreover, outward predictability is important to them only insofar as events and experiences involve their primary interests and emotional investments. For example, an ISTJ may be exacting about taking lunch at the same time every day, but oblivious to the clutter of books and papers on the desk or living room floor.

The very selectivity of the type's sensations gives ISTJs an extraordinary capacity for detail in the areas that strike them as important. Where data and figures are concerned, ISTJs are painstakingly thorough. Such types make persistent, informed, tough-minded finance officers, prosecutors, engineers, administrators, researchers, accountants, psychiatrists, professors, trustees, and the like.

Their powers of concentration are unequaled—and nothing escapes their attention, whether they're preparing a contract, assembling materials for a seminar, calculating a mortgage, repairing an electrical system, researching a legal precedent, or making sense of medical statistics. They prefer to work in an uninterrupted manner, and they are patient with routine undertakings that other types might describe as tedious.

Their capability and reliability in this respect often results in their attaining a position of administrative power. ISTJs oversee and supervise departments in far more organizations and institutions than their 6 percent representation in the population might suggest. They take their authority seriously, are always ready to solve a problem, and are scrupulous about their responsibilities. However, they may be perceived as emotionally distant and demanding.

They don't always understand what people want of them, and they may be uncomfortable and awkward about conveying warmth apart from a situation of personal intimacy. Although they enjoy socializing, especially the kinds of rituals and holidays that bring family and friends together, like other Introverts, they need a fair amount of time to themselves.

Privately, ISTJs are usually observing the world with a kind of detached irony. Their inner expectations are frequently contradicted by outer reality, and the incongruity would be exasperating if they took it too seriously. Made aloud, their observations are both pointed and funny, but they are also unexpected and sometimes have an "out in left field" quality. Most ISTJs don't share their private considerations with others unless they feel at home and among friends. Experience usually teaches them that their reactions to a situation are not necessarily the ones that others are having.

Indeed, ISTJs are not very well understood. Because they tend to be low-key sorts, responsible, and reluctant to make a change in an outward situation until they've considered all its ramifications, they can strike others as overly cautious and unyielding workaholics, without much color. ISTJs themselves are inclined to take their own skills for granted, as though they were doing no more than following through on their commitments. Oh, well, they say, a diamond is just a piece of coal that stuck to its job.

It should be recognized, accordingly, that ISTJs are not just conservators and loyalists. They are masters of gradual, almost imperceptible modification. They tinker here, shore up there, solve problems and rectify ambiguities, all the while preserving the best of what exists, scarcely recognizing that in the process, they've adapted form quite brilliantly to function. They can accommodate the requirements of a job so perfectly to their own strengths that the systems they create are unique and difficult to pass on to their successors.

It should be noted that ISTJs are most decisive when they're organizing things for other people. Such types can find it difficult to limit and organize the data of their own mental world without an external reference point to guide them. For example, they may overestimate others' interest in a project. Given no specified limits, they can easily lose track of time. For this reason, such types may experience themselves as undirected or indecisive.

This self-experience derives, in part, from the immediacy of the type's dominant function. Introverted Sensation motivates ISTJs to acquire facts and to retain them, but it offers no way to discriminate among them rationally. These types may need to deliberately quell their desire for more information in order to develop stronger Extraverted Thinking skills.

Without sufficient contribution from their secondary function, ISTJs feel that they never have enough information to make a good decision. They may be particularly cautious about decisions that will require a sustained emotional investment over time. Thus, they may settle for situations that strike them as practical or appropriate rather than exciting or desirable, or they'll defer to someone whose knowledge or investment in a project is greater than their own.

Beneath their apparent detachment, ISTJs can be badly hurt by criticism and rejection. They have a strong need to feel useful, appreciated, and valued. They may feel quite insulted when someone appears to question their word, their expertise, their experience, or their honor. Their vulnerability in this regard can be surprising, and it's usually in evidence only when the situation is already out of hand. An ISTJ whose pride has been hurt will become distant rather than argue, and it may not be at all clear what the type experienced as the last straw.

ISTJs take no pleasure in losing control and they don't like to be caught off guard by what they feel. They want to be able to master a situation by way of knowledge and practical expertise. Indeed, most ISTJs are inclined to guard their emotions—save, perhaps, for righteous anger—believing that feelings are private and can be overwhelming to the senses. Accordingly, they will sometimes engage in overly correct behavior, drawing from traditional forms of etiquette to keep a potentially volatile situation stable.

Male ISTJs, who constitute about three-quarters of this type, often relate to women, for example, with a kind of gallantry that can strike one as a little patronizing. The type's propriety in this regard can sometimes result in an impression of quaint virtue, but it can also suggest something coarse and instinctive just beneath the surface, held relentlessly at bay.

Indeed, ISTJ males are likely to be quite different in the company of men than they are with women, and they enjoy the opportunity to be "themselves" in an all-male situation. Other types can be surprised by this aspect of the ISTJ, because they've mistaken the type's interest in concrete facts for cool cerebralism rather than the Sensate investment it is. ISTJs, both male and female, nearly always maintain an interest in outdoor activities pursued alone or with others— handball, hiking, hunting, fishing, weaponry, camping, scouting, and so forth.

It should be noted that, demeanor notwithstanding, an ISTJ's impressions of a conversational exchange can be unexpectedly and intensely personal. A discussion that takes place around a subject of mutual interest may strike the type as a form of intimate revelation—to the extent that he or she will feel self-conscious afterward, as though the relationship had become prematurely close.

When this kind of exchange occurs between two ISTJs, they tend to alternate between enthusiasm and caution, cataloging mutual knowledge and experience, but also recognizing that acquired facts may be related to deeply private needs and feelings. Indeed, such conversations should not be mistaken for a dry game of one-upmanship. The way a person talks about a common interest will tell most Introverted Sensates exactly who that individual is and whether a friendship should be pursued further.

Of course, this entire style of conversation is typically Introverted. ISTJs do need to develop their Extraversion as well, in order to recognize and adjust to limits and interests that don't have anything to do with their inner selves. Some ISTJs develop their Judgment just far enough to discriminate among their many perceptual impressions, without learning how to relate them to the needs and expectations of others.

Such types can be exasperatingly inflexible, because they turn to Introverted Feeling, their tertiary function, when they're trying to stand firm. They become quite sure that their ideas about what is important are unconditional, and they use external rules to confirm and authorize their impressions. In control, an extreme ISTJ can come across as a martinet. As a subordinate, the type may be restricted and fearful of acting without permission.

ISTJs locate their own authority when they recognize that their way of seeing the world is unique to themselves and requires constant relationship to others' logical expectations. When these types accept their genuine individuality, they work hard to adapt their strengths and ideas to social reality as it exists, and they can sometimes move mountains.

Such ISTJs have no need to prove themselves, and they don't insist that others live life the way they do. They don't have to. People see them as models of responsible, caring, civilized behavior, and seek them out as advisors, teachers, and leaders.

ISFJ: Introverted Sensation/Extraverted Feeling

ISFJ	
dominant	Introverted Sensation
secondary	Extraverted Feeling
left-brain alternatives	**Introverted Intuition**
	Extraverted Thinking
right-brain double agents	**Introverted Feeling**
	Extraverted Sensation
tertiary	Introverted Thinking
inferior	Extraverted Intuition

Like ISTJs, ISFJs are most comfortable with facts and information about concrete reality. However, where ISTJs organize and apply what they know impersonally, preferring numbers, schemes, or logical premises, ISFJs relate to the outer world in a decidedly personal way, with Extraverted Feeling. ISFJs are highly alert to behaviors and gestures that suggest another's emotional attitude, needs, or expectations, and they generally acquire knowledge that allows them to be of service—preferably to one person at a time.

For this reason, many ISFJs are attracted to social work, pastoral counseling, nursing, or family medicine—fields in which they excel because they can concentrate on the needs and problems of individual clients. However, like all Introverted Sensates, ISFJs are good at following procedures, and they may have a flair for research and statistics.

Thus, they are sometimes attracted to more technical fact-based occupations—for example, in library science, biometrics, computer programming, engineering, or insurance. Even in these cases, ISFJs tend to personalize what they do, using their skills on behalf of an employer, an administrator, or a customer: someone who needs their assistance and expertise.

Indeed, ISFJs are so focused on others' goals and expectations that they can seem literally selfless, without a full personality of their own. Support staffs throughout business and industry are made up of these types, who function almost invisibly, in the background of an organization, implementing decisions made by others. For this reason, it may be difficult to appreciate the Extraverted Feeling nature of an ISFJ's expectations.

Like the Extraverted FJs, ISFJs need to feel needed. They have a hard time saying no, even when they've taken on more obligations than they can readily handle. Moreover, like EFJs, ISFJs need personal feedback. They want their efforts to matter to someone. In this ISFJs are often disappointed, owing, in part, to their self-effacement. Their tendency to shrug off what they're doing as no more than any decent person would do under the circumstances ensures that they are usually taken for granted. Their Introversion also contributes to the problem.

Extraverted FJs are drawn to roles and commitments that reflect prevailing social values, which assures them of feedback in predictable terms. ISFJs are more subjective in their motivations. Their behavior is dictated not by their social role—as a good parent, citizen, employee, and so forth—but by their self-experience as a helper, rescuer, or nurturer. Most ISFJs find that they are drawn to and attract individuals who need them wherever they go. Moreover, the response of an ISFJ to another's need is immediate, dictated entirely by the others' situation.

ISFJs will go out of their way to help a family member in trouble, a misunderstood coworker, or a perfect stranger sitting next to them on a bus. They rarely consider the amount of time or effort their involvement will require—or even the potential consequences of their actions. They may find it difficult to justify, or even to verbalize, their fundamental motives, but they are quite certain they are doing the right thing and will not be swayed from their perceived task.

For this reason, ISFJs can seem stubborn, even when their behaviors are demonstrably selfless, or unable to appreciate people who aren't in some way dependent on them. They may react to signs of a person's independence as a kind of betrayal, which leads to their feeling jealous and possessive of the people they care about.

ISFJs are puzzled and hurt when others bring this aspect of their behavior to their attention. They don't experience themselves as strong or controlling. If anything, ISFJs see themselves as too "easy," too influenced by others' opinions, too eager to please, too scattered, unable to decide when to take a stand and when to give in.

This self-experience derives, in part, from the ISFJ's other-oriented basis for decision making. ISFJs are both firm and decisive when they're in a one-to-one situation—such as caring for a patient or carrying out an employer's wishes—because their behaviors are being guided by the other's immediate needs.

In a group situation, however, or in a position of general authority, ISFJs often feel unsure of their position until they know how others in the group will be affected. They resist making plans that appear to give their own needs precedence. For example, ISFJ administrators may find delegation difficult—as though it were an admission that they need help—and they can end up doing all the work themselves.

The ISFJ's preference for basing decisions on others' needs or wants is magnified by the length of time it takes this type to process sensory information. ISJs in general have a difficult time with Extraverted Intuition—"taking in the big picture." They want a concrete grasp of all the details before they're satisfied they understand what's at stake in a situation. If they're listening to a story, for example, and a minor point doesn't make sense to them, they may spend all their time trying to get that fact straight before they can react to the story's other implications.

Consequently, most ISJs experience a certain degree of pressure from other types to make decisions before they're prepared to do so. Although this poses a problem for ISTJs, their grounds for appraising external demands are impersonal and logical, and they may insist on taking the time they need. ISFJs, however, take others' reactions and expectations to heart, and they may end up offering approximate information rather than taking the time to think out what they know.

The constant experience of people pushing them to make up their minds and then correcting their facts can encourage the type to develop an inaccurate self-image as inadequate or not smart enough, and they may defer to an external authority or go along with others rather than process facts and information to their own satisfaction. They're constantly wrangling with themselves over their need to be true to themselves and their desire to maintain interpersonal harmony, and they sometimes wonder if they're simply rationalizing their inability to stand up for their rights or beliefs.

Like ISTJs, ISFJs have an idiosyncratic view of reality, but they don't recognize how individual their perspective really is. Their comments and observations often precipitate reactions from others that surprise them. ISTJs, in the inimitable way of most TJs, are hurt by rejection, but generally conclude that the problem is with other people's intelligence. ISFJs are more likely to be wounded by an unsympathetic response, and they're inclined to conclude that their opinions aren't good enough or worth voicing.

In fact, many ISFJs develop a self-deprecating sense of humor—intended, presumably, to beat others to the punch. Where ISTJs will comment on the little absurdities of life, as much for their own amusement as for that of others, ISFJs will call attention to their own foibles—as it were, telling on themselves.

For example, an ISFJ nursing administrator, talking about an upcoming trip, claims that she has to pack three suitcases, even for a weekend, because she's never sure exactly what the weather is going to be and wants to be prepared for every possible contingency. This is a good illustration of the ISJ's constant need to control the discontinuity perceived between inner expectation and outer reality, but it also illustrates the way ISFJs will turn the humor of the situation back on themselves.

ISFJs can become overly dependent on others' ideas about what's appropriate in a situation, especially if these ideas coincide with their own ideas about integrity and commitment. For example, they may find it difficult to approve of those who don't behave or dress appropriately for their social position. Extreme types can place a great deal of weight on social signs and signals of all sorts. Like ISTJs, they may believe that men and women should comport themselves quite differently from each other.

In the best of all possible worlds, ISFJs prefer to have a clear and concrete understanding of what is expected of them. Once they have all the details in order, they will follow through on their obligations conscientiously and exactly. It should be said, however, that most ISFJs overestimate the expectations that anyone actually has of them.

They seem to believe that worth accrues to any pursuit only by "going the extra mile."

Like all ISJs, ISFJs may stay too long in a situation, out of loyalty or commitment, even when their potential is being limited or squandered. This kind of dedication can be a genuine virtue, but it can also indicate that Extraverted Feeling isn't doing its proper job in the ISFJ configuration. ISFJs tend to use this function only to link the objective needs of others to their self-experience as helpers. They need to learn to train it on themselves and to assess their own needs and goals in outer reality.

When ISFJs become too dependent on Introverted Sensation, they have no way to assess the worth of their investment in a situation. Instead of using Extraverted Feeling to balance their viewpoint, they may turn to their tertiary function, Introverted Thinking, for support in their accustomed behaviors.

Introverted Thinking can, under such circumstances, convince the ISFJ that his or her actions are part of a much larger scheme whose integrity must be maintained self-sacrificially—the future of the children, the survival of the much-admired employer, the Christian way of life. ISFJs are often praised for their loyalty to lost causes, but they can actually use this proclivity to avoid real intimacy.

For example, such types can become accustomed to relationships in which all emotional risks are taken by the other, and the ISFJ's own weaknesses and problems remain private. Indeed, some ISFJs unwittingly undermine the efforts of others to become independent for fear of losing the relationship, and they can make serious romantic mistakes—choosing partners who are likely to keep them in a service-oriented role. They may have a difficult time with stories or movies that don't end happily and in favor of emotional commitment.

Like ISTJs, ISFJs enjoy an exchange of acquired facts, and they will warm to their subject in the presence of a receptive listener. And like ISTJs, ISFJs are often interested in outdoor activities—hiking, camping, swimming, hunting, fishing, and so forth. As with all activities that matter to them, ISFJs acquire the facts, equipment, and expertise their pursuit requires and take seriously the rules and behaviors that govern its performance.

16

Extraverted Intuition

E<u>N</u>TP and E<u>N</u>FP Types

Left hemisphere		Right hemisphere
Tertiary function		**Dominant function**
Extraverted Judgment		Extraverted Intuition
Inferior function		**Secondary function**
Introverted Sensation		Introverted Judgment

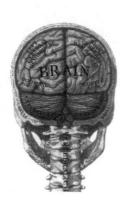

▲ AS A RIGHT-BRAIN PERCEIVING FUNCTION, Extraverted Intuition has a lot in common with Extraverted Sensation. Both push us to adapt, to relate ourselves to sensory data in our immediate environment. Sensation, however, draws our attention to objects, and we adapt immediately to their surface features. Intuition draws our attention to context and we adapt to sensory events in terms of it.

Although it's usually said that Extraverted Intuition gives us "the big picture," this image doesn't quite capture the cognitive process involved. If an editor-in-chief wants a "big picture" story, she's asking for an overview—a grand scheme, like capitalism or the evangelical movement, that will make sense of many different facts and events. If a CEO talks about "the big picture," he probably means the company's being downsized and people's jobs are less important than the system at large.

So it's important to understand that Intuition doesn't really work this way. The all-at-once right brain can't distinguish between the whole and the part. For example, when we recognize a piece of music, we're not distinguishing the tune from the individual notes that make it up. We've grasped the sensory data as a pattern of changing relationships.

We do the same thing visually when we recognize a face. We've unified the features as an integrated pattern. People who lose this ability have no problem seeing each component of a face, but they can't appreciate them as a structural arrangement.

Extraverted Intuition relies on this right-brain capacity for pattern recognition, and most of us use it to get the gist of a situation very quickly. For example, at its simplest level, Intuition will tell us that a panther in the jungle is dangerous but a panther in the zoo is not. Unifying the panther with its context gives us the "whole picture" before we've even had time to conceptualize it.

To be sure, Extraverted Sensation also outpaces our conceptual faculties. With Sensation, however, we're responding to the object itself. All that matters is past experience and whether it applies here and now. Or, as Ogden Nash once sagely advised, "When summoned by a panther, don't anther."

With Intuition, we're focused on the future. Once we've grasped a whole pattern, we can envision options that don't yet exist. Indeed, one of the drawbacks of Intuition is that it conjures up a future before we know very much about the present. For example, given enough elements to suggest a star or a square, we have a hard time not filling in the blanks and seeing the complete image. In the same way, a strong similarity between a familiar pattern and our immediate impressions of a person or event can lead us to make unwarranted generalizations.

Perhaps, for instance, someone's body language reminds us of someone we didn't like in the past. As a right-brain function, Intuition won't hand us an explicit memory of that earlier experience. It simply rummages through patterns we've encountered before, like an old jukebox selecting a 45 and plunking it down on our imaginal turntable.

Suddenly we're registering all the physical responses associated with that pattern. Our throat constricts and our eyes narrow, and we "just know" this person is going to be a problem. One or two analogous sense impressions have conjured up a whole set of anticipated options.

We usually call these experiences "gut feelings," and they may tell us something important about the possibilities in our present situation. But Intuition can be dead wrong and still feel like knowledge.

The Right Stuff

The hit-or-miss quality of Intuition is a lingering byproduct of its advantage to us as a species. If our ancestors had stopped to examine all the details before they recognized a stick in their path as a snake, they wouldn't have lived long enough to bequeath their Intuitive abilities to us. Evolution tends to favor the primates who find themselves half a mile away before they know they've Intuited danger— even if they're sometimes mistaken.

Of course, our objectives today are somewhat less dire than escape from hungry competitors on the open savannah. Most of us follow in the proud tradition of *Name That Tune* contestants, who raced each week to identify song titles from one or two familiar notes of music. That is, we're inclined to use Intuition as a mental short-cut—to get the gist of a situation by focusing on as few details as possible.

For example, we may sort mail by looking at the return address of an envelope. We've assimilated enough information about credit card offers, unpaid bills, and astrologers who can't wait to send us our special lottery numbers that we can infer the substance of an entire communication from one or two lines of text. We do the same thing when we realize from the first few scenes of a movie that we've rented the same video before.

Because most of us use Intuition in this casual way—to leap from a few immediate cues to a quick impression of the whole—we may

Calvin and Hobbes   by Bill Watterson

not realize how finely discriminating a skill it really is. We tend to apply the word intuitive as though it meant "suited by nature for a particular purpose in life."

For example, we speak of intuitive athletes, dancers, or film directors, and we mean that they're operating on the basis of untaught ability. We say that actors have intuitive chemistry with each other, meaning they "just know" what to do, without having to work at it. We speak of intuitive computer programs, which allegedly conform to our natural instincts. And we use the word somewhat disparagingly in the phrase "women's intuition," when an unsupported "feeling" has proven mysteriously correct.

Most of the people to whom we apply the word intuitive in this casual way aren't Intuitives—at least not typologically. They're usually Sensates and Introverted P types, whose right-brain abilities the left brain can't explain to itself.

The Real Thing

Whenever the word intuitive is applied to a genuine ENP, it's almost invariably followed by the word promoter or communicator. Such types strike us as "suited by nature" to sell themselves and their ideas. Charismatic, persuasive, and magnetic, ENPs are able to integrate diverse views in a larger pattern of meaning and to convince others that there are new and better ways of seeing reality.

Steve Jobs, the visionary who turned a hacker's gadget into the

Apple Computer industry, appears to be an excellent example of the type. So does Deepak Chopra, M.D., author of many books on the integrated relationship of mind, body, and cosmos.

In one of his ads, Dr. Chopra says: "The longer I practice medicine, the more I believe that the mind can change the very patterns that design the body. It can wipe mistakes off the blueprint, so to speak." No one but an ENP would make a statement that sweepingly optimistic about unrealized mental possibilities.

Apart from politicians, our most visible ENPs are probably those best-selling authors on the late-night infomercial circuit who are advocating new paradigms for understanding relationships. ENPs are possessed of great drive and vision, and they have an influence on society disproportionate to their 10 percent representation in the population.

Are Women Really More Intuitive?

Like the association of intuition with natural skills, the attribution of intuition to women has little to do with Intuition as it really exists. Historically deprived of a conceptual education, women have been presumed to be more instinctive than men, more liable to act on the basis of reflex, impulse, and emotions.

Although popular self-help books maintain quite flatly that men are "programmed by nature" to be "focused and logical," whereas women are "relational and take in the whole picture," two generations of type statistics reflect no such dichotomy. All functions are distributed more or less equally between the sexes.

Moreover, despite our assumptions, most of the apparent Intuitives in the social or political landscape are male. President Bill Clinton, for example, is almost certainly an ENFP. His ability to communicate persuasively is undeniable, even by his staunchest critics, and his penchant for generating new options at the point of decision has irritated almost everyone. No one ever suggests, however, that Clinton's behaviors are prompted by a feminine psyche.

Yet our associations persist, encouraged by increasing evidence that women have greater access to the right brain. The idea seems to be that female brains are "wired" differently from male brains, giving women more awareness of right-brain experiences and a greater incentive to conceptualize and talk about them.

From a typological perspective, however, the explanation doesn't account for the evidence. Right-brain skills *aren't* predominantly "feminine" in character. In fact, many of the tendencies governed by the right hemisphere—mechanical dexterity, an interest in graphic representation, the ability to judge spatial relationships—are traditionally associated with masculinity.

Finally, most of the traits that popular literature attributes to the female psyche aren't Intuitive so much as humane: compassion for others, empathy, the ability to "read" body language. If women appear to have a monopoly on these fundamental human properties, the issue is hardly one of natural programming but of resolute socialization. The point, in any case, is that functional preference doesn't support our insistent gender mythology.

The ENP Types

ENTP		ENFP	
dominant	Extraverted Intuition	dominant	Extraverted Intuition
secondary	Introverted Thinking	secondary	Introverted Feeling
right-brain	**Extraverted Sensation**	**right-brain**	Extraverted Sensation
alternatives	Introverted Feeling	alternatives	Introverted Thinking
left-brain	**Extraverted Thinking**	**left-brain**	Extraverted Feeling
double agents	Introverted Intuition	double agents	Introverted Intuition
tertiary	Extraverted Feeling	tertiary	Extraverted Thinking
inferior	Introverted Sensation	inferior	Introverted Sensation

Extraverted Intuition is so rapid and flexible an instrument that ENPs can operate almost like scanners, moving their attention widely over the environment, getting the gist of anything that happens to interest them. Such types are usually informed generalists, have a broad range of pursuits, basic knowledge about many things, and the ability to hold their own in a conversation about any of them.

Like Extraverted Sensates, ENPs are response-ready. Unless they can see new options, the possibility of change, or room for improvement, they're restless and bored. Indeed, because these types see life in terms of changing contextual relationships, they don't have much investment in the stability of material conditions—or take seriously the investment of others in those conditions. An unexpected juxtaposition of ideas, people, or images can reveal a larger pattern of meaning that changes all their priorities.

When their imagination is engaged, ENPs appear, for all the world, to be falling in love. They're not just interested in what they're doing. They're pulled in, like stars caught helplessly in a gravitational field, unable to think or talk about anything else. Whatever may have been felt or thought about yesterday is over, forgotten, without meaning. Their energies are devoted to anticipated prospects.

An ENFP analyst of my acquaintance, for example, became fascinated by chaos theory in nature. With great clarity he saw how psychological evolution could be understood as the same process in a different arena. The possibilities excited him and suggested any number of avenues to pursue.

Like most ENPs, the analyst was not motivated to work out his theory on paper or to research its practical applications. As far as he was concerned, the intuition was valid. What he needed was feedback from others to flesh it out and prove its viability.

To that end, he set up a conference series, inviting well-known chaos theorists to compare notes with interested psychiatrists and parapsychologists; offered a graduate course on psychology as a physical science; co-authored journal articles on relevant projects undertaken by his students; and promoted the subject at seminars all over the world. Within six months, he had established himself as a clearinghouse for an integrated field of ideas.

Like Extraverted Sensates, ENPs can make things happen very quickly. Sensates, however, are concrete pragmatists. They actualize people's expectations and in the process become their focal point. One might consider, for example, the evangelist in the film *The Apostle*. Within a week of walking into a small town, he acquires a church building, assembles a congregation, and becomes role model to people who barely know him.

By contrast, the ENFP analyst appealed to people's imagination, becoming a focal point for others' inventiveness and curiosity.

Like ESPs, ENPs enjoy "being on," and they're good at anticipating an audience. But they don't create an image that others envy and want to emulate, as Sensates do. Intuitives are screens for people's unarticulated hopes and aspirations. They recognize how circumstances may be changed to bring unexpressed potential into play.

The all-consuming enthusiasm of ENPs in the initial stages of discovery is infectious and charismatic. ENPs are not subtle about their ideas. In the throes of white-hot certitude, the type is an idealist, an advocate, the herald of a better way, the promoter of new enterprises—in Jung's terms, the "natural champion of all minorities with a future."[1]

Thus, where ESPs become the measure of a culture's external expectations, ENPs embody a culture's dreams and designs. Such types are inventors, evangelists, reformers, and kingmakers; if nothing else, they are intrepid motivators, able to persuade others to invest themselves in their plans and visions.

The flame of an Intuitive's enthusiasm blazes only so long, however. Potential exists, after all, only when it's unrealized. ENPs lose interest in a situation once its import becomes evident to others. This is why ENPs usually take jobs that offer a wide variety of situations, a turnover of clients, or the opportunity to devise creative solutions to a succession of problems—journalism, psychology, politics, education, public relations, the ministry, emergency medicine.

Of course, Extraverted Sensates also move on when their interest wanes, but their motives are mercilessly clear. The excitement is gone, and the experience is over. Extraverted Intuitives are more difficult to predict. They may lose interest before anything of consequence has even happened. A small part of the vision, once realized, suggests the whole thing, and the Intuitive feels no need to consider the matter further.

Perhaps one of the most interesting, and certainly one of the darkest, treatments of this aspect of Intuition occurs in *The Devils*, Dostoyevsky's novel about the forces of change in nineteenth-century Russia. In his notes for that book, Dostoyevsky describes his chief character, Nicholas Stavrogin, in terms that suggest an unmistakable ENP configuration. Stavrogin is a "man with an idea," which does not absorb him intellectually but merges with his own nature, so that he embodies it, and "having fused with his nature, it demands to be instantly put into action."

Like a demon lover, Stavrogin courses through the lives of others, becoming the focus of their unmet dreams, raising their hopes, and unwittingly laying the groundwork for revolution. But as soon as his effect becomes apparent, his interest disappears and he abruptly moves on, casting about for something new.

"Don't repeat my old ideas to me," he tells Shatov, unable to contain his impatience with the man's investment in him as a revolutionary messiah. And Shatov, having seen his highest aspirations reflected in Stavrogin, has no way to contend with his mentor's abrupt change of mind:

> "Do you suppose I don't see from your face that some new idea has taken hold of you? Why am I condemned to believe in you forever? Could I have spoken like this to anyone else? . . . I was not afraid of caricaturing a great idea by my touch because Stavrogin was listening to me. . . . Don't you know that I shall kiss your footprints after you have gone? I can't tear you out of my heart, Nicholas Stavrogin!"[2]

Intuitives are consistently surprised by the passionate responses they inspire in other people. Even the ENFPs, who identify strongly with people's feelings, don't react well to another's request for an investment deeper than they care to make. Their first instinct is to keep on moving before someone pins them down.

Thus, ENPs tend to live their lives in one of two ways: They become archetypal Seekers—curious, restless, living for adventure and passion, championing causes and underdogs, accumulating experiences in all manner of jobs and relationships. Or they become archetypal Companions, becoming close to people in whom they see potential, fueling inchoate dreams and ambitions.

Such types are so flexible and so quick to grasp the essence of a situation that they can do just about anything they set their minds to. But they may not stick with a situation long enough to realize the fruits of their labors. They depend on their supporters to take care of the follow-through and detail work, and those supporters wind up reaping the harvest.

Building a lifetime of temporary altars in the wilderness can, of course, be an honorable choice. ENPs are catalysts, and they can derive great satisfaction from quickening others' potential. However, ENPs need to develop enough Introverted Judgment to make that choice consciously. Without self-reflection, ENPs don't make use of their varied experiences. They "coast" on their Intuition, and life seems to have no lasting meaning for them.

Sometimes these extreme types settle into a situation that feels "right" to them, one secure enough to direct and motivate them, but flexible enough to keep them from feeling bored. For example, they may enjoy being creative mavericks in an otherwise structured job situation. But at home and in relationships, where structure must be self-generated, their lack of Judgment becomes apparent, and they can be impulsive, impatient, disorganized, and unpredictable.

In many cases, such types choose a Judging partner, who can supply them with stable reference points and a basic routine. However, this largely unconscious strategy of attraction gives them no contact with their own limits and values. Although ENPs will rely on the boundaries provided by others' Extraverted Thinking or Feeling, they also resent external limits as controlling and alien to their interests.

ENPs need to turn their Judgment inward to take personal limitations—of time, energy, resources, ability, even desire—into account. ENPs who resist this course assume that the people around them will anticipate what they need, read their moods, or fulfill the wishes they themselves don't know how to express. Given this egocentric assumption, they commit themselves to far more than they can or wish to deliver when the time comes.

ENPs don't recognize that they're overextending themselves. Without sufficient Judgment, they believe their intentions are as good as realized. It's just a matter of adding water, connecting the dots, filling in the blanks. They may not even start a project until the deadline has already passed. In consequence, ENPs are both surprised and frustrated by the problems that arise when their best intentions collide with material reality. They feel a sense of injustice, as though life were being unfair to them.

Indeed, these types can be badly hurt when people call them on promises they're not able to keep. After all, their heart was in the right place. It's circumstances that have changed. Extreme ENPs may even deny behaviors that have met with others' disapproval. An admission of wrongdoing would suggest that they *intended* to do wrong, and they didn't. The behaviors felt right to them at the time.

People who rely too heavily on their Intuition are usually caught between the devil and the deep blue sea. Unwilling to acknowledge their own limitations, they're forced to depend on the limits of others. Eventually, life confronts them with problems Intuition can't handle, and their psyche pressures them to grow. They feel the unexpected pull of their inferior function, Introverted Sensation.

As the ENP's least-developed function, Introverted Sensation is egocentric and not well-adapted to reality. Its unconscious influence overwhelms these types with the desire to stabilize their outer life in some unconditional way. However, an unmodified Intuitive standpoint generally persuades ENPs that priorities are dictated by the situation at hand. What seems required, therefore, is unconditional support from others—assurance that people recognize the worth of their intentions, even when things go wrong.

In consequence, ENPs don't see their Introverted Sensate impulses as part of themselves. Under pressure from this part of themselves, they suspect that others aren't supporting them well enough, and they lose faith in their ability to change things, to explore new possibilities. People who question their motives or behaviors strike them as spoilers, attempting to rein them in, control them, or deprive them of approval.

ENPs in this situation generally respond to the perceived problem by pushing the envelope. They test people's limits, attempting to force an expression of unconditional love and approval. What they actually need is more experience with their secondary function, Introverted Thinking or Introverted Feeling. When ENPs feel personally responsible to the situations they create, they set limits for themselves, and they're not so dependent on others' approval and reactions.

An interesting way to look at this kind of development is offered in an episode of *Star Trek: The Next Generation* called "The Host." The ship's doctor, Beverly Crusher, has fallen in love with Odan, a Trillian mediator en route to a diplomatic mission. In the course of the journey, Odan is mortally wounded, and Dr. Crusher is shocked to discover that a parasite is living inside him. Moreover, it turns out that the parasite is Odan himself. The Trill body he occupies is a host, a symbiotic arrangement common on the Trill home world. He can survive if a Trill replacement arrives in time.

Commander Riker becomes Odan's temporary host in the meantime, but Dr. Crusher is at a loss. She doesn't love Commander Riker, and it's difficult for her to relate to Odan in this new body. She finally overcomes her resistance and they spend a night together, but the symbiosis is ultimately harmful to Riker.

Dr. Crusher removes Odan from Riker's body, and the replacement Trill arrives just in time—a female. Now in a woman's body, Odan is still in love with Beverly, but the doctor is unable to make the transition. She vows to love the creature within, but she can't deal with the constantly altered conditions of its expression.

ENPs who rely exclusively on their Intuition are a lot like Odan. They feel centered by their Introverted Judgment, so they're not concerned with keeping outward conditions stable. This arrangement is a highly creative one, and it gives ENPs an unrivalled ability to adapt and roll with the punches of life. ENP politicians use this ability to great advantage, changing "host bodies" as needed to survive and prosper under unexpected circumstances.

ENPs need to recognize, however, that the person inside has consistent needs and values dictated by life experience. Some of these needs and values are important enough to honor under *all* circumstances. For example, Extraverted Intuition easily tells us that a punch in the nose and a verbal insult aren't the same situation. Even if our emotional reaction is the same, we recognize different options for behavior.

ENPs have the idea that paying more attention to their inner life means ignoring situational distinctions and doing whatever "feels" right to them at the time. But Introverted Judgment is a rational function. It helps us to see that our actions have effects that go beyond our immediate situation, and they need to be taken into account.

Such Judgment might suggest, for instance, that violence is unwarranted under any circumstances. To honor this subjective value is to forfeit some of our behavioral options, but it also gives our deeper intentions outward form, puts our humanity on the line.

ENPs are well accustomed to making personal sacrifices, but largely for the sake of their Intuition. They'll forfeit a great deal of material stability for the sake of increased options. But they need to reflect on a situation from an Introverted standpoint—to recognize that their responsibility to a situation outweighs some of the options available to them.

Odan, after all, had no doubt that he loved Beverly Crusher, and he was disappointed by Beverly's inability to accept him under all circumstances. ENPs are often in this kind of situation, certain that being true to themselves is enough and either fighting or leaving when others' expectations conflict with their outward options.

But honoring one's feelings is a different matter. Introverted Judgment might have moved Odan, instead, to limit outward change in favor of love's ongoing expression, thus acknowledging his investment in Beverly's fundamental needs.

When ENPs resist their Introverted Judgment, Introverted Sensation gets too far from their conscious self-experience, and they have a hard time resisting its influence on them. Such types ultimately turn to Extraverted Judgment, their tertiary function, attempting to keep their Intuitive self-understanding intact.

Like ESPs, Intuitives use their tertiary function to Judge others, to discriminate between people who support them and people who don't. ENFPs, for example, whose tertiary function is Extraverted Thinking, become increasingly critical of people who disapprove of their Intuitive behaviors, judging them to be negative, controlling, or threatened by their choices.

Like all tertiary defenses, this one contains a general truth. Extreme ENFPs are too dependent on others' approval and expectations, and they're right to seek their own way. But Extraverted Thinking can't help them do this. It gives them no experience with their own values and beliefs. It simply convinces them that others' values and beliefs are unreasonable.

ENTPs, whose tertiary function is Extraverted Feeling, handle things differently. They gear all their efforts to collective expectations—but for tactical advantage. They strive for others' support by *displaying* more relatedness. Such types are badly offended if their gestures don't have the intended effect. Their Feeling function suggests that their efforts are not being appreciated, and they find it difficult to forgive the insult.

Again, this tertiary viewpoint contains a grain of truth. Without a strong internal code of honor, extreme ENTPs types lack self-discipline, and their competitive drive keeps them striving for outward control. They're right to put more emphasis on human relationship. But Extraverted Feeling doesn't help them in this effort. It encourages them to disarm people rather than to recognize their responsibility to them.

When used self-reflectively, Introverted Judgment has a strong moral dimension, and ENPs ultimately develop a strong social conscience. Fully realized, these types are forces to be reckoned with. The better they develop their Judgment, the greater their motivation to address social inequity and unsatisfied human needs. ENPs not only fuel the creative energies of the people around them. They keep society in touch with its potential for change, improvement, and new ideas.

ENTP: Extraverted Intuition/Introverted Thinking

ENTP

dominant	Extraverted Intuition
secondary	Introverted Thinking
right-brain alternatives	**Extraverted Sensation**
	Introverted Feeling
left-brain double agents	**Extraverted Thinking**
	Introverted Intuition
tertiary	Extraverted Feeling
inferior	Introverted Sensation

ENTPs are aggressive, expansive, and opportunistic in the best sense of the word. They have no doubt about the importance of what they're doing, and they're at their best when they feel challenged and have to improvise. They want to be inspired, are rarely content with things as they are, and tend to have many projects going at the same time. Others are excited by, even propelled by, the relentless tide of their drive and enthusiasm.

In their self-motivation and hunger for experience, ENTPs are not unlike the ESTPs. Both are competitive and derive energy from playing the game very close to the edge. They know more than they can verbalize about how well they are getting across, and they use this knowledge pragmatically—with an eye toward winning. These similarities are largely the result of supporting their Extraverted Intuition with the impersonal wholistic logic of Introverted Thinking.

Unlike Extraverted Thinking, which is conceptual and generalized, Introverted Thinking motivates strategic action in a specific situation. When ENTPs use it, they don't start with abstract rules and apply them, step by step, to bring about a goal. They recognize themselves as part of an ongoing process, and they keep adjusting their behaviors in terms of the whole picture.

When combined with Extraverted Intuition, Introverted Thinking can be highly cerebral, and it usually involves a complex imaginal pattern of relationships. For example, an ENTP might enjoy playing chess, because such types can usually anticipate the results of many potential combinations of moves. An ENTP salesperson might pull together a host of small details and recognize in one mental image how a customer is likely to respond to a product. An ENTP cultural historian might see how a seemingly insignificant detail in a popular movie actually defines the underlying ethos of a culture.

Such types are so alert to systemic logic that they often see relationships among elements that no one has ever considered before. In this respect, their intelligence is more fluid than an Extraverted Thinker's, unpredictable, and given to idealism.

Indeed, an ENTP's curiosity, drive, and force of will are highly charismatic. These types are innovative, imaginative, and exciting to be around. They often attract people who rely on their energy and initiative to galvanize their own ambitions. However, ENTPs are not necessarily aware of others' needs or weaknesses. Their focus is usually on systems and how they shape reality.

Once engaged, ENTPs are completely invested in their work—eating, sleeping, and dreaming their particular vision. A quote attributed to comedian Jim Carrey accurately conveys the viewpoint of many ENTPs: "It's hard for anybody who's with me not to feel starved for affection when I'm making love to my ideas." Such types usually generate more possibilities than can be implemented, follow their own rules, and find it difficult to delegate any part of the creative process. They may, however, use their powers of persuasion to talk followers, admirers, and fellow travelers into doing the tedious follow-through chores once an idea is being implemented.

For this reason, others can experience the ENTP as alternately seductive, impatient, and indifferent, and such types are not above intimidating people with the mercurial nature of their mind. ENTPs assume that everyone is as strong and self-assertive as they are and as capable of defending their own interests. They may even feel manipulated and exploited by people who need too much from them.

ENTPs are easily bored, and their attention span can be ruthlessly short. Unless they are discovering something new, pursuing a hunch, or acquiring another angle on a persistent question, they are likely to be restless and agitated.

On the other hand, the type's disinterest in hierarchy and displays of status can result in a disarmingly direct and unpretentious style of relating. A shipping clerk who had been talking to a famous ENTP scientist in the hall of a major research center was amazed to find out who his conversational partner had been. "He didn't talk like he was important; he seemed like the kind of guy you'd go bowling with."

This is one reason such types often have broad public influence. They combine a grassroots appeal with a highly systemic view of reality. For example, ENTP politicians generally outline "wholistic" plans that paradoxically promise more localized control.

The full maturation of an ENTP usually depends on the type's willingness to use Introverted Thinking for perspective on—as well as support for—the aims of dominant Intuition. All Extraverted Perceivers emphasize the value of personal freedom, and ENTPs are inclined to draw from their tertiary function, Extraverted Feeling, to disarm people before they're able to exert control.

When they learn to apply Introverted Thinking to their own behaviors, they begin to work their will on the inner rather than the outer world. They develop more self-discipline, and they recognize their responsibility to others in the larger scheme of things. ENTPs who manage to do this are natural leaders, humanitarians, whose efforts may extend beyond their own lifetime to change the way we understand reality.

In this respect, well-developed ENTPs are like mature ESTPs. They have an effect on us, and we regard them as larger than life. ENTPs, however, are a different sort of hero. One might consider the difference between an ESTP Olympic athlete, who represents American ideals of mastery and discipline, and Steve Jobs, a probable ENTP, whose ideas for marketing the personal computer changed the way Americans understand everyday life.

Extraverted Sensates embody, in their actions and personhood, a way of being that we admire and want to imitate. Extraverted Intuitives foreshadow a new way of looking at things—a paradigm that reveals unsuspected connections and permits us to see the world differently.

ENTPs tend to be high-scoring Extraverts who want to exert an external effect on a grand scale. They have real vitality, enjoy life, like to laugh, and relish socialization that involves a freewheeling exchange of views and ideas. Like all Intuitives, they can be playful, but their sense of play is generally confrontational, and they may have a tendency to "test" people with a barrage of puns or bantering remarks.

Because they depend on being challenged to stay interested, they're likely to challenge others, and they enjoy being one up on almost anything that interests them—even if it's just knowing the latest gossip about mutual friends. Accordingly, they may not realize that others can be exhausted by their relentless pursuit of reactions and contest.

In fact, the thrill of being tested beyond their own resources is so pleasurable to ENTPs that they may take unnecessary chances simply for the opportunity to improvise and beat the odds. Sometimes this involves physical risk, particularly if the enterprise also involves the promise of discovery: deep-sea diving, white-water rafting. For the most part, however, ENTPs take chances by being mavericks. They will abandon a successful career for something unknown, challenge an authority, antagonize supporters, or try to get away with something just because they can.

Inevitably, they make some enemies. This happens, in part, because they enjoy a good skirmish. But they also underestimate the effect of their behaviors on others. They can be puzzled and irritated by people's expectations of them, especially if circumstances have dictated a change of heart or mind. They may even regard a person's anger or disappointment as a tactical maneuver that they need to counter or escape from. Like all ENPs, they will anticipate disaster or entrapment on the basis of one or two negative cues.

Because they depend so much on their dominant function, ENTPs may be somewhat deficient in the Feeling and Sensate aspects of life. This may not be apparent right away, because ENTPs can relate with great charm in the pursuit of a goal that interests them. Moreover, their expansive nature and appetite for life can make them seem more Sensate than they really are.

Although they can use Extraverted Sensation when they need to, and are very much concerned with their external sphere of influence, their material awareness is always geared to their dominant interests. It extends largely to the possibilities that interest them, the pragmatics of actualizing them, and the obstacles that stand in their way.

ENTPs can easily forget about their physical needs. They can get so caught up in a project or idea that they will work until they get run down and sick. They may forget to eat or subsist on junk food because it's quick and easy and gets them back to the drawing board right away. They need to pay attention to signals of fatigue and stress-related illness.

Introverted Sensation is the ENTP's inferior function, and the type's behaviors generally bear this out. Introverted Sensation encourages the maintenance of consistent inner priorities. ENTPs want the freedom to change their direction at any given moment. They find rules and regulations frustrating and confining—an affront to their individuality—and they have a tendency to flout them simply to prove their point.

It's a rare ENTP who hasn't thrown out the baby with the bathwater somewhere along the line. Extreme types can seem downright hypomanic—unable to contain their own energy, intolerant, impulsive, full of passionate conviction, certain that ordinary rules don't apply to their own behaviors.

These types often choose mates who can provide them with stable reference points and are willing to take responsibility for the maintenance of social relationships and the day-to-day chores of life. They tend, however, to regard these things as touchstones. They want the freedom to use them and disregard them as desired.

ENTPs need to turn deliberately to their secondary function in order to realize their full potential. Introverted Thinking gives ENTPs a sense of the ties that bind in the complex weave of life relationships. It tempers the type's need to resist control by taking it or disarming others. Instead, ENTPs recognize their responsibility to the situations they've created and to the people who care about them.

A self-disciplined ENTP is extremely attractive to others, because people sense the kind of power that has been harnessed to the task. Once Introverted Thinking is helping to balance Extraverted Intuition, ENTPs begin to draw from their less-developed functions more consciously—to recognize the value of others beyond their immediate utility and to stick with something until it is fully realized.

ENFP: Extraverted Intuition/Introverted Feeling

ENFP	
dominant	Extraverted Intuition
secondary	Introverted Feeling
right-brain alternatives	**Extraverted Sensation**
	Introverted Thinking
left-brain double agents	**Extraverted Feeling**
	Introverted Intuition
tertiary	Extraverted Thinking
inferior	Introverted Sensation

ENFPs are the most optimistic of the types—not because they're determined to see the positive, but because they focus on hopeful possibilities. Like ENTPs, they grasp patterns very quickly, but their interest in them is decidedly personal. They see people's potential

214

for loving, for learning, for making a difference, and they look for ways to nurture and encourage it.

Whether they're running a halfway house, teaching a class, mobilizing a task force, or waiting in line at the grocery store, ENFPs have a warm, empathetic approach to others, and they establish immediate affective connections. They have implicit faith in their ability to identify with people, and are often sought out by coworkers and acquaintances who have a problem to solve or need to confide in someone.

Even if they're tired or have other plans, ENFPs are receptive to these interactions, and they're unfailingly generous with their time and advice. Such types can find, however, that their deep personal engagement is sometimes misread. Although they're capable of identifying with another so completely that they anticipate sentences and take on the person's speech inflections, their exclusive attention is no indication of affective priority.

Like all Extraverted Perceivers, ENFPs are in the moment. They focus with equal intensity on whatever and whoever catches their attention. Indeed, because their experience of commitment is fateful and immediate, these types can easily burn themselves out. With each potential contact, the world becomes new again, and they're reluctant to hold anything in reserve.

ENFPs are so alert to circumstantial potential that they can adapt themselves to almost any job that interests them. However, they're usually drawn to professions that favor their immediacy, their social conscience, and their ability to forge common bonds—politics, sales, journalism, promotions, teaching, group therapy, the ministry, and so forth. Persuasive and charismatic, they're at their best in all-or-nothing situations, where they can invest everything they have in making the sale, ensuring the vote, or motivating people toward a specific goal.

Whatever career they choose, ENFPs have little patience for administrative detail. They prefer to think on their feet, as a situation is happening. Moreover, they have a hard time sacrificing their options to an organized routine. A pundit once suggested that if Bob Dole, Newt Gingrich, and Bill Clinton were doing yard work together, Dole would be telling other people how to mow their lawns,

Gingrich would be exploring a plan for mowing lawns on Mars, and Clinton wouldn't be able to decide whether to mow the front lawn or the back.

If Dole illustrates the ISTJ's inclination to manage life for others, and Gingrich the ENTP's willingness to entertain the speculative, Clinton suggests the ENFP's steadfast refusal to make absolute judgments. These types simply won't declare that one option is inherently better than another. They want to be able to do it all, and they invariably have more on their plate than they can reasonably handle.

This is one reason ENFPs are so keenly aware of systemic injustice. They're inclusivists of the first order, deeply concerned by standards or institutions that categorize people or limit their natural potential. If they have to make a decision, they want feedback from as broad a range of people as possible.

Although ENFPs can seem hesitant in this regard, unwilling to act until they've tested public opinion, it should not be supposed that they're yielding to popular consensus. As dominant Intuitives, these types are looking to the future. They see how a change of circumstances will make life better for people, but they're not sure yet about the means to realize their vision. ENFPs use their secondary function, Introverted Feeling, to make choices and to determine their agenda.

As a right-brain function, Introverted Feeling works differently from the Extraverted sort. Extraverted Feeling prompts us to reason in terms of prevailing social values. For example, when we say "You've been like a mother to me," we're presuming shared standards about what mothers do.

Introverted Feeling, by contrast, prompts us to reason in terms of fundamental human values, whose meaning and importance are conditioned by our own experience. We may believe, for example, that life is unconditionally sacred even though society sanctions military action. If we make choices in light of that value, we're calling prevailing social beliefs into question and may anger or disappoint others.

Introverted Feeling helps ENFPs to take responsibility for the decisions they make, to accept the social consequences of their choices. It allows them to distinguish between an expedient choice, which circumvents others' expectations, and an honorable one, which transcends them.

Although ENFPs usually develop Introverted Feeling quite well, it takes them a while to recognize what it asks of them in the way of personal accountability. The better their Intuition works, the more likely they are to use Introverted Feeling analytically to measure the prevailing structures of society against fundamental human values and to discern their potential for change. This is an infinitely fertile field for speculation, and ENFPs generate many ideas about improving the institutions that determine people's opportunities and experience.

When they seek feedback from others, these types are trying to gauge the relationship of their ideas to their immediate social resources. As they exchange information, they're limiting their options in terms of the people around them—what's important to them, what they bring to the task, what they know how to do.

This entire process is an important component of the ENFP's power to inspire and mobilize large groups. As they link their vision to others' hopes and aspirations, people feel that they're collaborating with a driving archetypal imperative—a force of nature that will change everything in its path—and they're led to accomplish extraordinary things.

Ultimately, however, the ENFP's outward focus takes its toll. For one thing, these types spend a great deal of their time trying to cover all the bases. Without enough Introversion, they're dependent on others' stake in their ideas, so they devote their energies to winning people's approval. Given their awareness that circumstances are likely to change, they try to make their case broad enough to incorporate all possibilities. In consequence, ENFPs can end up talking a better game than they're prepared to play.

Indeed, because ENFPs have done so much work in selling their idea to others, they tend to overlook problems of implementation until they actually occur. They're shocked and disillusioned when things don't work out as anticipated. It strikes them that doing the right thing should work *because* it's the right thing, so they have no recourse but to believe they've been thwarted by people with the wrong values.

ENFPs need enough contact with their Introverted side to appreciate the genuine diversity of people's experience and beliefs. Unless they recognize the subjective nature of their own value system, they have no way of understanding people whose values are legitimately different from their own.

Moreover, an exclusive reliance on Extraverted Intuition ensures that its opposite, Introverted Sensation, plays no part in the ENFP's self-experience, and it eventually works against the type's acceptance of material imperfection. Under the unconscious influence of this function, ENFPs yearn for a lasting investment, invulnerable to chance or circumstance, and they begin to wonder if they're tilting at windmills.

Like other types, ENFPs don't recognize their inferior aims as part of themselves. They simply feel dissatisfied with what they've accomplished. If these Sensate impulses surface around midlife, ENFPs become abruptly aware of the progression of time. They haven't done what they were meant to do—maybe they haven't even found themselves yet—but they're also hemmed in by the many obligations of an established job or household.

In point of fact, by midlife ENFPs have usually accomplished a great deal, which is why their psyche is pushing them to grow beyond their dominant perspective. Their first instinct, however, is to reinforce their Intuitive frame of mind—that is, to change their present circumstances: to quit their job, go back to school, start a new project, have a baby, take a vacation, sell the house. One might recall the hitchhiker in the classic film *Five Easy Pieces*, whose dream was to reach Alaska. Having seen a picture of it once, she perceives it to be the perfect place to start over—white, clean, uncorrupted. "Yeah, well," says the hero, "I think that was before the Big Thaw."

Sometimes ENFPs do need to start over and try something new; sometimes they need a quiet place for thought and reflection. But it's difficult for them to address this question until they get some *psychological* distance from their environment. They need to figure out how to honor their values in the everyday choices they're currently making.

There is a most interesting episode of *Star Trek: The Next Generation*, in which Worf, a Klingon officer raised by human parents, declines to defend his Klingon name—all that he possesses of his blood heritage—when his biological father is accused of treason. He endures the disgrace because unmasking the real traitor would plunge the empire into war. This is the kind of judgment that Introverted Feeling promotes in an ENFP: a recognition that some things are more important than Intuition can discern.

It should be emphasized that Introverted Feeling does not *oppose* Extraverted Intuition in this respect. It equips ENFPs to deal with questions that can't be addressed with their dominant skills. For example, if Worf had used Intuition to understand his dilemma, it would have counseled him that his best option was not to be in it.

Introverted Feeling told him, rather, how to be responsible to his situation—not because it was fair or his fault, but because it was happening to him, and its larger outcome depended on his hierarchy of values. Ultimately, he subordinated what was good for him (the name that connected him to his blood family) to what was good for his people as a whole.

ENFPs tend to make contact with their inner selves largely in their creative pursuits (in the music they love, the art they make, the poetry they write); their faith practice; or meaningful projects with like-minded colleagues. They make time for solitary walks in a natural setting or other sentient activities that foster communion with the larger fabric of life. When the psyche is pushing them to grow, however, wholistic experiences can take them only so far. ENFPs need to make a more deliberate effort to figure out how their values are influencing their life's direction.

For example, ENFPs are often eloquent in their arguments for social institutions that recognize the dignity of all people. Introverted Feeling asks them to come at this question differently. It asks them to locate, in their individual relationships, their responsibility to acknowledge human dignity, even when circumstances dictate anger or self-defense.

ENFPs resist this Judging point of view because it seems so implacable. To see life that way would be impractical; it would keep them from responding directly to experience. Besides, living out their values one person at a time is all very nice, but it has no effect on the systemic problems that need to be solved.

When ENFPs wrestle with this conflict long enough, they realize the enormous power Introverted Feeling actually confers. It gives them a way to embody their highest aspirations every day, in the world that really exists. And it offers self-awareness, helping them to set their own limits.

Types who resist their Introverted side eventually reach a point where they feel tired and overwhelmed, unable to follow through on much of anything. Too much seems to be coming at them, and they just can't manage all the details. Every situation they're in seems to require every bit of their energy, and no one seems to appreciate the pressure they're under.

ENFPs are not mistaken about these perceptions. If they've resisted self-reflection, they *are* overinvested and overwhelmed. However, their ideas about why this is happening are misplaced. They aren't overwhelmed because there's too much to do or because people expect too much. They're overwhelmed because they're constantly changing in response to their circumstances.

When ENFPs develop Introverted Feeling, they short-circuit this receptive mode and come to terms with who they really are. If they don't, Introverted Sensation gets so far from their conscious self-experience that they're sure people are working against them, fighting their attempts to improve life for others. Under such conditions, the only defense they can muster is their tertiary function, Extraverted Thinking.

Given an adequate Introverted perspective, ENFPs use Extraverted Thinking very well. It helps them to set logical priorities and to respect the priorities of others. Marshalled to protect an Intuitive function under siege, however, Extraverted Thinking is egocentric. It convinces ENFPs that others should respect their priorities. From an Extraverted Intuitive standpoint, of course, a priority is whatever the ENFP is responding to right now.

The defensive utility of this strategy is clear. It allows ENFPs to maintain their immediate approach to life, but it also gives them the idea that people who want something different from them are being unreasonable and depriving them of respect. The important thing is to do what's right for themselves.

In point of fact, ENFPs who are defending their Intuition against all limitations have no idea what's right for themselves. They only know what's immediately possible to them, and they want the freedom to respond as they like, without social consequences.

For example, if they miss an appointment or forget a promise, they have a hard time apologizing. They'll point out how overwhelmed they are by their many obligations, how much they're doing that isn't expected of them. Before the other person knows it, the question at hand is not the broken promise or missed appointment, but the ENFP's rights or well-being, or the absurdity of dismissing a relationship over one small issue.

Ultimately ENFPs need more than freedom and opportunity. They long for intimacy, relationships they can count on, people who will stand by them no matter what the circumstances. When they recognize that they're responsible for creating the kind of life that makes these things possible, they come to terms with their Introverted side. If their secondary function limits some of their options, it also offers new ones—for example, the opportunity to change people's hearts by being true to their own.

Once ENFPs are in touch with Introverted Feeling, they don't lose their charisma and persuasive gifts. They become more aware of their own needs, less vulnerable to the approval and disapproval of others. Such types often find that they're skilled at helping others to discover and cultivate their own values, and they make a consistent and positive contribution to society at large.

17

Introverted Intuition

INTJ and INFJ Types

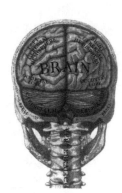

Left hemisphere

Secondary function
Extraverted Judgment

Dominant function
Introverted Intuition

Right hemisphere

Inferior function
Extraverted Sensation

Tertiary function
Introverted Judgment

▲ LIKE THE OTHER PERCEIVING FUNCTIONS, Introverted Intuition draws our attention to immediate sensory phenomena. However, Introverted Intuition is more cerebral than the three just discussed. It prompts an interest in perception itself—the process of recognizing and interpreting what we take in.

Whatever types we happen to be, we use all four means of Perception in one way or another. For example, if we were spending a day at the beach:

▲ *Extraverted Sensation* would prompt us to go with our sense impressions as they occurred: to lie in the sun, play in the surf, listen to the gulls piping overhead.

▲ *Introverted Sensation* would move us to stabilize our sense impressions by integrating them with facts we knew to be consistent.

We might bring our favorite book, a snorkel and flippers, a bag of snacks, extra towels because someone will probably forget one, and a watch to make sure we beat the traffic home.

▲ *Extraverted Intuition* would move us to unify our sense impressions with their larger context, thereby creating new options for meaning and response. For example, as we lie on our blanket in the sun, perhaps we hear music in the distance. Someone passing by mentions a great restaurant in town. Suddenly we're thinking: Hey, there must be an amusement park nearby. If it's on our way to town, we can check out the rides before we look for the restaurant that passerby was talking about. In fact, maybe the guy knows about other places we should consider. Where did he go?

▲ *Introverted Intuition* would prompt us to liberate our sense impressions from their larger context, thereby creating new options for perception itself. For example, we might find ourselves wondering why people feel so strongly about getting a good tan. We remember reading somewhere that before the Industrial Revolution, being tan marked one as a manual laborer, because it suggested work out of doors. After the Industrial Revolution, it was pale skin that suggested manual labor, because it indicated work in a poorly lit factory. Such correlations aren't relevant today, but a good tan is still considered attractive. Why is that? We consider raising the question as a topic of conversation, but we're pretty sure our friends will think we're observing a situation instead of enjoying it.

Because we usually associate Intuition with "feelings" and hunches, the conceptual nature of Introverted Intuition may be difficult to appreciate. Like its Extraverted counterpart, Introverted Intuition is a Perceiving function, but it's also a left-brain function. The left brain won't focus on many things at once. It depends on words and signs to make outward experience predictable and orderly.

This is most clear in the areas governed by Extraverted Thinking and Extraverted Feeling, the left-brain Judgment functions. ETJs and EFJs, whose Judging skills are dominant, wield language like a knife, separating meaningful sense impressions from all the nameless experiential stuff that surrounds it. Such types may be hard pressed to grant the reality of impressions that can't be explained or talked about.

The left-brain Perceiving functions are different. Introverted Sensation and Introverted Intuition make us aware of all our sensory impressions, notwithstanding prevailing categories of knowledge. In consequence, ISJs and INJs tend to have interests and priorities that strike others as unpredictable or esoteric.

On the other hand, as left-brain types, ISJs and INJs also need conceptual control over their outer world. For this reason, both types have a strong investment in the structure of public information. ISJs are concerned with making that structure secure, whereas INJs are interested in changing or improving it.

For example, at a recent board meeting, an ISTJ accountant told the group that he enjoyed recording the organization's income and expenditures, but he didn't want to be involved with the money itself—counting it, bringing it to the bank, and so forth. This is a classic Introverted Sensing approach. Material reality is just so much raw experience. It has to be controlled with a stable mental framework.

Introverted Intuition moves us in the opposite direction. It tells us that changing our frame of mind can change the world. For example, a recent article advises the parents of a fussy or demanding baby not to describe the infant as difficult but to recognize that such children have vivid, strong, and rich personalities. This is how Introverted Intuition works. The material facts remain the same, but we organize them in a new conceptual pattern that changes their meaning and gives us new options for behavior.

Introverted Intuition versus Extraverted Intuition

Because Extraverted Intuitives also see life in terms of new perspectives, it's important to recognize the difference between ENPs and INJs. Motivated by functions that implicate opposite sides of the brain, these types are mirror images of each other.

Extraverted Intuitives are right-brain types who deal with their sense impressions by unifying them into larger outward patterns. An ENP physician, for example, may realize, with sudden insight, that several unexplained symptoms are actually part of a single disease. As an Extraverted type, the physician has no doubt that the disease syndrome really exists. The pattern was always there, waiting for someone to discover it. What's important now is telling others about the discovery—getting people to see that the new model offers more options than the old.

Introverted Intuitives don't think this way. For INJs, patterns aren't "out there" in the world, waiting to be discovered. They're part of us—the way we make sense of the riot of information and energy impinging on our systems. A disease syndrome is a useful construct, but that's all it is—an aggregate of observations attached to a label, telling us what to see and how to deal with it.

Given their real-life consequences, mental constructs don't strike INJs as imaginary or irrelevant. They're merely arbitrary, derived from a particular view of life. For this reason, they can trap us into holding that view—say, that physicians are in the business of cure rather than prevention—without being aware of its effects.

Introverted Intuition in Practice

Most types rely on Introverted Intuition to contend with ambiguities of meaning and perception—that is, to see that a situation can be interpreted in more than one way. We may use it, for example, to acknowledge the possibility of both scientific and religious positions on life after death, or to deal with incompatible experiences of self and solidarity at work, at home, and among friends.

It may seem peculiar, therefore, to depend on this function for one's primary understanding of reality. If INJs are seeing things from many (sometimes conflicting) perspectives, on what basis would they ever take action?

It should be emphasized that INJs are very much like ENPs in this respect. Where Extraverted Intuitives see many behavioral options, INJs acknowledge many conceptual standpoints. They experience no need to declare one inherently better than another. Indeed, these types have the disconcerting habit of solving a problem by shifting their perspective and defining the situation some other way.

One might recall the movie *Star Trek: The Wrath of Khan*, in which Admiral Kirk reveals that he was the only cadet ever to beat a program designed to test people's responses to a no-win battle scenario. It turns out that he managed to do this by reprogramming the simulator to give him the advantage. On the horns of an apparent dilemma, this is the sort of thing INJs tend to do.

For example, years ago, when I was copy editor on a women's magazine, a disagreement arose among the editorial staff over an article about a film director. The piece included an anecdote about the director's early years as a seldom-employed performer, when she was working part-time at a fast-food counter.

Because the "look" for female stars at that time was pallid and doe-eyed, the olive-skinned director went to her day job in a thick layer of white pancake makeup, just in case someone called her in for an audition. She had no idea how people actually saw her until one day she overheard one of the cooks say to another, "Here come that chick with the green face!"

The argument among the editors was over the punch line. Some of the staff thought that printing the sentence in what was then called Black English was prejudicial. They wanted to change the word come to comes. The other staff members thought that adding the s was itself prejudicial—and lost the flavor of the original remark.

The editor in chief happened to be an INFJ, and she was determined to pull the question outside the framework of "correct politics." She advised us to add the s—because most of our readers would be unfamiliar with that particular use of the tense and would assume we were sloppy proofreaders.

This is a fairly typical example of Introverted Intuition when it's supported by the diplomatic tendencies of Extraverted Feeling. INTJs do the same thing, but their focus of attention is impersonal, dictated by the logical interests of Extraverted Thinking. For example, I remember a conversation with an INTJ researcher after the famous Bobby-in-the-shower scene had appeared on the program *Dallas*.

Bobby had been killed and buried on the show the year before, because the actor who played him wanted to leave the show. When he rejoined the cast, the writers solved the problem by explaining, within the context of the plot, that the entire previous season had occurred in his wife's dream. As the new season opened, Bobby's wife awoke from that dream to find her husband in the shower, very much alive, unaware of the events that had "happened" during the past year.

The researcher and I were discussing the difficulties created by this plot device, given the fact that Bobby's death and funeral had been worked into the story line of the *Dallas* spin-off, *Knots Landing*. Were the events on that show *also* part of Pam's dream?

The researcher's answer was typically INTJ. He said he'd decided that Bobby had died and been buried in a parallel time line. Although his wife remembered the alternate life as a dream, none of the other characters need be aware of it at all. I can't think of another type who would invoke a speculative aspect of quantum theory to impose causal logic on a soap opera narrative!

INJs often take jobs that draw on their ability to bring conceptual descriptions more closely into line with unrecognized aspects of a situation. However, they need enough Judgment to distinguish between frame shifts that bring new information into relief and frame shifts that merely avoid a problem.

Calvin and Hobbes   by Bill Watterson

The INJ Types

	INTJ		INFJ
dominant	Introverted Intuition	dominant	Introverted Intuition
secondary	Extraverted Thinking	secondary	Extraverted Feeling
left-brain	Introverted Sensation	left-brain	Introverted Sensation
alternatives	Extraverted Feeling	alternatives	Extraverted Thinking
right-brain	Introverted Thinking	right-brain	Introverted Feeling
double agents	Extraverted Intuition	double agents	Extraverted Intuition
tertiary	Introverted Feeling	tertiary	Introverted Thinking
inferior	Extraverted Sensation	inferior	Extraverted Sensation

Some twenty-five years ago, there was a riddle making the rounds that went something like this: "The surgeon's brother went out to sea; but the man who went to sea had no brother. So who was the surgeon?" At that time, the answer was a surprise and produced a laugh: The surgeon, of course, was the man's *sister*. Today, the answer may be so obvious that the joke seems pointless and insulting.

The issue here is the framework of beliefs and expectations that we maintain. Some are dictated by society; others are a matter of subjective experience—our gender, our name, our history, our vocation, our background. Knowledge is facilitated, limited, and directed by boundary conditions.

INJs have an unusual awareness of how such conditions determine our conceptual vocabulary, and their Intuition leads them to discern aspects of reality that aren't being acknowledged. Thus, many INJs choose professions that allow them to work with questions of language and terminology—as editors and proofreaders, for example, but also as mathematicians, psychologists, theologians, poets, and programmers. Any field that involves conceptual signs and categories is likely to interest these types.

The difficulty, of course, is that an INJ's Intuition often takes the type beyond the reach of an existing vocabulary. Consider again the joke about the surgeon's brother. It used to work because the word *surgeon* was synonymous with a male doctor. The idea that a surgeon might be someone's sister was beyond the reach of most people's expectations.

INJs are often frustrated by the limits of the language they're using to test the freight of their Intuitions—whether their means of expression involves the written word, mathematics, musical or scientific notation, metapsychology, or art. As they shift vantage points, they're obliged to invent new terms, reinterpret old ones, or use words like *post-modern* to avail themselves of the categories their Intuitions are pointing beyond.

One can see in Jung's body of work, for example, his long struggle to invent terms for what he Intuited about archaic levels of the human mind. Even when he had settled on words like *archetype* and *collective unconscious*, he spent the better part of his life attempting to work out their conceptual limits.

Because INJs can't develop their primary skills without analyzing the way things are generally described and understood, these types are likely to experience themselves as different from others. Constituting only two percent of the population, young INJs can feel isolated, unable to fit in even when they want to. Before their skills are well-developed, it's difficult for these types to justify the questions that occur to them.

After all, Introverted Intuitions are not really ideas. They're like trains at the edge of articulated knowledge. You can't claim them or advocate them. You put on a hat, grab hold of a boxcar door, and see where they go. Until these types acquire enough information to map out the path they're taking, all they can do is insist on their need to take it.

INFJs, in particular, who need others' encouragement and approval to establish a positive self-image, struggle with feelings of alienation, and they often develop an ironic sense of humor that protects them from self-revelation and assures them of positive relationships. INTJs do this too, but they're not as reluctant to ask questions and summarily reject the answers. One might consider, for example, the humor of comedians like Dennis Miller and George Carlin.

In either case, INJs have no choice but to cup Intuition's small flame against the hard wind of others' beliefs and opinions. If they lean too comfortably against the lamppost of someone else's knowledge, they never realize how illuminating that inner flame can be. They have to tolerate "not knowing" long enough to understand how an existing vocabulary works and to use it well enough to point beyond its limits.

Once INJs learn how to do this, they have to learn how to *stop* doing it. Such types are never satisfied with what they know, and it takes a real effort for them to set limits and make use of the knowledge they already have. In fact, an INJ who feels well-informed is likely to have so much information that imposing order on it and sharing it with others is almost impossible. INJs are so different in this respect from their Extraverted counterparts that it's worth noting their opposing behaviors.

ENPs are most visible in the first flush of discovery, when they're excited and optimistic. They aggressively seek feedback from the people around them, and they welcome others' involvement in formulating their Intuitions and carrying out their plans.

INJs are least accessible in the discovery process. Like the prince in the story of "Cinderella," they're solitary, sometimes obsessive, fitting Intuition to expressible terms like the glass slipper to potential brides. Until they've managed a good enough fit between their inner reality and an outward vocabulary, INJs may not even know what they're after, and they won't involve others in formulating their plans.

The goals these types posit are also inversely related. ENPs, as right-brain types, understand objects in terms of their larger context. They picture an integrated "whole" in which diverse people or diverse views are perfectly integrated—a global village, a unified theory, a consolidation of disciplines, a mind-body-spirit connection.

The left-brain INJs understand context as a mental phenomenon, something that people bring to the outer world from within. Thus, they don't see "wholeness" as an integrated endpoint. Wholeness, for INJs, is the chaotic beginning—raw sensory input without meaning.

Charles Williams, in a novel called *The Greater Trumps*, describes what he calls "the everlasting dance"—the reality that lies behind reality, and his image characterizes very well the INJ's perceptual experience of life:

> Imagine . . . that everything which exists takes part in the movement of a great dance—everything, the electrons, all growing and decaying things, all that seems alive and all that doesn't seem alive, men and beasts, trees and stones, everything that changes, and there is nothing anywhere that does not change. . . . Quick or slow, measurable or immeasurable, there is nothing at all anywhere but the dance.[1]

One might also suggest that the Internet is a pretty decent reflection of the way INJs think. Information is constantly proliferating in all different directions. One click of the mouse and your entire perspective shifts. You give away one idea and in return you get access to more data than you'll ever be able to look at.

Where ENPs will take action as soon as they have the gist of a situation, the more information INJs acquire about a subject, the more it strikes them there is to know before action is possible. As Spock maintained throughout the *Star Trek* series: Truth is not Oneness. It's infinite diversity in infinite variations. Indeed, most INJs use their secondary function, Extraverted Thinking or Extraverted Feeling somewhat defensively to dismiss the influence of perspectives that stop short of what they've already considered.

For example, an INTJ theology professor at the seminary I attended, who enjoys theoretical discussions and has no problem entertaining multiple paradigms, had the reputation of being dogmatic and impossible to satisfy because he consistently directed his Extraverted Thinking to pointing out the logical limitations of any idea a student ventured. He wanted his students to take an Intuitive leap—to move beyond the boundaries he was setting up, but his comments struck them as negative and critical.

INFJs are less likely than INTJs to diminish the views of others by subjecting them to logical analysis, but they're quite capable of surrounding themselves with people whose Judgment skills are undeveloped, which gives them the opportunity to conduct their relationships by advising others on the wisdom of their life choices.

INJs and Physical Reality

Like Introverted Sensates, INJs may collect objects or experiences that give form to their inner life. ISJs, however, give form to a consistent self-experience, and they often preserve cherished objects against changing tastes and times. One might recall, from chapter 15, the ISJ who was fascinated by cylinder phonographs, learned to repair them, and found, almost despite himself, that his expression of self had turned into his social identity and life's work.

INJs, by contrast, often collect things that represent their sense of emergent meaning, even if they can't explain why the objects matter to them. For example, an INTJ minister of my acquaintance collects carvings of the Green Man. The instinctual nature of this pagan image resonates with him but has no relationship to his present life structure. The INJ's self-experience nearly always involves the unknown, a state of being that's not yet embodied.

Accordingly, where ISJs maintain and enjoy their hobbies all their lives, INJs tend to lose interest when the fluid nature of unrealized meaning takes expressible shape and has meaning for others. One of my cousins, an INFJ, spent years following the career of an unknown character actor, mesmerized by what she saw in him but unable to explain the interest to anyone else. When he ultimately got a part in a popular TV show and won an Emmy, she felt vindicated but found that he no longer held the same fascination for her.

Although Extraverted Sensation is the INJ's inferior function, it should not be supposed that INJs are entirely in their heads or never leave their journals and computer terminals. They're bona fide Perceivers, and their senses may be very keen. INJs follow sports, enjoy outdoor activities, take up Tai Chi, drive fast cars, cook gourmet meals, make art—all sorts of things that involve a sensory engagement with life.

Their Extraverted Sensate skills are undeveloped in the sense that INJs have a hard time seeing themselves objectively. Physicality, for these types, is quite nearly another conceptual viewpoint, a way of looking at life. The aforementioned seminary professor used to work part-time on a moving van in order, as he put it, to "make room for a little body consciousness."

INJs tend to enjoy fantasies and myths in which the hero has evolved a perfect combination of visceral and cerebral skills, but in practice, the two usually run on parallel tracks. Indeed, INJs who lack Extraverted Judgment are likely to neglect their practical and material needs, regarding visits to the dentist or eye doctor as time wasters, letting everyday chores pile up, or assuming that bills, retirement plans, and health insurance will take care of themselves.

Predictably, our Sensation-oriented pop culture is merciless in its INJ stereotypes. While INFJs are portrayed as neurotic psychics, INTJs are depicted as nerds, absent-minded professors, and eccentric detectives with bad wardrobes and inadequate sex lives. This is how Fox "Spooky" Mulder on The X-Files was initially portrayed—as a classic INTJ obsessive, oblivious to work atmosphere, career status, and the need for relationship—everything except his private quest for truth.

As the series has moved from cult status to broad popularity, Mulder's character has been subtly redrawn. He's less like an INJ who sees conceptual possibilities excluded from the FBI's standard categories of knowledge and more like an ISP influenced by tertiary Introverted Intuition, certain that the government is conspiring to hide the presence of aliens from an unsuspecting public.

On the other hand, the decision to pair Mulder not with an ESP action hero (which is the usual gambit in a science fiction series), but with an ENTJ pathologist (Agent Dana Scully) is inspired. Scully's by-the-book Judgment is consistently subverted by Mulder's appeal to her secondary function. Consider this bit of dialogue between them:

> SCULLY: I'm struck by how much you're like Ahab [in Moby Dick]. You're so consumed by your personal vengeance against life—whether it be its inherent cruelties or its mysteries—that everything takes on a warped significance to fit your megalomaniacal cosmology. The truth or a white whale—what difference does it make? Both obsessions are impossible to capture.
> MULDER: Scully, are you coming on to me?

Extraverted Judgers almost always stereotype INJs this way: as peculiarly and obsessively driven, with a tenuous hold on morality. And like Mulder, INJs are liable to sidestep the observation by shifting perspectives and depriving it of meaning.

Developing Secondary Judgment

In point of fact, INJs would do well to take Scully's assessment into account. Such types spend so much time avoiding external influence to protect their evolving Intuitions that they learn to use their Judgment largely to dismiss others' opinions and to maintain their self-determined path.

There's an old Star Trek episode about an alien life form that had invaded the planet Deneva. Batlike creatures, these aliens would entwine themselves with people's nervous systems, manipulating their behaviors and driving them mad with pain. Ultimately, the crew discovered that the creatures could be destroyed by exposing them to intense light.

INJs tend to use their Thinking or Feeling in much the same way—to resist "infection" by a custom, method, ideology, theory, or set of expectations that feels alien to them and capable of malignant attachment. They throw light on such creatures, revealing them as arbitrary constructs, depriving them of the power to influence.

It takes a deliberate effort for INJs to use their Judgment for self-criticism, and not just to analyze the limits of others' ideas. Until they learn to do this, they're nearly impervious to criticism from anyone. Even INFJs, who can be seriously wounded by a rift in a relationship, are unlikely to take another's opinion of them at face value. A position that conflicts with the INJ's own is, after all, just somebody else's point of view.

In fact, a logical argument aimed at convincing the INJ of one specific truth will usually encourage the type to point out the speaker's need to see things that way. For INJs, truth isn't about logic. Truth is a frame of reference, a way of organizing information, which serves one set of needs or another.

It takes a fair amount of experience for these types to recognize that merely pointing out the limits of whatever happens to be in place is ultimately destructive. Two stock characters in films and novels exist for good reason: the INFJ whose local grievance unleashes mob fury and the INTJ scientist who sells his soul for knowledge and brings about the apocalypse. These stereotypes don't say as much about the INJ as they do about the effects these types can have on others. INJs have a distinct responsibility to develop their secondary function, because their Intuitions have power well beyond their own interests.

Introverted Intuition in a Sensate Culture

INJs throughout history have been prophets, poets, and heretics. But in a Sensate culture, whose focus is on immediate surface stimulation, the INJ's process of self-discovery inevitably coincides with some of society's blind spots. Without an adequate Judging perspective, these types can be influenced by society's unconscious needs without realizing what's happening to them.

Like all types, when INJs become too dependent on their dominant function, their psyche floods them with unconscious impulses from their inferior function, which pushes them out of their usual approach to life. This gives INJs a chance to grow, to get in touch with their secondary perspective, Extraverted Thinking or Extraverted Feeling. But INJs are less likely than other types to recognize the opportunity.

All types feel the pressure of their inferior function when they're stuck in one way of adapting to life. Their usual way of doing things isn't working, and they feel unhappy, unable to do what they've always done. It's natural to believe that the problem is one of circumstance.

INJs, however, have an additional incentive to blame their situation. The unconscious Sensate impulses they're experiencing share common ground with prevailing views outside them. So it's not difficult for them to conclude that their problems are the result of people's inability to see past surface boundaries.

Like all Introverts, INJs respond to a threatened self-experience defensively, by using their secondary function to get the outer world under control. This can happen in any number of ways, depending on the type's interests and concerns.

INJs may, for example, feel a strong need to express themselves creatively. But without sufficient Judgment, they don't know how to structure their ideas. Such types may not even know what they want to say. So they spend their time acquiring more information about the writing process itself—perhaps by reading other people's books or finding out more about publishing. Instead of applying their Judgment to their inner world and limiting their options, they apply it to the outer world and keep their Intuitive approach intact.

INJs also defend their Intuition by applying their Judgment to institutionalized bias. This is a valid concern, of course, and well developed INJs are often in the forefront of battles involving inclusive language. However, when these types are defending their inner world against inferior aims, they invariably focus on terms that suggest a Sensate viewpoint—that is, one determined by surface criteria: gender, race, color, and so forth.

The defensive nature of these efforts is apparent in the laws, charters, hymn books, and classroom agendas that issue from them. The language of these products is not inclusive so much as disembodied. Made to accommodate the INJ's purely conceptual approach to life, the terms don't support every point of view; they reflect no one's actual experience.

Like individuals, a Sensate society doesn't improve when it's compensated by its inferior function. A Sensate approach to life becomes morally responsible when it's tempered by Introverted Judgment—the recognition that human values transcend loyalties based on surface criteria. Introverted Intuition merely counsels that surface criteria should be discounted altogether as conditions for meaning. This notion completely negates a Sensate point of view.

Indeed, the only way a Sensate society can appropriate it is to conclude that every social structure is constructed around specific material conditions and excludes people whose conditions are different. No moral consensus appears to be possible. Respecting people's differences becomes a matter of tolerating any life choice as valid and valuable.

Moreover, the idea arises that having a moral perspective is impossible to a material being. One sees this philosophy afloat on the tide of culture in those cults that believe the body is a mere container for consciousness and in popular ideas about the intercession of angels.

Developing Extraverted Judgment

When INJs are defending themselves against unconscious Sensate motives, they start out by resisting others' conceptual boundaries. Gradually, however, their inferior Extraversion becomes apparent. The more their behaviors are colored by unconscious Sensate aims, the more they're aware of themselves as different from others. Such types want people to see them as special, but they often feel insecure and unappreciated.

Their unconscious Sensate impulses fill them with a yearning for

Calvin and Hobbes   by Bill Watterson

credit and recognition, but they may be increasingly critical of their opportunities to make a contribution or so dissatisfied with their efforts that they don't share them with others. This is generally the point at which the type's tertiary function, Introverted Thinking or Introverted Feeling, steps in.

As discussed in other chapters, our tertiary function is helpful and enriching when our secondary function is well developed. It provides an outlet for "the other side" of our personality. For example, it prompts INJs to recognize that truth can be appropriated experientially as well as conceptually as a way of being, one that they feel in their senses and their bones.

As a last-ditch defense against unconscious Sensate impulses, however, Introverted Judgment simply convinces INJs that they have no need to establish an investment in their outer situation. The real truth is the complicated inner stuff that can't be put into words because it's connected to everything else that matters to them.

The more INJs try to protect their inner world, the more they lose the Intuitive perspective they're trying to maintain. They lose their capacity to shift perspectives. They have the sense that truth is a core experience, archetypal, impossible to express in a way that captures its full significance. Their vision becomes a psychological castle and they stand in the highest parapet, warning people that they aren't worthy to come in.

It should be emphasized that INJs who feel like this aren't hiding from the outer world. If anything, unconscious Sensate impulses are generating undue interest in how they look to others. The problem is the type's inability to deliver what's gestating inside. It's too large, too unformed; it won't survive in the world if it's cut off from the INJ's Intuitive nourishment. The only way they know how to witness to it is to point out the poverty of others' positions, showing how they fall short of understanding. Such types may become so adept at this that people see them as oracles and prophets. But they don't really have a positive vision of their own.

When INJs develop Extraverted Judgment and train it on themselves, they begin to see life differently. They recognize their need to be understood, to make a genuine connection with others, to be a contributing part of something outside themselves. This recognition short circuits the INJ's focus on conceptual boundaries. Such types try to *reach* people instead, to formulate their ideas in light of what others believe and think and cherish. In the process, they find a way to bring their insights into the larger community.

INJs don't find it easy to make this effort. But developing secondary skills is always difficult; it forces compromises we don't want to make. For INTJs, saying things in a way that people can support and accept feels like selling out or watering down something important. For INFJs, it feels like being inauthentic and hypocritical. Extreme types may even believe they still need to figure out who they are and shouldn't be influenced by others' expectations.

The irony is that INJs figure out who they are *by way of* Extraverted Judgment. It's the attempt to give their insights outward form that ultimately shapes their social identity. Unless INJs find a way to honor their Intuitions in the public arena, they won't recognize themselves in the feedback they get from others. Even if they've been highly successful in their outward pursuits or spent many happy hours in solitary pastimes, they're likely to feel unfulfilled.

Once INJs are relating to people (rather than counseling them or analyzing their frame of mind), they recognize how different perspectives can be bridged by common ideals. Well-developed INJs are capable of unusual empathy on this basis. They may see, for example, how widely divergent political positions are derived from the same moral principle. Psychologist James Hillman speaks about psychological polytheism—the separate selves existing inside us, anchored by the soul.

Such philosophies are not social plans. They're descriptions of an interior point of view that enables a person to respect diversity without compromising important social values. INJs are often moved to write about interior perspectives—how they're cultivated, the power they have to change society, what they feel like when they're operating. Given a facility with language, INJs can be highly gifted in this area.

Such types also realize that some Intuitions will not bear fruit in a particular time and place. Sometimes the only responsible decision is to keep them alive and pass them down to the next generation. This is a hard notion in a culture that values the gratifications of the present moment, but INJs often make a difference whose consequences they will never see.

INTJ: Introverted Intuition/Extraverted Thinking

INTJ	
dominant	Introverted Intuition
secondary	Extraverted Thinking
left-brain alternatives	Introverted Sensation
	Extraverted Feeling
right-brain double agents	Introverted Thinking
	Extraverted Intuition
tertiary	Introverted Feeling
inferior	Extraverted Sensation

Because INTJs rely on Extraverted Thinking for their dealings with the outer world, they often have a scientific, somewhat skeptical approach to reality. They want to know how things work and what they're likely to do under varying circumstances. Impatient with wasted motion, words, and emotion, their outward demeanor may be difficult to read.

Indeed, an INTJ's bearing can seem downright Vulcan. The Vulcans, of course, are a fictional people in the *Star Trek* series—resolute logicians who barely change expression or use body language, even when they're puzzled or aware of danger. Thus, one might heed the words of Tuvok, the Vulcan tactical officer on the spaceship *Voyager*, who warns: "Exterior composure is no indication of a Vulcan's inner state."

Although they superficially resemble Extraverted Thinkers, INTJs are always guided by their Intuition. They are rarely committed to general assumptions about rules, laws, and hierarchy, and they may have an acerbic or wry sense of humor about such things. INTJs will use what works in the service of their ideas; and they will quickly discard or change what doesn't.

A (probably apocryphal) story tells of a delegation of sailors who went to the tribunal of the Inquisition in the seventeenth century, when the Catholic Church had forbidden the use of Galileo's astronomy as an affront to the Bible's account of creation. The sailors sheepishly confessed that Galileo's theory had both simplified their journeys and made their maps more accurate. They hoped that the Inquisitors would exempt mariners from the church's proscription against it. The tribunal considered the problem, consulted with the bishops, and sent an emissary to the pope. Finally, they conceded. They said, "OK, if the theory works, use it. *But don't believe it.*"

This is a pretty fair description of the INTJ's basic attitude. Fundamental truth is something different from expressed knowledge, which is always a fiction of one sort or another. If a theory works, it doesn't matter who supports it or what anyone thinks it means. If it doesn't, why bother with it?

Although both INTJs and ENTJs realize their Intuitions by way of rational criteria—principles, law, organizational structure, and so forth—ENTJs will not usually pursue a goal unless it strikes them as compatible with reason. INTJs are more classically Promethean. They will steal fire from the gods without any assurance that a reasonable hearth exists at which to tend it back home. For such types, knowledge is not information, but a way of looking at things.

Consider James Hillman's understanding of the soul as "a perspective rather than a substance, a viewpoint toward things rather than a thing itself." This is a typically INTJ antidefinition. Such types may expend a great deal of time attempting to winnow the actual logic of accepted theories and formulations from expedient or merely limited assumptions.

INTJs are accordingly drawn to science, mathematics, and medicine—fields in which new ideas about reality are constantly being forged and tested logically. They may also take an interest in psychology, theology, publishing, and linguistics. As they pursue their intuitions, they inevitably combine elements from varied fields, perceiving an underlying commonality of form or meaning.

This sense of underlying structure and meaning leads INTJs to value both elegance of form and subtlety of expression. Nothing exists that can't bear reediting and paring down to its essential components. The connections INTJs perceive among very different areas of knowledge may be sufficient to convince them they're headed in the right direction, even when they can't explain what they're after.

Like the ISTJs, INTJs cannot accept new information until they relate it to their inner world. However, ISTJs analyze new data by aligning it with what they already know. Once they've accepted a fact, it becomes part of their identity. INTJs explore information largely by rejecting its influence—examining it from other perspectives and determining its limitations.

Because this inner process is tied to their sense of self, INTJs can take a long time to figure out "who they really are." Their need to find "what's missing" from a system of information invariably takes them into their own mental world—to an imaginative reconstruction of ideas—and the effort necessarily becomes a search for part of themselves. Such types can develop the destructive habit of formulating their identity in terms of their ability to see a situation's limits, needing to find the flaws that will allow them to become spectators rather than performers.

For this reason, others don't usually recognize the need of the average INTJ for external structure. INTJs are invariably described as independent and self-motivated, and this is certainly true with respect to their strongest functions. Where technical and intellectual competence are concerned, INTJs have a kind of inner compass, and they prefer a situation in which they don't have to coordinate their work with or report to someone else.

Moreover, they don't take criticism of their ideas personally. Position, title, and reputation have no meaning for these types. They will not entertain another's judgment of their worth unless they believe the person intellectually qualified to make the assessment. And even a legitimate judgment will usually strike them as an indication of the other person's assumptions and expectations.

Personal relatedness, however, is a different matter. INTJs are much less confident in a purely social situation. It is no exaggeration to say that their primary relationship is to their inner world, and they will nurture that relationship at the considerable expense of social abilities and the art of compromise.

In a field that excites and interests them, they are often driven, and they tend to expect the same degree of investment from subordinates. They frequently convey impatience when a situation that had seemed impersonal and outwardly predictable suddenly requires free-form personal interaction.

INTJs don't like to say something more than once, and they may cut others short when conversation strikes them as unnecessary. Moreover, their need to find an alternate point of view in order to understand something can sound like disagreement or negativity—as though the speaker's ideas had been judged and found wanting. Thus, even people who know an INTJ well may believe the person is either indifferent to them or critical of them.

INTJs can also be lonely behind their reserve, not knowing how to fit in even when they want to be included. This aspect of the type is partly the result of the INTJ's comparative rarity. At 1 percent of the population, INTJs are usually the only one of their kind in a family. Throughout grammar and high school, they are often the only such type in a classroom.

Although this ratio changes at the college and graduate level, when INTJs specialize in fields that appeal to other INJs, for most of their developing years, these types have good reason to feel different from others. Because they relate to the outer world with Extraverted Thinking, they generally interact by trying to determine the logical relationship of others' views and demands to their own needs. Consequently, they get little experience in areas of relationship that don't interest them.

Many such types become articulate quite early, and they use their verbal abilities to fend off involvement in anything they don't understand or don't wish to do. However, their awareness of others' feelings does not keep pace with their verbal abilities. Young INTJs may be intellectually precocious but emotionally immature, exercising their dominant function by distancing themselves from others, engaging in ironic comments and somewhat juvenile sarcasm.

Sometimes, to their surprise, their observations make people laugh and afford them the group approval they were attempting to preempt. INTJs rather enjoy the paradox this sets up and will play to it—experimenting with the boundaries of humor itself. One might consider comedian Dennis Miller, who presents himself as a caustic observer and occasional saboteur of the images and conventions on which his livelihood depends.

Like all types, INTJs resist their least-developed functions and attempt to avoid situations in which they'll come into play. It should be granted, however, that Sensation and Feeling, the INTJ's weakest functions, cannot be avoided wholesale in the course of a normal human life. These functions are our means of concrete embodiment—our physical pleasures and desires, our emotional connections with others, our love of home and hearth, our sense of being grounded and real.

INTJs appreciate these things well enough, but more in the abstract than in the messy realities of everyday existence. Regarding most events as arbitrary arrangements of elements, to be dismantled and reassembled at will, they may find it difficult to assume the duration of another's affection or interest in them.

In general, these types deal with feelings the way they deal with ideas—by formulating and explaining them to themselves so they know what to expect, or getting far enough outside them to resist their influence. In an INTJ's mind, friendships require a particular kind of investment; sexual connections another; marriage another. Such types want to know which category they're dealing with before they get involved.

But real relationship is unpredictable, and real people resist the categories the INTJ attempts to apply. In fact, sexual attraction and romantic infatuation usually catch these types by surprise. And although they enjoy the distinct pleasures of sensuality, the careening roller coaster of emotions that comes with the territory ultimately forces them to use their inferior functions.

As opposed to their usual view of reality as arbitrary, they begin to experience the influence of primitive Extraverted Sensation and feel an anxious sense of material possession. They feel impulsive, out of control, and unable to take anything for granted. They worry that their intellectual life will never get back on track until the relationship becomes more ordinary and settled. Ultimately, they attempt to regain control—by pressing for declarations and permanency, even if their own intentions aren't clear to them yet, or by using their critical judgment to distance themselves from their emotions.

INTJs appreciate the security of a committed relationship, and given the ratio of Extraverts to Introverts in our culture, often marry Extraverted types. They enjoy their families and maintain an unusual respect for the individuality and independence of both spouse and children. However, they may not sustain the kind of Extraverted interaction their partner expects.

They're more likely to settle in and, at their first opportunity, reassert their primary relationship to their inner world. This is true of both male and female INTJs. When there is too much outer stimulation or conflict, INTJs lose touch with their intuitive process and become restless, bored, and emotionally exhausted. Thus, INTJs need a fair amount of time alone.

They also need a fair amount of intellectual challenge and exercise. If a partner can't provide it, INTJs are likely to seek it privately or with others. The same INTJ who gets bored at parties and looks around for the nearest bookshelf may well forget to eat or sleep when involved in a complex and intricate conversation about ideas. In fact, for an INTJ, the communion of like minds is a kind of cerebral analog to falling in love.

INTJs may even resist concomitant physical attraction to a kindred spirit for fear of compromising the relationship with the exigencies of chemistry and social expectation. Such types frequently envision an ideal way of life that would unify NTJ cerebralism with SFP physical immediacy, but in actual practice, they are most likely to understand such unification as something ultimately spiritual. For this reason, INTJs may have an abiding interest in Sufism, or the Buddhist warrior philosophy, or the kind of mystical poetry that celebrates this idealized state in language.

Ironically, INTJs can best engage their Feeling and Sensate qualities by developing more Extraverted Thinking. The inner world of an INTJ is so compelling that such types can let their physical and emotional needs go for long periods of time. Deliberate use of Extraverted Thinking gives them more of what they need—a sense of rootedness in the material world: the world of bills, train schedules, medical and dental appointments, shoe repair, and the like. As the Zen Buddhists are wont to say, "After ecstasy, the laundry."

Extraverted Thinking also connects them to the assumptions and expectations of others, so they are better able to analyze people's expressions and behaviors for social cues. Many INTJs find, for example, that their career ambitions push them into developing a serviceable repertoire of behaviors that convey goodwill and put people at ease. Ultimately, these behaviors are more predictable than the abstract categories of relationship INTJs are inclined to devise.

When Extraverted Thinking isn't working well enough, INTJs draw directly from their tertiary function, Introverted Feeling, which merely rationalizes and supports their worst tendencies. It encourages them to idealize their abstract ideas about life and to avoid real relationships as unworthy of their investment. Such INTJs are often credited with staying above the emotional fray of life, when they have actually never been in it.

INFJ: Introverted Intuition/Extraverted Feeling

INFJ	
dominant	Introverted Intuition
secondary	Extraverted Feeling
left-brain alternatives	**Introverted Sensation**
	Extraverted Thinking
right-brain double agents	**Introverted Feeling**
	Extraverted Intuition
tertiary	Introverted Thinking
inferior	Extraverted Sensation

Because INFJs use Extraverted Feeling to relate to the outer world, they may seem more outgoing than they really are. Their personal approach and ability to find common ground with others combines with their Intuitive need for innovation and alternative views, and they frequently find themselves in positions of authority. They may not seek leadership, but they are often elected by others to serve on boards and committees. People appreciate their ability to listen and to consider group feelings and values.

Thus, it should be recognized that INFJs are more like INTJs than they initially appear. Their primary relationship is to their inner world, and they are receptive to others only up to a point. Indeed, these types often find that their sympathy and perceptive listening have been mistaken for an overture of friendship, which they didn't intend.

The truth is that Introverted Intuition inclines them to keep a part of themselves in reserve—to locate their true identity outside the expectations and definitions of others. Unlike INTJs, however, their sense of the unexpressed is not impersonal and causal; it is intensely personal and oriented by emotional awareness. Their Intuition takes them into psychological areas that other types are likely to keep at bay.

Because they don't usually know right away the import of what they're Intuiting, they may "go along" with a questionable situation until they can get hold of how they actually feel about it. This tendency can be confusing to others, and it is often misinterpreted as reckless experimentation.

Some INFJs work to develop their Extraverted Thinking function, attempting to bring order to their Intuitions, but they usually end up using their Judgment defensively—to assert their right to feel exactly what they're feeling as they're feeling it. Such types are quite articulate in their resistance to others' analysis of them, but they're also wounded by criticism and may hesitate to reveal themselves again.

Like INTJs, INFJs have a penchant for abstraction and symbolic representation. If they are interested, they excel in the fields of science, mathematics, and medicine. However, they are not generally motivated by sheer intellectual challenge. INFJs require a sense of meaning in the work they do.

They are more likely than INTJs to personalize their skills—as teachers, psychologists, consultants, ministers, and family doctors. They're particularly sensitive to others' feelings of exclusion, and they may address or try to rectify inequities of status or opportunity within the context of their profession.

Such types can be quite tenacious in pointing out the discrepancies between stated beliefs and actual behavior. This is the arena in which their Intuition is most evident. INFJs wrestle all their lives with the conflict they perceive between maintaining harmonious relationships and expressing emotional truth, and it is a central issue in the books, novels, plays, and psychological articles that INFJs write. Their 1 percent representation in the population belies the tremendous influence these types have in shaping cultural ideas about identity and being true to oneself.

INTJs usually appreciate the interface of science and mysticism, but INFJs are genuine romantics. They can't help but Intuit the individual emotions and visions that lie outside the standard canons of generalized knowledge—in literature, in art, in history, in any area of expressed truth. They are frustrated, sometimes infuriated, by cultural myths that come in the guise of objective fact, forcing people into stereotyped behaviors, compromising their autonomy.

Thus, INFJs are exquisitely sensitive to nuance and suggestion—all the ways we unwittingly express how we feel, who we are, what we believe about ourselves and others. They are not interested in the precision of language, as INTJs are, but in its rich possibilities for metaphor and multiple layers of meaning. They often have a gift for verbal imagery or poetic expression, and they are sometimes capable of raising to consciousness something that others can only dimly sense. If INTJs value elegance of form, INFJs value the art of allusion—the current of shared experience that flows beneath our varied signs and symbols.

INFJs frequently express themselves indirectly, depending on unstated implication to carry their meaning, and they can be put off by too direct a reference to something that is of great value to them.

They much prefer a glance, a sign, a hint, a story, or a shared symbol to a clear-cut description. They may envision a perfect relationship in which thoughts and moods are so perfectly aligned as to constitute a communion of souls.

This ideal is understandable, given the complex nature of the INFJ's inner life. Because INFJs are so alert to the unsaid, they may find it difficult to sort out their own emotions from the moods and feelings they discern in others. Young INFJs, in particular, are sometimes labeled hypersensitive or melodramatic, because their self-experience is tied to others' emotional boundaries. Such types can be overwhelmed by the task of finding their own personal truth. Because they have a strong need for approval, they can feel literally split between their Feeling and Intuitive motivations.

Ultimately, that split strikes them as a fundamental condition of being human—echoed in the polar nature of conscious awareness. They may experience themselves, in this regard, as the breach in a divided kingdom, locating in their inner lives both the heights and degradation of emotional experience, unable to reconcile good and bad, false and true, male and female, flesh and spirit, and so forth. Optimally, they bring their emotional insights into the community as art, or they use them to help others come to terms with conflict in their own lives.

INFJs are also capable of turning their inner experience into trenchant social commentary—by finding their truest voice and using it, perhaps in the ministry, or in the kind of edgy comedy of a Richard Pryor. Types who do this can become a potent focal point for others' unexpressed fears and yearnings. However, the pressure of speaking one's own truth in a public forum is ultimately taxing for most INFJs.

The INFJ's sense of physical well-being is very much allied with their relationships and emotional investments. They want very much to be liked, but they're afraid of being hurt, and they often develop a sense of humor that helps them to maintain a wide range of friendly contacts. For example, they're likely to exchange jokes and stories by e-mail with a large number of people they seldom see.

Indeed, such types are by turns highly sociable and maddeningly inaccessible. They need a meaningful outlet for their sense of meaning and import—and they often find it in some form of creative work. A colleague, attempting to describe the frustrating behavior of his INFJ son, says that having pushed the boy to mow the lawn, instead of compliance, he received a brilliant poem describing the anger the boy felt at having been coerced. This is by no means unusual of the type.

INFJs have to find some way to sort out their feelings from the feelings of others—if not in writing or art, then in an expression of religious faith, or the effort to help others to express themselves. If they can't find a way to Extravert what they're Intuiting, they tend to cultivate an intricate and deeply felt fantasy life that means more to them than the real people who care about them.

Like INTJs, INFJs have a tendency to use their secondary function for protection—for example, to distance themselves from a relationship that demands too much of them emotionally. They are entirely capable of meeting the expected surface demands of a situation, all the while nursing secret criticisms of a partner or a friend.

INFJs need to watch that tendency, because as soon as they feel emotional distance, they begin to turn away and look for something new. Not that they will literally leave a committed relationship. They go through the motions of life, but inside the mind, they've mounted the dappled horses of imagination and are surveying inner kingdoms.

For example, a well-loved but somewhat remote INFJ minister in my neighborhood spends most of his free time in his church office composing poetry that few people will ever appreciate, given its liberal use of puns in Greek, Hebrew, and medieval English. This is the kind of pursuit that encompasses both the INFJ's fascination with multi-level meaning and the typical INFJ conundrum—the romantic quest for a spirit so perfectly kindred it can be found only within.

In general, these types do create their own reality, and it is one of great riches—a storehouse that artists, poets, and writers draw from for their material. However, if their inner life is not balanced with reality, they may feel so different from others that they become self-conscious and defensive. They may be drawn to dysfunctional people, romanticizing their ability to see something in them that others cannot see.

INFJs are a bit like Merlin, summoned by the voice of Nimue deep within the enchanted forest. The song they hear is calling them elsewhere, beyond the cultivated borders of common consensus. When they are able to use their Extraverted Feeling function well, they bring that song back into the public domain, finding a way to integrate it into the fabric of the community. INFJs who don't do this can get trapped, like the great wizard of Camelot, in a kind of enchantment that robs them of their very genuine powers of discernment and insight.

The Judging Functions

- ▲ Extraverted Thinking
- ▲ Introverted Thinking
- ▲ Extraverted Feeling
- ▲ Introverted Feeling

18

Extraverted Thinking

ESTJ and ENTJ Types

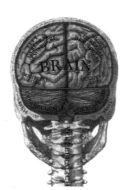

Left hemisphere

Dominant function
Extraverted Thinking

Secondary function
Introverted Perception

Right hemisphere

Tertiary function
Extraverted Perception

Inferior function
Introverted Feeling

▲ UNLIKE THE PERCEIVING FUNCTIONS, which encourage us to process sensory impressions as they occur, the Judgment functions are rational in operation. They prompt us to *organize* our sense impressions—by focusing on the ones that happen regularly enough to recognize and predict.

Although rational thought is usually discussed as a left-brain phenomenon, Judgment operates in both hemispheres, just as Perception does. Left-brain reasoning is more apparent because it depends on language—concepts and signs that tell us what things are and how they relate to each other. Right-brain reasoning is experiential and immediate, inherent in the situations in which it's operating.

Extraverted Thinking, the subject of this chapter, is a left-brain Judgment function. Like all left-brain functions, it gives us a conceptual, one-thing-at-a-time approach to life. It prompts us to notice sense impressions that are stable or occur regularly, so we can define them and focus on them as distinct objects and events.

Even the left-brain Perceiving functions, Introverted Sensation and Introverted Intuition, work this way. They encourage an awareness of sense impressions as they happen, but we acquire them as facts and ideas, one at a time, in light of what matters to us. The difference between these latter functions and Extraverted Judgment is that Introverted Sensation and Introverted Intuition are not rational.

In the inner Perceptual world, we need not organize acquired facts or determine their relationship to each other. It's in the outer world that the left brain requires predictability. Confronted with multiple objects in a sensory context, the left brain has to decide where to place its focus. To that end, it deploys Extraverted Thinking or Extraverted Feeling.

These functions enable us to make our knowledge systematic, so we have a basis for concentrating our attention. Extraverted Thinking is one way of creating this basis—an impersonal way. It prompts us to notice the qualities that objects have in common, and to use those shared aspects as a standard of sequential order. Whenever we Think, we're relying on such standards—to organize multiple objects and to establish logical relationships between them.

The process is as familiar as finding a name in a telephone directory. If we couldn't assume the logical relationship of each letter to others in the alphabet, we'd spend half our lives looking up a phone number. It's the same with celebrating a birthday. We're recognizing the logical position of a date in a calendar sequence of days and months.

Like all Extraverted functions, Thinking harmonizes us with general ideas about reality, so most of the standards of order we employ are collectively determined. Indeed, when collective Thinking standards are operating successfully, we take them pretty much for granted. We "know," for example, that letters run from A to Z, that numbers progress by tens, that a year has 365.24 days, that a day has twenty-four hours, that presidents have more power than vice presidents, that a high grade point average is better than a low one, and so forth.

It's natural to associate the capacity for reason with the conceptual systems we've learned to rely on. But this association can get in our way. Extraverted Thinking is a universal skill, and it need not lead to the systems of order we define as rational.

Of Logic and Letterman

Given the requisite neurological equipment, all humans are inclined to organize sensory experience by impersonal standards of order. The ability develops early, long before acquired concepts hammer it into a specific social shape. As soon as a child is coordinated enough to be the direct cause of a maddening effect—say, the clang of a spoon dropped from a high chair a few thousand times in a row—Extraverted Thinking is beginning to develop. The relationship between act and result is so utterly predictable that it suggests a fixed sequence of events—the idea that the same thing will occur with other kinds of objects.

This, properly speaking, is an exercise in logic—the discernment of a standard, or principle, that can be pried apart from its context and applied to a new set of objects. Long before we credit children with any capacity for scientific thought, they're determining the validity of the "dropped spoon" principle by setting up experiments—with a new vase in the parlor, for example, or an exceedingly tolerant cat. A great deal of our formative experience is devoted to cognitive exercises of this sort, by which we learn to distinguish logical predictability from so-called magical thinking.

The delight that accompanies successful experiments is not unlike the audience reaction to classic stunts on the David Letterman show, such as running over beer cans with a steamroller or pushing watermelons off the top of high buildings just to see what happens. Silly as they are, these routines are a nice illustration of the Thinking process.

When we Think in an Extraverted way, we're recognizing that certain principles of order are "always true." Letterman's routines

Mutts

Mutts. Reprinted with special permission of King Features Syndicate.

are funny because they're gleefully subversive, but also because their outcome is never in doubt. The only thing in question is how satisfying a mess an object is going to make when tossed out a window.

This tells us something else about Extraverted Thinking. Ultimately, the objects that illustrate our general principles are less important than the principles themselves. Even for a child, the spoon and the floor eventually lose their power to entertain. What's important is their relationship—the expectation we retain.

The entire house can blow away—utensils, high chair, kitchen, and all—but the relationship between the spoon and the floor endures, like a ghost in the mind. As we move from one context to another, a throng of such ghosts come with us, and we assess their possibilities for tangible embodiment.

One envisions the harried Letterman staff, week in and week out, locating ever novel material hosts for the same invisible idea—a bucket of chowder, a rotten pumpkin, a can of green paint. And one can see from the audience reaction how Extraverted Thinking ultimately portends a community. The people who watch the show regularly enough are united by the common vocabulary of the routine. They laugh because they know what to expect, and their expectations are confirmed definitively and viscerally.

Our societal Thinking vocabulary is more subtle, of course, but it works a lot like this. The principles "we hold to be self-evident" aren't really. They're ghosts, too. They're self-evident only so long as we translate them into material form and recognize their effects.

256

Thinking, in this respect, is not just a matter of acquiring a system and following the rules. It's an act of imagination. Left-brain imagination.

Right-brain imagination soars beyond the world as we know it. It issues in patterns untried by the fires of linear application. But left-brain imagination is always a compound of mind and matter. It has a kissing-cousin relationship to magic. It begins with an invisible intention and ends with material results.

When we Think, we're either extracting a logical relationship from its material context, turning it into a portable ghost, or we're translating our familiar ghosts into form in some new context. Either way, the process directly influences the structures we build, the aspects of reality that claim our attention, and the standards we count on for meaning and community.

The Collective Aspect of Thinking

Given the natural human ability to derive principles from predictable outward relationships, it should be clear that *every* culture uses Extraverted Thinking to establish structural expectations in its members. It doesn't matter whether a culture is literate, subscribes to the medical model, or keeps track of its finances. All humans make sense of their sensory experiences by relating them to principles they can count on.

Perhaps the quintessential illustration of the process is a prisoner, deprived of all other forms of identity and rational control, who scratches a crude calendar into the wall and charts the alternation of light and dark. Like the God of Genesis, he splits the inexorable tide of natural events into a sequence of predictable units, creating time and linear direction. Such things give us a way to manage what happens to us, to make plans, to establish routines, to know who we are with respect to our circumstances.

Even if a culture's ideas about the predictable are limited to the rising and setting of the sun, the phases of the moon, seasonal change, and distinctions of gender, the principles derived from these regularities ultimately shape a philosophy that portends an organized community. As far back as archaeology can reach, sexual icons, representing regular biological experience, have been used as an ideo-grammatic vocabulary to celebrate the foundation of order in the cosmos.

The "truth" of Extraverted Thinking, in this respect, is not its scientific accuracy but its rational utility. It doesn't matter that other cultures have conceptualized time, space, and seasonal progression differently than we do. Thinking can underlie theocratic stability as easily as it does technocratic change. The bottom line is that our Thinking principles are reliable enough to use as consensual bench-marks, thereby freeing us from the dictates of immediate experience.

Freedom's Just Another Word . . .

It may seem peculiar to describe principles as freeing one from immediate experience. From an Extraverted Perceiver's standpoint, freedom means the unfettered ability to *respond* to immediate experi-ence—the *absence* of structure and expectation. For Judging types, however, it's the absence of rational structure that traps us, forcing us to respond to things as they happen, to forfeit plans and goals, to depend on the bounty of fate.

This view is well illustrated by the comment of an INTJ seminary student, who was irritated by a classroom discussion about the Phari-sees. An ancient religious sect concerned with observing the law, the Pharisees are presented in the New Testament as foils for the Chris-tian message—as self-righteous generalists, more interested in peo-ple's surface behaviors than their interior life. Most of the students were expanding on the classic interpretation, but the INTJ saw things differently.

The Pharisees, he said, were forerunners of today's micromanag-ers. They weren't interested in surface behaviors. They were inter-ested in structural integrity. They were trying to shape a discipline certain enough to protect them from the clamor of the "ten thousand things." Without that kind of discipline, it's not even possible to develop an interior life.

Although the student's point reflects an Introverted Perceiver's understanding of Extraverted Thinking, it says a great deal about the kind of approach the function promotes. For TJs, freedom isn't the opposite of management. Freedom is management so adept that external reality all but takes care of itself.

Calvin and Hobbes   by Bill Watterson

Shifting Cultural Perspectives

The ability to adhere to a general principle of order, particularly when immediate experience inclines us to do otherwise, has traditionally been understood as evidence of character and self-discipline. In fact, Thinking types consider most forms of principled behavior as signs of integrity and respect for others—arriving on time, keeping one's promises, following through, playing by the rules, fitting into one's role, respecting the chain of command. Thus, when an ETJ's dominant identity reflects the structural expectations a society takes for granted, we regard these types as arbiters of moral obligation. We seek their advice, their counsel, their mentorship, their guidance.

As I've pointed out in other chapters, however, society has become increasingly oriented toward Perception, so that our ideas about Extraverted Judgment have changed over the last few generations. For one thing, we've become more aware of the biases enshrined in our impersonal principles.

Although standards of order are derived from observed qualities and behaviors, and hence are objective, they're also relative. For example, we can organize a rock collection in any number of ways—by size, by color, by age, by type, by name. Any of these qualities will

259

determine an objectively logical system. But each will result in a different sequence of order, which may be said to "favor" a different kind of rock. Choosing one over another will always involve subjective considerations—our sense of what matters.

ETJs can lose sight of this. As Extraverts, they accept the principles of order that exist, and their concern is to apply them. A Sensate society, however, will be acutely aware of limited options. The idea arises that the principles in force must coincide with the subjective self-interest of the people who rely on them.

For this reason, the marriage of a Thinker's dominant identity and traditional roles and institutions has come to look less like character and more like an attempt to maintain an accustomed power base. In one fell swoop, the ETJ can reduce an infinity of perceptual options to two: the way I do it or the wrong way.

One envisions media paradigms, two generations past, who reflect the strong association Extraverted Thinking once had with benign, institutionalized (male) authority: the Walter Cronkite–type news anchor; the straight-arrow cops who wanted just "the facts, ma'am"; all those Eisenhower-era patriarchs who knew best, whether they presided over a suburban family or a cattle drive on the old frontier. Within a generation, they'd evolved into the comically reasonable Dad on the *The Brady Bunch*, lost without his watch and his shoe trees.

Today, the movie remake of *Mission: Impossible* has no qualms about turning Jim Phelps, the highly principled task force leader from the late sixties' TV series, into nothing more than a self-serving double agent. Even Dana Scully, the responsible ENTJ pathologist on *The X-Files*, is cast as an overly rational skeptic, clinging to her FBI handbook and the scientific paradigms that tell her what should and shouldn't be done. The word *Scully* has passed directly into the pop lexicon as a verb that means to offer a conventionally logical explanation for an event that requires an open mind.

Extraverted Judgment in a Perceiving Society

Unquestionably, a Judgment-oriented society can be a conformist one, closed to information that lies outside its accepted framework of assumptions. Compensation from its Perceiving side becomes inevitable, and the result is a kind of cultural thaw— a spring wind that brings the possibility of change and new growth, the pleasure of experience for its own sake, opportunity for people whose potential has been overlooked or devalued. But a society oriented by Perceptual considerations has its own problems.

Perceiving functions make us aware of all the sense impressions available to us, but they give us no ability to set limits or to choose among our various options. Thus, one sure sign of our dependence on these functions is our understanding of life as a perpetual now, to be filled up with all the possibilities within our grasp. An information-saturated culture favors the right-brain penchant for improvising, skimming the surface, juggling multiple options and roles, and dispensing with niggling details for the sake of the larger picture.

In consequence, the balance of power has been shifting in our social institutions. A great many of our corporate executives and politicians are now ESPs and ENPs, impatient, opportunistic, constantly in motion. The ETJ's inclination to assess, evaluate, and finish one project before starting another has come to seem inflexible and too perfectionistic a method for getting enough accomplished.

But a principled approach to life, as suggested, involves more than outward structural stability. At bottom, Extraverted Judgment is a social language—a vocabulary that creates common ground, rights, and expectations among people whose life experiences may be very different. A society oriented by Perceptual priorities will be increasingly unable to appreciate these aspects of Extraverted reasoning.

As I've said in other chapters, a Perceiving society normally looks to Introverted Judgment for rational limits, emphasizing the effects of specific life experience. Well developed, however, Introverted Judgment has a wholistic character. It helps us to recognize that our immediate actions are an integral part of whatever exists, affecting it for good or ill. Thus, our moral decisions are being made at every moment, in light of our common human experience.

This idea has unmistakable power, and rightly so, but it's difficult to translate it into any kind of social vocabulary. Like all Introverted philosophies, it can be applied only by the person who holds it. It has come, however, to color the way society understands morality in general, creating disillusion with the more generalized Extraverted concepts of law and equal justice.

The students in my friend's seminary class, for example, clearly understood the Christian message from this Introverted Judging perspective, assuming that a concern with general standards of order is axiomatically hypocritical and beneficial only to the people who formulated them. As culture becomes more Perceptually oriented, the suspicion arises that Extraverted Thinking has no relationship to morality at all—that it's always a strategy for creating the right image, controlling people's behaviors, or enabling covert self-interest.

How Extraverted Thinking Really Works

In point of fact, dominant Thinking types usually have the opposite problem. They're so accustomed to *putting aside* their immediate interests for the sake of their principles that they lose sight of their own needs and priorities. They screen out so much direct information that their logic becomes theoretical. They lose touch with real life.

A real estate agent, for example, told me about an ESTJ sales representative who had accepted a two-year assignment at the local branch of his parent company. He was buying a house for the two-year period, and he had two mortgage options. One was variable, guaranteed at 7 percent for three years; the other fixed, guaranteed at 9 percent for thirty.

The agent naturally encouraged his client to take the variable mortgage. The 7-percent rate was guaranteed for three years, and the man was staying for only two. But the ESTJ insisted on taking the fixed rate—because it was the more responsible choice! He didn't want to take any chances. Rather than respond to a clear immediate advantage to himself, he held to his principles.

The ETJ's behavior can *look* self-oriented because these types will ignore *others'* immediate interests as well as their own. They don't trust exceptions to the general rule. Mitigating circumstances strike them as excuses, and they try not to take them into account.

The *Star Trek* franchise offers many episodes that deal with this aspect of Extraverted Judgment, because its Starfleet officers are, at bottom, military personnel, committed to a specific code of directives. Captain Kathryn Janeway, for example, in *Star Trek: Voyager*, is an unusually sympathetic portrait of an ETJ in conflict. The fact that this *Star Trek* series is the least popular of any is no surprise.

Janeway is in command of a lost ship, light-years away from home, helmed by a combination of Starfleet officers and renegade freedom fighters. Her task, in many of the episodes, is to recognize the value of the rebels' experience, as opposed to their credentials and training, which is not easy for her. She is also trying to enforce Federation rules among crew members who don't share Starfleet's assumptions about protocol.

As this series has unfolded, two things are worth noting. First, the Federation rules have, in fact, given the officers and the freedom fighters a common standard of order, despite their very different experiences and loyalties. Second, Janeway has come to recognize that her situation has no precedents. Federation directives could never have anticipated some of the crises she's had to resolve.

Thus, she's learned, very gradually, to take immediate events into account and to deal with them as they present themselves. Her first inclination remains, however, to maintain her principles—not because they support her position or keep people under control, but because they tell the crew what to expect from one another when nothing else is certain.

An even better illustration, because of its reverse morality, is Quark, the avaricious Ferengi barkeep in *Star Trek: Deep Space Nine*. The Ferengi are a business-oriented society whose transactions are guided by *The Rules of Acquisition*, a compendium of principles that require a good citizen to put profit above all else.

In one episode, believing he's about to die, Quark offers his body parts to the highest bidder. As it turns out, his health is fine. But now he has a problem. To break a contract ensures the loss of all his assets, tantamount to loss of identity.

Quark is confounded by the quandary. To fulfill the contract, he has to die. But to break the rules strikes him as thoroughly immoral. His integrity is at stake. Although *The Rules of Acquisition* support all manner of bribery, cheating, and dishonesty for the sake of self-interested profit, the idea of violating the rules themselves, even in the interest of self-preservation, gives Quark real pause.

And this is precisely the point. It doesn't matter how a culture or an organization conceptualizes its principles of order. Keeping faith with them always strikes a Thinking type as a matter of responsibility, honor, and knowledge of the "right" values. This is why ETJs need their secondary function, Introverted Sensation or Introverted Intuition—to recognize when immediate experience takes precedence over authorized procedures.

The ETJ Types

ESTJ		ENTJ	
dominant	Extraverted Thinking	dominant	Extraverted Thinking
secondary	Introverted Sensation	secondary	Introverted Intuition
left-brain	**Extraverted Feeling**	**left-brain**	**Extraverted Feeling**
alternatives	Introverted Intuition	alternatives	Introverted Sensation
right-brain	**Extraverted Sensation**	**right-brain**	**Extraverted Intuition**
double agents	Introverted Thinking	double agents	Introverted Thinking
tertiary	Extraverted Intuition	tertiary	Extraverted Sensation
inferior	Introverted Feeling	inferior	Introverted Feeling

ETJs represent about 18 percent of Americans. Toss in the Introverted TJs, who use Extraverted Thinking as a secondary function, and the number rises to one-quarter of the population. All but 6 percent of these TJs are STJs, which is one reason we tend to associate Extraverted Thinking with an investment in what already exists.

All ETJs have a strong sense of responsibility. They are not fuzzy about the principles they hold. They can articulate them, and they regard them as a basis for the kind of life they actually live. Knowledge, they might say, with Isaac Bashevis Singer, is a small island in a sea of nonknowledge. The integrity of that island strikes such types as a matter of personal obligation.

One might recall the "living books" in *Farenheit 451*—people who "became" the classics the government had burned by memorizing them and reciting them to others. As their memory failed, they trained others to take their place. ETJs are something like these "living books." They try to live up to the roles they play in society. They are faithful to the categories of knowledge they've received, and they're proud of their ability to fit themselves into a larger system and succeed on the terms specified. Such types have a great deal of momentum and direction in this respect.

ESTJs, prompted by Introverted Sensation, enjoy contributing to an existing organization, particularly when their ability to meet specified goals is recognized as superior. Such types depend on reason and analysis to deal with life, and they are careful about getting the facts they need in their area of expertise. In general, they support a "measure twice, cut once" philosophy of life.

ENTJs, by virtue of Introverted Intuition, are more likely to see around the corners of an existing structure. They are usually motivated to streamline goals or tactics, and they may be gifted in their ability to solve problems that require imagination. They are something like INTJs in this respect, but their sense of possibility doesn't take them as far afield of structural priorities. ENTJs want to create a better mousetrap; they don't question whether mice should, in fact, be caught.

Both ESTJs and ENTJs require the confirmation of hard evidence before they'll deal with a situation. To paraphrase Aristotle (perhaps the quintessential Thinking type), if you can't measure something, you can't predict its behavior, and hence it isn't real. This, admittedly, is a very loose paraphrase, but it's close enough. Aristotle's belief is echoed in the words of every ETJ physician who finds no measurable basis for a patient's chronic pain.

The bottom line is that reason can't be used to analyze the unknown. Unless one can determine the sequence in which one thing follows another or the functional contribution of a part to a whole, a situation is not a logical one and, to the Thinker's mind, probably doesn't exist.

ETJs reason quite literally in a step-by-step manner. Asked to explain one aspect of a problem, they will begin at the beginning and explain the entire linear process. Such types tend to plan and set goals even when they're doing something "for fun." And they are just as interested in "retrodiction" as they are in prediction. That is, they will analyze their actions after the fact, attempting to prepare for similar situations in the future.

Thinking versus Feeling

Although the Feeling functions are discussed in their own right in chapters 20 and 21, it's important to understand what motivates Extraverted Thinkers to see life differently from Extraverted Feeling types. Our everyday use of the words *thinking* and *feeling* can give us the idea that Thinking is rational in operation and Feeling emotional. But this stereotype doesn't hold where typology is concerned.

Thinking and Feeling are *both* rational functions. When they're Extraverted, they're left-brain functions, concerned with organizational structure and relationship.

▲ When we Think, we use an impersonal basis to organize objects, thus establishing logical relationships between them.

▲ When we Feel, we use a personal basis to organize objects, thus establishing their value and relationship to us.

As soon as we hear the words *personal* and *value*, we contrast them with rational objectivity, as though Feeling were a matter of immediate emotional reactions. But it isn't. Extraverted Feeling is a form of reasoning based on objective signs—the things we do and say to make our relationship to a situation manifest and predictable.

For example, in American culture, when a man wears a tie, we generally conclude that he considers the event important. The relationship between the sartorial display and the communication of respect is not logical. But it isn't emotional either. It's rational. It's a standard of Judgment that tells us how the man is related to the situation, that he appreciates its value.

Unlike Extraverted Thinking principles, Feeling standards are not portable ghosts. They can't be pulled apart from their context and applied to new situations. They consist of ritualized behaviors that we understand by way of cumulative social experience. This is why the attention of Feeling types is focused on people and what they do and say.

So Why Choose One or the Other?

Clearly, we all make use of both Thinking and Feeling vocabularies in the course of our lives. However, we usually have a decided preference for either impersonal or personal reasoning strategies. The question is, why?

The Body and the Body Politic Commonsense observation tells us that Feeling types are more expressive than Thinking types. They laugh and cry more easily, grow red when they're angry or embarrassed, are more likely to gesture when they speak. This is one reason they seem more in touch with their emotions.

Common sense, however, can take us only so far. Throughout history, Thinking types have been willing to die for the sake of their principles. Their capacity for emotional investment is no different from anyone else's. Thinkers differ from Feeling types in their *registration* of emotional effects. This is not a choice on their part. It's a biological distinction, and it makes for a different experience of reality.

When signs of emotion are visible to others, they're forms of communication. People notice them and respond to them, thereby giving them social meaning. This kind of interaction is our earliest form of structured experience. It helps to shape our values and our expectations. Over time, the visible components of our feeling states become harmonized with general ideas about appropriate and inappropriate behaviors.

Feeling types, whose emotions are readily apparent, depend on such interaction for their dominant approach to reality. They care about the effect they have on others, and they're aware of people's social behaviors—their meaning, their necessity, their worth, their appropriate or inappropriate nature. They're concerned to convey the right relationship to a situation and to let others know they're appreciated and valued.

This is why it's inaccurate to believe that Feeling standards reflect immediate emotional bias. They're an objective social language. It's entirely possible to use this language strategically, without "feeling" anything at all. However, FJs are more likely to jettison their "real" feelings if they're in conflict with the collective standards they're trying to maintain. Their first instinct is to keep faith with their social obligations, at whatever cost to themselves.

It should be noted that Perceiving types will also express a broad range of feeling states and are highly alert to the reactions of others. They don't, however, have the FJ's left-brain incentive to capture the predictable and use it as a general standard. For Perceivers, the beauty of feelings is their sheer unpredictability—their connection to immediate sensory experience.

How ETJs Deal with Feeling Issues

Thinking types, to whom biology has granted the luxury of emotional privacy, tend to rely on conceptual predictability for rational decision making. This doesn't mean that Thinkers are suppressing their emotions or don't have any. It means that experience doesn't educate them, as it does Feeling types, to set their goals by way of others' reactions to their expressive cues. So they're likely to associate displays of feeling not with caring and sensitivity but with the dependency of childhood and being out of control.

This is why ETJs ultimately have a hard time conveying their personal relationship to a situation. The social signs that tell Feeling types whether people value them or not aren't connected in an ETJ's mind with the inner states they're supposed to represent. Displaying them strikes the type as a form of playacting, and the results are never predictable in a logical way.

Herb and Jamaal

Herb and Jamaal. Tribune Media Services, Inc. All Rights Reserved. Reprinted with permission.

Women are usually socialized to recognize and use some Feeling standards in their relationships with others, whether they're Thinking types or not, but ETJs in general, both male and female, believe their intentions should be apparent in their consistency and discharge of responsibility. They won't make a promise unless they're ready to stand behind it, and once they've stated their objectives, they see no reason to say more—unless the situation changes.

This approach ensures, of course, that ETJs make few appreciative comments about a normal course of affairs. They're likely to be most expressive in their description of problems that need to be solved. They can, for this reason, appear to alternate between inexpressive neutrality and critical assessment. Ironically, both states indicate an ETJ's ongoing interest and involvement in a situation.

Such types are almost always surprised to find that others regard their analytical remarks as indications of anger or disapproval. Thinkers consider their thoughts quite separate from their emotional life. They don't use verbal exchange the way FJs do, as an attempt to establish common ground with others. They ask questions, describe things, examine them, criticize them, take a position.

In fact, notwithstanding others' experience of their aggressive verbal style, ETJs tend to believe they hardly ever get angry. This is because they associate anger with being out of control. No matter how sarcastic they get, or how cruelly they exaggerate to make a point, as long as they can reason verbally, ETJs don't feel out of control.

As Strong As Our Weakest Think

Because Extraverted Thinking encourages a problem-solving task orientation, ETJs are usually hard driving and driven, the classic workaholics. They are deeply invested in and identify with whatever job they've taken on. They may not leave much room for "play," but they do enjoy socialization and recreation, particularly when it intersects with traditions in the family or community.

They aren't drawn, like Extraverted Perceivers, to play for its own sake. They tend, rather, to explain to themselves why they're doing what they're doing—getting some exercise, furthering a relationship, visiting family, seeing the sights, taking a break from routine. It is this need to justify what they do apart from their routine obligations that keeps ETJs from fully developing their secondary function, Introverted Sensation or Introverted Intuition. They tend to mistake its subjective and irrational voice for emotional need.

As noted, Introverted Perception is a left-brain operation. It's compatible with and can broaden an ETJ's usual way of doing things. It gives the type access to new information—a means of recognizing ideas and potential that exist outside familiar categories of reference. But Introverted Perception conflicts with a Thinker's dominant attitude. It's supposed to. Coming to terms with this conflict is the way ETJs grow.

Thinking types are like surveyors, measuring the tides of experience against a fixed part of the social landscape. They need a way to get into the water and swim for a while. Introverted Perception helps them to do that. It suggests that outer reality has no fixed reference points. We make sense of life, as individuals, by recognizing what matters to us, what priorities we maintain even when circumstances change.

ETJs usually bump into their secondary function by accident—because a life crisis has forced them to reassess their rational principles. And it can plunge them into a crisis of faith. If there are no absolute standards, what is there? Exploring the question strikes them as dangerous. They don't want to be overwhelmed by subjective motives beyond their rational control.

But ETJs who resist their inner experience of life ultimately reach a state of imbalance. They're screening out too much information. Their least-developed function, Introverted Feeling, gets out of their control and begins to flood them with impulses that undermine their accustomed point of view. Because these impulses are unconscious, ETJs don't recognize them as part of themselves. They believe that other people aren't being logical or responsible enough, obliging them to take control and be the grown-up.

As stated in other chapters, Introverted Feeling is a right-brain form of Judgment, immediate and subjective. Well developed, it fosters an inner moral compass—a recognition that everything we do affects a situation for good or ill. This wholistic perspective calls into question the ETJ's principled approach to life, which is guided by general rules, notwithstanding people's subjective value judgments.

Pressured by impulses in conflict with their accustomed strengths, ETJs feel threatened, as though someone were depriving them of their logical expectations. Like all types, they don't see this unconscious drama as part of themselves. They see it as part of their outward situation. For example, they may be frustrated by people who don't play by the rules, or people who want personal benefits without taking social responsibility. The needs of loved ones may strike them as disruptive, particularly if addressing them means modifying their priorities or changing their routines.

Such types can seem egocentric or insensitive, but their focus is squarely on their logical self-image. The problems they're noticing can't be solved with Extraverted Thinking, and as long as they're resisting other approaches, their only option is to defend the one they've got. They do this by eliminating, ignoring, or complaining about the things that can't be explained by or fit into their Thinking framework.

ETJs in this situation need more contact with their secondary function—the private motives that swim beneath the surface of their logic; their need for play and pleasure and creative dreaming. When they accept this part of themselves, they recognize that responsibility means more than striving for external goals; it means coming to terms with who they really are. ETJs who manage this don't take themselves so seriously, and they're better able to deal with the frailties and needs of others.

Without some access to their Introverted world, these types confuse being logical with being objective. They lose sight of the fact that an objective view would encompass both rational and irrational aspects of life. Indeed, Introverted Feeling gets so far out of their control that their logic is gradually compromised. They aren't weighing pros and cons and drawing reasonable conclusions. They know the right way and the wrong way to do almost everything.

Once they've reached this point, ETJs are dissatisfied most of the time. They can't relax. They feel that unless they're supervising, nothing will get done the way it should. The pressure of Introverted Feeling is so great that they turn to their tertiary function, Extraverted Sensation or Extraverted Intuition, to protect what's left of their accustomed self-image.

Like all tertiary functions, Extraverted Perception is helpful when ETJs are in touch with their secondary function. It prompts them to meet their physical needs, to have fun, to make room for their desires and appetites. As a last-ditch defense against Introverted Feeling, however, it keeps the ETJ's focus on the external world. It overwhelms the type with temptations on "the other side" of life—to run away, to rebel, to be self-indulgent, to be impulsive, to be irresponsible.

There is some irony in this, of course. ETJs resist their secondary (Introverted Perceiving) function because they're worried about the consequences of irrational thoughts and ideas. But their tertiary (Extraverted Perceiving) function ultimately pressures them to live out their irrational impulses, with no consideration of the consequences.

ETJs of this sort focus all their energies on maintaining their surface image as reasonable people. The FP traits that strike them as tempting, but potentially out of control, are projected onto people who depend on them. One can see this psychic dichotomy writ large in our traditional Extraverted Judging social vocabulary. It's in the stereotypes bedeviling people "dependent on the system"—welfare recipients, illegal aliens. It's in the premise of those popular books that describe men as Martians (hardworking, logical, and linear) and women as Venusians (play oriented, childlike, unfocused).

It's important to recognize that extreme ETJs need not fit our more contemporary stereotype of the social or political conservative. There are more than enough hooks in society on which to hang disowned FP traits and keep them under control. Projection has its limits, however.

The ETJ's Judging and Perceiving worlds can become so polarized that the type is actually living two different lives—productive and principled in public but surprisingly amoral in private. This dichotomy is built into so many of our social expectations (for example, about workweek versus weekend behaviors) that we don't think about it until it involves a serious discrepancy between surface image and private reality—say, when a pillar of the community is revealed to maintain a decidedly unprincipled sideline interest.

Such people generally protest, when their private pursuits come to light, that they've done a good job professionally and should be judged only on that basis. The choices they've made on "the other side" of life are no one's business but their own. Extraverted Perceivers tend to focus on this kind of ETJ, because it confirms their own ideas about the hypocrisy of Judging behaviors.

Developing Introverted Perception

In the film, *The Last Wave*, a highly principled Australian attorney is drawn into a case involving tribal Aborigines, whose understanding of legal obligation is very different from his own.

"But surely," the attorney says, "you believe that man is greater than the law."

"No," his Aboriginal client tells him, "the Law is greater than just man."

Dominant Thinkers are not unlike the attorney. They recognize principles as necessary to human organization but regard them as servants of the human will. Such types usually run into their secondary function by surprise, while they're "busy making other plans." Life deals them a hard blow, which they're unable to master with logic, so they come to terms with Introverted Perception unhappily, recognizing that principles have no absolute force against the genuine unpredictability of being alive.

Plunged unexpectedly into an experience larger than themselves, forced to take things as they happen, ETJs may recognize the opportunity to make peace with the inner self, which knows how to let things be. For example, they may see, for the first time, that unfamiliar situations can bring out the best in them. Or they may realize that other ways of structuring life are not only possible but more realistic, and require less directed energy.

ETJs who get in touch with their secondary function gradually see the Aboriginal client's point. The universe is lawful, but archetypal Law doesn't correspond to human ideas about what is and is not rational. Experience irrelevant to our impersonal goals can be ignored or set aside, but it's part of life, and it has real-life consequences that must, inevitably, be taken into account.

This recognition can wake ETJs up to a very different kind of world. When they aren't trying so hard to keep their circumstances conformed to their logic, they find, to their astonishment, that life is not out of control. Rather, the paths they chart keep logic in contact with circumstances as they exist. Such types have no need to rush in to solve others' problems. Their principles inspire others and help to build real communities, making the best of people's potential.

Developed ETJs are genuine teachers. They have an unshakable sense of security and self-understanding, and they know how to laugh at themselves. They're clear-eyed and realistic. We seek them out for advice and guidance—not because they'll prescribe the "right" behavior, but because they have integrity. Their vision incorporates all the elements of a situation and is legitimately without bias.

ESTJ: Extraverted Thinking/Introverted Sensation

ESTJ	
dominant	Extraverted Thinking
secondary	Introverted Sensation
left-brain alternatives	**Extraverted Feeling**
	Introverted Intuition
right-brain double agents	**Extraverted Sensation**
	Introverted Thinking
tertiary	Extraverted Intuition
inferior	Introverted Feeling

ESTJs see reality as a kind of puzzle whose pieces must fit together logically if they are to understand the whole picture. They have an incisive understanding of organization and complexity. Theirs is not, however, the nuts-and-bolts approach to life that characterizes a born technician. ESTJs reason conceptually, one step at a time. The problems that absorb them are too complicated to be solved by common sense or intuition. They require the negotiation of structural relationships by way of logic.

ESTJs observe facts, draw tentative conclusions, predict what will happen next, then check their predictions against real-life consequences. Anything that can't be proved by hard evidence is ruled out. In the inimitable words of Sherlock Holmes, "When you have eliminated the impossible, whatever remains, *however improbable*, must be the truth."

ESTJs generally want their abilities to be useful to others. They're like ISJs in this respect. However, they don't have the ISJ's self-experience as a rescuer or caretaker. ESTJs see themselves more as advocates—people whose position and knowledge permit them to represent a system and to negotiate its structure for others. Such types may be administrators, salespeople, lawyers, public officials, business managers, detectives, financial advisors, teachers, investigators, and so forth.

Although ESTJs need interaction with people, they're not group oriented in the way ESFJs are. They don't want to make their plans in terms of others' ideas and approval. They want to play their part in a larger system and be accountable for meeting their objectives. When they socialize, their conversation tends to be impersonal and factual—about the work they do or information that strikes them as interesting.

Such types have a strong sense of principle. They know what they believe about how things should happen, and they try to live according to the rules they've set for themselves. Unlike Introverted Thinkers, they're not interested in purely abstract reasoning or speculative theories that can't be practically applied. For example, they may discuss the pros and cons of a potential strategy, but they want the analysis to culminate in a concrete decision that makes sense to them and meets their standards.

ESTJs think hierarchically. They define their priorities and attend to them, one by one, in descending order of importance. They understand the value of the proper chain of command. They want to know where they stand in the assessment of others, and they want this standing to be deserved.

For ESTJs, people are like buildings: The deeper the foundation, the higher they can go. Progress is earned by the hard work one invests, and it's always a step-by-step affair. Each stage requires the genuine mastery of defined tasks and is marked by specific rewards. To skip a step or to be rewarded for merely personal reasons strikes them as unfair and a potential threat to the system as a whole.

Because they think in terms of organizational structure, ESTJs are able to put aside their immediate interests for the sake of a principle or procedure. They can make and act on hard decisions that require personal sacrifice. This is one reason ESTJs have traditionally been in managerial positions in Western society. They gain people's cooperation by earning their respect and making them feel safe and contained. No matter how lousy they feel or how hard the snow is falling, they can be counted on to show up and do their part.

It should be noted that ESTJs are inclined to assign higher priority to impersonal obligations than to personal ones. Their impersonal responsibilities are usually to an organized social system, whereas affective priorities strike the type, inaccurately, as self-oriented, and they're accustomed to putting aside subjective interests for the sake of collective demands. Accordingly, a partner may accuse them of being incapable of showing or acting on their feelings.

In general, they believe their investment and consistency in maintaining a personal relationship are evidence enough of their emotional commitment. On the other hand, these types can be quite sentimental about the personal traditions of a family or society—birthdays, holiday get-togethers, rites of passage, and so forth—which have a strong collective aspect and can be justly treated as high-priority affective obligations.

In general, ESTJs are cautious about sharing their personal life unless they feel close to someone. They are also cautious about physical proximity. They tend to associate physical contact somewhat indiscriminately with an infringement of personal boundaries, which may be either violating or arousing—or a combination of the two. A casual touch on the hand or a shared hug of victory can be awkward for them.

ESTJs are probably most comfortable in relationship when they're sharing their knowledge or using it on behalf of another. They may relate best to their children, for example, when they're helping them with homework, showing them how to do things, or clearing a path for and supporting their career ambitions. They're frequently drawn to the camaraderie of teaching and mentoring. Retired ESTJs will often train the people who follow them and enjoy advising others who are starting out in the same profession.

In truth, the identity of these types is tied to what they know how to do, and they may need to work or teach in order to feel "like themselves." Those ESTJs who elect to be homemakers are likely to systematize and run a highly efficient household. All such types can experience a serious "loss of self" if they discover that their knowledge is no longer useful to others.

ESTJs don't have the determined need of ESTPs to know something before everyone else does. They want to know enough to stay on top of their game. If the parameters of a profession change, they may resist starting all over again at the "entry level" of how-to knowledge. They may try to find a place for themselves where they can continue to do what they know best. However, once they realize that ideas or procedures are becoming an accepted part of the "system," ESTJs will generally adjust and stay with the collective flow.

People sometimes take the ESTJ's gradual approach to change for an investment in the status quo, as though such types didn't want to try anything new. But ESTJs are not conservative by temperament. Like all J types, they need a sense of the predictable before they act. They won't embark on a quest until they have a plan that's likely to work. The only way to make such a plan is to base it on what they know—the facts they can count on, the experience they really have.

Once they've mapped out the territory between intent and objective, ESTJs become resourceful and inventive. They're excited and inspired by the challenges of implementation. If a new device will do the job, they'll try it. If something doesn't work, they'll drop it. If they can't find the right tool, they'll fashion a makeshift one out of what they have on hand.

This isn't improvisation so much as a matter of directed focus. ESTJs are persistent, patient, and able to gather all their energies in the service of the task they're working on. They divide projects into a series of steps, and they complete each one in turn.

This is one reason ESTJs dislike being interrupted in the middle of a project. They lose their momentum. They also lose their place. Once distracted, they can't return to their stopping point and begin again. They have to regroup. They may go back and repeat the steps already taken, so they're sure they understand what the next step should be.

The ESTJ's systematic approach is of inestimable value in the impersonal realm, particularly when an enterprise requires that nothing important be left to chance. The type can run into problems, however, when others' priorities are in conflict with the ones they've established. The classic stereotype is the ESTJ who has organized a vacation trip in advance and is frustrated by the unpredictability of the real experience.

It is in this respect that ESTJs can lose sight of options and possibility. They may hold with a predictable method of doing something simply because it has worked in the past, even if it isn't the most realistic or humane one under the present circumstances. Such types need to take in enough immediate data to keep their logic flexible and geared to situations as they really exist.

This is the purpose of their secondary function, Introverted Sensation, their best source of immediate subjective information. By using this function, ESTJs become aware of the data that lies outside their rational categories, some of which must be taken into account when they make their plans.

Like all Extraverts, ESTJs tend to believe their Introverted life consists of the impulses and desires left over once they've adjusted to the shape of a social role. These types, however, have a particular problem in this regard. They're motivated to ignore all aspects of life that can't be logically justified by their outward responsibilities.

As a result, ESTJs may dismiss experience that controverts their general ideas about what a situation's priorities are. They may ignore real-life problems that don't relate to their perceived obligations. They may not take others' personal or physical needs into account—or their own—until conflict in these areas forces their attention to matters of human or subjective welfare.

When ESTJs use Introverted Sensation only to support their Extraverted Thinking assumptions, they're inclined to mistake being impersonal and logical for being objective and realistic. As a result, their Thinking function becomes too narrowly focused. They lose sight of the variables that don't make rational sense to them.

The more impersonal and logical they try to be, the more they push the personal and subjective aspects of life out of awareness. Introverted Feeling, their least conscious function, gets out of their control, and it begins to work against their dominant position.

ESTJs who are flooded with the personal and subjective motivations of inferior Feeling usually respond by increasing their efforts to stay impersonal, logical, and in control. They stick firmly to what they know how to do. They don't realize how emotionally invested they are in the specifics of this knowledge. They become one-sided, and their careful systematics congeal into a penchant for perfectionism.

For example, they may not recognize when a task requires a "good enough" approach or even a "quick and dirty" one. They approach all situations with the same relentless attention to what they consider important. They literally don't see other options, and they may have little curiosity apart from their particular arena of expertise.

Ultimately, they draw from their tertiary function, Extraverted Intuition, which permits them to rationalize their imbalanced approach. It focuses their attention on the negative possibilities for action that conflict with their image of a reasoned way of life.

Such types experience a sense of conflict, but they see it as an exterior one. They worry about others' weakness and impressionability. They believe that people need them to take over and manage things for them. Indeed, they may keep others in a position of dependency, making decisions on their behalf, oblivious to needs or potential that can't be related to their particular understanding of life.

These extreme ESTJs don't experience themselves as controlling. They genuinely believe they're doing the right thing. They simply don't recognize the value of much beyond their own structure and resources. This unfortunately includes their own needs—insofar as they exist apart from their ideas about how things should be.

For example, such types may be starved for genuine personal contact, but their options for intimacy seem to exist apart from the rational framework they've set up for themselves. They may experience a division of self in this regard. Their tertiary function will encourage them to satisfy that hunger only perceptually—by overeating, drinking too much, or engaging in impulsive behaviors apart from their everyday routines.

For many ESTJs, life itself eventually forces a crisis of the secondary function. The type can, as Jung so nicely put it, coerce "the untidiness and fortuitousness of life into a definite pattern" for only so long. The so-called acts of God are always part of the fabric.

Moreover, an ESTJ who shuts out inner conflict is merely projecting it into the outer world, where it causes problems that can't be solved without a conscious Introverted perspective. Such types may, for instance, unwittingly push others to live out their inferior functions, and the resulting relational conflicts can shatter the ESTJ's illusions about partnership, family roles, or the institution of marriage.

When ESTJs recognize that their rational concepts fall short of real life, they are plunged into the experiential realm of Introverted Sensation, and they undergo a conflict of faith. This inner conflict is never entirely resolved. But ESTJs who accept it and wrestle with it gradually come into their own. They develop a sense of principle that goes beyond the aspects of life they know how to control and justify. They become realists in the true sense of the word—able to accept and take into account the irrational and personal aspects of life.

Well-developed ESTJs are more than advocates for an organized system. They are advocates for the sake of principle itself. They may find themselves standing with and for the real people a society's institutions are meant to serve. Their reason doesn't lock them into an impersonal, logical straitjacket. It gives them the ability to see the essential truth of any situation.

Such ESTJs have the courage of their convictions, which gives them a certain generosity of spirit. They know what they believe, they live their lives accordingly, and they are willing to stand for right against wrong, but they're also confident enough in the power of truth to be tolerant, allowing others the freedom to recognize it in their own time and in their own way.

ENTJ: Extraverted Thinking/Introverted Intuition

ENTJ	
dominant	Extraverted Thinking
secondary	Introverted Intuition
left-brain alternatives	**Extraverted Feeling**
	Introverted Sensation
right-brain double agents	**Extraverted Intuition**
	Introverted Thinking
tertiary	Extraverted Sensation
inferior	Introverted Feeling

Like ESTJs, ENTJs reason conceptually, with deductive and in-ductive logic. But these types are not content to negotiate structural relationships within a system. ENTJs want to be in charge of a system, to improve it, to realize its functional potential.

Such types are not advocates and administrators so much as natural leaders—decisive, charismatic, impelled by the courage of conviction, and able to manage power with confidence and determination. Their energy and ambition in the service of an idea can put one in mind of ENTPs. But ENTJs don't share the Perceiver's holographic visionary perspective. Like all types who use Extraverted Thinking, ENTJs need factual and material predictability for their skills to operate well, and their left-brain orientation gives them a ruthlessly linear approach to goals and decisions.

Given their common primary functions, ENTJs are most like INTJs in their process of thought. Both types are fascinated by the translation of mental concept into material form. INTJs, however, are oriented by the subjective, irrational, Perceiving viewpoint of Introverted Intuition. Such types are alert to the limits of a rational theory or vocabulary. They're driven to pull unexpressed possibilities into the existing framework.

ENTJs are oriented by the objective, rational, Judging viewpoint of Extraverted Thinking. They're alert to aspects of an organized system that have no functional purpose, and they're driven to rid the system of their influence. They're immediately aware of a discrepancy between a stated objective and the procedural strategies designed to bring it about. They can't tolerate wasted efforts, repeated problems, or the need to say something more than once.

It may be useful in this regard to note that the word *decision* comes from the same French root as the words *scissors* and *excise*. An ENTJ's decisions corroborate this etymological history. The intelligence of these types is incisively critical. They're almost compelled to point out an illogical premise or an unjustified conclusion and get things in rational order.

Like ESTJs, these types think hierarchically, but always with an eye toward appraisal and discrimination. Just as INTJs believe that nothing expressible can be finally true, ENTJs believe that nothing exists that can't be improved. One of my ENTJ college professors was consistently in trouble with the school's board of directors because he believed that no one could accumulate and use knowledge well enough to deserve an A +.

ENTJs have an abiding sense of their own authority, and they often find themselves in a position to lead. They don't push for direct control. They assume it, and people respond accordingly. A recent T-shirt slogan, "Team effort . . . is a lot of people doing what I say," pretty much covers their frame of mind.

Like ESTJs, they have the capacity to sacrifice everything to the realization of a plan. Their strength, their strategic ability, and their pragmatic approach to rules and policy (if it works, use it; if it doesn't, change it) motivates others to follow them—and to earn their respect. It should be granted, however, that ENTJs don't pay much attention to the effect they have on others in the emotional realm.

Of all the types, ENTJs are probably most inclined to separate the cerebral from the feeling level of life. A verbal exchange about ideas requires no basis in friendship and has nothing to do with liking or disliking someone. Verbal communication is quite flatly a means of knowledge and information. ENTJs can experience a kind of hunger for verbal input. They may have the sense that all the information in the world is available, can be sifted through, possessed, applied, if one just had the time and opportunity.

Their determined focus on the conceptual makes for a great deal of tolerance for alternate points of view. So long as a belief can be logically justified, the type will grant it validity and discuss it, without feeling any need to approve or disapprove its existence. It is the type's investment in logic itself that tends to be unyielding.

Indeed, these types have a deep investment in the precision of conceptual form. They are invariably articulate and aggressively verbal, and they discover quite early in life that the well-chosen phrase is a many-splendored thing: it convinces, dissuades, and wounds as well as communicates.

Young ENTJs quickly learn the utility of cold sarcasm to distance themselves from a situation that strikes them as unreasonable or not worth their time. And they're astonished by the power inherent in the form, because they themselves are nearly impervious to signs of criticism from others. Introverted Intuition gives them a sense of being outside the framework that determines people's ability to judge them accurately. They may even escalate the situation just because they can.

From an ENTJ's perspective, most people are illogical, and their opinions don't matter—except insofar as they determine the nature of our social assumptions. And it is here that the ENTJ's powers of analysis are usually trained—on the gulf between our Thinking-oriented system and people's actual capacity for Judgment.

It should be emphasized, in this respect, that ENTJs are motivated by the collective nature of their dominant function. Their focus is ultimately not on people's inability to Judge so much as on the possibility of improving the systems that enable people to Judge soundly and well. These types regard knowledge as power, and they have a genuinely democratic approach to its dissemination.

Like ESTJs, the identity of ENTJs is tied up in what they know how to do, and they generally need to work or teach in order to feel like themselves. These types are far more impatient than ESTJs, however, because they're driven by the concomitant need to set things right. They can have a hard time recognizing that others are motivated differently than they are and may need signs of praise, approval, and personal interest. They may even see these motives as a sentimental weakness that ought to be overcome.

The cutting edge for ENTJs is their tendency to dismiss the importance of direct experiences that don't meet their standards of principle or logic. The abstract nature of impersonal knowledge can move them to construct systems that are highly efficient but leave no room for human value. ENTJs need more input from Introverted Intuition than they're usually willing to entertain.

Because Introverted Intuition coincides with our Sensate society's least developed inclinations, ENTJs share with INJs the burden of the collective unconscious. However, where INJs can be pushed by society's imbalance into a compensatory use of their dominant function, ENTJs are more likely to deny the existence of Introverted Intuition in themselves. They associate it with its inferior use in culture at large—irrational ideas about how things are, for example, along with the suspicion that secret knowledge is being hidden behind "official" explanations for social policy.

Sometimes ENTJs will, in fact, maintain complicated conspiracy theories about why bureaucracies work the way they do. But most such types work hard to hold a line of defense against anything that can't be proved with hard evidence. They experience themselves as the last bulwark against a rising tide of inferior Perception, and their weapon of choice is Occam's razor, a rule in science that requires any explanation for the unknown to be attempted in terms of what is already known.

In truth, ENTJs need a way to get *outside* the terms of what they already know—not in order to entertain irrational theories of causality, but to recognize the value of experience that doesn't fit into their rational framework. If they use Introverted Intuition only for critical purposes, in the service of their Thinking approach, they gradually lose sight of any objective but conceptual mastery.

Like ESTJs, the more logical and impersonal ENTJs become, the less objective and realistic they are. Their least conscious function, Introverted Feeling, moves outside their conscious control, flooding them with motives they don't understand. ENTJs experience the resulting conflict as something that's happening to them, caused by others. For example, they may feel controlled by people's needs or expectations, or hampered by institutional inefficiency and authoritarianism. Ultimately, they begin to draw from their tertiary function, Extraverted Sensation, to keep their Thinking boundaries intact.

Like all tertiary functions, Extraverted Sensation is not well developed in these types. It can overwhelm them with impulses they normally keep at bay—encouraging, for example, a strong attraction to graphic images of perceptual and visceral intensity. Under most circumstances, ENTJs regard this side of themselves as potentially out of their control, and such impulses push them to hold more firmly to their dominant Thinking position.

However, because our culture has become increasingly Sensate, ENTJs are actually encouraged to live out this part of themselves, as though it were more "authentic" than the behaviors demanded by the social roles they've assumed. For example, there are any number of institutionalized programs and movements designed to push people beyond their logical perspective to "get in touch" with their "real feelings."

ENTJs who are resisting their secondary function are indisputably out of touch with their subjective perceptual side. However, a concerted effort to bypass their rationality and gain access to behavioral immediacy doesn't make them more aware of what they feel. It plunges them into their inferior functions. They're moved to act on primitive, unadapted Sensate impulses—as though authenticity of self required the translation of these impulses into direct behavior and they were strong enough to risk others' disapproval for the sake of personal truth.

ENTJs who cultivate their secondary function don't experience impulses that directly conflict with their rational approach to life. They experience doubt about the absolute nature of logic. Reality is never going to be perfect. It's here and now, with all its messiness, missteps, and myriad possibilities for understanding.

When ENTJs wrestle with this Introverted point of view, they don't try to locate their wilder selves outside the boundaries of what they've established. They recognize that they've been systematically eliminating the untidy aspects of life from their focus of attention. Their situation isn't the problem. It's the way they've conceptualized it. The freedom to change and the ability to love are all tied up with life's imperfections, and they can't be eliminated from the picture.

Well-developed ENTJs are nearly transcendent in their ability to see all sides of an issue. Their reason is clear-eyed and sound, and they use it generously—not only as a source of analysis and judgment, but as a means of relationship and empathy. They see a situation's real possibilities, and they have the drive and energy to realize them.

19
Introverted Thinking
IS*T*P and IN*T*P Types

Left hemisphere

Inferior function
Extraverted Feeling

Tertiary function
Introverted Perception

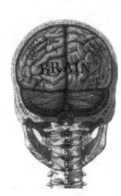

Right hemisphere

Secondary function
Extraverted Perception

Dominant function
Introverted Thinking

▲ LIKE EXTRAVERTED THINKING, Introverted Thinking is a Judging function that prompts us to reason logically and impersonally. However, as a right-brain function, Introverted Thinking operates differently than its left-brain counterpart.

The difference may be easiest to see by considering a game or a sport. Take baseball, for example. We know the rules of the game by way of *Extraverted* Thinking. Like all general standards, the rules exist apart from the real-life experience. They specify the impersonal structural relationships that constitute a game's meaning.

Once we recognize these relationships, we have an objective basis for Judging what happens in a game. No matter who a player is, whether we like him or not, or what we believe about his intentions, if he doesn't touch base on his way around the diamond, we can logically conclude he's out.

But let's say it's the top of the ninth, the score is tied, and we're actually rounding second base. The Judgments we're making—whether to stay at second or to try for a home run—also require impersonal logic. But knowing how baseball games are supposed to be played won't do us much good. What we want is *subjective* logic—a way to coordinate our behaviors logically with immediate sensory data: the position of the ball, the skill of the batter coming up, the distance we can probably slide, the actions of the other players.

This is the province of *Introverted* Thinking. When we use it, we're not structuring experience before it actually exists. We're engaged by conditions here and now, and we're adjusting to them in light of their impact on our goal.

As a right-brain function, Introverted Thinking is not conceptual and linear. It's body based and wholistic. It operates by way of visual, tactile, or spatial cues, inclining us to reason experientially rather than analytically. There are countless situations in which subjective Judgment is preferable to—and more effective than—the objective sort.

For example, if we're in a supermarket, trying to fit all our groceries into one bag, Extraverted Thinking is too exacting. We'd have to buy a ruler, measure the boxes, cartons, and coffee cans, and relate the numbers to the volume of our container. What we want here is Introverted Thinking—a way to eyeball the groceries and work out the spatial arrangements as we're packing.

Similarly, if we're connecting a splitter to a cable converter, a TV set, and two VCRs, Extraverted Thinking is too complicated. We don't want instructions that divide the task into linear steps, such as "Connect TV Output A to Splitter Input A, and Splitter Output B to Input A on VCR-1." We want a diagram of the completed project, so Introverted Thinking will kick in and "just do it."

The left brain, with its one-thing-at-a-time approach to life, requires exact predictability before it takes action. This is a clear advantage in situations we don't know much about. As long as we have a set of instructions or understand the principle involved, we don't need firsthand experience in order to proceed. However, when an enterprise involves random data, or there are many variables to consider, left-brain logic has no recourse.

The right brain, with its all-at-once approach to life, doesn't require exact predictability before it takes action. Its decisions are based on probabilities, and it leaves room for the random and the unexpected. But right-brain logic *does* require hands-on experience. We have to recognize, in the midst of action, which variables are best taken into account and which are irrelevant to our goal.

Thus, Introverted Thinking always involves perceptual skills, and using it may not feel like "being reasonable." In fact, when Introverted Thinking is combined with Extraverted Sensation, as it is for the ISTPs (and ESTPs), it feels a lot like instinct.

Athletes, for example, talk about being "in the zone"—a state in which the mind allegedly "gets out of the way," so the body can take over. What's actually going on is the left brain yielding its prerogatives to the right. Once left-brain logic gets out of our way, we have no expectations, so our Judgments are immediate and perceptual, and they seem reflexive.

As mentioned in the chapter on Extraverted Intuition, those types who favor right-brain functions are frequently described as "intuitive." The word has become a kind of catchall term for cognitive processes the one-thing-at-a-time left brain doesn't know much about. Although prevailing gender mythology ordinarily associates intuition with women, it's interesting to note that the "intuitive" mechanical skills Introverted Thinking promotes are invariably associated with men, or at least with behaviors men believe they're supposed to exhibit—such as having a "feel" for tools and equipment (being naturally "handy") or good spatial judgment (never needing to ask for directions).

When Introverted Thinking is combined with Extraverted Intuition, as it is for the INTPs (and ENTPs), its cognitive nature is more apparent, NTPs have a strong interest in patterns and their structural relationship to an immediate context, that fuels careers in architecture and production editing. But the logic of NTPs is equally equipped on direct experience and body-based skills. INTP music producers, for example, can "hear" in their minds how different combinations of effects will contribute to the sound and energy of

Sally Forth

Sally Forth. Reprinted with special permission of King Features Syndicate.

an instrumental pattern, and their Judgments translate directly into hand movements on a console.

Understanding Introverted Thinking

Because Introverted Thinking feels instinctive, the types who use it best may be least likely to recognize it as rational. Most of them are ESTPs (about 13 percent of the population) and ISTPs (about 6 percent), who associate its right-brain character with physical dexterity and the ability to improvise. So it's easy to get the impression that ESTPs and ISTPs are pretty much alike—action-oriented sorts who inhabit a completely different world from the more intellectual INTPs.

The outward resemblance of "SP" types in general has led David Keirsey and Marilyn Bates, in their famous type book *Please Understand Me: Character and Temperament Types* to question whether ISTPs are Introverted Thinkers at all:

> Behaviorally, the ISTP is more like the ESTP than any other type.
> . . . Jungians think ISTPs are just like INTPs with only minor
> differences, but this is based on the definition of ISTPs as "intro-
> verted thinking types." INTPs are logicians, philologists, and ar-
> chitects in the way they think, but ISTPs are completely
> disinterested in these pursuits. Even a cursory observation of a
> few clear-cut ISTPs will show how striking the contrast, and how
> trivial the resemblance.[1]

ISTPs and ESTPs share common strengths, of course, so behavioral similarities are inevitable. But the idea that INTPs are bona fide Thinkers because they're interested in systemic logic, whereas ISTPs are motivated purely by a hunger for action, represents a misunderstanding of Introverted Thinking in general.

If I Had a Hammer . . .

As indicated earlier, Introverted Thinking is *not* just a matter of responding to immediate perceptual stimuli. It's a decision-making process. When we're Thinking in an Introverted way, we're coordinating our behaviors with the variables in a situation related to our intended effect. This is a matter of logic, limitation, and goal orientation—all the things we associate with a rational approach to life.

Introverted Thinking is hard to see when it's oriented by Sensation because it can't be isolated from the perceptual context in which it's occurring. It operates tacitly—in the background of awareness, as we're focusing directly on something else.

The classic illustration of "tacit" information is the act of hammering a nail into a board. Our attention is on the nail and what we're doing to it. But we're also responding to all sorts of perceptual data relevant to our goal. As the nail's angle changes, we're making adjustments, appraising the distance between our present state and the completed task. We're moving our palm and fingers to change the impact of the hammer, its spatial relationship to the board, and so forth.

These perceptions aren't peripheral. They're crucial to our intended effect. And they aren't reflexive. They're *unspecified*. As we're selecting and responding to them, we're not defining them and telling ourselves about them in a left-brain way.

This is what constitutes our right-brain process of Judgment—the unspecified perceptions that are important to us, here and now, in light of our intentions. We can't specify them because we're not focusing on them directly. They're informing our actions, keeping them logically related to our goal.

Indeed, if we turn our attention to any one of them, the fluid, experiential nature of our logic disappears. For example, if we focus on the sensations of the hammer in our hand, our hammering goes awry. We've lost sight of what we're doing.

This is why STPs appear to be (and believe themselves to be) using their reflexes when they're actually using their reason. Their Judgments aren't known to them in a focused, verbal, left-brain way. They're being translated directly into physical adjustments.

Once it's clear how Introverted Judgment works, its logical character is apparent in all the types who use it—as are the differences in their Judging motivations.

ESTPs and ENTPs   ESTPs and ENTPs are dominant Extraverted Perceivers. For these types, reality is immediate perceptual engagement. They use Introverted Thinking to assess or exploit a situation's potential for action or excitement.

▲   ESTPs are risk takers, quick to see opportunity and advantage.
▲   ENTPs are animated by systemic possibility—the variables in a situation that can exert change on the whole.

Until life pushes them to slow down, ETPs won't use Judgment to limit their intake of sensory information. They'll use it to compete wherever they happen to be.

ISTPs and INTPs   ISTPs and INTPs are dominant Introverted Thinkers. Reality for these types is not the stimulation of the external world but the tacit information that guides their direct experience— the perceptual logic of a situation. Where ETPs need action for its own sake, enjoying the thrill of challenge, ITPs need to be engaged in a way that brings their logic into play.

To be sure, ITPs enjoy competition as much as the ETPs. But they're not generally drawn to situations merely by the likelihood of risk and sensory excitement. They need to be part of a process—the dialogue between a situation's structural potential and its material realization.

One can see this more clearly in the INTPs, because Intuition pushes them to explore the idea of structural potential in its own right. This is why such types seem more conventionally rational than the ISTPs. Such types will talk about the relationship between form and context, and they'll wrestle with its implications by way of architecture, design, systems analysis, or the physical sciences.

Although ISTPs appreciate this relationship in more direct physical terms, its fundamental nature remains a mental one. Consider the description given by Robert Pirsig, in *Zen and the Art of Motorcycle Maintenance*, of the dialogue between the idea of a motorcycle and the steel that gives it shape:

> People who have never worked with steel have trouble seeing . . .
> that the motorcycle is primarily a mental phenomenon. They associate metal with given shapes—pipes, rods, girders, tools,
> parts—all of them fixed and inviolable, and think of it as primarily physical. But a person who does machining or foundry work
> or forge work or welding sees "steel" as having no shape at all.
> Steel can be any shape you want if you are skilled enough. . . .
> Shapes . . . are what you *arrive* at, what you give to the steel. . . .
> The *steel*? Hell, even the steel is out of someone's mind. There's
> no steel in nature. Anyone from the Bronze Age could have told
> you that. All nature has is a *potential* for steel. There's nothing else
> there.[2]

This viewpoint may be recognized as typically Introverted. Unlike the Extraverted TPs, who take the material world for granted, Introverted Thinkers understand reality only in terms of their ability to "converse" with it, to take part in its "becoming."

This way of seeing the world is not unlike the sort described by alchemists or magicians, who say that the realm of "patterns" exists on a different plane from the materials they inform. To practice magic, one must be in harmony with this other realm, where shape is still fluid and can be manipulated before it gets tangled up with matter and congeals into an object.

ITPs wouldn't describe their approach this way, but they understand very well what it means to be in harmony with the parts of a situation that are still in flux. When they're involved in something that interests them, they don't distinguish their thoughts from the tacit level of information they're relying on. They're part of the process, changing its nature by changing themselves.

This is one reason ITPs are so challenging for their left-brain counterparts, the Extraverted Thinkers. ETJs make a firm split between observer and observed. They set objective goals and will sacrifice their own needs to bring them about. ITPs will do the inverse. They'll sacrifice objective considerations for the sake of a project or experience that "feels right" to them. The resulting behavior looks impulsive and may even be destructive. But the ITP's decision-making process is simply not objective.

ITPs are, of course, capable of formulating a plan and taking steps to reach a goal, but this is not their primary response to reality. They don't fully recognize their outward needs, or their responsibility to others, unless they cultivate their secondary function (Extraverted Sensation or Extraverted Intuition) well enough to value experience for more than its subjective appeal. Until they manage this, they can be naive and careless about the Extraverted choices they make—particularly in the area of relationship.

Like all P types, ITPs know less about where they're headed than they do about where they don't want to be. Unlike Extraverted P types, however, they will not fake a show of interest long enough to locate the nearest door. ITPs simply won't do what strikes them as not worth doing, and they feel little need to consider the interests of others in the matter.

For example, an INTP architect I know was thoroughly nonplused when his family expected him to show up at the hospital to see his ailing father. The idea of hanging around, saying comforting things to people, struck him as impractical. It was very clear to him that his value to the situation was to call the doctors involved and to find out what tests they'd scheduled and how they were likely to affect his father.

Although this behavior can be interpreted as defensive, touching as it does on inferior Extraverted Feeling, it's very much integrated with an impersonal Introverted Thinking approach. Unless the man had direct involvement in the unfolding process and could exert some effect on its logical outcome, he didn't know how to relate to it.

When ITPs do feel related to a situation, they are unfailingly generous and almost without boundaries. Thus, these types can seem like entirely different people in different contexts. They may be intensely private at work or at home—in the inimitable words of Ann Landers, "like a clam with a broken hinge"—but open, engaged, spontaneous, funny, and giving when they're with people whose sense of priorities is like their own.

This in itself suggests how dependent such types are on their immediate environment for their understanding of reality, and how important it is for ITPs to get enough experience outside the contexts in which they feel comfortable and at home.

The ITP Types

ISTP		INTP	
dominant	Introverted Thinking	dominant	Introverted Thinking
secondary	Extraverted Sensation	secondary	Extraverted Intuition
right-brain	**Introverted Feeling**	**right-brain**	**Introverted Feeling**
alternatives	**Extraverted Intuition**	alternatives	**Extraverted Sensation**
left-brain	Introverted Sensaton	**left-brain**	Introverted Intuition
double agents	**Extraverted Thinking**	double agents	**Extraverted Thinking**
tertiary	Introverted Intuition	tertiary	Introverted Sensation
inferior	Extraverted Feeling	inferior	Extraverted Feeling

All Introverted Thinkers are guided by the perceptual logic of a situation, but INTPs and ISTPs can easily appear, at first glance, to have little in common. Their similarity is not in their surface behaviors. They share a common need to make contact with the structural potential of a situation, and to have an effect on its material possibilities.

INTPs, whose Intuition prompts an interest in pattern itself, are fascinated by the internal architecture of systems, the fluid relationship between form and context that determines a living process. This interest can manifest itself in art, architecture, design, or musical composition, but it also moves INTPs into fields like physics, economics, and mathematics.

It should be emphasized that these types are not like Extraverted Thinkers, who break objects down into parts and see how they fit together. INTPs are interested in the active relationship of a pattern to its immediate environment, and they try to get at its essential nature by making models. In many ways, the unfolding dance of variables between a design and its surrounding conditions is more important to them than the practicality of the objects they create.

A striking example of the type is the architect Frank Lloyd Wright, whose leaky rooves are the stuff of legend, along with his disregard for the clients who objected to them. For him, the important thing was the idea a building could express. He thought of architecture as a medium that brought together the will of a specific culture and the underlying structure of nature.

Although ISTPs tend to be artisans rather than architects—athletes, surgeons, guitarists, leather workers, technical wizards, mechanics, and so forth—they experience the same kind of symbiotic relationship between their intentions and the underlying structure of a situation. For example, ISTP musicians speak about the creative merger of audience and band in a free-form joint effort.

The difference between INTPs and ISTPs in this regard is simply one of Intuition versus Sensation. ISTPs are entirely present oriented, tied perceptually to their context. INTPs are motivated by Intuition to recognize systemic possibilities. They're excited by the changes a particular environment can make in the way people think or live their lives.

This approach is not quite at home in an intellectual climate that insists on the split between observer and observed. In the Renaissance, churches were deliberately constructed with the idea that their design and structure could align a worshipper's psyche with a deeper pattern of reality. The same principle lies behind the art in traditional Islamic institutions, whose lines and dimensions are meant to bring one into harmony with the perfect design of the cosmos.

The experiential nature of their logic gives most ITPs a problem in a traditional Extraverted Judging system of education. The type's intelligence can be experiential to the extent that he or she finds abstract reasoning tedious and difficult to understand. Even Albert Einstein, a clear-cut ITP, was reportedly an average student who struck no one as a budding genius.

ISTPs are more vulnerable than INTPs to misunderstandings along these lines because they depend on firsthand experience for what they know, and they won't relate to situations in which their body-based logic can't be utilized. Such types may excel in shop, music, and gym, where hands-on activities bring Introverted Thinking into play, but they're regarded as underachievers in their academic classes. An unusual number of rock bands seem to be made up of such types, who dropped out of school for lack of discipline but happily spend eight hours a day perfecting guitar chords.

Indeed, because rock music requires the sort of physical interaction that marries art and technology, young ISTPs are often deeply invested in it. Bruce Springsteen talks about realizing one day that his guitar could speak for him—express all the things he couldn't otherwise put into words.

Most ISTPs think of tools this way, whether instrument, brush, or weapon—as extensions of themselves, part of their bodies, capable of expressing their passions and potential. There is often an erotic component to the relationship, either implicit or explicit, as befits a sensory understanding of reality in general.

Introverted Thinking in Pop Culture

Although the Extraverted Judging nature of our cultural institutions can work to an ITP's disadvantage, it's interesting to see how popular images of Thinking in general have shifted over the last few generations to accommodate our increasing Perceptual outlook. The recent film *Men in Black* offers a particularly good example of Introverted Thinking writ large.

Designed as a parody of alien conspiracy theories, *Men in Black* is about a secret federal agency that tracks the coming and going of extraterrestrials and protects the public from potentially malicious alien influence. The principals of the story are Mr. Smith, a senior government agent, and Mr. Jones, a new recruit, a former New York street cop with unusual athletic skills and a penchant for bending the rules.

The ISP nature of the movie is apparent in the fact that these latter qualities are precisely the ones the agency is looking for. Mr. Jones is tested along with a group of academics and military officers who are ultimately disqualified because they have a conventional approach to authority and wait for instructions before taking action.

The senior agent is an appealing variation on Sgt. Joe ("Just the facts, ma'am") Friday of the old *Dragnet* series—terse, laconic, and war weary—but it's the differences that are telling. Friday was conceived as an Extraverted Thinker, and his application of the law was guided by a very sure sense of right and wrong. Many of *Dragnet's* stories point up the ETJ's difficulty in maintaining an uninterrupted personal life in the face of pressing impersonal priorities at work.

Mr. Smith is conceived as an Introverted Thinker. His job requires that he surrender *all* claims to external identity, including relationships with others—a clear-cut reflection of the Introverted Judging idea that a moral commitment must claim the whole person, not just his or her public behaviors. Moreover, the rules Mr. Smith follows are not societal generalizations. They're derived from years of direct experience: his real-life knowledge of what works and what doesn't with varied alien species.

Indeed, the education of the agent's successor consists entirely of apprenticeship—trial by fire. The recruit's survival depends on his learning to improvise within the parameters of situational logic. When he attempts to ignore his superior's greater wisdom, mistaking it for rule-oriented inflexibility, the apprentice puts both himself and others in immediate danger.

The popularity of this movie says a great deal about how many Sensate types understand reality. It also tells us why so many ISTPs are bored and contemptuous of traditional standards of education and law but have superior abilities as coaches and military strategists. They excel in situations that allow them to formulate tactical parameters based on real people and real circumstances.

INTPs are less likely than ISTPs to drop out of school and seek camaraderie in sub- or countercultural arenas. They have more interest in the art of rhetorical persuasion, which gives them an incentive to write and to publish. Their process of thought, however, is wholistic and imaginal, and they can run into difficulties attempting to express their ideas in academic circles.

Albert Einstein's understanding of his work, for example, is typical of an Introverted Thinker's, particularly his idea that the driving force behind scientific research is "the cosmic religious experience."

This is the sort of wholistic image that will push a scientist to seek a unified theory beneath nature's infinite diversity, but it can't be fit into the Extraverted Thinker's general categories of observation.

Another interesting example, in this regard, is the head of the Nation of Islam, minister Louis Farrakhan. Many of Farrakhan's speeches suggest a classic INTP perspective, in that he believes the structure of American culture deforms and degrades the self-understanding of its Black constituents. Moreover, his manner of defending his ideas is not analytical but analogical, designed to unify his audience in terms of shared contextual experience.

The Moral Perspective of Introverted Judgment

Whatever may be said about Farrakhan's views or politics, his process of thought tells us something about Introverted Thinking's prophetic power. At the societal level, this function will bear the burden of moral imperatives a culture has not acknowledged, keeping the outward face of law in touch with the immediate experience of real people.

In fact, Introverted Thinking is frequently used this way by all types. A good example may be the pressure brought to bear on the medical examiner by the families of those victims lost in the crash of TWA flight 800 in 1996. The coroner had been doing autopsies methodically, attempting to find evidence of a bomb or missile, thereby delaying the identification of bodies. The families appealed to the authorities on subjective moral grounds, pointing out that the coroner's objective standards of investigation were not taking into account their immediate situation.

In response, the coroner adjusted his methods, much as one would respond to tacit information. The families' priorities didn't become the focal point of his attention; they helped to guide his actions, bringing the generality of the Extraverted system into balance with the issues of a real situation.

This balancing act is a normal and legitimate part of any organized community, and it's important to recognize the value of Introverted Thinking in this respect. It's also important to recognize the specific needs of those types who use Introverted Thinking for their dominant approach to morality. Unless such types recognize the connection of Extraverted Judging generalities to their own direct experience, they will depend on parochial considerations for moral direction.

One can see from recent legal cases how easily a Perceiving society will suspect that Extraverted Judging standards are merely the fruit of someone else's perceptual experience. The idea is all but accepted that a fair verdict is possible only when a jury is made up of people of the same racial or ethnic makeup as the defendant. This perspective has also issued in the increasing practice of "jury nullification," whereby jury members attempt to rectify perceived inequities in the law by taking the defendant's direct experience into account.

The ITP's Tertiary Function

One of the dangers of society's parochial understanding of shared experience is that ITPs can fall too far outside the societal orbit. They can come to believe that their only necessary allegiance is to their immediate local environment and to the people who have firsthand experience of its influence.

This understanding of moral obligation results in fierce loyalty to the brothers and sisters of a common group identity, and the enduring nature of such loyalty can be noble and courageous. However, the basic motivation of ITPs is an Introverted one—to keep their external responsibilities in line with the perceptual cues familiar to them,

Unlike Extraverted Perceivers, who are likely to accumulate varied experiences but may not discriminate among them or recognize their responsibility to them, ITPs are likely to stick to what they know because its meaning is very clear to them and it's under their control. Such types will become past masters of a particular craft or activity, but they may have no experience at all with areas of information that can't be harmonized with their accustomed approach to life.

In fact, ITPs usually find an outward niche for themselves in just this way—by contracting their services in a specific area of technical expertise. And the problem with this kind of investment is simply that it keeps them locked into their dominant function. They develop their Extraverted skills only well enough to engage life in terms of the challenges they enjoy and feel comfortable with.

So, eventually these types run into problems. Their least-developed function, Extraverted Feeling, gets too far away from consciousness. Indeed, these types can be nearly oblivious to the social rituals and signs of relationship that Extraverted Feeling regulates. If they become aware of this aspect of life, it can strike them as a kind of strategic game. For example, an INTP mathematician of my acquaintance, whose relationships were often difficult and confounded him, had a successful sideline career running singles parties and writing how-to manuals on picking up women.

On the other hand, the ITP's spontaneous emotional expressions are likely to be downright impetuous. A relationship that "feels right" to the type can prompt life-changing decisions without much consideration of their Extraverted consequences.

Ultimately, these types wind up in situations that can't be solved without developing more Extraverted Perception. They need to see themselves more objectively, through the eyes of others, because they don't entirely realize their effects on people. The more they resist this aspect of themselves, the more unconscious their Extraverted Feeling function becomes, until it floods them with impulses they don't understand.

Well developed, Extraverted Feeling prompts us to find our identity in relationship to others. When Extraverted Feeling is unadapted, however, it's likely to be primitive and egocentric. An ITP who loses touch with it can be overwhelmed by unconscious desires for others' approval and appreciation. These impulses push ITPs away from their usual subjective approach to life and give them a chance to grow.

But like all types, ITPs don't recognize the influence of their unconscious side. What they experience is an increasing sense of being *deprived* of approval and appreciation. The price of relationship seems too high, so they try to shut out affective claims that might cause them to be hurt or suffer rejection. The more emotionally unavailable they become, the more vulnerable they feel.

For Better or For Worse

For Better or For Worse © Lynn Johnston Productions Inc./Dist. by United Feature Syndicate, Inc.

Like all extreme Introverts, ITPs invest the outer world with too much power, and they attempt to use their secondary function to get things under control. Instead of using it to modify their Introverted approach, they brandish it like a weapon, to keep their dominant function intact. This defensive behavior is easier to recognize in types like the ITJs, who are clearly using their Extraverted Thinking skills to analyze others instead of organizing the data of their inner world.

When ITPs use Extraverted Sensation or Extraverted Intuition defensively, their behaviors don't look like attempts to control others. But they are. They keep others from having any influence over what they do. Such types use Extraverted Perception to stick with experiences they know how to handle, which gives them control of their immediate environment.

Unlike ETPs, who involve themselves in whatever turns up and may not know what really suits them, ITPs know exactly what they're good at, and they don't feel the need to do much else. Once they're using familiar skills, every situation is unique, its variables subtly different, its randomness exciting. So these types are content to divide all their time and energy between one or two areas of technical or physical expertise.

Because Extraverted Feeling is so profoundly unconscious, ITPs feel little responsibility to situations uncongenial to their accustomed sense of self. It may even strike them that true freedom requires people's indifference to one another's separate pursuits. Others' reactions to them have so little influence on their understanding of a situation that they can appear to have no conscience.

It should be emphasized, in this regard, that an ITP's secondary function is not Extraverted Judgment. Even those ITPs who differentiate more Extraverted Sensation or more Extraverted Intuition don't "get with the program" and do what others think they should. Introverted Judgment doesn't issue in allegiance to general standards. It fosters responsibility to actual situations.

ITPs often develop this sense of individual responsibility by seeing it modeled in someone they admire. They begin to realize that a person's behaviors are one of a situation's variables, capable of influencing circumstances for good or ill. This insight forges links between their logic and the Extraverted choices they make.

ITPs who restrict their arena of experience to activities that suit them ultimately lose touch with the Extraverted character of their Perception. They have no faith in any environment they can't control. They draw instead from their tertiary function, Introverted Sensation or Introverted Intuition, as their source of information.

Introverted Perception, as we've seen in chapters 15 and 17, fosters a strong identification with ideas and priorities that exist apart from prevailing cultural assumptions. This kind of identification is crucial for Extraverted Thinkers, who are likely to subordinate their inner perceptual life to their social roles. But Introverted Thinkers already find social expectations suspect. Introverted Perception adds fuel to their suspicions, persuading them they're right. The problem lies outside them. Such types use their tertiary function to rationalize a kind of vigilance.

INTPs, whose tertiary function is Introverted Sensation, generally focus their defenses on their material well-being. They may worry about the harmful effects of certain environments, or the effect of particular behaviors on their health or stamina.

For example, an otherwise delightful INTP psychologist is convinced that tomatoes are poisonous when combined with dairy products, and friends have learned by hard experience not to invite him out for pizza. Such types may experience physical conditions that are analogically related to unrealized emotional states.

ISTPs, whose tertiary function is Introverted Intuition, are more likely to focus on patterns of social or institutional hypocrisy. Such types love gadgetry and technology, but they despise the commercialism that comes with the territory, and they tend to see bourgeois sham and sanctimony everywhere. Many of the films and TV shows that suggest "the system" is hiding the truth from its citizens appeal to these types.

The convictions of extreme ITPs have a slightly paranoid quality, as though a nucleus of supportable facts had attracted to itself a primitive complex of fears and defenses. Thus, it can be difficult to persuade them that the conclusions they're drawing, under the influence of inferior Extraverted Feeling, are illogical. Their dominant perspective gives them a strong sense of moral outrage, while tertiary Introverted Perception ensures that they see all manner of things that can't be reconciled with prevailing social canons. When such types make art, they often mix cynical social commentary with graphics that are visceral and upsetting.

The fact that such commentary strikes a genuinely prophetic note can belie its somewhat peripheral relationship to external conditions as they actually exist. ITPs in contention with their inferior function are attempting to limit their perceptual intake to what they recognize and can count on, but the unconscious Extraversion of their inferior function is moving them to do it in a way that draws attention to themselves and points up the darker side of Feeling motivations.

In fact, the more ITPs defend themselves against the Extraverted Perception they actually need, the more powerful their Extraverted Feeling impulses become. Such types pay a good deal of attention to the way people react to them. The famous scene in *Taxi Driver* in which the main character rehearses his response to perceived disrespect, "You talkin' to me? You talkin' to me?" is a larger-than-life illustration of the kind of concern extreme ITPs experience.

Their indifference to others is paradoxically combined with the idea that people are trying to make them look bad or treating them with disregard. Both types tend to take such disagreements into the public arena. ISTPs may respond in a direct physical manner. INTPs spend time and energy worrying about their professional reputation or defending their thoughts against perceived attacks in scholarly journals.

303

The Development of the Secondary Function

When Introverted Thinkers use Extraverted Perception to broaden their base of experience, they begin to see life in a new way. It's useful to consider, in this respect, ITP heroes as they're portrayed in our movies and TV shows.

Like the principals in *Men in Black*, such heroes are depicted as loners, the beneficiary of experience that separates them from others. For example, the heroes of syndicated fantasies such as *The Highlander* and *Forever Knight* are not quite human. One is immortal, the other a vampire. Silly as the plots may be, they pose questions difficult to frame in other contexts. It's probably worth noting, in this regard, the widespread popularity of comic book superheroes, whose stories involve similar issues.

All such characters have been obliged, for one reason or another, to stay true to their "secret identity" in terms that others will recognize and accept. In the case of the Highlander and the vampire detective in *Forever Knight*, this balancing act has been perfected over centuries, in many countries, among very different peoples. In the process, both characters have developed a moral code that raises questions about the fate their true identity would ordinarily portend.

Barring the mythological aspect, this is the problem ITPs experience when they get in touch with their Extraverted side. They're obliged to balance their accustomed way of life, shaped by individual experience, against the needs and views of others. As they deal with the conflict, they discover that responsibility is both deeper than Extraverted consensus and broader than Introverted identity.

Perhaps the quintessential portrait of the type is the mysterious ISTP stranger of traditional Westerns whose hard-won moral code brings order to a community where the legal system cannot. This image says something important about an ITP's very real potential to teach and to lead.

Well-developed types don't avoid conflict by rejecting Extraverted principles in favor of their own agenda. They feel responsible to any situation they're in, as it exists, and gradually recognize the far-reaching influence of ordinary human decency. This influence, like all perceptual variables, extends in terms of probabilities. It can't be entirely controlled or predicted.

There's a scene in the movie *The Big Chill* that addresses this question in something closer to everyday terms. A group of friends from the sixties has come together for a funeral in the eighties, and all but one now inhabits a recognizable social shape: a franchise king, a journalist, a lawyer, and so forth. The one who hasn't "made it" appears to have forfeited his considerable potential. He's a sometime drug dealer, determinedly present-tense, self-protectively cynical about the countercultural years his compatriots recall with nostalgia.

In the scene I'm talking about, this character wakes up, for virtually the first time, to who he really is. He's telling a young woman about a time when he worked as a radio psychologist. He's embarrassed by that now, because he was so sure then that he had all the answers. As it turns out, the young woman remembers the show. She was in high school at the time, and had called him up one night when she was unhappy.

The character asks if she remembers what he said to her. She says he told her to do her homework and live her life and she'd be okay. He says, "Oh, Christ! I didn't really *say* that?" And she says, "No, you were right. It *was* okay. You helped."

This is the kind of subtle awakening ITPs tend to experience. They abruptly realize that what they do and say has meaning for others that can't be entirely calculated and links them to the larger community, whether they acknowledge it or not. The mutually shaping dialogue that goes on between form and context in their skilled activities also goes on between themselves and others.

ISTP: Introverted Thinking/Extraverted Sensation

	ISTP
dominant	Introverted Thinking
secondary	Extraverted Sensation
right-brain alternatives	Introverted Feeling
	Extraverted Sensation
left-brain double agents	Introverted Sensation
	Extraverted Thinking
tertiary	Introverted Intuition
inferior	Extraverted Feeling

ISTPs relate to the world by way of Introverted Thinking, a form of logic that's tied to their direct perceptual experience. It works in the background of awareness, guiding their actions, facilitated by visual and tactile cues in an unfolding situation.

Because Introverted Thinking works like this, as a means of negotiating immediate experience, ISTPs have to be active in order to use it. They need hands-on involvement so they can feel a situation's impact and gauge the effects of their behaviors on it.

Unless they experience this kind of contact, they're likely to be bored and restless. They can't get enough perceptual feedback to sustain their attention. Even their language may reflect their hands-on preference—in phrases such as, "I get it," "Can you handle that?" "Stop pushing me around," "This is really hot!" "Cool!" and so forth.

For this reason, ISTPs can be misunderstood as impulsive or hyperactive. They don't reason conceptually, like Extraverted Thinkers. They reason with their bodies as a situation is happening. For J types, who see the world in terms of general rules and predictable structural relationships, ISTPs appear to be out of control, unable to delay gratification, insistent on doing whatever they want.

But Thinking is always discriminating and logical, whether it's Extraverted or Introverted. Extraverted Thinking is objective. It operates by way of signs that represent what is generally true about experience. Introverted Thinking is subjective. It operates by way of participation and a grasp of what's structurally possible in an immediate situation.

The difference is very clear when it comes to styles of learning. For example, the classic approach to learning to play the piano is an Extraverted Thinking one. We start with the objective tasks of reading music and practicing the scales. ISTPs don't learn this way. Indeed, these types may have a difficult time understanding the point of conceptual systems. They usually learn to play by ear, because they need to recognize the underlying structure of music, the way it takes shape as an unfolding pattern.

This kind of perceptual learning ultimately trains the ability to improvise. Once ISTP musicians grasp the internal structure of a song, they're free to experiment with its possibilities, depending on their mood, their audience, and their immediate context. Such improvisation is far from doing "whatever they want." Their skill is to find a reasoned balance between structure and freedom.

ISTPs live for that kind of balance—in everything they do. It makes every situation one of a kind. Indeed, it was probably an ISTP who invented the phrase "You hadda be there." The point of life for ISTPs is to be fully present to it, so that their direction becomes clear in the process of living it.

One can see this perspective very clearly in the tendency of such types to freelance their services. These are not the sorts who opt for a fast track to a career and the American dream. They prefer to remain independent, to get paid for their time and skills, and not for their loyalty to a particular institution.

ISTPs may be photographers or painters, mechanics, welders, construction workers, visual effects mavens, chefs, surgeons, musicians, and so forth, but the jobs they do always involve hands-on involvement and the opportunity to improvise. ISTP arc welders are constantly anticipating the results of their actions and adjusting the intensity and angle of the current accordingly. ISTP film actors immerse themselves in a role, harmonizing themselves with their character's internal structural pattern, allowing it to take them into areas of psychological risk.

ISTPs tend to "freelance" their relationships as well. Part of the pleasure of being with friends is that structure is an immediate phenomenon. It doesn't exist before the situation unfolds, so the element of surprise is always a factor. When too many expectations dictate an ISTP's behavior, the type may be disruptive, attempting to get in touch with the real world of immediate data. In this regard, ISTPs resemble ESTPs.

This resemblance is only superficial, however. Average ESPs are somewhat indiscriminate. They depend on their past experience to understand reality, but they need novelty to stay interested, so they're excited by new situations that require familiar skills.

ISTPs are not like this. ISTPs are utterly present oriented, so they don't require novel perceptual experiences to stay interested. Once they're using familiar skills, every situation is new. Such types may leave school for lack of Extraverted discipline but spend hours every day perfecting the same Introverted Judging skills—in a sport, the martial arts, the playing of an instrument, technological construction or repair—and every day the experience is completely different for them.

Moreover, ISTPs are not indiscriminate. ESPs try to enjoy whatever is happening. If they don't want to be in a situation, they'll "play along" until they can find a way to escape. If they can't escape, they'll create a humorous diversion to keep things alive.

ISTPs are either "with" a situation or they're not. If they're not, they will make no effort to pretend they are. They won't exhibit initial interest, explain, or apologize for their inattention or lack of compliance. When these types are disruptive, they aren't being playful. They feel trapped, isolated from the information they need to feel alive and aware.

ISTPs may do something they don't want to do for someone they respect, but they will not fake goodwill in the process. The commitments these types make are based on shared experience, not shared thoughts or feelings, and they have no reason to trust people who haven't proved themselves in areas they consider important.

The image created by this kind of behavior has a certain resonance in the Sensate pop ethos, manifested by the many film heroes whose perceptual logic, sensory skills, and laconic unpredictability manage to extract civilization from the jaws of corporate hypocrisy and greed. In real life, however, ISTPs may narrow their world to the extent that they have no idea what's going on outside their own environment.

Many ISTPs find a niche where their reliance on direct experience is necessary and rewarded. For example, such types can be excellent tacticians and, given the interest, have the potential to lead and inspire others. They know what individuals are likely to contribute to a team, and they have a "feel" for the synergy of a group in action.

This skill is evident whether they're coaching a sport, rehearsing a band, or working out a military strategy. Because they work with a situation's logical implications and not in terms of principles or hierarchy, they have an egalitarian attitude and can usually manage others without making them feel like subordinates.

Such types have also benefited from the advent of computers and interactive video games, which has shifted some of the emphasis in a school curriculum to individual sensory skills. The visual effects crews on films always seem to be composed of these types, who enjoy exercising their skills in the creation of realistic explosions, disasters, outer space scenarios, monsters, and computer-generated stunts for movies.

It should be granted, however, that ISTPs are still the most likely of the types to drop out of school or to graduate without acquiring much in the way of basic Extraverted reasoning skills. Ironically, given the highly Sensate nature of society, these types actually need more contact with the Extraverted Sensate world than they usually get.

As stated earlier, ITPs are not generally interested in novelty. They're interested in hands-on activity, and the Sensate world provides a great deal of opportunity to satisfy this interest. ISTPs may race cars, pilot small planes, snowmobile, play sports, or join a band to get the kind of action they need, and they're often credited with being in touch with their feelings because these pursuits so completely and passionately absorb them.

In general, however, these types experience their feelings only in the course of using their subjective logic. Their ability to sort them out and recognize their meaning is not usually well developed. Somewhat like ISTJs, ISTPs tend to acquire things that will give form to their inner lives. They establish collections and tend to display them in a somewhat ritualized way. The structural and aesthetic integrity of the arrangement may be highly important to them.

For example, many rock performers acquire extensive collections of guitars, which no one is permitted to touch. The many stores that have arisen devoted to comic book and trading card collectors may appeal to ISPs in general.

However, this Introverted manner of expressing their inner life doesn't give ISTPs any experience with the social vocabulary that tells people they're cared about and mean something to them. An ISTP's Extraverted Feeling function tends to be undeveloped to the point of being unconscious.

Verbal assurances mean very little to them, and they don't tend to offer them. If someone asks too much of them, they will simply walk away and seek the company of like-minded companions. These types are not motivated to be unfaithful, but they're liable to lose interest when a partner changes direction in life or the connection seems to have run its course.

Extreme ISTPs, who rely exclusively on Introverted Thinking, may attempt to avoid any situation that will require them to do something that doesn't come naturally to them. And they may be quite angry about the ways in which others are trying to control them and make them fit into a particular social niche. They may believe that people who have not had their background and experience have no right to judge them or expect anything from them.

These types need to get in touch with the Extraverted nature of their Sensate function. They need to make an actual effort to adapt to contexts they can't negotiate in their usual way. Extreme ISTPs think this will compromise their freedom or force them into a social straitjacket, but they're wrong about this. Such types need to get enough experience to keep their perceptual logic sharp. If they don't, they aren't taking in enough information, and they begin to feel alienated.

When ISTPs have developed Extraverted Sensation well enough to recognize the validity of experiences unlike their own, they are likely to use their tertiary function, Introverted Intuition, to great advantage. It prompts them to improvise in a way that is highly original and makes a contribution to their field.

However, when they use Introverted Intuition defensively, to keep their dominant function intact, these types identify very strongly with ideas that call the present structures of society into question. They attract to themselves not only the disenfranchised and the iconoclast but the psychotic and the troubled, without being able to offer anything beyond the common experience of feeling disrespected.

In general, these types are pushed by life to recognize that some experiences are the same for everyone, regardless of what they know or have or do. Human need and aspiration aren't variables that can be ignored; they're part of a situation's structural pattern, and logic itself dictates an alignment with them.

ITPs who learn how to do this realize a great deal of personal power. They don't withdraw from expectations that strike them as alien; they align themselves with the common human experience in a situation and improvise in the best sense of the word.

INTP: Introverted Thinking/Extraverted Intuition

INTP	
dominant	Introverted Thinking
secondary	Extraverted Intuition
right-brain alternatives	**Introverted Feeling**
	Extraverted Sensation
left-brain double agents	**Introverted Intuition**
	Extraverted Thinking
tertiary	Introverted Sensation
inferior	Extraverted Feeling

Like ISTPs, INTPs depend on Introverted Thinking, a form of reasoning that operates on the basis of immediate perceptual information. They, too, are able to grasp, all at once, the structural logic of a system or process. ISTPs, however, relate to the outer world with Extraverted Sensation, so the perceptual nature of their reasoning is apparent. They obviously need visual and tactile contact with a process in order to understand it. INTPs relate to the outer world with Extraverted Intuition, so their need for direct experience is not as clear.

Such types are interested in the logical *possibilities* of structure: the way form and context interact with and exert change on each other. Thus, they're more at home than ISTPs with theoretical reasoning. INTPs do, however, require visual and tactile contact with a system in order to reason properly. Their primary method of exploring structural possibility is almost always a form of design or model making. Such types compose music, render blueprints, perform lab tests, work up magazine layouts, draft construction schemes, and so forth.

Because their focus of attention is on possibility, INTPs are likely to be more interested in the idea that animates a system and its impact on reality than they are with the system's objective utility. In fact, there's an old joke, intended to implicate economic theorists, that offers a bit of insight into the type's approach.

A chemist, a physicist, and an economist are stranded together on a desert island, with only a crate of canned tuna to keep them alive. The problem is how to get the cans open. The chemist suggests putting them in the ocean for a while, until the salt compromises the tin. The physicist says, "No, let's put the cans in the sun until they explode." They both turn to the economist, who says thoughtfully, "Let's assume we have a can opener."

Galvanized by Intuition, INTPs will strive for theoretical systems that include all possible variables, but such theories can fall short of application in the real world. Accordingly, these types can be frustrated by the need to defend their ideas in terms of Extraverted logic, which begins and ends with material application. Even when they develop high-level communication skills, INTPs aren't really talking about the same things that concern left-brain Thinking types. Or they're talking about them in a way that leaves too much room for speculation to suit an Extraverted analytical mind.

The biologist Rupert Sheldrake, for example, developed a revolutionary theory about recurring patterns in nature, which derived, he says, from an attempt on his part to picture God less as an embodiment of unchanging law than as an evolving organic process. This is the sort of metaphor an INTP might use to make clear the underlying idea informing a project, but it has no means of evaluation in left-brain Thinking terms.

On the other hand, because INTPs see logical implications in terms of systemic change over time, they are often well ahead of the curve on issues of cultural evolution. They seem like ENTPs in this respect, but the two are actually mirror images.

Like all Extraverts, ENTPs take the outer world for granted. They use Extraverted Intuition to gauge a situation's possibilities, then strategize with Introverted Thinking to bring them about. For example, the man who developed the Wal-Mart conglomerate might well have been an ENTP. He Intuited the venture's commercial potential, then worked out the structural design for making it happen.

INTPs approach reality from the other way around. They use Introverted Thinking first, to get a sense of a situation's structural pattern, then use Extraverted Intuition to recognize its impact on what actually exists. The architect Frank Lloyd Wright, for example, recognized how prefabrication could lead to superhighways, suburbs, and shopping malls long before Wal-Mart was even a gleam in an entrepreneur's eye.

Clearly, most people recognize that color, space, light, and order have a great deal to do with their experience of a restaurant or a housing project or a government building, but most of us are not thinking about the internal logic of our technical creations. An INTP designer, however, might spend a lifetime exploring Western culture's attachment to angled frames as opposed to ovals.

Because INTPs represent only 1 percent of the population, they're not well understood, and their interests may be just rarefied enough to make them feel isolated. This sense of isolation is compounded by the Introverted nature of their thought process. All Introverted P types run the risk of losing contact with objective reality apart from the areas of knowledge and experience that suit them.

Unlike the ISTPs, whose physicality can look like emotional volatility, an INTP's feelings are not usually visible in the type's demeanor. In fact, these types may find it difficult to know what they're feeling until they experience themselves as out of control. Their ability to sort out their emotions and recognize their meaning is not well developed.

For this reason, romantic attachment can pose a problem for INTPs. They usually develop enough Extraverted Sensation to engage in experiences that draw on their primary skills, but they don't fully appreciate the objective image they display to others. And because Extraverted Feeling is their least-developed function, INTPs can be shy and awkward about affectional connections. At midlife, they may abruptly realize they haven't given enough thought to issues of marriage, children, or domestic stability. They may not even be certain about what they require from a partner. Their sense of predictability involves matters of impersonal design; the personal realm strikes them as utterly without rational order.

Thus, such types tend to marry other INTP colleagues or find themselves blindsided by attractions to people who can make up their deficit in Extraverted Feeling. These latter attractions are not easy to sustain in the long run. INTPs require a great deal of time to be alone with their thoughts. They're also likely to overlook, or to regard as unnecessary, the ritual signs of affection that Extraverted Feeling types depend on for a sense of well-being.

Most INTPs need more contact with the Extraverted nature of their secondary function. They're accustomed to using their Intuition only to assess logical probability in a system. They have to make a deliberate effort to apply it to themselves—to see the effects they have on others in the larger picture, or to entertain possibilities outside their familiar framework of expectations.

Without this Extraverted ability, INTPs get locked into their dominant function, and their least-conscious function, Extraverted Feeling, gets too far away from their will and aims. Such types are gradually flooded with unconscious desires for others' approval and appreciation, which undermine their impersonal approach to life.

This internal drama is a healthy one. INTPs who are pushed away from their usual frame of mind can get some perspective on their accustomed behaviors. Like all types, however, they don't experience unconscious pressure as part of themselves. They experience it as something that's happening to them—a problem with their situation, caused by other people. They may believe, for example, that they aren't getting the appreciation they deserve.

In response, INTPs sometimes seek reassurance—by turning to Extraverted Sensation and attempting to cultivate a better image. They're more likely, however, to reassert their familiar Thinking-oriented sense of self, concluding that they've become too dependent on others' views. They worry that their needs are right on the surface, so they attempt to increase their self-sufficiency. As a result, they become more self-oriented, disinclined to accommodate others, or to do anything they don't want to do.

The more emotionally unavailable these types become, the more they experience themselves as emotionally vulnerable, constantly open to heartache and rejection. They begin to isolate themselves from others, persuading themselves that most people are too pedestrian to grasp what they can see. This is the point at which INTPs tend to lose touch with their secondary function altogether and turn, instead, to their tertiary function, Introverted Sensation.

Well developed, Introverted Sensation helps us to recognize information that has consistent meaning for us, apart from prevailing social assumptions. Such information is crucial for ESJs. Extraverted Judgers are likely to ignore their own priorities for the sake of a job or a social role.

INTPs, however, whose Judgment is Introverted, don't need more reasons to ignore social expectations for the sake of their inner needs. Introverted Sensation makes such types highly critical of others' expectations. Their Thinking becomes complicated and speculative, less and less related to reality as it actually exists.

Introverted Sensation also focuses the type's defenses on issues of material well-being. Such INTPs worry about the effects of others on their health, or about the harmful aspects of food or the environment, and they circle the wagons accordingly. Sometimes they strike others as hypochondriacs, but their physical states often mirror the emotional states they aren't recognizing in themselves.

INTPs of this sort are attempting to limit their perceptual intake to the familiar, but the result is the increasing influence of Extraverted Feeling. As Extraverted Feeling gets less conscious and more powerful, it begins to actively oppose the INTP's dominant approach. INTPs in this position are likely to draw attention to themselves. They're hyperaware of people's reactions to them, and they respond with vehemence. Extreme INTPs are frequently embroiled in disputes with people, and they spend a great deal of time and energy defending their thoughts in journals or on the op-ed pages of local newspapers.

INTPs who make a deliberate attempt to apply Extraverted Intuition to themselves feel an immediate sense of conflict. Like Extraverted Thinkers, these types confuse their ability to be impersonal with the ability to be objective, and Intuition is usually their first recognition that objectivity has nothing to do with removing oneself from the situation. It offers them an image of themselves as part of the larger picture, with effects on others that can't be entirely calculated and a dependence on others that is not entirely under their control. INTPs ultimately get in touch with their Feeling function this way—through their Intuitive objectivity.

The late Corita Kent, an American artist noted for her silk-screen prints, offers a nice illustration of this perspective in her description of her work:

> A painting [is] a symbol for the universe. Inside it, each piece relates to the other. Each piece is . . . answerable to the rest of that little world. So, probably in the total universe, there is that kind of total harmony, but we get only little tastes of it. . . . That's why people listen to music or look at paintings. To get in touch with that wholeness.[3]

INTPs who come to terms with relationship by way of Intuition recognize their responsibility to others in the way Kent describes. They feel answerable to the people who share their situation. Such types have a strong sense of purpose, but they don't feel the need to calculate their behaviors in terms of logical probability alone. They recognize the existence of the unpredictable and the improbable: those aspects of life that require a leap of faith, or the ability to trust someone besides themselves.

20

Extraverted Feeling

ES_FJ and EN_FJ Types

Left hemisphere		Right hemisphere
Dominant function		**Tertiary function**
Extraverted Feeling		Extraverted Perception
Secondary function		**Inferior function**
Introverted Perception		Introverted Thinking

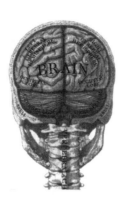

▲ AS DISCUSSED IN PREVIOUS CHAPTERS, the left brain prefers to focus on one thing at a time. Its global limit seems to be about seven pieces of information. For this reason, left-brain functions always encourage us to define boundaries. When we use them, we're deciding that some perceptions are more important than others and restricting our attention accordingly.

The left-brain Judging functions, Extraverted Thinking and Extraverted Feeling, prompt us to do this rationally—by defining familiar perceptions and organizing them in a systematic way. As Extraverted functions, they also adapt us to consensual reality—that is, to the standards of reason that characterize a given society, which determine its conventions and expectations.

As discussed in chapter 18, Extraverted Thinking supports an impersonal standard of reasoning, based on general principles. Essentially, principles tell us how things are supposed to happen. Under specified conditions, a principle says, things always proceed in the same sequence: first this, followed by this, then this.

Once we know the principle that governs a system, we can focus our attention selectively. For example, if we're looking for "Zerbe" in the phone book, we can disregard the names from A to Y. The principle of alphabetical order tells us how Z is logically related to the other letters, so we don't have to consider data irrelevant to our goal. Even principles of behavior work this way. They tell us how to proceed and what should claim our attention, despite the influence of other kinds of perceptual information.

But general principles are not the only way to manage direct experience.

Say we're making a list of the people we call every week, so their numbers are handy whenever we pick up the phone. Although it's possible to organize these names impersonally—by alphabet, for example, or frequency of contact—most of us don't do this. Most of us list the people we know in order of their relationship to us: family members first, then friends, then coworkers, and so on.

This, roughly speaking, is the domain of Extraverted Feeling. When we use this function, we aren't organizing data sequentially and logically, by way of principles. We're organizing data by relatedness to ourselves. The categories of relationship we maintain in the external world—and the way we maintain them—reflect our *values*.

But Isn't Feeling *Opposed* to Reason?

Because Feeling involves personal relationship, it's easy to assume that using it is a matter of emotional preference. But like all left-brain functions, Extraverted Feeling is conceptual and analytic. It encourages us to make rational choices, to measure our options for relationship against an external standard of behaviors.

What distinguishes this function from Extraverted Thinking is the fact that relatedness involves human beings, not impersonal abstractions. Thus, the systems that Feeling determines aren't logically accessible. For example, if we know the alphabet, we can always anticipate the logical order of names in a phone directory. Not so with a list of calling partners. Its specific order depends on the human being who taped it to the refrigerator. But the absence of *logical* predictability doesn't make a system unpredictable or based on individual preference.

"Family," "friend," and "coworker" aren't states of emotion. They're categories of human alliance, organized by *degree* of relatedness. What we're doing, when we use these categories, is accommodating our specific experiences of people to the conceptual shapes the terms offer. This is a rational process, not a sentimental one.

Cathy ©1997 Cathy Guisewite. Reprinted with permission of Universal Press Syndicate. All rights reserved.

Even if we're trying to decide whether a person is more of a friend than a co-worker, we aren't making this decision by consulting the depths of the heart. We're measuring our external experience of the relationship against the behavioral standards we associate with the category of "friendship." These standards constitute one aspect of our societal value system. They set up conventions that tell us how relationships are "supposed" to be conducted, and what responsibilities they entail.

For example, if the clerk in the supermarket tells us that his cellar was flooded in the last big rain, we have no reason to believe he expects more than our sympathy. If our best friend is bailing out her living room, however, the nature of the relationship will determine a different standard of response—like showing up at her door with a mop and a pail.

To be sure, our categories of relationship result in a myriad of assumptions about appropriate behaviors, and our emotions ultimately operate in concert with them. But the fact remains that we use these categories for rational purposes: to set our priorities, to make decisions, to understand our obligations to others, and to anticipate others' behaviors toward us.

Subjective and irrational approaches to life have their own merit, as type studies make clear, but they don't result in expectations, conventions, or external systems of order. An *irrational* approach to a list of phone numbers—say, tossing the names in a hat and writing them down as they came to hand—would create a random pattern, without meaning to anyone. And a purely *subjective* approach might incline us to organize our list differently every time we had a pleasant or unpleasant conversation with someone.

But Aren't Feeling Types Motivated by What They *Feel*?

Of course. Everyone is. The point, however, is that our functions are *mental* processes. They operate separately from our emotional system. When we use a function often enough, we're emotionally invested in the choices it encourages, but this is true of all functions, and it's not the same thing as acting directly on what we feel.

As far as type theory is concerned, *all* Extraverted functions are objective, because they focus our attention on the outer realm of observable phenomena. Extraverted Feeling is no exception. It focuses our attention on people's outward behaviors and prompts us to interpret them in a standardized way.

Given this outward focus, Extraverted Feeling is likely to prompt the *disregard* of immediate emotional preference. Consider, for example, the Feeling type who dislikes his father's new wife but is obliged by her category of relationship to include her in all the family get-togethers. What the man actually "feels" doesn't matter. There is no way to leave out his stepmother and also meet the conventional standards of familial behavior.

All those TV movies in which the cost-conscious hospital administrator accuses the research director of emotional blackmail because she says a cut in funds will hurt innocent children are trafficking in stereotypes. The research director's argument is a rational one, based on value. She's saying that society's behavior toward children is regulated by standards that conflict with the administrator's focus on logical efficiency.

Ultimately, an exclusive reliance on Extraverted Feeling leads to anything but a reliance on emotion. Extreme Feeling types *ignore* their immediate impressions and focus *only* on people's social obligations.

Garfield ©1997 Paws, Inc. Dist. by Universal Press Syndicate. Reprinted with permission. All rights reserved.

OK, but Values Still Seem Subjective

The word *objective* simply means "having material existence." We're disposed to hear this, however, as though it meant "existentially indifferent." Thus, general principles seem objective to us because they have nothing to do with our behaviors as people; they're abstractions—like the letters of the alphabet, or the concepts of unity and duality. Values, on the other hand, are personal and human. When they change, our behaviors change.

The term *family values*, for example, isn't an impersonal truth that can be abstracted from reality; it's a behavioral ideal, dependent on what we know about the relationships actually involved. In ancient Mesopotamian societies, where responsibility for a woman's children resided in her brother, people's family values would have been different from our own—particularly their standards for "paternal" and "avuncular" behaviors.

Cultural specificity, however, is not proof that people's values are just a matter of what they happen to believe. Our knowledge of alphabetical order won't do us a bit of good in a Moscow phone booth, where the equivalent letters run A, B, V, G, D . . . , but this hasn't convinced us that the alphabet is "just" a parochial belief system.

It's the *personal* specificity of our values that gives us a problem—the fact that they refer to standards of human relationship. When we try to conceptualize them, we end up universalizing our own experience, or, like Huck Finn, reducing them to "civilizin' tendencies": manners, decorum, being "nice," waiting our turn, apologizing, saying thank you for gifts. In point of fact, Extraverted Feeling does preside over "civilizin' tendencies," but their evidence is systemic, not individual.

The Collective Power of the Function

In myths, Extraverted Feeling is associated with Hestia, goddess of the hearth. After Prometheus stole fire from the gods and gave it to humankind, Hestia taught people how to maintain it—both at the center of the community and at the center of each home. When someone left a household to found his own, he took a bit of the home fire with him to start a hearth in his new dwelling.

This sort of custom isn't a matter of emotion, impulse, or doing what we learned in kindergarten. It's a secular ritual—a visible sign that marks a participant's membership in the community at large. Such rituals can touch us, but they aren't occasions of sentiment. They're a vocabulary, part of our Feeling lexicon. They submit to collective form an experience ordinarily confined to individual history, allowing us to express the kinds of relationships important to us as a people.

It may be easier to see how this vocabulary works by considering an episode of *Star Trek: The Next Generation*. Captain Picard has met with a Tamarian ship in the system El-Adrel, but communication with these potential allies has proved impossible. Tamarian words translate as names and places, but they don't seem to mean anything.

Picard is about to give up, but Dalthon, the Tamarian captain, takes a different tack. "Darmok and Jalad at Tenagra," he says, and shows Picard two knives. The men are then transported to a hostile planet, where a predatory creature obliges them to join forces. Handing Picard one of the knives, Dalthon says again: "Darmok and Jalad at Tenagra."

Meanwhile, the crew, shocked by this turn of events, is trying to beam Picard back to the ship. For a brief moment they succeed, and Dalthon, at the creature's mercy, is mortally wounded. In his grief and horror, Picard begins to understand.

The names and places in the people's language operate as metaphors, their meaning derived from a common stock of myths and historical events. Darmok and Jalad are characters in a Tamarian myth: strangers who learned to understand each other by facing a common enemy at Tenagra. Picard's relationship with Dalthon now has meaning in those terms.

Armed with this knowledge, Picard pays tribute to the dying man by telling him a story from Babylonian mythology—the tale of Gilgamesh and the comrade who stood by him: "He who was my companion through adventure and hardship is gone forever."

The customs that constitute our Feeling vocabulary are very much like the language of the Tamarians—inherited forms that shape the relationships we establish and maintain. Their meaning is not straightforward but cumulative, becoming apparent as we use them and recognize their effects.

Among the bones and ashes of our long-dead forebears, anthropologists routinely look for artifacts of such Feeling vocabularies: rites of transition and commitment; ceremonies of planting and harvest; customs of birth, family, caretaking, and burial. These conventions testify to a society's values. They tell us about the relationships that mattered enough to organize—relationships between men and women; between children and parents; between the community and its helpless, its old, its dying; between the community and the land; between the community and the divine.

Without question, social values have a strong moral component, enjoining the "right" ordering of our alliances and loyalties. Our increasing emphasis on direct experience has encouraged us to question traditional moral expectations, to note their effect on individual freedoms. But this is to miss the point of collective responsibility. Social values mark those areas of decision making that go beyond one person's immediate experience to affect the community as a whole.

Picard, for example, recognized in Dalthon's actions the moral sensibilities of the society that formed him. In the same way, an act of rape or child abuse is not one person's violation of another but a collective responsibility, because the society that tolerates such behaviors ensures that all its vulnerable members live in fear.

Apart from questions of moral rectitude, our behaviors toward others have implications, whether we intend them or not. When we have clear-cut standards, we know what to expect and what's expected of us in return. In the absence of collective expectations, we're constantly negotiating these behaviors, attempting to correct people's misreading of our motives. This is particularly evident when the responsibilities accruing to one social role conflict with those of another.

A recently retired minister went to the hospital to visit a sick friend who was also a member of his former congregation. As it turned out, two other of his former parishioners were in the hospital at the same time, and they were aggrieved and insulted that the minister had not visited them as well. As far as the minister was concerned, he was visiting his friend *as* a friend, not as a former pastor. He didn't even *know* the other people were in the hospital. But as far as those church members were concerned, the man's ministerial role was primary, and he should have checked the hospital register.

Embarrassed about the oversight, the minister called the two members to apologize. The next day, his pastoral successor got in touch with him, infuriated by his attempt to reinvolve himself with hospital visitation, which, of course, was no longer his official responsibility.

What "should" have happened in this situation? Which priorities obtain? If we can't rely on social consensus to resolve questions of everyday behavior, our only recourse is our own experience, and ultimately, subjective preference.

Tradition . . .

The dilemma of choosing rightly from a multitude of individual preferences is generally referred to as a postmodernist one, but typologically speaking, what we've got here is the natural outcome of a Perceptually oriented approach to life. If we can't depend on a stable social framework (Extraverted Feeling) to make our decisions, our only recourse is to rely on our direct experience of good and bad behaviors (Introverted Feeling). This shift has given us more subjective freedom, but it also forfeits cultural consensus, an objective sense of community.

It's worth discussing, in this respect, the dilemma that drives the plot of *Fiddler on the Roof*, a play that says a great deal about values and the stability of a community. The principals in this play, Tevye and Golde, preside over a Jewish family in nineteenth-century Russia whose Judging traditions have prevailed for generations. They have five marriageable daughters, and custom dictates the use of a matchmaker to find them husbands. But each daughter, in turn, falls in love outside the prevailing system.

The play is interesting from a typological standpoint because it doesn't draw the usual head/heart distinction between Thinking and Feeling positions. Tevye and Golde are both Extraverted Judgers. Both have a stake in the organized community.

When the matchmaker selects a husband for their eldest, Tzeitel, Tevye reacts impersonally, in the manner of an Extraverted Thinker. He knows that his daughter will never find the man attractive—he's the village butcher, a coarse widower twice her age. But these issues strike Tevye as circumstantial. The butcher is clearly the logical choice: he's financially comfortable, has a strong work ethic, can support children. These principles help to maintain the external structure of the family as Tevye understands it.

The match also satisfies Golde's Extraverted Feeling values. She, too, recognizes that Tzeitel doesn't love the man. But love, for Golde, is largely irrelevant to a stable marriage. Indeed, when Tevye asks her if she "loves" him after twenty-five years of wife- and motherhood, she scarcely knows what to make of the question. Relationship, on the other hand, is a manageable entity. The butcher was faithful to his first wife; he's a good friend and neighbor. He can be trusted to make a marriage work.

Tzeitel, for her part, has fallen in love with the village tailor. She didn't plan for this to happen, but now that it has, she wants the freedom to choose her own husband. Her conflict is a familiar one, because it's ours: a Perceiving versus Judging approach to life. Tzeitel understands freedom as the absence of social coercion, but it may be suggested that she's captive to the effects of her subjective experience.

It's instructive, therefore, that Tzeitel does not try to solve her problem by confiding in her mother and enlisting her support. If Extraverted Feeling really presided over issues of individual preference, she'd expect Golde to empathize, perhaps advise her to "follow her heart." But Tzeitel has no such illusions. She goes to Tevye, the Thinking type, and asks him to deal with Golde.

Why? Because Tevye's reasoning is impersonal, and Tzeitel can count on its objective flexibility. In the abstract realm of general principles, any number of routes can take us to the same goal. If Tzeitel can make a case for the tailor's youth and compatibility as variables comparable to the butcher's wealth and status, Tevye may see the logic of her choice.

Like all Extraverted Thinking types, Tevye works out the question by weighing the pros and cons. "On the one hand," Tevye muses, "being rich couldn't hurt. On the other hand, the butcher is older than I am; they have no common interests. Besides, Tzeitel is committed to the tailor, so she'll make the sacrifices poverty requires."

Extraverted Feeling is equally objective, but it doesn't have the same flexibility, because values are not abstract variables, like the principles of wealth or youth. Values are tied to the specific behaviors that maintain them, which link us to a place, a time, a family, a society.

Just as Thinkers who neglect issues of value may find that one variable seems as likely as another, Feeling types who ignore logic tend to make decisions in all-or-nothing terms. As far as Golde is concerned, either Tzeitel marries the butcher or the world as she knows it falls apart. There are no "other hands."

What's at stake, of course, is the community—its history, its continuity through time. To circumvent the matchmaker is not an issue of personal taste; it degrades all marriages in the village, suggests that a family can be predicated on the random attractions of children. The logical argument that persuaded Tevye—that there are other ways of ensuring familial stability—is not a hypothesis that Golde will entertain.

Indeed, Tevye knows that the only way to change Golde's mind is to bypass her dominant Feeling viewpoint and make contact with her subjective Perceiving side. He tries to do this by persuading Golde that the "right" way of doing things will exact too high a price under the present circumstances.

To this end, Tevye fabricates a dream. He tells his wife that Grandmother came from beyond the grave to celebrate Tzeitel's impending marriage—to the tailor. The ruse nearly fails. She must have heard wrong, Golde says. She meant the butcher. So Tevye embellishes the story with a visitation from the butcher's late wife, who threatens vengeance on Tzeitel if the arranged wedding should ever take place.

This is information that Golde can hear. Grandmother's access to the supernatural grapevine is one thing, but the butcher's wife was volatile enough as a flesh-and-blood neighbor. To tempt her malice as a jealous ghost is too high a price for Golde to contemplate. The community may not care what happens to Tzeitel, but she does, and that's all there is to it.

Fiddler on the Roof is particularly interesting because it's presented as a cautionary tale. With each daughter's marriage, Tevye further breaches his accustomed principles, until his logic bumps squarely into a priority he considers inviolable. His third daughter marries outside the faith, and he severs the relationship.

Significantly, this is where Golde is willing to compromise. How moral is the dissolution of a family, even for the sake of religious principle? But it no longer matters. The winds of change that have been blowing through the household are part of a much larger social upheaval that is beyond their power to control. The entire village is razed, and the people are forced to begin anew, somewhere else.

Values in a Perceiving Society

Most of us can identify with the terms of conflict in *Fiddler on the Roof*, because the struggle to reconcile individual potential with others' expectations is quintessentially human. If we had to choose, however, most of us would come down on the side of individual freedom. Although we empathize with the parents' discomfort, we understand very well Tzeitel's yearning to be the architect of her own destiny.

This is why the play works so well as a commentary on our own society. Typologically speaking, Tzeitel recognized the claims of subjectivity, which cracked open the frozen pact she'd made with community standards. Like a spring thaw, that recognition liberated the free-flowing potential beneath the surface of organized relationships in the village.

We support her position because the cards are pretty well stacked in her favor. "Falling in love" with the socially inappropriate person has set stories in motion for as long as people have been capable of telling them. Few of us would advise the heroine of this one to sacrifice her rich interior life on the altar of an inherited social compact.

It should be recognized, however, that Tzeitel's dilemma is emblematic. As human beings, we're always caught between individual aspiration and the interests of society at large. The point of developing our secondary function is to take on the burden of this conflict—to recognize competing claims for our loves and loyalties. Tzeitel's response to this universal dilemma was a defensive one, and it forced her to choose between self and other. Understandably, she tried to make that choice without price.

I am not, in this respect, suggesting that Tzeitel should have married the butcher and conformed her life to others' expectations. Like the heroines of most such stories, she's locked into a social structure that won't support female independence, and her realistic options are few. I'm suggesting that taking on the burden of her secondary function would have moved her beyond the terms of her apparent either-or situation.

For example, if Tzeitel had spoken to her parents honestly before the match was made, she might have persuaded them to take her feelings into account, or at least apprised them of the price she was willing to pay to honor her own experience. In the process, she might also have generated positive social change. When her sisters' turns came up, her parents might have handled things differently; or they might have talked to others in the community about the drawbacks of the matchmaking system as it existed.

Tzeitel's attempt to escape her portion in the larger community led her to determine that her problem was merely external—a systemic obstacle to her individual satisfaction and well-being. This moved her to use her tertiary function to devise a solution: that is, to use *Extraverted* Perception. It is here that the play is instructive with respect to our own society and our consistent elimination of perceived obstacles to individual aspiration and desire.

The more a society determines its priorities on the basis of Extraverted Perception, the more individual experience becomes primary and the less faith its members have in law and custom to set limits applicable to everyone. Under such circumstances, *Introverted* Feeling, which is subjectively determined, comes to seem like a more honest approach to moral decision making. One can see this shift happening simply by looking at our media heroes—people impelled by an elemental sense of good and evil to make choices beyond the constraints of community expectations.

The prophetic nature of such choices is real and positive. However, as a primary societal approach to Judgment, Introverted Feeling is dangerous because its power is not collective. A society that substitutes it for the Extraverted sort gradually trains its members to believe that *all* values are a matter of individual experience. We find ourselves thinking, "Well, I believe this is wrong, but that's just me. I can't tell *you* what to do. You have to take responsibility for your own behaviors."

This is one reason we've resorted to legislating our standards of relationship. In the absence of an objective sense of values, we have no other means of ensuring our rights and responsibilities to each other. One can see how this happens simply by looking at the gangs that flourish where family systems have broken down. Although members regard normative socialization as alien to their needs and background, the peer communities they've established are unified by highly rigid codes of external conduct, ensuring relationships more predictable than those of a Victorian social club—formal rites of passage and precisely determined hierarchies, along with exaggerated ideas about postures of social respect and disrespect.

The EFJ Types

	ESFJ		ENFJ
dominant	Extraverted Feeling	dominant	Extraverted Feeling
secondary	Introverted Sensation	secondary	Introverted Intuition
left-brain	**Extraverted Thinking**	left-brain	**Extraverted Thinking**
alternatives	Introverted Intuition	alternatives	Introverted Sensation
right-brain	**Extraverted Sensation**	right-brain	**Extraverted Intuition**
double agents	**Introverted Feeling**	double agents	**Introverted Feeling**
tertiary	Extraverted Intuition	tertiary	Extraverted Sensation
inferior	Introverted Thinking	inferior	Introverted Thinking

Like Extraverted Thinkers, EFJs make up about 18 percent of the population. If we include the Introverted FJs (who use Extraverted Feeling as a secondary function), about a quarter of the population takes an Extraverted Feeling approach to outer reality. Almost all these FJs are ESFJs (13 percent) and ISFJs (6 percent), people and service oriented, with strong values that link them to their families and to the communities they support.

ENFJs (5 percent) and INFJs (1 percent) share these characteristics, but they're galvanized more by people's potential. Such types usually express their values in counseling, teaching, the ministry, or writing. All EFJs identify with the roles they play in society, and they enjoy careers in which they can give others the benefit of their experience and knowledge.

As Judging types, EFJs have a good deal in common with ETJs. They want things settled and organized, and they want an external guide they can rely on. Pragmatic, disciplined, and inclined to take on too many responsibilities, they want others to keep their promises, to follow through, and to show up on time.

Unlike ETJs, however, the EFJ's primary focus of attention is people. These types are not only energized by their relationships; they need peoples' opinions and reactions in order to make objective decisions. Accordingly, EFJs spend a fair amount of time in conversation—exchanging observations, getting feedback, offering advice, volleying plans and ideas, telling and hearing stories about things of mutual interest and concern.

Thinking types sometimes dismiss this kind of interaction as "small talk," but an ETJ's impersonal priorities dictate a view of social conversation as a "break" from what someone is actually "doing." For Feeling types, talking is doing. It's a purpose, something that people plan for, make time for, engage in.

EFJs have a hard time understanding how people can get together without exchanging information about their lives. Unless they know real facts about people—where they grew up, where they live now, what they do for a living, what their family's like—they don't have enough data to relate to them.

It should be noted that EFJs are not social butterflies in this regard. They're no more tolerant than Thinking types of "idle chitchat" that simply passes time or keeps them from meeting their obligations. Feeling types are too conscientious to use time frivolously, and they invariably have a full dance card of responsibilities to others.

If they're not serving on committees, they're meeting colleagues for lunch; visiting relatives; driving the kids to Scouts; making meals for a sick friend; attending graduations, school plays, and concerts; getting people together for celebrations, picnics, dinners, and so forth. EFJs are constantly reaching for their calendar or date book.

It is this broad range of social interactions that separates EFJs from IFJs, although some of their behaviors look similar. As discussed in chapter 15, IFJs experience themselves as helpers or nurturers, and they're guided by the immediate needs of the people around them. They tend to resist social leadership, particularly the onus of making decisions for a group, but will take a great deal of authority in a service position.

EFJs, by contrast, experience themselves as coordinators who can anticipate and handle the needs that arise in the normal interplay of established relationships with others. This is what makes EFJs so good at careers in sales, teaching, and group motivation. They have no doubt that their way of organizing a situation will benefit all concerned, and they're good at making decisions and delegating tasks as required.

Indeed, such types have a hard time *not* coordinating the situations in which they find themselves. At a party, they're likely to make sure that everyone feels at home and included, and they may get involved in preparations or cleanup if no one tries to stop them. They keep lists of names and birthdays; show interest in other people's welfare, homes, and families; make others feel important and valued. They celebrate with those who are happy, cry with those who are not; remember the ages and hobbies of everyone's children; and stay current with news about people's joys, sorrows, and problems.

These behaviors strike us as warm, related, and caring—and they are. Feeling types laugh and cry easily, are "there" for people in trouble, referee arguments, soothe egos, are nurturing, concerned, attentive. It should be emphasized, however, that their behaviors are also part of our social lexicon—a vocabulary that signals the concern and attention we read into it.

Fluency in this language is the type's strength, and it gives EFJs the ability to engage people's trust and cooperation—to teach, to inspire, to lead, to reach out. However, their reliance on social cues to interpret reality in general inclines them, almost inevitably, to merge sign and substance. The absence of an expected social gesture can hurt and offend them, as though a relationship *had* to be expressed in the appropriate way in order to be genuinely experienced.

Many of the letters that appear in the advice columns are seeking clarification of such issues. For example, a woman wrote to Ann Landers asking if she were right to feel demeaned and cheated when her fiancé bought her a piece of land in Texas rather than the diamond engagement ring she was expecting. Ann Landers, a veritable bellwether of traditional social values, agreed with the writer, maintaining that a ritual declaration of intent is simply not interchangeable with an ordinary property investment.

Tellingly, the resulting mail ran against her. Our ideas about what's important are no longer well matched by Extraverted Feeling gestures. But the entire issue is a good illustration of the way EFJs themselves understand reality.

How Extraverted Feeling Develops

As discussed in chapter 18, a preference for Extraverted Feeling appears to coincide with a tendency to register physical signs of pleasure and displeasure in a visible, predictable way. Because these signs are apparent to others, they become forms of communication, and people respond to them.

We all rely on such responses, of course, to organize our social experiences and to gauge the nature of others' expectations. For example, almost all children, when negotiating the unfamiliar, look to a parent or peer for the smile or frown that signals encouragement or caution. Over time, we associate certain kinds of responses with validation, approval, and warm relationships. One can see this happening even in the preschool years, when children experiment with exaggeration and denial, attempting to gauge, elicit, and avoid the reactions of the people around them.

EFJs, however, are motivated to use their interaction with others as a primary basis for decision making. They're highly alert to signs of pleasure and displeasure in others, so they generally consider the effect their behaviors will have on the people around them.

Don't Women Care More about Social Cues Than Men? We hear this all the time, of course—that women have a strong grasp of social expectations even in childhood, whereas men regard a social exchange as something that kills time between innings. Current research even suggests that an awareness of social cues is genetic to females, determined by the X chromosome supplied by the father.

The fact remains, however, that such distinctions don't show up on type tests. Men and women prefer Extraverted Feeling in nearly equal numbers. Moreover, as stated, EFJs constitute less than a quarter of the population, which wouldn't be so if women were "naturally" disposed to a Feeling orientation.

What's undoubtedly true is that men and women are socialized to recognize different *categories* of relationship, along with the specific behaviors they entail. Some of these social incentives may reflect biological propensities, but they're just as likely to keep FJs locked into the forms they've inherited lest they express themselves in the "wrong" terms.

Hagar the Horrible. Reprinted with special permission of King Features Syndicate.

It should also be emphasized that genetic potential is no insurance of good interpretive skills. Like logic, an understanding of expressive cues requires training and cultivation, along with strong cognitive and analytic abilities. Young EFJs can be surprisingly awkward in social situations—particularly when compared with the more outgoing Extraverted Perceivers. Until they know how to gauge people's expectations well enough, they're self-conscious and reluctant to take action.

Moreover, these types can find it difficult to negotiate our culture's self-oriented priorities. ESFJ children, in particular, anticipate criticism for failure, and they want to know how things are "supposed to be." In a culture that values independent action, they can experience a kind of catch-22 situation, in which social approval appears to require that they have no need for social approval.

The Objective Nature of Extraverted Feeling

Because EFJs learn to use their dominant function by anticipating the effects of their decisions on others, they may not be comfortable with internal states that can't be harmonized with the values of the group to which they belong. Asked how they actually "feel" about something, EFJs react uneasily, as though the question were designed to elicit a negative response and create disharmony.

For example, I overheard a conversation during the coffee hour at church one Sunday in which someone asked an ESFJ whether she really believed in life after death. The ESFJ was embarrassed and defensive. She said it was no one's business what she believed; her faith should be apparent by the fact that she came to church every week and served on the board of trustees.

As stated earlier, this distinction—between public behavior and subjective experience—has come, in our Perceptually oriented society, to seem like evidence of calculation, tantamount to cultivating the right image. But EFJs aren't thinking about their image in the way that P types imagine. They're concerned about the *meaning* their behaviors have for others. They feel guilty about expressing needs and impressions that would cast doubt on their values and commitments.

The ESFJ just described, for example, didn't hear the question about eternal life as an invitation to discuss theology. She heard it as a criticism, a suggestion that her relationship to the church wasn't good enough. As far as she was concerned, that relationship was *evidenced* by her outward behaviors. She had no intentions of questioning it or causing a problem.

Indeed, EFJs will deny negative thoughts or opinions for the sake of social harmony, particularly if the category of relationship warrants the strategy. Such denial strikes them as the better part of valor.

Thinking types, with their penchant for impersonal accuracy, regard the whole business of tailoring truth to the category of relationship as dishonest—and more than a little irrational. But, of course, TJs spend most of their lives trying to *separate* their judgment from degrees of relationship. For EFJs, right and wrong behaviors can't be determined until the category of relationship is established. To behave otherwise strikes them as dishonest and irrational.

Cathy ©1997 Cathy Guisewite. Reprinted with permission of Universal Press Syndicate. All rights reserved.

Of Ritual and Romance

The nature of an EFJ's values is nowhere more apparent than in the gestures and signs EFJs describe as "romantic." Because the word implies a situation that enthralls or enchants, it's often applied to right-brain Perceptual experiences—events in which we're caught up in the moment, without reservation or expectation. For example, we talk about the "romance" of sailing, exploring, falling in love at first sight.

These experiences, however, are transient by their nature. A recent cartoon depicts a small mouse, dead drunk, slumped over an empty bottle. The bartender explains: "He says life just hasn't been the same since he spent those few, glorious hours as one of Cinderella's horses."

As left-brain types, EFJs appreciate the all-consuming nature of immediate engagement, but they're more likely to apply the word romantic to behaviors that sustain the experience in time, deliberately kindle or renew it, or testify to its ongoing power. We use the word in this way, for example, when we talk about romantic devotion to a cause.

Traditional literary romances concern themselves primarily with behaviors of the latter sort, and such stories tell us a great deal about the way EFJs understand questions of relationship and conflicts of obligation. The typical Medieval romance, for example, includes a plot about star-crossed lovers—usually a knight in love with a married noblewoman.

We're meant to recognize in this doomed relationship the possibility of perfect communion; however, the pair's behaviors are ultimately dictated not by that compelling promise but by their responsibility to commitments already made. The noblewoman struggles to feign indifference, while the knight sets off on a Crusade, wearing her scarf like a banner.

Such decisions not only show strength of character—the ability to sacrifice immediate advantage for the sake of one's values. They also keep the promise of the forfeited relationship intact. And it is here that one sees the primary significance of romantic signs and gestures. They testify to the ideal nature of a relationship, which exists despite the inevitable claims of finitude, imperfection, and competing obligations.

EFJs are masters of ritual declarations, whether they're cultivating a friend, reassuring a partner, or making children feel special and important. They buy small gifts that echo important conversations, display mementos of happy occasions, create family traditions, and make time for events that symbolize commitment to the ideal, even if everyday interactions tend to fall short of it.

Although the yearning for symbols of this sort is sometimes stereotyped as feminine, a great many of our romantic media images involve Perceptually oriented males caught off guard by their own capacity for romantic idealism. One might consider, in this respect, the war-weary protagonist in the film *Casablanca*, undone by a song, or the "Sorry, honey, gotta ramble" photographer in *The Bridges of Madison County*, who finds himself gathering flowers and dancing by candlelight.

Like *Casablanca*'s Rick and Ilsa, the protagonists of *Bridges* are clear descendants of our medieval twosome: the knight-of-the-road with a poet's heart, passions contained by the prerogatives of chivalry, and the woman imprisoned by marital convention, whose soul mate shows up one promise too late. Both recognize, almost despite themselves, the power of ritual intimacies to idealize the relationship and acknowledge its promise; and both (albeit in late-twentieth-century fashion) sacrifice its potential to the cause of fidelity and honor.

Although most types employ ritual declarations when they're obliged to do so by standardized social occasions—such as Mother's Day, Father's Day, Valentine's Day, and the like—for EFJs, displays of ongoing interest and devotion are a primary means of communication. Their absence almost inevitably persuades them that the other person doesn't care enough about the relationship, doesn't feel its effects.

Thinking types, in particular, who append the word *romantic* primarily to the word *illusion*, can easily strike EFJs as oblivious to romance in general. And in truth, Thinkers don't pay much attention to states of relationship that otherwise elude their cognitive grasp. Even when they're trying to use Feeling signs and rituals, they're likely to understand what they're doing in terms of logic, not ideals.

The character Seven of Nine, in *Star Trek: Voyager*, nicely illustrates the extreme reaches of a Thinker's general attitude. Seven of Nine is a human female, raised from childhood by the Borg, a cybernetically enhanced race with a hivelike structure of collective logic. Now separated from the collective mind, Seven of Nine is trying to work with *Voyager*'s crew but has no idea what human relationships are all about.

When one of the helmsmen flirts with her, asking if she'd like to see a simulated moonrise on the holodeck, she's puzzled. "Why?" she asks. "Because it's beautiful," the helmsman says. "Beauty is irrelevant," she snaps. "Unless," she says thoughtfully, "you mean to change the nature of our alliance with ritual deception. . . ."

This is not far from what Thinking types actually believe—that romance is basically strategic deception, pleasurable perhaps, but utterly goal oriented. Thus, Thinkers have a hard time understanding why the characters in literary romances are so annoyingly impractical.

In a Thinker's medieval narrative, a knight who had withdrawn from a relationship for the sake of honor would scarcely advertise his ongoing interest in it. And if he were willing to sacrifice his principles and pursue the woman, by God, he'd execute a plan—hire an attorney, acquire a title, seek grounds to annul her loveless marriage. Such campaigns, for TJs, evidence devotion no less enduring but of more efficient outcome than the display of a lady's scarf amid the wreckage of Byzantine kingdoms.

Thus, it should be emphasized that ritual signs have meaning for EFJs because they *don't* represent a logical problem-solving approach to relationship. Their purpose is frankly sacramental, requiring an investment of faith: a belief in the existence of infinite possibility in a finite and imperfect world.

Secondary Considerations

Because EFJs concentrate their attention on standards of relationship, they tend to use their secondary Perceiving function (Introverted Sensation or Introverted Intuition) largely to acquire immediate information about others' reactions and expectations. Like Thinking types, they aren't comfortable with the indiscriminate content of their subjective life—disruptive thoughts and fantasies, questionable motives, unpredictable impressions, unmet needs. They don't react to this content, however, the way Thinking types do.

As noted in chapter 18, ETJs experience their Perceiving side pretty much the way Spock experiences the human half of his personality: as illogical and potentially out of control. EFJs understand their inner life differently. Accustomed to measuring behaviors against collective standards of good and bad relationship, many of their subjective thoughts strike them as negative, because they're self-critical or disapproving. EFJs believe such thoughts are unworthy of them and shouldn't be entertained.

A cartoon comes to mind from a few years back, meant to illustrate the difference between East and West Coast attitudes. The cartoon consists of two panels, one labeled New York, the other California. Both panels contain the same two people, one of whom is talking to the other. In the New York panel (with all due apologies for language), the person is saying, "F**k you!" but he's thinking, "Have a nice day!" In the California panel, the person is saying, "Have a nice day!" but he's thinking, "F**k you!"

EFJs appear to believe that people who are truly good would say "Have a nice day!" and mean exactly that. They try very hard to change or eliminate what they see as negative thoughts and reactions. If they can't, they try to live above them, hoping to inspire themselves to do better. EFJs feel this way because their approach to life is guided by rational ideals, and rational ideals are maintained by focusing on the predictable—things that can be anticipated and controlled.

When EFJs rely too heavily on Extraverted Feeling, they have no way of perceiving the messy, unpredictable, irrational side of life—except in negative terms: as something to be gotten under control. This is why their Introverted secondary function is a valuable source of information. By paying more attention to their immediate reactions, EFJs learn to deal with areas of life that can't be addressed with rational Judgment.

For example, the classic EFJ has a hard time saying no, even when time and energy are in short supply. Such types don't want to let people down, so saying yes satisfies their Extraverted Feeling ideals. Their inner reactions, however, are correspondingly realistic, based on life as it's actually happening to them. They may feel resentful, wondering why people don't realize they're overextended, or anxious, because, given their other commitments, the job won't get done as well as it "should."

In the long run, EFJs swallow their resentment and live with the anxiety. They'd rather maintain a harmonious relationship than put their own needs first. But they always feel bad about the part of themselves that won't "get with the program." They figure a good parent/partner/friend/neighbor wouldn't "feel like this."

And, ultimately, because Extraverted Feeling is the type's strength, the EFJ's ability to put others first, despite the clamor of that inner voice, becomes a source of pride. EFJs are like ETJs in this respect, who pride themselves on staying in logical control—even when self-interested immediacy is the healthier option.

The EFJ's viewpoint becomes particularly clear in Bible study classes when the discussion turns to the story of Martha (Luke 10:38–42). Such types hear this story as a criticism of the strengths they've worked so hard to develop. Indeed, it's worth considering the Gospel narrative, because it raises so many of the issues that EFJs associate, negatively, with their secondary function.

Jesus, on his way to Jerusalem with disciples, stops in to see his friends Martha and Mary. Martha immediately welcomes these unexpected guests and sees to their needs, while Mary, her sister, settles in at Jesus' feet and listens. Finally, overwhelmed by the work, Martha asks Jesus to take her part. "Lord," she says, "don't you care that my sister has left me to do all the serving myself?" "Martha, Martha," Jesus answers, "you're distracted by so many things. Only one thing is necessary. Mary has chosen it, and it won't be taken from her."

A generation ago, feminist theologians heard in this corrective an implicit criticism of women's traditional roles in society—which is precisely why many EFJs are uncomfortable with the story. Why should Mary's self-interested choice be considered superior to Martha's? Why is it wrong to show love in a traditional way?

This is how EFJs usually experience the promptings of Introverted Perception. It makes them aware of needs they ordinarily discount, and their reaction is to feel defensive. Like Martha, they know they're doing too much, but they feel caught between two inadequate solutions: they can exhort others to work harder, or they can ignore their responsibilities and do as they like.

It's important to note, in this respect, that the Gospel story doesn't set up this kind of choice. It doesn't pit responsibility to others against immediate desire. At the time of his visit, Jesus was a marked man, an outlaw. Within a week, he'd be sentenced to death.

He was asking Martha to recognize her immediate subjective *priorities*. *Under the circumstances*, her obligation to provide for guests was not the most important consideration.

This is always the issue for EFJs—not the will to escape the roles they've taken on, but the ability to take circumstances into account, to recognize when immediate priorities are more consequential than objective standards, to know that receiving is sometimes a more responsible choice than giving. EFJs can be so distracted by taking care of things that they miss the import of life as it's really happening to them.

Unquestionably, Thinking types share the EFJ's tendency to confuse responsibility with taking care of things. The entire city could be flooded and ETJs would drown before giving up on getting to work. But a personal crisis—of health or relationship, for example—can shock Thinkers into using their secondary function. If they can't master a situation with logic, they have little choice but to accept it on its own terms.

Feeling types are different. Their reason isn't anchored by impersonal logic. It's anchored by the people who depend on them, and they work hard to divide their time and energy among family members, employer, neighbors, friends, clients, and all the others in their life who expect their loyalty and devotion. Given these objective priorities, a life crisis may not test their faith so much as increase their resolve. I've seen EFJs put off surgery rather than let someone else organize the annual card party. Letting go, for any reason, strikes these types as a misplacement of values, a willingness to put their own well-being above the people who are counting on them.

In consequence, EFJs frequently end up being the person who does everything for everybody. They may be completely swamped, but their ability to keep things organized confirms their self-worth, so they don't have much incentive to do things differently.

Introverted Thinking: The EFJ's Inferior Function

EFJs who rely too long on their dominant strengths eventually leave their inferior function, Introverted Thinking, far behind. As discussed in chapter 19, Introverted Thinking is a right-brain form of Judgment that makes us aware of a situation's many variables. When we use it, we recognize our power, as individuals, to exploit some variables at the expense of others.

This kind of awareness is not only impersonal; it's graphic, immediate, and wholistic. It prompts no assignment of predetermined categories of good and bad. Variables that have unusual or perverse potential are accorded the same consideration as variables that assure a socially appropriate outcome. EFJs can't acknowledge this viewpoint as part of their own makeup; it's too alien to the way they see themselves.

As I've said in other chapters, all types are capable of using the *skills* their inferior function offers. EFJs who crochet or play softball are obviously aware of the impersonal variables involved, and they may be highly talented in using them to advantage when the outcome is compatible with their Feeling goals. What's at issue here is the *approach to life* Introverted Thinking makes possible. The impassive curiosity it fosters strikes EFJs as cold and inhuman, tantamount to pulling the wings off flies to see if they feel pain.

EFJs need experience with their secondary function, Introverted Perception, to even *recognize* Introverted Thinking in themselves, much less consider its moral potential. Until that point, the function remains primitive and egocentric, the source of prejudice and stereotypes about others. Whenever EFJs feel stuck, because a situation can't be handled with Extraverted Feeling, Introverted Thinking gets out of control, flooding them with impulses that undermine their usual Feeling behaviors.

Like all types, EFJs don't recognize this psychological pressure as an opportunity to move beyond their accustomed choices. When they can't handle a situation in their usual way, they project their inferior impulses outward and see their conflict as a problem they're having with others. They focus on other people's selfishness, inconsiderate behaviors, poor judgment, seduction by negative options.

It should be emphasized that well-developed EFJs are instrumental in supporting people's strengths. They listen sympathetically, interpret problems, brainstorm solutions, bring out the best in others. EFJs pressured by Introverted Thinking aren't motivated this way. Such types consider themselves authorities on human relationship, and they're always ready to tell others how to live their lives. Fearing that people aren't as strong or as logical as they are, their advice is often unsolicited, intended to keep people from making bad decisions.

EFJs of this sort are deeply affected by unconscious Introversion, and many of their social concerns are focused on creating safe and secure environments. They work hard to set up rules and systems that will guard people against dangerous influences. Such types believe they're taking action on behalf of others, but they're increasingly stubborn about getting their own way. They don't recognize they're *deciding for* others, limiting people's opportunities to take responsibility for themselves.

In truth, the wholistic perspective of Introverted Thinking has persuaded them that they need to control *all* the variables of the situations that matter to them. But given their dominant left-brain viewpoint, they're trying to do this by changing or eliminating the variables that strike them as negative and unworthy of selection; and given their defense against inner conflict, they're focusing all their attention on the outer world.

Because it's manifestly impossible to be everywhere at once and get everything under control, these types are never entirely satisfied and always under pressure. Moreover, because their standards are unrealistic, they consistently feel that others aren't doing their share of the work, that they're stuck with it all.

Turning to the Tertiary Function: Extraverted Perception   As Introverted Thinking gains unconscious power, it begins to seriously color the type's behaviors. Such EFJs are socially motivated, but they're self-protective and insecure, all their energies devoted to controlling their relationships. They need increasing reassurances that they're important to people, but they can't accept them even when they're offered. Any show of independence or interest in something they don't approve of impresses them as a betrayal of the relationship. People see them as jealous, possessive—and, ironically, unaware of others' feelings.

This is generally the point at which the type's tertiary function, Extraverted Sensation or Extraverted Intuition, steps in. As stated in other chapters, our tertiary function normally provides an outlet for "the other side" of our personality. It prompts EFJs to make room for pleasure, to laugh at themselves, to take life less seriously.

However, as a last-ditch defense against Introverted Thinking, Extraverted Perception simply convinces EFJs that others are to blame for *all* their negative thoughts. Indeed, these types can be overwhelmed by the need to escape the constant external conflict—to walk out on people who don't appreciate them, to tell them all to go to hell.

Just as extreme Thinking types project their unruly FP impulses onto people who depend on them, thus to keep them under control, extreme Feeling types project their rebellious TP traits onto the people they love, thus to keep *themselves* under control. They see themselves as victims, obliged to carry all the burdens of relationship, and they're determined to do so, despite others' apparent selfishness and lack of appreciation.

It should be recognized, in this regard, that the success of a tertiary strategy is not in its capacity to make us happy but in its ability to keep us from experiencing inner conflict. Because extreme EFJs have projected all their questionable motives onto others, they feel decisive and morally strong, quite certain they're on the side of the angels. They may even consider themselves role models.

Indeed, the tertiary influence of Extraverted Perception pushes these types to place increasing emphasis on how things look. As with extreme ETJs, their Judging and Perceiving worlds can become quite polarized, so they're actually living two different lives—the public one, in which all the appropriate behaviors, grooming, and rituals are in place; and the private one, which is devolving into a series of stormy arguments, silences, and recriminations.

Although extreme EFJs can sometimes lock themselves into relationships that are genuinely exploitive, most such types feel mistreated because others won't conform to their unrealistic expectations. They aren't taking people's individual needs and experience into account. Extraverted Perception ultimately persuades them that they're justified in interfering in people's life choices: doing, as it were, what people aren't doing for themselves—behind their backs if necessary. They talk constantly about the sacrifices they've made on others' behalf, the love and involvement they've shown—and does anyone thank them? No. They get heartache, grief, ulcers.

The fact is that extreme EFJs really *are* working hard to maintain their relationships. But the problem isn't people's ungrateful receipt of their efforts. It's the EFJ's insistence on controlling others' behaviors, the impossible standards they've set as evidence of people's devotion. In many of these situations, people are thwarting the EFJ's expectations not because they're irresponsible and unappreciative but to force the type's receptivity, to make contact somewhere outside the Feeling frame.

Developing Introverted Perception

In Australian aboriginal society, there exists a method of self-recovery called walkabout. Native peoples who have lived or worked in the city for a long period of time begin to forget who they are, so they return temporarily to aboriginal life and "walk about" in the bush until they "meet themselves" again. This is the sort of thing that happens to Extraverted Judgers when they get in touch with their secondary function. Something pushes them out of their rational framework and they're forced to deal with experience on its own terms.

As stated earlier, Extraverted Thinkers are often shocked into using Introverted Perception. Sometimes EFJs are, too, especially at midlife, when relationships can change rather abruptly. But most EFJs simply reach a point where they aren't sure who they are anymore. The identity they've established with and for others doesn't give them large enough answers. Despite all the people in their lives, they feel lonely.

This vague feeling of loneliness is a hallmark of unresolved secondary issues. When EFJs have depended too long on Extraverted Feeling, their relationships aren't mutual. The feedback they're getting is based on their social roles, not on who they are. The living, breathing human being who experiences things exactly as they happen isn't being perceived—not even by themselves.

A rather interesting look at the phenomenon occurs in an early episode of *Star Trek* called "Metamorphosis." Nancy Hedford is a Federation diplomat in the throes of a terminal illness. Kirk, Spock, and McCoy are taking her to the *Enterprise* for medical treatment when a peculiar cloud creature draws their shuttle craft off course and brings them to the planet Gamma Canaris N. There they meet Zefram Cochrane, a famed scientist thought to have died in old age many years before.

It turns out that he, too, was diverted by the cloud creature, whom he calls the Companion. The Companion periodically envelops the man in a kind of mist, and merger with the immortal creature has kept him young; but Cochrane has been lonely. The creature evidently captured the shuttle craft to solve the problem. With the aid of a universal translator, Kirk questions the entity and discovers that she's female. She's in love with Cochrane and, despite Nancy's deteriorating health, has no intentions of letting any of them leave the planet.

Cochrane is repulsed by this revelation. He had no idea the Companion's merger with him was an act of love, and he feels violated. Moreover, the fact that the creature would allow Nancy Hedford to die strikes him as literally inhuman. He can't even imagine returning the entity's declared affections.

Meanwhile, as her life ebbs away, Nancy is realizing that she's even more of an alien than the Companion, who at least knows what it is to be in love. Nancy has spent her entire adult life resolving conflicts in the galaxy, and she's never experienced either love or romance with anyone.

Recognizing that Cochrane will never love her as she is, the Companion makes a fateful decision. In the moment before Nancy's death, she unites with the young woman, preserving her life at the price of her own immortality. Nancy rises from her sickbed, vibrant and warm, feeling human love for the first time. The Companion part of her, unable to survive outside the planet's atmosphere, is astounded by the loneliness and limitations of human existence. Her vulnerability moves Cochrane, who now feels needed, and he elects to stay behind and grow old with her.

Like the Companion, EFJs relate to people by caring for them, taking responsibility for their welfare and their needs. This is the way they know how to love, and they want to be loved in return. But

EFJs who have relied exclusively on Feeling for relationship aren't in touch with their mortal human nature—the need to be cared for as well as to serve; the need to be sustained and loved as they are, imperfections and all.

When EFJs aren't in touch with this aspect of themselves, they experience their very real desires for space, relaxation, and self-interest as weaknesses to be overcome. This is what makes their relationships unequal. They unwittingly assume a position of superiority, as though they were intended by fate to Companion others, without needs, flaws, feelings, and potential of their own. Like Nancy Hedford, the vulnerable part of themselves has never loved or been loved on its own terms.

In many cases, EFJs recognize this other part of themselves only when it's in desperate need of attention and it sends frantic messages from the inner world. Such types may experience these messages as external events—aches, pains, depression, anxiety, obsessive worry, sleep disturbances, and the like. Unaccustomed to looking within, it's hard for them to get hold of their subjective impressions until they exist as entities that others recognize and identify with.

In fact, these types have a tendency to treat their symptoms as external problems that can be talked about with others, defined, treated, and made to disappear. It should be emphasized in this regard that Nancy Hedford would not have fared better if she had reached the Enterprise and been "cured" of her illness. Rather, she might never have found her true path. This is the value of an EFJ's experience of loneliness. It pushes EFJs to accept their subjective experiences as part of themselves.

Many of the unfocused anxieties these types experience turn out to be not symptoms of illness but information about the life path they're taking and how it relates (or doesn't relate) to their inner Perceiving nature. Although they're resisting this information, it's crucial to their health and well-being. If they aren't in touch with who they are apart from their social roles, then they aren't really sharing themselves with anyone, and they won't feel truly appreciated no matter how much they do for others.

EFJs who struggle with their actual needs and potential often need encouragement to contend with the conflicts that arise in the process. To that end, they may need to share their thoughts and ideas with other people—perhaps just one other, who can be counted on to accept the new information and give them nonjudgmental feedback.

However, it's also important for these types to enjoy themselves in activities that don't involve others at all. They need to find out what makes them feel truly alive and whole—whether this involves listening to music, spending time in creative pursuits, or just taking walks in the sun now and then.

EFJs who cultivate their inner life never lose their fundamental Feeling orientation. As they bring their values into harmony with their real needs and potential, their dominant goals are broadened and deepened. Moreover, because they know what it is to be vulnerable themselves, they're able to accept people for what they truly are. This capacity, along with their warmth, humor, and understanding, makes them genuine leaders and guides.

ESFJ: Extraverted Feeling/Introverted Sensation

ESFJ	
dominant	Extraverted Feeling
secondary	Introverted Sensation
left-brain alternatives	Extraverted Thinking
	Introverted Intuition
right-brain double agents	Extraverted Sensation
	Introverted Feeling
tertiary	Extraverted Intuition
inferior	Introverted Thinking

ESFJs are the people we usually describe as "wearing many hats." Popular magazines are filled with articles advising them to take time for themselves, but ESFJs know who they are, quite literally, by way of their relationships, and they thrive on their multiple roles and responsibilities.

It's not that ESFJs spend all their time looking for clubs and organizations to belong to. They're not necessarily "joiners." These types have a natural sense of community, and it informs everything they do. Whether they're part of a household, a religious group, a workplace, a team, or a car pool, they're quick to assume the responsibility that marks them as supportive and contributing members.

For this reason, ESFJs are the quintessential volunteers. They may have wall-to-wall commitments and a calendar full of Post-it Notes, but when people need their help, they show up and pitch in. If they're not helping a brother-in-law paint his den, they're organizing someone's shower or retirement party, making costumes for a community play, taking magazines to a friend in the hospital—all the while striving to keep their professional life, house, property, family, and pets in order.

In their sense of responsibility and need for organization, these types resemble ESTJs; however, their process of reasoning is very different from a Thinking type's. ESTJs reason impersonally, with logic, which operates *despite* the nature of their relationships. Accordingly, their primary source of identity is usually their accomplishments—what they know how to do well.

ESFJs reason personally, *in terms of* their relationships, so their identity derives from the roles they play in people's lives. Where Thinking types talk about things of general interest, ESFJs are concerned with social time and space, their questions centering around common values and connections in the community: Are you married? Do you live in the neighborhood? Do you have children? Do you know so and so?

ESFJs are not only conscious of their place in an organized network of relationships; they live by the values associated with the roles they've taken on. They want their behaviors to stand as evidence of right relationship to others: as a good parent, a good neighbor, a good friend, a good brother or sister, a good employee, a good coworker, and so on.

These values are also the ESFJ's primary criterion for appraising others' behaviors. Such types may, for this reason, have a strong sense of how things "ought" to be. They're deeply invested in the activities and holidays that bring people together in shared celebration, triumph, and sorrow. Conversely, the absence of behaviors they associate with a particular role or social occasion can hurt or offend them. They may conclude, for example, that there's something wrong if families don't eat dinner together at the same time every night, or if children don't send cards on Mother's Day.

It should be emphasized that the ESFJ's values are not a matter of individual preference. These types won't act on their subjective observations and reactions until they've measured them against the prevailing social current. If ESFJs run into a problem, for example, they don't withdraw and work it out logically, the way Thinking types do. Feeling types use logic to assess their options, but they *solve* a problem by seeking consensus—talking to friends, asking colleagues for advice, getting a partner's input.

Indeed, the ESFJ's inclination to talk things out with others can make these types outstanding networkers, consummately skilled in gaining others' cooperation for plans and new ideas. By the time they've interacted with everyone involved, the information has been integrated into the larger social pattern and people accept it as a given. All well-developed ESFJs demonstrate this gift in one way or another—the ability to listen sympathetically, to interpret problems, to brainstorm solutions, and to gain people's trust within the context of a supportive social framework.

ESFJs are able to offer this kind of support because they have an innate understanding of people as members of a larger community. Like ESTJs, they're often in a position of advocacy, helping others to negotiate their relationships and to get their lives in order. These types need more, however, than praise for a job well done, which usually satisfies a Thinking type. ESFJs need to know that people like and appreciate them.

Dr. John Carter, the young emergency room intern on the medical drama ER, is a nice illustration of an ESFJ in this situation. Initially on surgical rotation, Carter had good skills, but he felt inadequate, torn between his natural talent for patient advocacy and the impersonal standards of his supervisor, who misread his values as lack of professionalism. Until Carter met other physicians who shared his viewpoint and encouraged him to be who he was, he felt demoralized and without direction.

Just as Thinking types need sufficient distance from personal bias for their logic to work well, ESFJs must have sufficient support from the people in their lives for their values to find expression. Without this support, ESFJs may squelch their best skills in an attempt to meet others' expectations. Sometimes, for example, when an ESFJ is partnered romantically with a strong TJ, the type will get nearly even scores in all test categories, being unwilling to declare *any* preferences that might undermine the relationship.

One can see the same phenomenon in the ESFJ's concern with how people in their social role are "supposed" to present themselves—not only in terms of behavioral standards, but in terms of style, grooming, fashion, and so forth. ESFJs can, in this respect, resemble ESFPs, because their grasp of social images is nearly instinctive. However, their motives are very different.

ESFPs are cultural surfers, riding the waves of emerging paradigms long before they break on the shores of mass acceptance. ESFJs are cultural *swimmers*. Waves of social change, if anything, are a problem. These types pride themselves not on their trendiness but on their ability to stay with the current—to know what to do, wear, or say to make their statement within the context of others' expectations. If their own perspective is broader than an existing context, they may feel bored or trapped, but they'll generally respect community standards as they happen to be.

An ESFJ's home usually reflects the same kind of awareness, expressing the type's interests and tastes, but in a way that others will recognize and admire as emblematic of his or her social role or position. These types often have a flair for color and pattern, and they may coordinate their home furnishings and art around a theme that reflects a romantic ideal. They notice the atmosphere of other people's homes, and they assume that others are doing the same.

Of all the types, ESFJs are likely to surround themselves with people who share their approach to life, which ensures them of the support and approval they need. However, this strategy also keeps them dependent on their dominant skills. ESFJs are so alert to people's reactions and spend so much time exchanging observations and opinions with others that it's easy for them to believe they're in touch with how they really "feel" about things. In truth, however, these types may not know how they stand on an issue until they find out how others do. Ironic as it sounds, the greater their reliance on Extraverted Feeling, the less in touch with their own feelings these types are likely to be.

Although Extraverted Feeling motivates a strong interest in social interaction, it doesn't necessarily promote intimacy. It focuses the ESFJ's attention on standards of outward predictability—that is, on right and wrong behaviors. Despite their strong emotional investment in the behaviors that reflect their values, ESFJs who don't get sufficient contact with Introverted Sensation, their secondary Perceiving function, are like theoreticians without a real-life laboratory. The gap between their rational ideals and their actual nature strikes them as a weakness, something to be overcome.

For example, surprised by a spare half hour before guests arrive, ESFJs may feel guilty about taking the time to relax; they'll find something else that needs doing—or re-doing. They subordinate their immediate needs to their rational ideals. But without some acceptance of their experiential side, ESFJs literally *can't* perceive the unpredictable, uncontrollable aspects of life in general—except in negative terms: as something to be eliminated, ignored, or held at bay.

A letter appeared in a recent advice column from a man whose father had remarried, adopted his new wife's children, and subsequently had two more. The writer said that his own wife was the problem. She sent birthday gifts only to the second two children, claiming that the adopted ones weren't "really" related to him.

This is the way Extraverted Feeling operates when ESFJs don't pay enough attention to Introverted Sensation. The unpredictable side of life begins to incorporate any experience that isn't accounted for by prevailing categories of relationship. Without enough Sensate development, these types end up using their Feeling strengths defensively, to avoid information that doesn't fit inside their rational framework.

One can see this most clearly in the difficulty such types have in accepting negative feedback. ESFJs need Introverted Sensate skills to accept a disagreeable statement of fact without interpreting it as a statement of disapproval. If they can't make this distinction, they have no way to experience criticism except as a threat, an invalidation of relationship, and they use their Feeling skills to defend themselves from it.

They mount this defense not by addressing the point at hand, which would require a focus outside their rational ideals, but by listing all the good things they've done and deserve credit for, all the behaviors that make the relationship a valid one. If all else fails, they'll discount the person's qualifications to make the judgment. In the movie In and Out, there's a wedding preparation scene in which the groom's niece says to the groom's mother, "My Mommy says the marriage won't last." The mother smiles sweetly and says, "Your Mommy is an alcoholic, dear."

ESFJs who won't deal with facts and possibilities that lie outside their rational ideals have a particular problem facing the messy, irrational side of the social groups to which they belong—their families, their political organizations, their churches. They don't believe it's right to "air dirty laundry." Even an attempt to talk about a bad situation can strike these types as a mark of disloyalty to the group.

Ultimately, ESFJs who rely too heavily on their Feeling skills invite compensation from their own psyche, because their least-developed function, Introverted Thinking, gets too far away from their conscious aims and goals. When this happens, their accustomed strategies don't work as well to defend them against disagreeable information. Every time they make the effort, Introverted Thinking floods them with impulses that oppose their Feeling strengths.

As a right-brain Judgment function, Introverted Thinking makes us aware of immediate logical variables, without regard to others' expectations. ESFJs who can't tolerate facts at variance with their Feeling standards have no way to recognize Introverted Thinking as part of themselves. It's too alien to their accustomed perspective.

Under its unconscious influence, they feel a sense of conflict, but it's an external one. They're unable to focus on the ideal, because too many things are going (or could go) wrong. They attribute the problem to people's weaknesses or their refusal to do what they "should" be doing, and they spend a great deal of time advising, counseling, and correcting others, trying to eliminate the negative variables or get them under control.

Ultimately, because their external focus is defensive—an attempt to avoid inner conflict—the variables these types are concerned with seem a little petty, like the aforementioned distinction between "real" and adopted siblings. As an instrument of reason, Extraverted Feeling easily determines that adopted children are related to a family by *marriage*, liable to the same standards of treatment as children related by blood. The letter writer's wife was focusing on the uncontrollable outward variable in the relationship because she was unwilling to resolve the more serious conflict within—her resentment of social obligations irrelevant to her own priorities.

ESFJs who resist their own feelings inevitably become involved in an unwitting sleight of hand, focusing on variables that can't be changed under any circumstances, or are so inconsequential as to illustrate the Biblical injunction against "straining at gnats while swallowing camels." The further the type's attention is diverted from issues that really need to be taken into account, the more powerful Introverted Thinking becomes, until these ESFJs have no recourse but Extraverted Intuition, their tertiary function, to keep internal conflict at bay.

Ordinarily, Extraverted Intuition is the source of an ESFJ's well-roundedness. Adolescent ESFJs tend to experiment with its Perceptual immediacy while they're still forming their identity—enjoying their power to play hard, stay late; daring people to draw the line. In a well-developed ESFJ, it prompts the entertainment of new possibilities, the ability to see that traditional values look different in different life contexts.

When it's wielded defensively, however, Extraverted Intuition simply convinces ESFJs that the problem not only is outside them but needs to be straightened out right now, at any cost. Such types are overwhelmed by the need to change things: to get rid of the perceived problem once and for all, no matter who gets hurt; to take over and get things under control, not only for others, but behind their backs if necessary; or to shut it out of awareness in whatever way they can manage.

Ironically, the external conflicts these types generate by turning to Extraverted Intuition are far more dramatic than the inner conflict they're trying to resist. When ESFJs cultivate Introverted Sensation, they aren't assailed by impulses to tear down everything they've worked to build. The conflict Introverted Sensation brings to awareness is psychological—the breach between the willing spirit and mortal flesh.

ESFJs resist this awareness because they have the idea that good people don't experience such conflicts, and if they do they keep it to themselves lest they discourage others. However, when ESFJs wrestle with their needs, fears, and doubts long enough, they become like Jacob wrestling with the angel. That is, they lose the battle, but the encounter changes them forever.

The film just mentioned, In and Out, is about a well-regarded high school teacher who realizes, at the very point of taking his wedding vows, that he's gay. The teacher had never thought through his own subjective experience, because his self-image was integrated with the way his family, community, and fiancée saw him. He felt responsible to the people who loved him and counted on him. The film is a comedy, but it's also an interesting exploration of how people come to terms with questions they can't solve with Extraverted Feeling.

In one scene, the groom's mother is sitting in the empty church reception hall, in the company of several friends, trying to salvage what's left of her dreams. One by one, with self-consciousness and difficulty, these friends offer their support—by recounting events from their own experience that don't match up with the images they've presented to the world. By the time they've all taken a turn, they're laughing at themselves and recognizing the nature of true friendship.

In another scene, the townspeople, gathered for the high school graduation, recognize that the teacher's sexual preference—his subjective impressions of relationship—doesn't change the way they've experienced him all their lives: as a decent, caring, gifted man with roots in the community and a will for its survival.

These scenes are a good illustration of what happens when ESFJs accept the gap between their ideals and human nature. They become more honest with people and, in the process, find out who their real friends are. Moreover, they find, to their surprise and pleasure, that unpredictability and circumstance unite them with others just as surely as predictable social behaviors.

When ESFJs discover the pleasure of being received as they are and not simply for what they do, they also find that they can separate themselves from people's opinions of their outward behaviors; they aren't so wounded by criticism. They're able to risk more of themselves, to be vulnerable, to take new directions. In turn, they become more accepting of others' ways of looking at life, recognizing that unfamiliar behaviors can be related to their own values.

These well-developed ESFJs are the people we turn to when we need both empathy and clear-eyed realism. They have a genuine love of life that others recognize and want to be around. They know how to listen, how to laugh, how to forgive, and they have a gift for bringing out the best in others.

ENFJ: Extraverted Feeling/Introverted Intuition

ENFJ	
dominant	Extraverted Feeling
secondary	Introverted Intuition
left-brain alternatives	**Extraverted Thinking**
	Introverted Sensation
right-brain double agents	**Extraverted Intuition**
	Introverted Feeling
tertiary	Extraverted Sensation
inferior	Introverted Thinking

Like ESFJs, ENFJs reason in terms of relationship, but their motives and ambitions are somewhat different. On the great highway of life, ESFJs are car-poolers, making sure that everyone has a ride, wears a seat belt, and gets where they're going, safe and sound. ENFJs are more like road rangers, patrolling life's detours and alternate routes, rescuing lost drivers, giving them decent maps. They have a psychological turn of mind, an interest in the journeys people take and how they're negotiated.

Although ENFJs are sometimes drawn to the health, sales, and service careers that appeal to ESFJs, they're more often found in the professions we loosely describe as "the care of souls"—counseling, psychiatry, the ministry, education. Both types tend toward supportive advocacy, but ENFJs are usually in the business of social redemption. They have a strong need to improve the systems that determine human relationship and to help people find meaning in their lives.

ENFJs are almost always good writers and editors, and the combination of Feeling and Intution can give them an interest in linguistic translation. But they enjoy face-to-face communication, and they're usually good with an audience. Indeed, their charismatic interaction with a group, and their focus on systemic improvement, can put one in mind of ENFPs.

It should be emphasized, however, that ENFJs don't inspire world-changing visions so much as life-changing decisions. Like INFJs, these types are interested in the way people see things, and the possibility of seeing things from another, better perspective. In fact, it's worth comparing the ENFJs and INFJs, because they're oriented by the same two functions.

INFJs, who rely on Introverted Intuition for their approach to life, emphasize perspective itself, particularly the effects that an accepted social pattern can have on individual self-experience. For example, last generation's INFJs pointed out that traditional gestures of social respect, such as holding a door for a woman, could encourage women to experience themselves as dependent and in need of protection.

ENFJs, who are dominant Feeling types, see the situation from the other way around. As far as these types are concerned, people's self-experience can deform their social relationships, encouraging irrational expectations and assumptions about others. For example, the popular psychologist John Gray says that men and women have inaccurate ideas about each other, derived from the perspective of their own gender. ENFJs want to make people aware of their inner scripts so they can get past them and develop more realistic ways of acting in the world.

Such types, accordingly, tend to counsel and motivate others in whatever career they happen to choose, whether they're directing a play, coaching a team, advising an author, or preaching a sermon. Because Introverted Intuition gives them the ability to acknowledge a person's viewpoint as subjectively valid without requiring its logical justification or factual accuracy, they're highly receptive listeners who may find themselves the recipient of people's problems whether they intended to be or not.

These types can be exceptionally inventive and insightful as group leaders. They seem to have a sixth sense about how a group can operate as a crucible for individual growth and development. They genuinely believe that, deep down, people want to contribute to the system that supports them, and they're certain that communication, understanding, and identification will ultimately bring anyone under the judgment of collective values.

The type's idealism in this respect is so well developed that ENFJs can have a difficult time saying no, even when their time and energy are in short supply. Because they see the potential good in anyone's point of view, they feel guilty if they don't nourish it and bring it into being.

For example, the late John Denver regularly did benefits and donated his time and money on behalf of many social causes. Yet in his autobiography, *Take Me Home*, he admitted that his commitment to these projects wasn't nearly as strong as his empathy with the people who requested his time. He thought that *their* commitment was good and honorable, and he didn't want to let them down.

This is often the danger for ENFJs. Their ability to see the positive aspects of anyone's position can make them feel indecisive, as though they had no firm position of their own, or inadequate, because their standards for themselves are so high. In consequence, they rely on Extraverted Feeling for grounding, gravitating to people who need them, so they can take their stand on collective values. One can see this very clearly in the way these types drive toward social harmony, a tendency they share with their ESFJ kindred.

Say, for example, that someone in a group accuses another of hypocrisy. Both ESFJs and ENFJs will head off conflict by steering the conversation in a more positive direction. ESFJs, who understand statements as Sensate facts, have no choice but to circumvent a disagreeable one—by changing the subject or registering polite disapproval. ENFJs, however, handle the situation differently. They use their Intuition to see the potential good in the accusation—to see where the person's perspective can be shifted. "Let's look at hypocrisy," the type might suggest. "Don't our high standards always fall a little short in the arena of real-life choices?" What the ENFJ has done is to restate the person's position from an Extraverted Feeling viewpoint, thus "modeling" a more empathic way of looking at the situation.

The type's ability to bring subjective perceptions into the collective framework, where they can be managed with Feeling, is an inestimable gift, and ENFJs almost invariably use it well. The point, however, is that these types gradually develop the habit of bringing alternate views into harmony with their own. They need to recognize that they themselves aren't grounded until they accept the aspects of experience that can't be harmonized with their Feeling assumptions.

Indeed, the psychological bent of these types pushes them to understand life's irrational aspects, as though immediate existence were a perspective that could be reformulated, like any other perspective, and fit into their rational framework. As Feeling types, ENFJs seek consensus on their problems, but they're inclined to do so in the academic forum. Thus, although they constitute only 5 percent of the population, their ideas have an abiding influence on our collective understanding of the issues at stake.

As ENFJs take classes, conduct research, read self-help books, and share their ideas with others, their secondary conflicts help to shape the larger societal dialogue: Why is life the way it is? Why do bad things happen to nice people? Why do we make foolish choices? This is Extraverted Feeling writ large, in contention with the random, unmerciful nature of life as it occurs.

Such questions are not answerable in rational terms, and ENFJs who wrestle with them ultimately find themselves contending with the limits of their Feeling skills. But sometimes these types aren't wrestling with the questions so much as holding the irrational at bay, and Introverted Thinking, the ENFJ's inferior function, begins to get out of their control.

As a right-brain Judgment function, Introverted Thinking is directly opposed to the humane concerns of Extraverted Feeling. It directs our attention to the logical variables in an immediate situation, and it dictates a dispassionate interest in their potential, without reference to people's needs or values.

When ENFJs are resisting their Introverted side, they don't see this viewpoint as part of their psychological makeup. It's alien to their self-image and accustomed goals. But each time they encounter a problem that can't be addressed with Feeling skills, they're flooded with impulses from this inferior function that undermine their accustomed way of looking at life.

Like all types, ENFJs don't recognize this internal pressure as part of themselves. When they can't handle a situation in their usual way, they project their inferior impulses outward and see them as part of the external world. They focus their attention on the aspects of life that seem alien to human values, and they try to handle them as they would any other negative variable. That is, they try to see the good in them so they can be harmonized with their Feeling outlook, or they try to eliminate them from the picture.

Like all Extraverted Feeling enterprises, the theories ENFJs devise to domesticate the unpredictable have unmistakable social utility. In a culture short on collective values, these types offer standards, strategies, and a common vocabulary for the kinds of relationships we regard as decent and worth pursuing. They help us to negotiate our expectations of each other, to make order in the otherwise random course of human events. But this is very much the point.

Extraverted Feeling encompasses what is averagely attainable in a particular social system. The goals it encourages are not transcendently fulfilling; they're collectively appropriate. ENFJs need more contact with Introverted Intuition to recognize that pursuing rational ends doesn't, by a long shot, take the whole self into account. Without sufficient Intuition, they're prone to mistake the elimination of conflict for intimacy and good relationship, so they inevitably find new variables that threaten the ideal picture.

Ironically, the more ENFJs focus on ideal relationships, the less they recognize people as individuals. They generalize about human behavior, unable to appreciate the unique nature of another's experience. Introverted Thinking, meanwhile, becomes so powerful that these types begin to draw from their tertiary function, Extraverted Sensation, to keep their Feeling standpoint intact.

In a well-developed ENFJ, Extraverted Sensation is a source of balance; it encourages such types to engage in pleasurable pursuits, to make art and music, to enjoy the effect they have on others. ENFJ actors, for example, use their Introverted Intuitive skills to understand the perspective of the character they're playing and their Extraverted Sensate skills for the performance.

When ENFJs use Extraverted Sensation defensively, however, they focus all their attention on others' painful experiences, attempting to preserve their position as advocates and counselors. Such types are overwhelmed by the difficulties people have, but they try to keep their reactions under control. It's important for them to maintain a positive, calm, and reassuring manner. Believing that they should be able to handle anything that arises with reason and understanding, they may have a particular problem with displays of anger.

Although they're trying to model the values they hold—to be perfect examples of a decent, compassionate, insightful person—they can strike others as unable to tolerate negative information, particularly about the group or social system they represent. One can see how this Sensate defense works simply by looking at the controversies that erupt in psychological literature.

When an unusual number of female patients told Freud they had been seduced by their father in childhood, he had a hard time accepting the stories as memories. He ultimately determined that they were infantile fantasies, common to all women. As Freud's change of mind became apparent to the psychiatric community, people naturally wondered if Freud had simply psychologized a disagreeable social fact he didn't want to believe.

My point is not to address this question but to note how well this controversy preserves the Extraverted Feeling stance of the therapist. Even if it were proved that the stories were memories, they would still be regarded as a holdover from the past—a subjective experience that's interfering with relationships in the here and now. The therapist remains the advocate of a better way.

ENFJs need Introverted Intuition to recognize that perceptual experiences are not just part of the past. They're part of every situation we're in. They tell us about aspects of life that don't fit into our conceptual frame. For example, Freud's female patients knew rationally that the therapeutic relationship was a professional one, but they *perceived* the interaction as it really happened. Freud's own reports make clear his intimate manner, his seductive questions, his suspension of personal boundaries.

Such behaviors had implications beyond the reach of the women's rational expectations. But they existed nonetheless, working their way into persistent claims of inappropriate sexual relationship, until Freud was obliged to admit that some boundaries should be unconditional. Little wonder that he concluded the images were fantasies and had no implications for living, breathing paternal figures.[1]

ENFJs are accustomed to using Intuition largely for purposes of empathy—to put themselves into someone else's shoes. It's harder for them to train it on their own self-experience. It raises too many questions, suggests that every point of view is valid in its own way.

But ENFJs who depend too much on Feeling to set their course are ultimately robbed of life's immediacy. One can see this in the difficulty such types have with unsocialized STPs, who challenge their value system and resist their attempts at empathy. ENFJs want to bring out the potential of STPs in a socially acceptable way, but they also envy the type's spontaneity, appetite for life, and ability to live in the moment.

Indeed, the Sensate nature of popular culture can encourage extreme ENFJs to feel trapped by the very accomplishments they've worked hard to achieve. Their relationships may strike them as good enough but not exciting, not capable of inspiring the passion and joy they're looking for; and they feel guilty about harboring that kind of dissatisfaction. They feel out of touch with themselves and the people they care about, uncertain of what they really want or who they really are.

These feelings, it should be noted, are not unjustified. ENFJs who resist the aspects of life they can't control usually trap themselves in a position where they're always the person who takes care of others. They're highly dependent on social admiration and approval, but they aren't sharing their real selves with anyone. Under the influence of their tertiary function, however, they can be persuaded that the answer to this problem is to liberate their pent-up emotions—to escape their current context or to shed what they see as irrational guilt and inhibitions.

These efforts are rarely successful beyond initial feelings of relief.

Because the behaviors are defensive, they aren't truly liberating. In point of fact, they serve to reinforce the type's dominant perspective, convincing ENFJs, for a while at least, that they've found a more "authentic" relationship or a more caring community than the one they've left behind.

ENFJs who cultivate their secondary function don't experience impulses that "free" them from their Feeling standpoint. They become aware of subjective experience that can't be addressed by meeting Feeling goals, experience they haven't yet tapped or taken into account. This other part of themselves requires a different kind of nourishment—kinesthetic, artistic, contemplative: a way to take shape apart from questions of a collective nature.

Recognizing this part of themselves grounds ENFJs; they begin to feel at home in the world in a new way. They become more honest about their feelings, able to tolerate disagreement with others and the effects of radically different life experiences. Moreover, they see people's genuine possibilities, and they have the drive and energy to bring them out in a way that benefits society as well.

21

Introverted Feeling

ISFP and INFP Types

Left hemisphere		Right hemisphere
Inferior function		**Secondary function**
Extraverted Thinking		Extraverted Perception
Tertiary function		**Dominant function**
Introverted Perception		Introverted Feeling

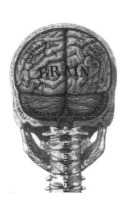

▲ LIKE THE OTHER JUDGING FUNCTIONS, Introverted Feeling prompts us to reason and to give meaning to our experiences. This function is somewhat less accessible, however, than the three already discussed. Although it encourages us to evaluate a situation, like Extraverted Feeling, its right-brain character ties us to experience as it's happening. Thus, we may not recognize Introverted Feeling as a form of Judgment. We tend to regard the viewpoint it encourages as "intuitive" or empathic.

Whatever types we happen to be, we use all four means of Judgment in one way or another. For example, if we were assembling a bookcase:

▲ *Extraverted Thinking* would prompt us to reason with causal logic: to make sure we understand the instruction manual and the predictable consequences of following the steps.

▲ *Introverted Thinking* would prompt us to reason with situational logic: to deal with immediate variables as they happen. Perhaps the holes in the second shelf don't line up with the holes in the groove it's supposed to occupy. Our step-by-step instructions don't cover this possibility, so we have to consider our options and their probable effects on the whole project.

▲ *Extraverted Feeling* would encourage us to Judge the finished bookcase in terms of general social expectations. For example, we might page through books and magazines about interior design, trying to determine whether this particular bookcase would look "right" in the living room.

▲ *Introverted Feeling* would prompt us to make the bookcase our own—that is, to give it a place among the things that matter to us. Maybe we'll use it for the books we love best. Maybe we'll put our collection of miniatures on the top shelf. We'll try something, change it, try something else, until the elements come into harmony for us and we're happy with the arrangement.

Although Introverted Thinking and Introverted Feeling both prompt us to reason perceptually, as a situation is happening, they preside over different areas of Judgment. Introverted Thinking is dispassionate and impersonal, prompting an interest in systemic logic: the probable consequences of immediate choice. For example, if we drill new holes into our shelf groove, will we have to compensate at other points in the process?

ITPs, for whom Introverted Thinking is primary, are usually creative technicians of one sort or another who reason literally in terms of patterns and emerging variables. Paul Simon, for example, talks about the constant evolution of a song as he exploits its structural potential, incorporating a snatch of Bach here, a gospel chord change there, each decision affecting the whole, creating new consequences and possibilities.

Introverted Feeling focuses our attention differently. It encourages a *personal* relationship to an evolving pattern, a will to gauge the situation by an experiential ideal. For example, if we use Introverted Feeling to make a good spaghetti sauce, we won't follow recipes or measure ingredients. We'll sample the sauce as we're making it, gauging its taste, smell, and texture by their ideal outcome and adjusting for circumstantial variables so the emerging pattern stays on track.

Although this process might be called aesthetic judgment, it doesn't operate on the basis of artistic *principles*. Its basis is living, breathing, firsthand experience. If we've never encountered a decent spaghetti sauce, we wouldn't use Introverted Feeling. We'd turn to *objective* Judgment: acquire a recipe (Extraverted Thinking) or ask a friend for advice (Extraverted Feeling). We might even use Introverted Thinking and experiment. To invoke Introverted Feeling, however, we have to know the difference between a good outcome and a bad one—know with our senses, in our bones.

The Moral Dimension of Introverted Feeling

As noted, using Introverted Feeling doesn't make us "feel" reasonable. We may not even feel like we're acting on "knowledge." We feel receptive, creative, guided by perceptions we can't explain. We tend to make this distinction, however—between a rational approach to life and a creative one—because we associate reason so firmly with the left-brain functions, particularly the generalized standards and logical control encouraged by its direct opposite, Extraverted Thinking.

The situation is complicated by the fact that only 6 percent of Americans use Introverted Feeling as their primary approach to life. This means that a great many types associate this function largely with its bottom-rung potential for impressionism and sentimentality. The stereotype is particularly common when aesthetic Judgment takes on a moral dimension.

Moral choices prompted by Introverted Feeling are not derived from legal principles or the social obligations that accrue to our roles in the world. They're derived from the subjective experience of being human, our will to deal with a situation in terms of human ideals. Decisions made on this basis are frequently misunderstood as a product of emotion or a deliberate rejection of structural authority.

For example, in an episode of the syndicated series *La Femme Nikita* about a hit woman in training, the heroine is led by Introverted

Feeling to ignore statistical risk and rescue the kidnapped child of a fellow recruit. Afterward, her immediate superior counsels, "You're a good operative, Nikita. Don't let your humanity get in the way."

This is precisely what Introverted Feeling does: it bypasses structural considerations and puts human value first. Such discrimination is unquestionably illogical, but it's in no way irrational. Indeed, to place human value above statistical risk isn't *possible* without the ability to reason.

One might even suggest that it's the rational character of Introverted Judgment that separates us from the species who share most of our DNA. Our closest primate relatives can be observed to use Extraverted Judging skills. They recognize a hierarchy of relationships, react to social cues, sacrifice their options for a wounded mate or an infant. They can be taught to perform calculations, to manipulate signs, to abstract general concepts. But they can't be taught to defy statistical odds purely for the sake of human value.

In fact, no one learns to make such decisions by way of formal instruction. As stated, Introverted Feeling is trained by subjective life experience. IFPs, who depend on this function as their primary means of reasoning, need enough *objective* experience to recognize the moral potential of their Judgment. Without it, they don't appreciate the difference between purely circumstantial values and values that link them with the larger human enterprise.

Some of our values, after all, are shaped by a specific context, and they're irrelevant when circumstances change. Others are quintessentially human and, as such, unconditional. Unconditional values can't be erased from the human psyche, no matter what kind of social system is in place. To express them is to see through the divisions external distinctions reinforce.

One might consider, in this regard, the famous incident in 1880, when Texas Rangers rounded up a group of Apaches in New Mexico and began lynching three an hour until someone revealed the hiding place of their chief. A U.S. Cavalry troop rode in and not only objected to the tactics but arrested the Rangers for murder. These troopers were the "buffalo soldiers," former slaves who had been recruited for duty on the Western frontier. Hard experience had taught these men a good deal about institutionalized inhumanity.

Indeed, they anguished over the conflict between proving themselves competent soldiers and colluding with their former masters in the kind of discrimination they had known firsthand. This conflict has nothing to do with sentimentality. It measures the basis of collective identity against the criterion of unconditional human value.

As suggested, Introverted Feeling is not a substitute for Extraverted Judgment. It won't solve the analytic problems that logic and causal reasoning are designed to address, and it won't establish a basis for predictable social interactions. But, conversely, it addresses aspects of human reality that Extraverted reasoning cannot.

Without a Song

Star Trek: Deep Space Nine offers an interesting portrait of a people who operate *without* Introverted Feeling—a species called the Vorta—and it's instructive to consider the way these humanoids understand life. The Vorta were genetically engineered by a race known as the Founders, who have no permanent form. Their purpose is to manage the Founders' objective affairs (politics, business, military strategy) among the "solid" species on satellite planets.

In their malevolent wisdom, the Founders left Introverted Judgment out of the Vorta's genetic code, and although an occasional administrator regrets his inability to appreciate art or to carry a tune, the Vorta believe such capacities irrelevant to their basic commission. What the Vorta don't recognize is their consequent lack of wholistic perspective—at all levels of application.

For one thing, they can't appreciate military strategy, which requires Introverted Thinking. They understand battle plans only in terms of the limited goals they're meant to achieve and the time it "should" take to reach them. More significantly, these creatures have no conscience. They don't recognize the possibility of questioning what the Founders have ordered them to do, and they're not capable of empathizing with the people their actions affect.

As stated, aesthetic judgment has a moral valence that goes beyond matters of art and music. It gives us the capacity to see a situation whole, apart from the assumptions we've absorbed from a particular community—and to determine, from that broader perspective, the integrity of our actions. Extraverted Feeling, with its emphasis on prevailing social behaviors, can't provide this wholistic aspect of decision making.

Indeed, the Vorta are perfectly capable of demonstrating social affinity with others. They smile when required, say the right things—but no one *ever* believes them. One might consider a recent cartoon character who describes social correctness as the ability to smile and lie, as in "Nice to see ya! Have you lost weight? How's the family?" Without some capacity for Introverted Feeling, our relational behaviors are purely strategic; they have no subjective content.

It should not be supposed, in this regard, that Introverted Feeling is *opposed* to Extraverted Feeling. Both involve the "right" ordering of our relationships and loyalties. Their different effects in the brain, however, see to it that they produce inverse results.

Extraverted Feeling relies on the outward, left-brain criteria of custom and law to mark off decisions that go beyond our immediate experience to affect the larger community. For example, in chapter 20, I mentioned rape and child abuse, which are not matters of individual choice, because they poison the society that tolerates them.

Introverted Feeling relies on the inward, right-brain criteria of experience and empathy to mark off decisions that go beyond our roles in society to affect us as human beings. Law and custom, after all, are the lowest common denominator of a defined community. We associate character and humane behavior with the moral imperatives shaped by inner values.

One might consider the following story from *Chicken Soup for the Soul: 101 Stories to Open the Heart and Rekindle the Spirit*:

In one bus seat, a wispy old man sat holding a bunch of fresh flowers. Across the aisle was a young girl whose eyes came back again and again to the man's flowers. The time came for the old man to get off. Impulsively, he thrust the flowers into the girl's lap. "I see you love the flowers," he explained, "and I think my wife would like for you to have them. I'll tell her I gave them to you." The girl accepted the flowers, then watched the old man get off the bus and walk through the gate of a small cemetery.[1]

The meaning and force of this story depend entirely on whether the listener has an inner point of reference, one trained by personal experience. Who the people are, what city they're in, what faith they practice, their racial and social makeup—none of it matters. The story bypasses all that to focus on the quintessentially human.

IFPs, who use Introverted Feeling for their dominant approach to life, are drawn, more than any other type, to medical and religious occupations, and particularly to organizations like the Peace Corps, Doctors without Borders, and Habitats for Humanity, which allow them to take humane action transcending conventional Extraverted conceptual and social boundaries. But Introverted Feeling can also precipitate feelings of self-doubt, because the type's ideals generate expectations that are larger than an Extraverted life can accommodate.

IFPs may, for example, have the sense that they don't fit in, and they can be lonely underneath their "live and let live" exterior. They feel called to do something meaningful and good, something that will bring their values into the fabric of the community, and if they have no way to do this, they don't know how to define themselves. They may believe they're "making do" until their purpose becomes clear to them and their "real life" begins.

Secondary Influences

Although ISFPs and INFPs are both motivated by Introverted Feeling, they're prompted by their secondary Extraverted function to develop and express their values differently.

▲ ISFPs, who relate to the world with Extraverted Sensation, are engaged by material reality as it exists, and their values, accordingly, are a product of concrete experience.

▲ INFPs, who relate to the world with Extraverted Intuition, are engaged by patterns of meaning, and their values are a mixture of experience and the mental impression of alternate patterns.

Extraverted preference plays such a strong role in determining the IFP's interests and behaviors that core similarities between ISFPs and INFPs can be difficult to see. ISFPs literally *require* sensory engagement to bring their Judgment into play, so they're inclined to be physically active and may be restless when they aren't. They resemble ESPs in this respect more than they do their speculative INFP kindred.

Indeed, the behavioral distinctions between ISFPs and INFPs have led David Keirsey and Marilyn Bates, in *Please Understand Me: Character and Temperament Types*, to dispute the idea that ISFPs are Introverted Feeling types at all. As mentioned in chapter 19, Keirsey and Bates believe that ISPs should be classified together with ESPs as SP types.

> SPs, they say, are temperamentally distinct from INFPs: insubordinate; easily bored, wanting excitement, risk, chance, and tests of luck; uncomplicated in motivation. . . . ISFPs are misunderstood . . . because the Jungians have cast them as "introverted feeling types," and therefore very much like the INFPs. Watch a few thoroughgoing ISFPs and you'll find they have very little in common with INFPs.[2]

Although the outward behaviors of ISFPs and INFPs are unquestionably influenced by opposing Extraverted preferences, Keirsey and Bates have been led by the demands of their temperament theory to ignore the IFP's *inner* motivation. Introverted Feeling is a way of looking at life, a lens ground by direct experiences of good and evil, but it has to be adjusted for immediate outward conditions, rather like a camera.

ISFPs understand these outward conditions by way of Extraverted Sensation, so they're adjusting their lens for concrete changes in their physical environment. INFPs understand external conditions by way of Extraverted Intuition, so they're adjusting for hidden patterns and unrealized potential. The clarity of focus IFPs are trying to maintain, however, is consistent, and this is determined by Introverted Feeling.

How Introverted Feeling Works

Introverted Feeling works in the background of awareness, very much like Introverted Thinking. It moves us to adjust rationally to a situation while it's happening. As stated, the process is a bit like using a camera whose lens has been ground by our personal experience of good and bad situations. We're looking through this lens at the outer world, but we're also making adjustments for unexpected variables, for circumstances as they exist here and now.

It's easiest to see the nature of this process when IFPs make art—that is, when they "take a picture" with their typological camera and bring a bit of their vision into the objective world. Elvis Presley, for example, illustrates a classic ISFP perspective, in which outward expression is determined by one's concrete interests and experience.

By the time he was eighteen, Presley had absorbed as many forms of music as existed around him—blues, gospel, hillbilly, pop—but he drew no formal distinctions between them, had no Extraverted Judgments about the "slots" American society had determined for them. All he saw was what was "good" and what wasn't. The consistency of his Judgment unified those influences into a sound that changed the direction of popular music—and forced people to recognize some of the racial and social barriers in the music business.[3]

It should be emphasized, in this respect, that ISFPs who use their subjective experience to focus on what is unconditional in human nature don't necessarily make art that coincides with social prescriptions for "good" behavior. They're more likely to do as Elvis did—touch on some vital human principle that society has attempted to isolate as a class or racial problem.

INFPs demonstrate exactly the same kind of Judgment, but their Extraverted arena is more likely to involve patterns of meaning. For example, director Errol Morris uses film to explore the mystery of human endeavor—why we persist in doing things that may well disappear when we do.

In Fast, Cheap & Out of Control, he finds overlapping themes in four disparate pursuits, interviewing a lion tamer, a topiary gardener, a robotic scientist, and an expert in mole rats. None of these fields has an apparent external relationship with the others, but each man is obsessed with what he does, and Morris weaves his subjects' remarks in a way that ultimately manufactures a whole narrative. Both interviews and visuals begin to blend into each other, revealing patterns, themes, and relationships that turn the film into a poetic elegy to the entire human project.

IFPs don't need to be artists in the conventional sense of the word, but they do need some way to integrate their outer and inner realms. An INFP psychologist of my acquaintance addresses this problem by hosting a regular gathering of people who have influenced, at various points in her life, her ideas about spiritual growth and practice.

The ages, professions, and religious persuasions of these people are broadly diverse but not important to her. She convenes the group because the members have nourished her inner life and helped to give it verbal expression. In turn, the group is guided by her subjective values to interact in terms of their common human quest.

How Introverted Feeling Operates in Different Types

Once it's clear how Introverted Feeling operates, its character is apparent in all the types who use it—as are the differences in its outward expression.

EFPs

EFPs, as dominant Extraverted Perceivers, take outer reality for granted—as it happens to them. They like people, enjoy the unpredictable nature of direct experience, and have a tendency to live in the present. Accordingly, most EFPs take jobs that involve a rapidly changing environment and interaction with others, and they use Introverted Feeling to find common human ground with the people they're meeting.

When Introverted Feeling is minimally developed, EFPs use it only to support their Extraverted motives, and they rely too much on outer experience for their self-image. Such types are good at identifying with others, but they seem unpredictable, because their basis for relationship is shaped by whatever people they happen to be dealing with. They're hurt and puzzled, however, when others question their inconsistency, because they're trying so hard to connect with others in an empathic way.

The better EFPs develop Intraverted Feeling, the more they recognize their power to support unconditional human values in those aspects of life that society has overlooked. ESFPs tend to do this concretely, by acquainting themselves with the facts and reaching out to people who need them. The late Princess Diana, for example, took her Sensate world for granted but used her advantages in that realm—her wealth, fame, and charisma—to attract the world's attention to the poor, the sick, and the displaced.

ENFPs are more likely to focus on patterns of understanding, attempting to change people's ideas about prevailing social or psychological structures, or to show people, by prophetic example, the creative benefits of a new approach.

IFPs

Oriented by Introverted Feeling itself, IFPs don't reinvent themselves with each experience they have. They depend on Extraverted Perception to *control* their outward experience—to ensure its connection with their values. The difference is immediately clear if we compare Princess Diana, who lent her Sensate celebrity to popular causes, and Mother Teresa, who limited her Sensate world to an arena of direct service.

When Extraverted Perception is minimally developed, IFPs use it only to support their Introverted motives and don't get much experience outside the situations that engage their Judgment. They need enough Sensation or Intuition to recognize the difference between subjective preference and unconditional human values. Otherwise, they're inclined to use their lens like a magnifying glass, emphasizing the importance of their own experience at the expense of everything else. Or they'll depend on others for objective structure and social relationship, "going along" with required Extraverted activities without being fully engaged by them.

Even an artist as successful as Elvis Presley ultimately used his wealth and social status to conform his environment to exactly what he thought worth his time and effort, and his total absorption in that world became legendary. For all his savvy as a self-schooled musicologist, he reneged on any task that required an Extraverted

Thinking perspective, and so depended on others to make his objective decisions: he established no organized way of paying his session men, allowed his manager to determine his professional direction, and set no limits on his own appetites.[4]

The more IFPs develop their Extraverted Perceiving skills, the less they discriminate among their experiences, and the more they accord value to direct knowledge of many areas of life. Such types acquire the ability to take life as it comes, their values like rocks beneath the surface of moving water, giving them a certain path.

For example, the popular Sister Wendy Beckett, of *Sister Wendy's Story of Painting*, was led by her values to construct a cloistered life for herself, and she spent much of her time absorbing information on art. It was her ability to locate the common human aspects of art that brought her to public attention, and she took the opportunity to teach on film. Although her consequent celebrity may seem paradoxical given her primary vocation, IFPs who develop their Perceiving skills pay little attention to outward distinctions.

The IFP Types

ISFP		INFP	
dominant	Introverted Feeling	dominant	Introverted Thinking
secondary	Extraverted Sensation	secondary	Extraverted Intuition
right-brain	**Introverted Thinking**	**right-brain**	**Introverted Feeling**
alternatives	**Extraverted Intuition**	**alternatives**	**Extraverted Sensation**
left-brain	**Introverted Sensation**	**left-brain**	**Introverted Intuition**
double agents	**Extraverted Thinking**	**double agents**	**Extraverted Thinking**
tertiary	Introverted Intuition	tertiary	Introverted Sensation
inferior	Extraverted Feeling	inferior	Extraverted Feeling

As stated, IFPs constitute about 6 percent of the population—nearly all of them ISFPs, who rely on their Sensate skills for information about reality. INFPs, who make up scarcely 1 percent of us, rely more on their ability to find meaning and potential in what they see.

This difference is amplified by popular culture, in that some 40 percent of Americans deal with external reality by way of Extraverted Sensation. Thus, ISFPs have more opportunity than INFPs to develop their secondary function and to relate to others on that basis. Most are drawn to hands-on professions that allow them to meet the sensory and physical needs of others—medicine and social work, for example, or cooking, or making music. They're also likely to be artists—painters, potters, jewelers, instrument makers, and so forth.

INFPs, on the other hand, have more flexibility than ISFPs, because they're not as dependent on physical action to express their values. They're more inclined to seek meaning and depth in their work, in areas like psychology, spiritual development, editing, and special education. INFPs resemble ENFJs in this respect, who go into many of the same professions.

It should be emphasized, however, that ENFJs are Extraverted Feeling types, who act as social advocates. They help people to realize their potential in a way that society will ultimately accept. INFPs are advocates of the inner world, the values that connect us to other living beings in a fundamental way. They go where they feel needed, helping to nurture these values or to support people who have fallen through the cracks of a prevailing social system.

Although ISFPs don't have the same interest in psychological and social theory, they have the same drive to connect their outward experience to fundamental human ideals. They, too, go where they're needed—healing the sick, tending to the lost, taking care of animals or nature. But these types are also attracted to Sensate activities that make them feel in harmony with a whole environment: playing a sport or an instrument, spending time in the woods, letting go of attachments and just "being."

Indeed, most IFPs have some investment in an activity that will express their fundamental sense of harmony with life. If their career can't satisfy them in this way, they'll create a "space" for themselves in their off-work hours, where they can make contact with that still point inside. Such activities are not necessarily "artistic," but they usually involve some medium in which the type can grasp the structural patterns of the inner world—listening to music, painting a mural, tending a garden, practicing a discipline, attending worship.

For example, a young ISFP of my acquaintance collected comic books and spent his leisure time drawing larger-than-life heroes and villains. Having lost his father in childhood, he identified very strongly with fictional characters like Batman—Introverted heroes for whom tragedy had galvanized special powers and the ability to fight for the common good. He had a particular affection for film star Brandon Lee, charismatic son of the late martial arts expert Bruce Lee.

As suggested earlier, the Sensate nature of popular entertainment tends to be consistent with an Introverted manner of Judgment, and ISFPs are able to use it for rational perspective. It gave this particular young man a way to construct meaning from an otherwise random childhood event: to see a universe in which all events, however pointless and irrational they may seem at the time, have a larger archetypal purpose.

When Brandon Lee also died, in a freak accident, the young man felt a sense of grief he could scarcely explain. The integrated universe he had glimpsed by way of Lee's image seemed lost, along with the connection he felt to others who appreciated Lee's work. He finally came to terms with the situation by creating a ritual of his own. He set up an altar in his room and every year, in the month of Lee's death, places fresh flowers at the altar and says special prayers.

One of Jung's enduring ideas is that the unconditional aspects of human reality are normally mediated by cultural images and rituals, which tie prevailing social assumptions to larger human truths. When collective images no longer make this connection for people, individuals are forced to appropriate those larger truths for themselves. IFPs, in some respects, are living illustrations of how this psychological process works.

They recognize by way of their own experience an unconditional value that links them with humanity as a whole, and they're moved, accordingly, to sacralize the event that revealed it to them. The will to make art or perform is an extension of this motive, in that it universalizes the IFP's experience, making it a window on larger meaning.

IFPs thus have a wide range of self-presentations. Some are drawn to a life pared to the human essentials, and they seem Zen-like or otherworldly; others are determined to help others, apart from conventional assumptions about status and power. Some make art that weds the individual situation with its universal import; yet others put themselves on the line, breaking the law for a higher moral purpose, and willing to pay the price.

In all these cases, IFPs are holding with ideals that are larger, and more stable, than a universe of chance and possibility can contain, and the effort to do so gives them an almost karmic sense of good and bad. To be attached, to care about objects sets in motion the archetypal drama of opposites. One cannot seek the good without contending eventually with the other side.

Between Friends

Between Friends. Reprinted with special permission of King Features Syndicate.

Like ITPs, Introverted Feeling types can be challenging for left-brain Judgers. Types oriented by Extraverted Feeling, for example, believe that having values is to do the right thing in the right circumstances, even when subjective desire encourages them to do otherwise.

IFPs have the inverse idea. Value, for these types, is a fateful claim from within that aligns one's behaviors with a larger purpose, notwithstanding perceived circumstance or social obligation. This is what makes the IFP's behaviors seem irrational to an outside observer. They can't be causally deduced from the objective situation.

Indeed, this is why matters of spiritual motivation are almost invariably couched in Introverted Feeling terms. One might consider the following quote used by Dorothy Day, the founder of the Catholic Worker movement:

> To be a witness does not consist in engaging in propaganda or even in stirring people up, but in being a living mystery; it means

379

to live in such a way that one's life would not make sense if God did not exist.[5]

Introverted Feeling in Pop Culture

The increasingly Sensate nature of popular culture has ensured a corresponding increase in the popular association of spiritual awareness with the development of Introverted Feeling. One can see this association in the extraordinary number of books devoted to creating sacred "space," workshop altars, and personal rituals that resonate with our "authentic self."

One can see it as well in our media pantheon of SFP icons. From Luke Skywalker to Buffy the vampire slayer, these heroes are usually quiet, reluctant sorts, their values ripening under force of dysfunctional social paradigms, pressing them into action against the chaotic forces of darkness.

This is clearly Introverted Feeling writ large, and as I've implied, such images have genuine typological valence. They reflect the hunger of a Sensate society for values more enduring than the pleasures of surface experience. Moreover, as the story of the "buffalo soldiers" makes clear, to bear the brunt of a society's inhumanity can train a viewpoint that has evolutionary potential for human consciousness.

There are a number of problems, however, with the iconization of Introverted Feeling imagery. One is the fact that however easily it lends itself to expressions of spiritual awareness and political prophecy, Introverted Feeling is *not* tantamount to spirituality. Although it offers a profound way of witnessing to the sacred, each function provides its own means of spiritual witness and vocation.

More significantly, the human values that Introverted Feeling brings to awareness are just that—Introverted. They don't offer a basis for an objective social system. If anything, they offer a basis for *disattachment* from social conditioning. This is what gives them the power to change hearts. The only kind of world in which Introverted Feeling could possibly obtain as a primary source of *social* Judgment is a chaotic, unpredictable one in which the systems designed to protect the community have no power to do so.

This is precisely the sort of world that syndicated saviors like Hercules, Xena, Sinbad, Conan, and Buffy inhabit week after week—a world in which spiteful gods and demons prevail, and our only hope is to recognize our fundamental connection to "the force," "the roar," or the "eternal energy" that permeates all living things. The undeniably engaging Hercules can scarcely make time for a pleasant dinner with Mom before the cosmos goes awry and he's obliged to return to his singular destiny.

Well beyond the comic book fictions of TV and film, the award-winning play *Angels in America* depicts exactly the same kind of apocalyptic world. The merciless reality of AIDS has knocked down familiar social boundaries and political agendas, and the dying recognize themselves called to the Great Work: that of uniting people around common human values in an otherwise horrific life experience.

The insistent theme that runs through these FP myths is the hopeful idea that if everyone developed Introverted Feeling, external boundaries wouldn't matter anymore. We'd realize that all people are unique, have their own gifts, and are valuable as fellow humans. And it may be noted, in this respect, that people whose subjective experience has led them to champion this kind of vision almost always get high INFP scores on type tests.

The hard reality, however, is that Introverted Feeling acquires prophetic power only by virtue of its relationship to a framework of common expectations. It indisputably calls a society to account, but it doesn't suggest a substitute paradigm for social relationships.

The Water of Life   An interesting anecdote speaks to this last point. Mother Teresa was reportedly giving a speech on a hot summer's day. Her voice was becoming hoarse, so a man in the audience went out of the crowded auditorium into a nearby kitchen and poured her a glass of water. When he walked up the long aisle to the podium and gave it to her, Mother Teresa scarcely looked at it. She handed it off to one of the people seated on the dais.

So the man went back into the kitchen and poured another glass. The same thing happened—not once, but again and again, until everyone on the dais had a glass of water, along with several members of the audience. The man was in a quandary. He envisioned himself spending the rest of the afternoon trying to serve all the people in the auditorium.

This story gives us a perfect capsulated image of Mother Teresa's IFP strengths: her disregard for issues of status or privilege; her single-minded selection of variables related to her values; and her ability, in that single-mindedness, to offer her audience an object lesson. With utter clarity, the people who watched the little drama could appreciate the immensity of the task Mother Teresa had set herself in the world.

But the story also illustrates, with equal clarity, how Introverted Feeling will invert collective standards of Judgment, elevating subjective values over Extraverted social expectations. If Mother Teresa's behavior was deliberate, an attempt to show her audience what reality looks like when unconditional human value supplants conventional assumptions about status and power, it was also shrewd, because her ability to make this point was dependent on those social assumptions.

A society that trains its members to rely only on Introverted Judgment for their choices doesn't turn out members who are more charitable and caring; it turns out self-oriented people who judge every social situation in terms of their own experience. For example, a recent ad for a workshop on alternative holiday celebrations reads:

> Images of merriment and warm, loving relationships can be painfully contradictory to one's personal experience of the holidays. Bring your authentic self as together we seek to forge connections that will carry us through the holidays in a new, enlivened way.[6]

This viewpoint is empathic and well meant. People who are grieving when others are celebrating may need help to see beyond commercial imagery to the deeper Christmas message of renewal in a time of darkness. But the ad also suggests the frame of mind that develops when Introverted Judgment becomes our primary source of moral perspective. Collective rituals lose their objective character: they no longer shape our relationships with others; they seem, merely, to exhort us to false conformity.

The characters in *Angels* are contending with the fallout from this subjective standpoint. Drawn together by a common Introverted quest in a world decimated by disease and failed social institutions, they have no idea how to conduct or sustain more permanent relationships with each other.

Louis, the ENFP visionary, talks endlessly about the moral problems of a society whose laws condemn his sexual identity, but he can't bring himself to stand by his terrified, dying partner. Nothing in his own experience compels him to go beyond what he knows how to handle, and nothing in the social compact obliges his fidelity. The author clearly intends this paradox, but the premises he's set up don't allow a resolution.

I mentioned earlier the psychological deficit in the fictional Vorta people, members of the *Star Trek* universe. Without Introverted Feeling values, their Extraverted Feeling behaviors have no connection to real human experience. They're just performances. But the converse is also true. Without Extraverted structure, Introverted values lock a Sensate culture into an eternal present where nothing matters but one's own experience, and social systems are always perceived as inadequate because they don't address the injustices of life itself.

The IFP's Inferior Function

Like all Introverted functions, Introverted Feeling is an individual viewpoint: something we bring to reality from within ourselves. As stated earlier, it can't be used without direct experience. This is what makes it so hard to legislate the behaviors it impels. To advance toward a society organized beyond external distinctions requires the will to ignore conflicting interests and needs.

Indeed, IFPs feel precisely this kind of tension when they try to adapt the objective world to their inner one. It's as though some unformulated answer that would reveal the interconnectedness of the universe were trapped inside them, and all the questions people ask are too small, can't contain what they have to give. This is one reason IFPs turn to archetypal imagery—media figures, Gothic or Arthurian romance, goddesses—to represent their deepest values.

These all-encompassing images resonate with their inner sense of passion and idealism. But archetypes that have no organic connection to real experience are so all-encompassing that everyday life falls short of them. IFPs can end up living frugally on anticipation, waiting for the right situation to claim them. Meanwhile, the Extraverted tide of social expectations carries them into situations they haven't entirely thought out.

Such types seem laid-back, accommodating themselves to others' routines and structures, doing what's required of them and more, but they aren't really engaged. Congenial, good-natured, positive thinking, impressionable, and somewhat unassertive on the surface, their inner life is a tinderbox of yearning for something they can't define.

Like Introverted Thinkers, IFPs need to develop their Extraverted skills well enough to invest themselves in life as it really is. Otherwise, they spend too much time protecting themselves from situations uncongenial to their inner realm, and their least-developed function, Extraverted Thinking, gets out of their control.

As stated in other chapters, all types use the *skills* their inferior function supplies, and IFPs are no exception. When their values lead them to pursue mathematics, accounting, medicine, or science, for example, IFPs are just as motivated and capable as Thinking types.

What's difficult for these types is the *approach to life* Extraverted Thinking fosters. To understand reality by way of general principles strikes IFPs as cold and dehumanizing. It reduces people to categories, robs them of their self-experience. IFPs don't see this viewpoint as part of their own makeup, so it remains primitive and undeveloped, forming the basis of their stereotypes about others.

If IFPs don't develop enough Extraverted Sensation or Extraverted Intuition, they get no Extraverted experience to speak of, and Extraverted Thinking gets too far away from their conscious goals. It floods them with impulses in conflict with their self-image, pushing them to use other functions.

Like all types, IFPs don't recognize this internal drama as an opportunity to grow. They simply feel unhappy, and an inferior Thinking perspective focuses their attention on impersonal structures in the outer world.

Such types acquire an increasing impression that they aren't fulfilling their purpose in life—that they've compromised their values for the sake of others' structural priorities. This impression may involve a personal relationship, the workplace, a school situation, a church organization, or a political structure, and it's important to recognize that it always has some basis in reality. IFPs who haven't developed their Extraverted side can't help but drift into situations determined by others' needs and interests.

The solution to this problem lies in sharpening their Sensate or Intuitive skills. IFPs need to see their situation for what it is and figure out how to nourish and express what they believe in a creative way. If they're contending with Extraverted Thinking impulses, however, IFPs have no incentive to do this. They're too busy defending their beliefs against perceived external threats. They zero in on the boundaries they've been accommodating, hoping to eliminate them from the picture.

To their surprise, others are threatened by their self-assertion, and the type feels hurt and angry. After all, if IFPs have spent half their lives accommodating boundaries uncongenial to themselves, they expect the people who support these boundaries to make some compromises in return.

Using Extraverted Perception as a Defense

It's very hard for IFPs to see their part in this kind of external conflict, because the structural boundaries they're confronting are very real. They simply feel stalemated. They're dissatisfied with the situation as it is, but they don't want to leave, and they don't know how to change it. This experience of paralysis is always an indication that a type is avoiding a secondary conflict within.

IFPs who develop Extraverted Perception invariably see the difference between purely subjective values, which make them feel personally comfortable, and values that are unconditional, part of every human situation they encounter. Once they recognize this distinction, they don't have to change people's minds. They see right through the Extraverted limits of a situation and align themselves with its fundamental axis, thereby changing people's hearts.

Sometimes this happens by virtue of necessity. An INFP pianist of my acquaintance was led by his inner values to pursue a career in ministry and found himself assigned for ten years to a music development program in Taiwan. That assignment forced him to develop his Extraverted Intuition, because his accustomed behaviors had been shaped by a culture vastly different from the one he was now in.

Given the fact that all his experiences were brand new, he had no opportunity to focus on the limits and boundaries he was encountering. He simply played the cards he was dealt, contending with the self reflected back to him from his colleagues and students. In the process, he *consciously* recognized the utility of Extraverted Judging structures to collaborate with others and to organize the information he needed.

As a result, his perspective broadened. He found that he had a real gift for unifying people of diverse backgrounds and theologies, and when he returned to his home province, he was put in charge of some 150 churches.

IFPs who are resisting their Extraverted side invest the outer world with too much power over them. Under the influence of Extraverted Thinking, they use their secondary function not to take in information but to categorize it as congenial or alien to their inner values. In consequence, they devalue the aspects of a situation they find unacceptable.

ISFPs tend to mount this defense with their Sensate immediacy. Convinced that people are trying to define and predict them, they frustrate these expectations, usually by refusing social identity or doing something patently illogical. Mother Teresa did this con-sciously when the nice man was trying to bring her a glass of water. She wanted her audience to see the difference between rendering service to a person and making no distinctions whatsoever among people. But undeveloped ISFPs will do this kind of thing uncon-sciously, attempting to maintain subjective control.

INFPs are more likely to use their Intuition to distance them-selves from others' categories and definitions. These types will meet people's expectations in a job or relationship that doesn't really claim them, while investing their "real" selves elsewhere.

Ultimately, IFPs in contention with unconscious Thinking im-pulses find themselves in a quandary because their dominant func-tion urges them to make peace—to find common ground with others, to grant people's right to be who they are. Such types may double their efforts to see the good in people and to be charitable about all else, but the effort simply perpetuates situations they don't want to be in.

cathy®   **by Cathy Guisewite**

Cathy © 1997 Cathy Guisewite. Reprinted with permission of Universal Press Syndicate. All rights reserved.

Turning to the Tertiary Function

The more these types struggle to conform the outer world to their inner one, the less contact they have with the Extraverted char-acter of their Perception. They begin to rely, instead, on their tertiary function, Introverted Sensation or Introverted Intuition, for informa-tion about reality.

As we've seen in chapters 15 and 17, Introverted Perception fosters a strong identification with ideas and priorities that exist apart from prevailing cultural assumptions. This kind of identification is important for *Extraverted* Judging types, who are inclined to subordinate their immediate experience to others' expectations.

Introverted Feeling types, however, already believe they're subordinating their authentic selves to others' expectations. Their tertiary function persuades them they're absolutely right about this. The problem is their situation—others' behaviors, others' beliefs, others' ideas, others' lack of tolerance and understanding.

INFPs, who turn to Introverted Sensation, become deeply concerned about the discrepancies between their self-experience and others' expectations of them. They may literally avoid situations that force them to compromise, narrowing their perceptual world to the people and experiences that make them feel "like themselves."

ISFPs, whose tertiary function is Introverted Intuition, are more likely to pursue an alternate lifestyle, attempting to embody their social critique. Sometimes INFPs do this, too, but they don't anticipate the conflict this will generate in their lives.

An INFP minister, for example, spent a great deal of his time preaching the virtues of vegetarianism to a congregation raised on meat and potatoes, quite certain of his moral rectitude, and was shocked when he was fired because church members didn't trust him to care about their domestic and spiritual problems.

It should be emphasized that many IFPs are involved in issues of social justice and work hard to make systems more compatible with human values. Some opt for pacifism or maintain a diet in harmony with their values. These are honorable choices, and I'm not suggesting they shouldn't be made or that making them is an indication of a problem.

My point is that IFPs who make these choices under the influence of their tertiary function are doing so defensively. They've turned their values into a left-brain system of classification that allows them to categorize other people as good or bad and defines their experiences before they actually have them.

Developing the Secondary Function

I want to share a story here because it focuses on the question of defining experience in advance of having it. Sometime in the mid-seventies, when I was passionately interested in Sufi philosophy, I went to a conference on new methods of education. I think it was "Education for the Right Side of the Brain." I went because a number of presenters were Sufi thinkers, one of them a man named Idries Shah, whose books I treasured.

I was so excited about seeing Idries Shah in person that I invited several friends to the conference to hear him. As it happened, his presentation was the last before lunch, and people were already a little restless. He was introduced with great fanfare, and I was really surprised to see him walk up to the podium. He was uneasy and a bit irritable, and he seemed woefully unprepared. He could barely get through a sentence without stuttering and clearing his throat and starting over again.

We all looked at each other. He was terrible! He hemmed and hawed and made a number of crass jokes and seemed annoyed about being there at all. People started to walk out. I thought about walking out, too, but I had such respect for the man's books that I didn't want to abandon him. I was definitely uncomfortable and embarrassed, however, because I had told my friends how special he was.

Well, within ten minutes of the start of that presentation, the audience had dwindled from five hundred to about fifty people spread out all over the auditorium. Dr. Shah looked around, satisfied, and then asked those few of us left to come up front and sit together. I no longer remember exactly what he said, but it went something like this:

You are here because you're interested in alternative kinds of education. One of the things standing in the way of changing a system is the expectations that people bring along with them. The people who left were disappointed because I did not meet their expectations as a teacher. You, who put aside your preconceptions and gave me a chance, are the people I want to talk to.

Now, I'm not going to tell you that the man thereafter turned into the best speaker I ever heard. He didn't. But he turned out to be an excellent teacher. And what he did—by frustrating the expectations of the people who wanted him to confirm what they already thought—explained a lot of what I'd seen in other Sufi teachers who seemed to deliberately disappoint their followers in order to show them how their expectations were closing them to real experience.

I remember one teacher who scandalized people at a weekend retreat by roasting a pig and inviting everybody to eat and drink with him. Many of his staunchest followers went home incensed because they were expecting two days of fasting and praying and chanting. The man was showing us how a relationship with God transcends our investment in outward form, even a good and proper outward form.

Dr. Shah's point can help IFPs understand what's at stake in the cultivation of their secondary function. When they resist an experience before they actually have it, life can no longer teach them by way of surprise. They're surrendering their strongest skills.

Well-developed IFPs are so present to their immediate situation that they seem utterly without expectation. They know that unconditional values are truly unconditional, so they have no reason to make predictions about how an experience will meet or not meet their needs.

This frame of mind doesn't blind IFPs to objective reality; it opens their eyes to it. It tells them exactly what's important and exactly what isn't.

Indeed, IFPs sometimes resist their secondary function because it strikes them that accepting reality for what it is will make them ordinary. They want to fight for the good, to make a difference. A classic *Mash* episode speaks poignantly to this issue. As in most stories that deal with Introverted Feeling, the world portrayed is an unpredictable one, the system inadequate to relieve pain and suffering.

It's Christmastime, the doctors are demoralized, the patients maimed and dying, and Father Mulcahy feels utterly ineffective. He isn't a doctor; he can't save anyone's life. No one is asking him for advice; his confessional is empty, his services unattended. All he can do is give people the last rites. By Christmas Eve, however, he realizes that it's his consistent kindnesses in a world gone mad that keeps the others going and gives them faith in a higher moral order.

IFPs need to take a cue from the Sensate mythologies around them and recognize that when a social system isn't doing enough, being exactly who they are can transform lives. Like Father Mulcahy in that classic *Mash* episode, IFPs are not always seen as heroic, but the cumulative effects of their actions accomplish extraordinary things.

Well-developed IFPs are at home with themselves, in harmony with life, and they teach largely by example. They don't have to preach; their values are expressed in the dispatch of ordinary life choices. Indeed, they're the most compassionate of the types, recognizing that even the most wretched of lives can be changed by hope and an appeal to dignity and human worth.

ISFP: Introverted Feeling/Extraverted Sensation

ISFP	
dominant	Introverted Feeling
secondary	Extraverted Sensation
right-brain alternatives	**Introverted Thinking**
	Extraverted Intuition
left-brain double agents	**Introverted Sensation**
	Extraverted Feeling
tertiary	Introverted Intuition
inferior	Extraverted Thinking

Literature that advises us to find our inner child probably has in mind the fresh, uncomplicated vision that ISFPs bring to their world. Oriented by Introverted Feeling and Extraverted Sensation, these types are very much in the here and now. Naturally spontaneous, they live as though each experience were newly discovered and their primary purpose were to be in harmony with it.

Such types understand outward reality by way of sensory skills so finely tuned that they're likely to have a strong identification with nature. One might picture all those deceptively easygoing film heroes who make their statement by breaking into the psych lab and uncaging the chimps or by driving the horses out of the corral and watching them thunder back into the wild. Almost all ISFPs have a special gift for communicating with children and animals, and they may have a green thumb as well.

Such types are frequently drawn to medical specialties, where their perceptual acuity has practical application, and to veterinary work, where it is imperative. Animals sometimes hide pain and illness, because signs of weakness make them vulnerable to predators, but ISFPs seem to know what to look for, and they treat all creatures with respect for their dignity.

The unconditional nature of this respect may be illustrated by an ISFP of my acquaintance who "adopted" a computer-generated puppy. When a friend asked her to squirt the creature with virtual water from a spray bottle that came with the program, she was horrified. "How can I do that?" she asked. "It's playing so happily!"

Whenever this sensitivity comes into play in the social arena, ISFPs have a sense of mission. They may, for example, opt for a pacifist, vegetarian, or anticruelty lifestyle, or volunteer their services to movements like Greenpeace and Amnesty International.

Like other types who use Sensation to deal with the outer world, ISFPs learn by experience, and they need hands-on contact in order to know something well. Unlike Extraverted Sensates, however, they don't require perceptual novelty to stay interested in something. When their Judgment is engaged, ISFPs are focused, contained, and nearly inexhaustible. Whether they're athletes, artists, paramedics, or nurses, whether they make music or take care of stray animals, these types are likely to regard their work as a vocation rather than a profession.

Indeed, their engagement has nothing in common with the goal-oriented Judgment of ESJs. ISFPs don't think in terms of objective limits and requirements. They think in terms of values—what's right in the situation at hand. They lose sight of themselves as objects, rushing in where angels fear to tread.

I knew an ISFP who worked in a community program locating resources for people who ordinarily lived in boxes and tunnels and under bridges. After work, he'd go out on his own trying to find program dropouts in an effort to persuade them to return. He'd often end up in dangerous situations, but it never made him more cautious. The vulnerability of those people struck him as more important than his emotional and physical security.

ISFPs are often like this in an activity that truly captures them. They're not attempting to "go the extra mile." It's who they are. In fact, their lack of objective boundaries usually keeps them from freelancing their skills the way their ISTP kindred do.

ISFP artists, for example, tend to seek ongoing support for their activities—in the way of grants, contributions, seed money, opportunities for performance, and so forth. These types don't want to think too much about the objective conditions of their employment. They want a space that allows them to do what they feel called to do.

It may be noted, in this respect, that as Fox Mulder, of *The X-Files*, has gradually metamorphosed (with the show's success) from a rumpled INTJ obsessive into a peripatetic ISP folk hero, he spends nearly all his time outdoors, investing himself in cases as they come to hand, happy to avoid the confines of the institution that provides his objective means. Moreover, his partner, the hyperrational Scully, now serves him less as an analytical counterpoint than as a frustrated protector, advising him of his bureaucratic options.

ISFPs tend to attract Extraverted Thinkers of this sort, whose anchorage in the world of established systems keeps the type aware of objective responsibilities. ISFPs don't seek this kind of relationship so much as let it happen to them, granting another's investment in material stability and welcoming the structural touchstones, without according them much larger importance.

Although ISFPs are warm, generous, and develop deep connections to people, they have a certain resistance to attachment for its own sake. One might consider Zoe, the twenty-something daughter on the comedy *Cybil*. Zoe is portrayed as an ISFP musical prodigy, romantically drawn to a young man much like herself. Recognizing the worth of the relationship, the two have agreed to keep the connection platonic, lest the social repercussions of sexual involvement rob them of immediacy and the natural rhythms of life as it happens.

All ISFPs aren't like this, of course, but the image catches the flavor of the type's caution with respect to ownership and material possession. Where ISTPs regard a tool, brush, or instrument as an extension of their body, ISFPs are like those rock musicians who break their instruments at the end of a performance. They want to *see through* the objects that serve their talents and ambitions, lose themselves in the creative act itself.

ISFPs will even take up disciplines designed to free them from material dependence, but this is a bit like taking coals to Newcastle. They're more likely to abdicate responsibility for their objective situation than they are to be trapped by what they own.

In fact, ISFPs are most likely to feel bogged down by possessions and material constraint when they're too dependent on their dominant function. Their inferior function, Extraverted Thinking, is too far away from their conscious aims and goals. Whenever they encounter a situation that can't be addressed with their dominant skills, Extraverted Thinking exerts a strong unconscious influence on them, and they lose touch with their accustomed sense of values.

This is the normal course of affairs when a primary function is too strong. The psyche pulls us away from our usual behaviors, giving us room to develop more of our potential. Like other types, however, ISFPs don't recognize their Thinking impulses as part of themselves. They simply feel that they're losing contact with their deepest self, and the only way they know how to solve the problem is to reject the claims of anything that doesn't support that contact.

For example, ISFPs who join a spiritual organization to nurture a contemplative life can be shocked to discover that structural containment has no organic relationship to their aspirations. Their values are being standardized and directed rather than nourished. Once these types define the problem this way, however, they don't know what to do. The right-brain character of their Feeling goals suggests a life lived in surrender to their craft or commitment, but they aren't sure how to make that happen on their own.

So frustration gradually pushes ISFPs into using their secondary function defensively, to assert their existential freedom. Their devotion to a vocation becomes paralleled by an equally strong need to prove their objective self isn't important. This need doesn't necessarily result in a crash-and-burn lifestyle, although it can. Such types may simply do whatever it takes to stay aware of the creative force within—without much thought for the logical consequences. The image these ISFPs construct has quite a bit of resonance in the Sensate pop ethos, and such types can acquire what may be called a tragic sense of cool.

It's ironic, therefore, that what they actually need is *more* contact with their Extraverted Sensate side—not to defend themselves against inferior aims, but to balance their primary needs against their real circumstances. When ISFPs don't get enough Sensate development, they end up using Introverted Intuition, their tertiary function, to keep their dominant self-image intact.

Under most circumstances, Introverted Intuition keeps ISFPs well-rounded. It helps them to recognize that their way of seeing reality is important and real—even when they can't find a way to express it. Used as a defense against Thinking impulses, however, Introverted Intuition simply increases the ISFP's resistance to others' influence on them.

In one of the X-Files episodes, for example, Scully asks Mulder, "Have you ever thought about dying?" "Yeah," he says, "once when I was at the Ice Capades." ISFPs who are trying to resist others' claims on them are almost always defensive in this flip way, believing that others will merely appropriate their deepest feelings for their own purposes.

Such types can end up feeling like Kevin McCarthy in *Invasion of the Body Snatchers*, faced with two bad choices: they can go to sleep, let the pods take over, and wake up happy to be programmed, or they can fight to stay awake and spend the rest of their lives resisting cooptation.

When ISFPs develop sufficient Extraverted Sensation, it takes them outside the terms of this either-or dilemma. They begin to see that their inner potential dictates outward responsibilities. An image given to me by Dr. Ann Ulanov, a Jungian analyst, addresses this situation in an interesting way.

She said that if you live in close contact with your inner world, it's a lot like living by the sea. You can get flooded unless you can build a structure that suits your needs. Your first instinct, however, is to build the kind of house the townspeople live in, because that's the kind of shelter others will help you construct. This is precisely the kind of house that will be ruined when the tide rises. For a while you think, "I should have built a better townhouse." But gradually you reject others' advice and you live without structure.

Why not build the kind of house that will serve your actual needs? Build the kind of house the fishermen build, one the water can go through without knocking it down. And when visitors show up, warn them not to wear their good shoes, because their feet may get damp during dinner.

This is really the primary task for ISFPs: to recognize their need, as it were, to live by the sea of their inner world. Their secondary function helps them to construct a life for themselves that honors their genuine gifts and calling. It doesn't impel them to reject everything they already have and know. It moves them to recognize their purpose for being alive and to find their own path.

Well-developed ISFPs live, as it were, between the sea and the town, doing what they need to do. In consequence, their creations, their choices, their way of being can remind people of important things the community has forgotten.

INFP: Introverted Feeling/Extraverted Intuition

INFP	
dominant	Introverted Feeling
secondary	Extraverted Intuition
right-brain alternatives	**Introverted Thinking**
	Extraverted Sensation
left-brain double agents	**Introverted Intuition**
	Extraverted Feeling
tertiary	Introverted Sensation
inferior	Extraverted Thinking

INFPs are the type of whom people say, "Still waters run deep." Oriented by Introverted Feeling and Extraverted Intuition, they're both highly idealistic and quietly tolerant of others' choices.

Although Feeling always determines a form of idealism, the values determined by Introverted Feeling are different from the Extraverted sort. Extraverted Feeling presides over social values—current ideas about how relationships in the community are best conducted.

Introverted Feeling determines subjective values—convictions about how a life is best lived.

Such values are trained by direct experience of good and bad behaviors, and they claim us from within. But relationship gradually teaches us that some of them transcend our individual circumstances, linking us irrevocably with other human beings.

Found in only 1 percent of the population, the INFP's understanding of reality is quite nearly like the one described by mystics, who believe that spiritual energy descends to earth by way of eternal ideals—structural patterns that bring order out of material chaos. By aligning their behaviors with these ideals, mystics can, presumably, bring life into harmony with its divine potential.

INFPs may not describe their approach to life in metaphysical terms, but it's a rare INFP who doesn't see in nature's underlying pattern intimations of a larger purpose. Whether they write, teach, nurture, conduct research, make art, or devote their lives to spiritual service, their work becomes the agency through which they can grasp those "distant deeps and skies" in which such "fearful symmetries" are framed.

INFPs yearn to experience oneness with their circumstances, but Intuition prevents them from satisfying this longing as ISFPs do, by losing themselves in a physical activity. Intuition doesn't push INFPs to act. It pushes them to interpret: to see the potential of their thoughts and behaviors in terms of their ideals.

Because their ideals are wholistic, INFPs feel responsible not only for their actions but for their desire to take action, and they have a nearly karmic idea of balance. If they betray their ideals in either deed or feeling, they try to make restitution. When good things happen, they may worry about paying a price.

It's instructive to compare these types to ENFPs, who share the same two functions but understand life very differently. ENFPs rely on Intuition to gauge the nature of an external context and Feeling to recognize the values of the people in it. The best illustration of how this works is President Clinton's unrivaled ability to identify with an audience and sympathize with their aspirations. ENFPs generally believe that people will recognize their good intentions, even if their behaviors fall short of them.

INFPs approach reality from the other way around. Introverted Feeling prompts them to hold unconditional human values, and they use Intuition to figure out what that means in terms of their existential context. Asked whether he had ever had an extramarital affair, President Jimmy Carter said no but allowed that he had experienced "lust in his heart." This is a quintessential INFP perspective. Such types feel responsible for their hidden intentions, even if their behaviors *exceed* people's expectations.

Given their focus on what it is to be human, INFPs are not always easy to recognize as types. Their outward behaviors vary widely. Some are reserved and prefer one-to-one conversations, but a surprising number of INFPs enjoy performing and may be singers, actors, and comedians. In all cases, however, INFPs need a fair amount of time to themselves.

Although they identify strongly with expressions of joy, sorrow, pain, and vulnerability in others and respond compassionately to people who need them, they're accessible only up to a point. Once that point is reached, they've genuinely depleted their social capital and need to recoup.

It's easy to misunderstand INFPs in this regard, because they relate to others in the same low-key, easygoing way that characterizes ISFPs. They're often wry, and if they're comfortable, they'll contribute a running patter of perceptive remarks and observations. Thus, it surprises people when the INFP abruptly winds down and wants to be alone.

Moreover, these types are sympathetic listeners, genuinely interested in what others do and believe, which encourages people to anticipate a more extensive relationship than the INFP may have bargained for. Until they recognize what's happening, INFPs may be constantly obliged to extricate themselves from situations they got into simply by virtue of warmth and goodwill.

Along the same lines, these types have high romantic ideals, and express this aspect of their personality somewhat tentatively. This can lead people to believe that they're shy or not interested in physical intimacy. In actuality, INFPs long for communion of mind, body, and spirit, and they envision a partner who can appreciate the nature of their inner world and give them access to it in sexual terms.

However, like all P types, they don't want to set goals for their relationships; they want good things to happen naturally, to grow out of the situation as it exists. Moreover, their finely tuned Intuitive skills lead them to believe that the right person would see through all the surface nonsense to the inchoate potential within, read it in their body language, their musical tastes, the images that move them, the underlying meaning of their words.

This ideal picture is also a consequence of their wholistic point of view. INFPs have a hard time articulating who they are inside, and they keep hoping the objective situation will give them enough reference points to express themselves in a way that feels true and right. Indeed, INFPs can have a hard time figuring out what they're called to do in life.

Unlike Extraverts, whose primary self-image is tied up with their outward behaviors, INFPs may get at their self-experience only when it conflicts with their external choices. Even those INFPs who have plugged themselves into a career that allows them to do something meaningful and good may not feel sure they're doing enough. They're nagged by an impression that something else is supposed to happen, something that will tell them what they're *really* meant to do.

Al Capp used to draw a syndicated cartoon called Long Sam, in which a grizzled, pipe-smoking mountain woman dispensed hard-won wisdom about life. When it came to human values, however, all she could say was, "Being nice is better—because it's nicer." INFPs can find themselves in the position of saying something very much like that when they try to articulate what they believe and why. Their values have no predictable reference points in law and social convention. They cut through all that to the heart of a matter.

In order to actualize their certainties and ideals, INFPs generally find a place for themselves in the prevailing social system that allows them to focus on human potential. But given the fact that their values are more fundamental than institutional priorities, they're constantly frustrated with the time and energy they spend on structural mainte-nance—society's "edifice complex."

So they're in a quandary. Because, apart from jobs of this sort, they don't have a clear idea of what it would mean to act on their values. The right-brain character of their Feeling goals suggests a life spent in pilgrimage, free from objective attachments—even a sense of home.

And some INFPs do, in fact, give their lives to missionary work or the priesthood or a spiritual community. But most INFPs, by the time they're wrestling with this question, have established a home and family and/or a place for themselves in the community, and they're not inclined to hurt the people they love for the sake of an ideal they can't quite define.

So frustration gradually pushes INFPs into using their Intuition defensively, to protect what feels like their "true" self against the imperfect outer situation they're living in. They feel guilty about this, too; because they think they ought to be satisfied with what is, after all, a perfectly decent life course.

INFPs who are relying on their Intuition this way usually take one of two directions. Either they become permanent seekers—good at many things but disinclined to stick with any for long—or they become somewhat passive, unable to articulate what they want but dissatisfied with what they're doing.

These latter types generally feel that they don't have enough initiative, but they don't get much accomplished apart from others' routines and structural expectations. Left to their own devices, they tend to procrastinate or do unnecessary tasks to avoid more important ones.

When INFPs spend most of their energy protecting their inner realm from attachment to an imperfect outer situation, their least-developed function, Extraverted Thinking, doesn't get very conscious. Such types are often excellent at managing time and resources for others but have a harder time structuring and organizing their own lives. In fact, they may become romantically involved with a strong J type, who can anchor them to the objective world, but can't provide what they actually crave: something to pull them to the surface of their own personality.

INFPs need to use their Intuition in a genuinely Extraverted way. They're accustomed to using Intuition to figure out how to deal with an existing context; they need to apply it, instead, to the task of defining what an objectively good situation would be like.

This is by no means easy for INFPs to do. When they stop using

Intuition to defend themselves, their first instinct is to assert the importance of their Feeling goals. They challenge people, question the aspects of the situation that strike them as problematic. This "feels" like Extraverted behavior, but it isn't. Extraversion moves us to take the objective world for granted. It's Introversion that strives to adapt the objective situation to itself.

Meanwhile, the Extraversion these types actually require goes underground. Extraverted Thinking becomes so profoundly unconscious that it floods them with impulses directly opposed to their Feeling aims.

Like all types, INFPs don't recognize this internal pressure as an opportunity to grow. They feel the influence of their Thinking function, but they mistake it for an outward problem. They feel increasingly thwarted and boxed in, false to their real selves, and they're sure the reason is their accommodating spirit. Thus, they go back to using Extraverted Intuition as a defense, but more aggressively, because the stakes are higher. They decide to fight some of the things that are hemming them in.

INFPs don't like conflict, so their rebellion is often subtle and passive-aggressive in form. They drag their feet when someone pushes them to do something they don't want to do, sometimes until the person gives up, or they "yes" people, then do as they like. None of this helps INFPs to find their own truth; it actually takes them *away* from the quest, concentrating their attention on all the wrong things.

One might consider, in this respect, the characters in the movie The Big Chill—friends from the sixties who come together, twenty years later, for the funeral of their compatriot, Harold. Harold had been a role model for them, a free spirit guided entirely by Introverted Feeling ideals. His suicide makes them realize how far afield subsequent choices have taken them from the values he inspired.

Thus, they each attempt to prove that they're not locked into the social roles that appear to define them: the unmarried lawyer decides to get pregnant; the upscale franchise king gives his friends illegal stock information; the society matron has an extramarital affair.

INFPs under the influence of Extraverted Thinking are not unlike these characters. They're self-conscious rather than idealistic. Their actions aren't being guided by an inner code, leading them to positive action, but by a need to defend themselves against others' priorities.

In fact, such types usually find that ignoring others' expectations doesn't give them enough protection, and they turn to Introverted Sensation, their tertiary function, to keep their Feeling values intact. They literally avoid situations that don't accord with their primary self-experience, forfeiting relationships rather than experience inner conflict.

Ironically, the more unconscious Extraverted Thinking becomes, the more INFPs call attention to themselves in their attempt to keep their environment congenial to their values. Their objective preferences become idiosyncratic, forcing others into unusual accommodations in order to relate to them. Given the fact that they've projected their STJ impulses on to the impersonal structures of society, they feel morally vindicated. What can they do to change a whole system? What's important is to be true to themselves; others have to take responsibility for their own choices.

It should be emphasized that INFPs aren't wrong about this. They do need to be "true to themselves." However, Introverted Sensation doesn't help them do this. It keeps them locked into things as they are. It turns their ideals into an external value system that defines some situations as congenial to their needs and others not, leaving them no choice but to stay out of the ones that aren't.

When INFPs develop sufficient Intuition, they *stop* focusing on things as they are and begin to see new possibilities for action. One might consider, again, the characters in *The Big Chill*. Among the mourners at the funeral is a young woman who was living with Harold when he committed suicide. She strikes the old friends as shallow, a silly adolescent, unable to appreciate who Harold really was.

When INFPs first make contact with the Extraverted character of their Intuition, they see it in the same terms—as a shallow approach to life, without meaning. It invites them to give up their expectations, live in perceptual harmony with anything that happens. This strikes them as irresponsible. As the song says, "If you don't stand for something, you'll fall for anything."

The more they wrestle with this perspective, however, the more they see that their values have nothing to do with their comfort or discomfort in a situation. They constitute a way of seeing life, a way of relating to *any* situation. When INFPs use their Intuition to figure out how to make this relationship manifest, they see that they have many options to take positive action.

It may be noted that at the end of *The Big Chill*, one of the friends, the one who had been resisting social definition, decides to help the young girl finish a house Harold had been building in the wilderness. This is the sort of thing that happens to INFPs who wake up to the wholistic nature of their inner life. They realize that being responsible to their values isn't about fighting what exists; it's about building, recognizing that they can do things, *want* to do things, that might not even occur to others.

INFPs who reach this point don't ignore the problems of society or betray commitments they've already made. They simply play from their strengths. For example, an INFP social worker of my acquaintance, after much reflection, left his position to design a unique company of his own, which helps corporations restructure their organizations in terms of human values. He no longer feels quite at home in the world, but he's at peace with himself, working on the things that truly drive him.

Sometimes INFPs simply need to make room in their lives to give their strengths a chance to grow. For example, they may take up creative pursuits—writing, composition, design, art: something that allows them to give their ideals material form. Sometimes they volunteer their services or take care of homeless animals.

In general, however, well-developed INFPs live lives that don't look much different from anyone else's. What's different is their perspective. They strike others as unassuming, even deferential, because they treat people with unconditional love and compassion. In consequence, their actions, their choices, their way of life can awaken others to human values the community has not acknowledged.

For example, a small Midwestern church had hired a pastor from the New York area, and there were many discussions on the church board about the difficult transition for the congregation. An INFP board member saw the situation from the other way around, empathizing with the minister and his family, uprooted from their home and friends in the East to make a new life among them.

When the family arrived, a day ahead of the moving truck, picturing themselves eating pizza on a bare floor, they walked into the parsonage and found a table set with flowers and good china, a refrigerator full of dinners and staples, and soap and towels in the bathrooms. Such actions see through external distinctions of role, background, and status to focus on our common human links.

INFPs sometimes underestimate their strengths because there are so many problems in the world that can't be solved by changing people's hearts. But they shouldn't. The effects of their decisions are often incalculable, renewing people's faith in human nature.

Notes

Chapter 1. This Door is Not the Door

[1] This is a paraphrase of a story told in the film *Chan is Missing* (1982), directed by Wayne Wang.

[2] Version told by Idries Shah, *The Sufis* (Garden City, N.Y.: Doubleday & Company, 1964; Anchor Books edition, 1971), 40–41.

Chapter 2. Casting Types

[1] Aryeh Maidenbaum, Ph.D., director of The New York Center for Jungian Studies, Inc., is the author of *The Maidenbaum Personality Inventory*, which served as the initial basis for the test in this book.

Chapter 8. Personality Types Are Also Brain Types

[1] Diagrams of the functions and how they relate to activity in the two brain hemispheres rely on information provided in Jonathan Niednagel, *How to Choose Your Best Sport and Play It* (Laguna Niguel, Calif.: Laguna Press, 1992).

Chapter 13. The Attitudes

[1] David G. Myers, "Pursuing Happiness," *Psychology Today* (July/August 1993), 35.

[2] C. G. Jung, "General Description of the Types," in *The Portable Jung*, ed. Joseph Campbell (New York: The Viking Press, 1971), 180.

[3] Idries Shah, *The Sufis*, 67.

[4] William Shatner with Chris Kreski, *Star Trek Memories* (New York: HarperCollins, 1993), 131.

[5] Shatner, *Memories*, 130.

[6] Idries Shah, *The Way of the Sufi* (New York: E. P. Dutton & Co., 1970), 213–214.

Chapter 14. Extraverted Sensation

[1] Robert M. Pirsig, *Zen and the Art of Motorcycle Maintenance: An Inquiry into Values* (New York: Bantam Books, 1975), 161.

[2] Jon Krakauer quoted in Anne Stephenson, " 'I Wish I'd Never Gone': How Mount Everest Expedition Spiraled Downward to Tragedy," *Milwaukee Journal Sentinel* May 20, 1997, sec. E.

[3] See Diane Werts, "Dudley Do-Right Gets His Due," *New York Newsday FanFare* Dec. 3, 1995, 22.

Chapter 15. Introverted Sensation

[1] C. G. Jung, "General Description of the Types," 254.

Chapter 16. Extraverted Intuition

[1] C. G. Jung, "General Description of the Types," 224.

[2] Fyodor Dostoyevsky, *The Devils*, translated by David Magarshack (Baltimore: Penguin Books, 1969), ix, 261.

Chapter 17. Introverted Intuition

[1] Charles Williams, *The Greater Trumps* (Grand Rapids, Mich.: William B. Eerdmans Publishing Co., 1976), 94–95.

Chapter 19. Introverted Thinking

[1] David Kiersey and Marilyn Bates, *Please Understand Me: Character and Temperament Types* (Del Mar, Calif.: Prometheus Nemesis, 1978), 203.

[2] Pirsig, *Motorcycle Maintenance*, 194–195.

[3] *Newsweek*, December 17, 1984. Quoted in James B. Simpson (compiler), *Simpson's Contemporary Quotations: The Most Notable Quotes Since 1950* (Boston: Houghton Mifflin Co., 1988), 257.

Chapter 20. Extraverted Feeling

[1] In discussion with Robert Langs, M.D. See *A Primer of Psychotherapy* (New York: Gardner Press, 1988).

Chapter 21. Introverted Feeling

[1] *Chicken Soup for the Soul*, by Jack Canfield and Mark Victor Hansen, quoted in Shirley Basfield Dunlap,"Romancing the Soul," *Prologue: Milwaukee Repertory Theater* (Dec. 1997/Jan. 1998), 1.

[2] Kiersey and Bates, *Please Understand Me*, 206–7.

[3] See Lou Carlozo, "Elvis' Mid-Death Crisis," *Chicago Tribune*, Sunday, Aug. 3, 1997, sec. 7.

4 Carlozo, "Elvis' Mid-Death Crisis," 15.

5 Dorothy Day, quoted in Tom Heinen, "Activism of 'Catholic Left,' Day Recalled," *Milwaukee Journal Sentinel* Oct. 11, 1997, sec. B.

6 Holiday Workshop advertised in "Holiday Making: Exploring Some Alternatives." *Kirkridge Upcoming Events*, Bangor, Pennsylvania, 1997.

Index